"Linda Przybyszewski takes her readers on an imaginative journey through a largely forgotten universe of women writers in the twentieth century who wrote about the art of dressing well. The book is sprightly and well-written, and it suggests new directions for research in the history of fashion and of women. Przybyszewski offers useful critiques of the restrictive clothing of the nineteenth century, the sloppy clothing of the 1960s, the periodic infantilizing of women through dress design, and the increasing commoditization of products and pleasures. She mourns the loss of the elegance of the 1930s, when women looked both liberated and chic."

—Lois Banner, Professor Emerita, Department of History and Gender Studies Program, University of Southern California, author of *Marilyn: The Passion and the Paradox*

"This is an important work. In *The Lost Art of Dress,* dressmaker and historian Linda Przybyszewski skillfully delineates the rise of the Dress Doctors in the early twentieth century to their demise in the turbulent sixties. Przybyszewski excavated the lost texts of home economists and others who taught the art and science of dress through the application of five principles of art. Although Przybyszewski laments the decline of the teachings of the Dress Doctors during the 1960s, she sees their legacy in the recent rise of the craft of dressmaking and is encouraged by a renewed interest of Americans in the art of dressing well and with good taste."

—Patricia Cunningham, Associate Professor Emerita of
Fashion and Retail Studies, Ohio State University

The
Lost
Art
of
Dress

The
Lost
Art
of
Dress

The WOMEN *Who Once*
Made AMERICA STYLISH

LINDA PRZYBYSZEWSKI

BASIC BOOKS
A Member of the Perseus Books Group • New York

Published by Basic Books,
A Member of the Perseus Books Group

Designed by Pauline Brown
Typeset in 11.75-point Adobe Caslon Pro by the Perseus Books Group

Library of Congress Cataloging-in-Publication Data
Przybyszewski, Linda.
The lost art of dress : the women who once made America stylish / Linda Przybyszewski.
     pages cm
 Includes bibliographical references and index.
    ISBN 978-0-465-03671-4 (hardback) -- ISBN 978-0-465-08047-2 (e-book) 1. Fashion--United States--
History--20th century. 2. Women fashion designers--United States. 3. United States--Social life and
customs--20th century. I. Title.
 TT507.P79 2014
 746.9'2--dc23
                                      2013045448

10 9 8 7 6 5 4 3 2 1

To John,
who promised me a good time

CONTENTS

INTRODUCTION

WANDERING THROUGH A USED BOOKSTORE YEARS AGO, I spotted a thick volume called *Clothes for You*. I've always been interested in fashion, so I pulled it off the shelf. It turned out to be a college textbook from 1954, but it was like no textbook I had ever seen before.

The book's five hundred pages taught the art and science of dress, explaining that beauty in dress can only be achieved by applying the principles of art to clothing. These principles hold true no matter the season, the year, or the century. A woman can use them to choose the beautiful from whatever current fashions have on offer, and it won't cost a fortune so long as she follows some basic rules of economics. If necessary, any girl can learn how to sew and create whatever she needs. The book's message was artistic, logical, and democratic: knowledge, not money, is the key to beauty in dress.

The book aroused my curiosity on two counts. First, I'm a dressmaker from a long line of sewing women. One of my grandmothers could make anything her daughter pointed out to her in a shop window; the other left me her Singer Slant-O-Matic sewing machine, the very latest in high tech from 1952. My mother sewed and knit clothes for my sister and me when we were little. Sewing came in especially handy when I had to live on a low budget while earning my doctorate from Stanford University. Second, I'm a professor of

American history. My first book was a biography of a justice on the United States Supreme Court. I may be the only historian to lecture at the Supreme Court in a suit that won a blue ribbon at a county fair.

Clothes for You inspired me to find out more about the art of dress. My hunt took me from the basements of bookstores to the archives of universities. I discovered that hundreds of books and pamphlets were written to teach the American woman how to dress for the twentieth century. Millions of girls read them in home economics classes and in 4-H clothing clubs.

The books were written by a remarkable group of women who worked as teachers, writers, retailers, and designers. They offered advice in classrooms, on radio broadcasts, at women's clubs, and in magazines. They even enlisted the federal government in their efforts through the Bureau of Home Economics. I call these women the "Dress Doctors" after a story told by Mary Brooks Picken, the first among them.

Born on a farm in Kansas in 1886, Picken was a prodigy who could spin, weave, and sew by the age of five. At eleven, she made the layette of clothes and bedding for her newest baby brother. Widowed young, she supported herself by teaching dress design and sewing to everyone from the respectable young women at the YWCA to the female convicts doing time at Leavenworth Penitentiary.

A skilled woman physician turned to Picken for help, she recalled in 1918. The good doctor realized that people thought her less intelligent than she really was because she dressed so badly, but she had no idea what to do about it because clothes mystified her. So she asked Picken to "diagnose" her case. Picken examined the doctor and prescribed a professional wardrobe. When the doctor donned her new clothes, she noticed a marked difference in the way people viewed her. Her fellow doctors treated her with more respect. So did the hospital nurses who worked under her. People who had never before bothered to consult her professionally now made a point of doing so. She had been cured.

Fig. 1: Mary Brooks Picken at the time that
she cured a physician of a bad wardrobe in
1918. PICKEN, *THE SECRETS OF DISTINCTIVE
DRESS*, 1918

"Do we not express ourselves through the clothes we wear as much as through what we say and what we do?" asked Picken.[1]

The makeover is a story as old as Cinderella, but the Dress Doctors reinvented it for the modern age. Picken's doctor wasn't trying to land a prince. She was struggling to succeed in a profession in which women were few and far between.

Picken eventually moved east and made herself into the most important authority on dress in America. She wrote dozens of books, including the first dictionary penned by a woman, *The Language of Fashion*. She helped found the Costume Institute, which is now part of the Metropolitan Museum of Art, and became the first woman to serve as a trustee of the Fashion Institute of Technology in 1951.

Picken and the other Dress Doctors took traditional ideas about beauty and art and used them to help American women to flourish in the twentieth century, an era they viewed as one of unprecedented opportunity for their sex. They considered art a spiritual force that encouraged an appreciation of the beauty of all God's creation. They taught their students to study the Five Art Principles of harmony, rhythm, balance, proportion, and emphasis, and to observe them at work in famous paintings, such as Leonardo da Vinci's *The Last Supper*. They explained that these same principles should be used in the design of clothing. Their aim was the creation of what they called "artistic repose," the moment when the discerning eye takes in a design as a whole and finds it perfectly satisfying in color, line, and form.

The Dress Doctors followed the lead of the Arts and Crafts movement, which first blurred the distinction between what was beautiful and what was useful in the late nineteenth century. Any everyday object could be beautiful if it was suited to its purpose and designed according to the principles of art. Clothing fit the bill. By teaching dressmaking, the Dress Doctors made women into creators, not just shoppers. "Beautiful clothes should be part of contemporary art," declared one Dress Doctor in 1925, "not beautiful clothes for the few, but beautiful clothes for everybody, and at a cost that all can afford."[2]

The Dress Doctors were eager to prepare women for new roles in American life. World War I had called upon women to replace men in factories, while housewives learned to conserve food and clothing. Women gained new civic duties when the Nineteenth Amendment guaranteed them the right to vote in 1920.

Against this backdrop, the Dress Doctors identified Six Occasions for Dress—school, business, housework, sport, afternoons, and evenings—and explained which designs and fabrics were best suited for each. The girl at school wore tailored dresses that allowed her to focus on her studies. Sober colors and restrained lines were good for women working in business, while cheerful and washable housedresses suited women looking after their children and their homes. Outfits for sport allowed the athlete—another new, modern role for women—to move with strength and grace everywhere from the tennis court to the skating rink. Afternoons and evenings let a woman indulge herself in fragile fabrics and rich colors, whether she was a social butterfly headed out for the evening or a quiet homebody curled up with a good book. Gently but firmly, the Dress Doctors urged all American women to wear clothes that let them work efficiently and that brought the elevating power of beauty into their lives.

And such a wardrobe would not break the bank, because it need only be made up of a small number of beautiful garments. During the Great Depression, the Dress Doctors showed farmwomen how to recycle flour sacks into dresses. When World War II redirected the American economy to provide for the troops, the Dress Doctors explained how to cut down a man's suit to make a woman's suit. When the 1950s brought prosperity, the Dress Doctors explained how best to choose a dress from the multitude offered in department stores. And through it all, the Dress Doctors reminded the American woman that a few perfect outfits, assembled according to the art principles, and suited to the occasions of her life, were all that she needed.

The Dress Doctors also advised what suited a woman at different ages. The schoolgirl's clothing, whether day wear or evening wear, remained simple in cut so that she could move her energetic body freely. The bright and playful colors she wore reflected her youthful energy and simplicity. Aging meant gains in worldliness. The Dress Doctors reserved for the woman over thirty the most complex dress designs and the subtlest color schemes. They explained how a woman can age with grace and dignity by using the right hues and fabrics.

The Dress Doctors offered solutions to perennial problems of style. They reminded their students that fad stands for "For a Day," because that's about how long it will last. Instead, they counseled avoiding the spectacular and the weird in favor of the beautiful. The Dress Doctors knew women must deploy the erotic power of clothing sparingly if they wanted to be taken seriously in other arenas of life.

The businesswoman and the housewife required very different ward-robes, so no list of fashion "must haves" would suit them both. Instead of advising on trends that would soon be obsolete, the Dress Doctors taught the rules of good design. Armed with these truths, a woman in any era could determine for herself what was beautiful, while the lessons on budgeting from the same advisers kept her out of debt.

The art and science of dress was once a standard part of a girl's education, but even historians have overlooked the Dress Doctors' work. How were they forgotten so completely?[3]

The cultural rebellion of the 1960s undermined the Dress Doctors from all sides. The home economists among them had claimed a place at the vanguard of professional women in the 1920s, but now they seemed hopelessly old-fashioned as women demanded the right to work in all fields. When radical feminist Robin Morgan spoke at the annual meeting of the American Home Economics Association in 1972, she told the women in her audience, many of them teachers, that the best thing they could do for young women was quit their jobs. By the mid-1970s, funding for home economics programs in public schools was being slashed on the grounds that their classes encouraged sexual stereotypes. Ambitious young women turned to other professions.

The art principles also came under attack during the "Youthquake" movement of the 1960s. The Baby Boomers opted for shocking color schemes that created anything but the artistic repose espoused by the Dress Doctors. The sophisticated fashion models of the 1950s sometimes worked into their forties, but now the fashion world cel-ebrated youth and youth alone. Clothing manufacturers abandoned what they called "Sophisticated Styling" in favor of "Young Styling" and "Youthful Styling," because grandmothers and granddaughters were wearing the same dresses.

The results were not pretty. Jessica Daves, former editor of *Vogue* magazine, was herself a *grande dame* born in 1898. Taking in the state of fashion in 1967, she wrote, "The absurdity of a busty lady with a dowager's hump and substantial legs appearing in the streets in a sleeveless shift, above the knees, is something horrible to contemplate." The hallmark of Young and Youthful Styling—simplicity—led to the simplemindedness of garments like the dish-towel dress in the 1970s.[4]

The Dress Doctors may have been forgotten, but they deserve our attention. How valuable would this advice be today when American women are mired in credit-card debt, urged to shopping frenzy, and when the most common yardstick of attractiveness is who's wearing the shortest dress? Many voices offer fashion advice today, but, unlike the Dress Doctors, they say little about overarching principles of style. In order to distill the teachings of the Dress Doctors of yore, I have collected and studied more than seven hundred books and magazines on dress and sewing. I have re-created vintage clothing from every decade of the twentieth century. I even made that dish-towel dress (not that I enjoyed it). I also mastered the art of millinery, because hats were once part of every woman's wardrobe. This book explains what I have discovered.

Today, Americans are known for their sloppy dressing, but it was not always so. An Englishwoman who came to the States after World War II marveled at "the inherent good taste" of the American woman. But American women weren't born with good taste. They learned it from the Dress Doctors. And we can learn it again.[5]

❊ 1 ❊

Introducing
the Dress Doctors

I N 1913, THE SECRETARY OF AGRICULTURE, David F. Houston, was worried about the decline in the number of Americans living on farms and determined to make rural life more "comfortable, healthful, and attractive," so he sent out a survey asking farmwomen what the US Department of Agriculture might do for them. He got some surprising letters back.[1]

There were plenty of requests for plans for efficient kitchens and methods for banishing pests, but there were also letters that revealed how much American women hungered for beauty in dress. A girl would not be so eager to leave the farm, wrote a lady from Tennessee, if she could "really see that there is an art in the farm life, and that she can dress as prettily and have her home as neatly furnished as the city girl can." A woman from Idaho thought that a pamphlet on "the art and appropriateness of dress" would be much appreciated. Who would answer these requests? The home economists, who soon found a headquarters at the USDA.[2]

Home economics got its first footing in the land-grant colleges created by the states under the Morrill Act of 1862, which granted federal lands to the states for them to sell in order to raise money to establish colleges of agriculture and mechanical arts. (This is what put the "A" and "M" in Texas A&M.) In a world that divided the sexes into separate spheres of activity, men got control over the worlds of agriculture and industry, while women were given the home. By 1905, thirty-six land-grant colleges had departments of home economics.[3]

Yet the USDA had always spent most of its efforts helping farmers with research and programs, and some thought that it was time to pay more attention to the profession of homemaking. As the American School of Home Economics put it in 1911, "we believe . . . that the upbringing of children demands more study than the raising of chickens." The Smith-Lever Act of 1914 called for the USDA to cooperate with the states on public programs—called "cooperative extension work"—to bring instruction to farmers and farmwomen. Three years later, the Smith-Hughes National Vocational Education Act increased federal funding for vocational education, including home economics, which led to a 300 percent increase in the number of women teaching vocational skills over the next fifteen years. The first "Dress Doctors" began their careers at this time.[4]

Over the 1920s and 1930s, they rose in prominence. Lucy Rathbone and Elizabeth Tarpley, for example, started as adjunct assistant professors in the 1920s teaching home economics in portable shacks with paper-thin walls and leaky roofs at the University of Texas. By 1933, they had moved into a new Department of Home Economics building, a lovely Spanish Renaissance structure with a red-tiled roof and balconies. They worked there for decades. The congressmen who voted for instruction in home economics were thinking only of practical skills for the future wives and mothers of America, but the home economists themselves set their sights on the full breadth of domestic science and on careers for their students. Their leader was the remarkable Ellen Swallow Richards, who had studied chemistry at Vassar College and then discovered, upon her graduation in 1870, that no one would hire a woman to work as a chemist. She decided to continue her education and was admitted to the Massachusetts Institute of Technology. The men there treated her, as she reported, "very much as a dangerous animal." Richards earned a bachelor's degree in 1873, becoming the first woman to earn a degree from MIT, but the professors made it clear they would not help her earn a doctorate. That did not stop her from directing her energies elsewhere. She taught sanitary chemistry at MIT, wrote books on sanitation, and, in 1908, organized the home economists into a professional organization, the American Home Economics Association, which later became the American Association of Family and Consumer Sciences.[5]

Despite the domestic focus of their work, home economists did not see their field as limited. To them, a well-run home was essential to human health, happiness, and prosperity. By researching how best to run that home, they created a professional niche in a world that did not welcome career women. "The educated woman longs for a career," wrote Richards in 1900, "for an opportunity to influence the world. Just now the greatest field offered to her is the elevation of the home into its place in American life." Their scientific ambitions sometimes sparked criticism, as chemist Isabel Bevier learned when her program at the University of Illinois came under attack from farmwomen for not offering basic sewing classes. Yet such ambitions also explain why 303 of the 474 women faculty doing science at the leading American universities in 1960 were working in departments of home economics.[6]

Domestic science had a reach beyond the home that justified women taking part in public life. Everything that touched the home was of interest to home economists and became a specialty within their profession: truth in labeling, public sanitation, theories of child development, nutritional discoveries, architecture, and dress. Their

earliest efforts reflected the spirit of the Progressive Era, circa 1900
to 1920, when many Americans believed that government could be
reformed, even purified, and put to work to solve the problems of
the day. Science could be brought to bear on everyday life. The home
economists wanted to give the modern homemaker the knowledge she
needed to keep her family safe from germs, poor nutrition, and shoddy
goods, and to offer her the insights of business efficiency to make the
most of her time and energy. Homemaking required knowledge of art
when it came to designing homes, gardens, and clothing if they were
going to be both beautiful and functional. The added challenge for
clothing is that it should be comfortable to live in.

Home economists proved their value to the nation during World
War I, when their scientific knowledge of fabrics and food became
vital. Which fibers last longer under hard wear? What's the best way
to protect military bedding from mildew? What foods are most nutri-
tious? How can they be preserved? The home economists were ready
with the answers.

With the help of the home economists, the US Food Administration recruited some 750,000 women to help teach the rest of America's
women about food conservation. Their slogan became "Food will win
the war." The recruits got a pin, a badge, and a pattern for an apron.
The white apron was named after Herbert Hoover, who was then
head of the Food Administration. The Hoover apron's claim to design
fame was that it completely wrapped around your dress and protected
it from spills, opening in the front with a large overlap. Since it could
overlap it in either direction, you could wear it twice as long as a regular apron before it was too filthy to wear. It was practical, and sort of
disgusting, but it became a popular design. Renamed "Hooverettes" or
"bungalow aprons," done up in perky prints with ruffles at the neck and
sleeves, they were sold in stores as dresses over the next two decades.[7]

Having proven their value during the war, home economists got
their own bureau at the USDA in 1923. Its first head was Louise

Stanley, a PhD in biochemistry from Yale University, who soon became the largest employer of women scientists in the country. The Division of Textiles and Clothing at the Bureau of Home Economics hired two physicists, two chemists, a "cotton technologist," two specialists in clothing design, and a dressmaker. Their chief was Ruth O'Brien, who had a master's degree in chemistry from the University of Nebraska. O'Brien looked like a mild-mannered scientist, but beneath her large, round spectacles lay a dynamic personality that rose up in wrath at the suggestion that "girl chemists" learn how to type instead of aiming for jobs in laboratories.[8]

The bureau's Food and Nutrition Division tended to get more press coverage than Textiles and Clothing—which makes sense, since botulism can kill you, while an ugly dress only makes you wish you were dead—yet the members of its staff were eager to prove their scientific chops. They put to use an invention created by Professor Wilbur O. Atwater, a specialist in nutrition, which he called the "respiration calorimeter." It could calculate how much energy a person took in as food and how much energy they expended as activity. (Yes, Professor Atwater is the man responsible for your counting calories.) In 1896, he constructed a giant box and sealed a graduate student inside to determine how many calories he used studying and weight-lifting. Then Atwater put in a champion cyclist to see how long he could pedal a stationary bike on one egg. He appalled teetotalers by proving that alcohol was food by sealing a man in the box who lived on the stuff for six days.[9]

Ruth O'Brien's question was more mundane: How much labor did a sewing machine save? They put a woman in the box and learned that she used six times as much energy using a treadle machine as she did sewing by hand but got fourteen times more work done. When she used an electric sewing machine, she managed to get sixteen times more work done using no more energy than hand sewing.[10]

Fig. 1: The Dress Doctors ushered out the demure Victorian maiden, who spent her spare time on samplers and the treadle machine, and ushered in the modern girl, who played tennis when she was not sewing on her electric machine. DULCIE G. DONOVAN, *THE MODE IN DRESS AND HOME*, 1935

No wonder women had purchased these machines in droves the minute they had shown up decades earlier. *Godey's Lady Book*, the most popular women's magazine of the nineteenth century, called the sewing machine "The Queen of Inventions" and a "Household Fairy." In 1858, the editor of a farm journal said he was sorry he'd ever written a column about sewing machines, because his office was flooded with letters from women demanding advice about which model to buy. One Anna Hope had written to a farm journal in 1857 arguing that women needed sewing machines as much as men needed new farm machinery. (One wonders if Mr. Hope had been acting mulish about such a purchase.) The cost of the machine had to be weighed against the time saved by using it and what a woman might do with that time. "Next to the gospel, I consider the general introduction of the Sewing

Machine the best gift to woman," she concluded. "For it gives her time to cultivate her own higher nature, and to devote herself more fully to the best interests of her children." Some 98 percent of farm families and 92 percent of city folk owned a sewing machine by 1925.[11]

The home economists believed that the study of clothing required the sciences of physiology, psychology, hygiene, physics, chemistry, bacteriology, and sociology, not to mention history and economics, but they added art to that list for the same reason that Anna Hope praised the sewing machine: its ability to improve women's spiritual lives.[12]

That art should be part of American lives was a shift in more ways than one. Early in American history, the artist was considered dangerous because he created a useless luxury, pandered to aristocrats, and ogled nude models; but by the nineteenth century, art seemed to have a potential as a teacher of morality, and even ministers saw the artist as imitating God's own creative acts. Americans now identified art with spiritual concerns at a time when women were thought more naturally spiritual than men. At the opening of a fine arts college for women in 1889, a hymn proclaimed:

> God speaks in Art: all beauty, grace,
> And symmetry their models trace
> In His Perfections; there we view
> The Good, Beautiful, the True.[13]

No wonder the farmwomen longed for information on beauty in dress. The home economists were determined to satisfy their needs. One of the first of the Dress Doctors, Leona Hope, who taught at the University of Illinois, set the pattern in 1919 by writing an extension pamphlet called *Fashion: Its Use and Abuse*. The *Chicago Tribune* praised her as a "university apostle of sanity in feminine dress."[14] She followed up with pamphlets on artistic dress and color. The Dress Doctors directed their message largely at girls and women for two reasons. They assumed that boys would be trained in the art of dress by their mothers, and they knew that women's dress veered into discomfort and goofiness far more frequently than men's clothing.

Government became interested in teaching art as a way of improving industrial design and increasing profits for American industry in the late nineteenth century, but it was women who championed the movement to make art a part of everyday life so that all Americans could share in the spiritual benefits of beauty. William Morris of the English Arts and Crafts movement said, "Art should be no more for the few than liberty is for the few."[15]

Morris, and the Americans who would create their own Art and Crafts movement, believed that the rise of mass industry had destroyed the vital link between the work of the mind and the work of the hand by setting factory workers to mindless, repetitive tasks. All people needed to both design and make. Dressmaking answered this need perfectly.

When the USDA began offering cooperative extension work in the 1920s, clothing clubs were far and away the most popular option. In 1932, more than 324,000 girls joined clothing clubs. Cooking came in a distant second, with only 193,000 girls. (The rabbit club attracted a mere 275.) Extension programs were segregated, but both black and white women were enthusiastic members of clothing clubs. Extension agents from thirty-nine states published more than 250 publications for clothing clubs by 1932. Even the weekly radio broadcast of the *Farm and Home Hour* featured tips on sewing clothing.[16]

Clothing clubs at 4-H taught skills year by year. When a twelve-year-old girl joined 4-H in Ohio in the 1940s, she got a storybook about Molly, also age twelve, who learned how to hem a tea towel only to have her dog, Scamp, make off with it. Not to worry. The towel was recovered and would be as good as new after a washing. By age seventeen, a clothing club girl was skilled enough to make herself a graduation or prom dress. The clothing clubs remained overwhelmingly popular for decades. Whatever the extension agents were selling, farm girls were buying it.[17]

In fact, all of America was buying it. "Every woman has to think of clothes," said a New York City sewing club member in 1890, and no one wanted to pay too much for having them made up by a professional dressmaker. To earn the coveted rank of Golden Eaglet, a Girl Scout had to earn fourteen badges in the 1920s, including her Needlewoman Badge, which required her to make an apron, and her Dressmaker Badge, which meant making a dress or blouse.[18]

The home economists convinced the public that their work was valuable enough to be part of public education. By 1939, more than 90 percent of all but the smallest towns in America offered home economics programs in their schools, and 90 percent of junior-high-school girls were required to take courses. The Dress Doctors' books were published by the major houses, such as J. B. Lippincott, Charles Scribner's Sons, Funk & Wagnalls, Macmillan, D. C. Heath, Houghton Mifflin, and McGraw Hill, and they were so successful that they came out in multiple editions.[19]

The Dress Doctors came from all backgrounds and in all varieties. Women used the presumption that their sex had a claim on good taste to make themselves more valuable to manufacturers and retailers. That claim amounted to "cashing in on woman's sphere," as an advertising woman once put it. But most of the Dress Doctors sounded much less cynical.[20]

Some Dress Doctors came to the work by accident. Mary Schenck Woolman was born the daughter of privilege, but death and illness devastated her family. She was on the verge of bankruptcy when a fellow boarder's request for her to review a sewing book led her to write her own. It revolutionized the teaching of sewing. Eleven years later, she was professor of domestic arts at Teachers College at Columbia University. Dorée Smedley was a middle-aged frump when the editors at *Good Housekeeping* decided to make her over in 1939. Pictures of the apparently younger, thinner, and more attractive Smedley stunned readers, who denounced her as a fake. She launched herself on a national lecture tour to prove that she was real and then wrote her own dress book for other middle-aged women.

Other Dress Doctors were trained in their fields. Elizabeth Hawes, a dress designer who apprenticed in the United States and Paris, made a name for herself by denouncing the myth that only the French could design beautiful clothes. Ruth O'Brien studied textile dyes, but her obsession was standardized sizing. (Yet her greatest achievement, a study of the measurements of nearly 15,000 American women, could not end the practice of vanity sizing.)

Some of the Dress Doctors wanted to inspire women, such as Grace Margaret Morton, who wrote like a poet. Others seemed keen on shaming them into dressing well, such as Mildred Graves Ryan, the author of *Clothes for You*. A former high-school teacher, Ryan never stopped scolding teenage girls about their bad wardrobe choices.

The Dress Doctors who were home economists created a professional network among themselves. They reviewed one another's books, worked together on state and national committees, and saw one another at annual meetings. Because they were teachers, they thought about dress systematically and became prolific authors of dress textbooks.

Women trained outside of the field of home economics expressed many of the same ideas. Mary Brooks Picken, who ran her own fashion academy, learned her skills from her grandmother, from a neighbor, and from classes she took in Kansas City and then Boston. That Picken had no degree in home economics did not stop those who specialized in the field from using her books. Harriet and Vetta Goldstein were trained in art, taught applied art at the University of Minnesota, and did extension work. Many home economists came to rely on their book for their understanding of the art principles.

Sometimes a woman's career blurred the lines between home economics, retail work, and industry. Bernice G. Chambers got a bachelor's degree from Oregon Agricultural College, now Oregon State University. She then earned her master's degree in textiles research from the University of Washington with the help of a Bon Marché Fellowship (named for its sponsor, the largest department store in Seattle). In exchange for its funding, the store expected Chambers to test its merchandise in the university's textile laboratory. Chambers later moved to Washington, DC, to work as a textile specialist for the Bureau of Home Economics. She next taught fabrics, design, and fashion at New York University's School of Retailing. She also worked in advertising, consulted for Dupont Rayon, and taught at Pennsylvania State College, now Pennsylvania State University. Along the way she wrote books on color and design in dress and home decoration, on selling fashion merchandise, and on choosing from among the many possible careers in the fashion industry.[21]

If the Dress Doctors were a kind of extended family, Mary Brooks Picken was the grandmother of the clan, someone whose vast number of publications meant that almost everyone referred to her work. An entire branch of the family settled on the prairie at Kansas State College, now Kansas State University, under Margaret H. Justin, the ambitious dean of home economics there for more than thirty years. When her faculty complained early on about a lack of good textbooks, she told them to write some, and they did.

Alpha Latzke got both her bachelor's and master's degrees at Kansas State, then led the college's Department of Clothing and Textiles for twenty-four years, coauthoring book after book on dress along the way. Latzke was one of the spinster aunts of this large family. And for a woman, spinsterhood was often a prerequisite for a faculty position at a land-grant college in the early twentieth century. Any woman who married was usually fired.[22]

As in any family, there were a variety of temperaments. While Kansas produced industrious cousins, this family also boasted cheerful aunts like Dorée Smedley, who urged all middle-aged women to rejuvenate their lives, and cranky aunts like Mildred Graves Ryan. Elizabeth Hawes was the equivalent of that cool teenage cousin who wears black eyeliner, smokes, and makes cynical remarks. She wrote that high-school home economics courses, and later, art courses, had taught her nothing of value; she only learned to design clothes successfully by first spending several years trying and failing.

The distant cousins worked on fashion magazines and in the advertising industry and voiced the same core set of ideas. In fact, the Dress Doctors' ideas were eventually expressed by prominent women such as First Lady Eleanor Roosevelt, who remarked in the depths of the Great Depression, "I have seen women who spend very small amounts on their clothes but who plan them carefully, frequently look better-dressed than women who waste a great deal of money and buy foolishly and without good taste."[23]

Fashion is ever-changing, but the Dress Doctors' advice transcends their own time and its now vintage looks. Their principles offer a way to achieve the art of dress today and into the future.

Art

Principles for Beauty

T HE US DEPARTMENT OF AGRICULTURE issued a great many scorecards to ensure fair judging of the entries at hundreds of county and state fairs held across the country each summer. There were scorecards for judging butter and beef cattle, swine and sweet potatoes.

In 1927, the department issued a new scorecard that looked a little different from the others; it distributed its 100 points among a number of categories, including the following:

Artistic aspects . . . . .10 pts

Occasion . . . . .10 pts

Posture and carriage (if worn by contestant) . . .5 pts

Effect of underwear . . . . .5 pts

This was a scorecard for a Dress Revue, not a stock pen. It was designed for use by the judges of the work produced in the clothing clubs, the most popular clubs that the USDA organized for women and girls. With such a scorecard, the women working at the Bureau of Home Economics hoped to establish standards for "economical, becoming, and healthful apparel." They also wanted to end squabbles among judges and clothing club leaders over such vexing questions as whether an entry of colored underwear should be marked down in favor of one made in demure white.[1]

Centuries earlier, the rulers of Renaissance Europe had passed sumptuary laws to make sure it would be easy to distinguish at a glance a duke from an uppity merchant, or a respectable matron from a professional whore. The USDA never went quite so far, although some Americans would not have minded if it had. One Arkansas woman wrote the department in 1914 to insist that there ought to be a law to stop American women from dressing like "disreputable Parisian women." Instead, the women who ran the Bureau of Home Economics, and their sisters-in-arms at the nation's colleges, high schools, and junior high schools, embarked upon a campaign of persuasion in dress that would reach into practically every American home.[2]

Their campaign blended women's old responsibilities with the new opportunities opening up to them in the twentieth century. The nineteenth century had seen women as the guardians of religion and morality, two realms that were closely linked to an appreciation of art. In the new century, science entered the domestic realm in the name of healthier and more efficient living. Plus, women had gained the vote in 1920, launching them more fully into public life.

Helen Binkerd Young, a graduate of the Cornell University architecture program as well as an instructor in its Home Economics Department, wrote, in an extension pamphlet on household furnishings for farmwomen, that if a woman could "learn to see the relation between orderliness of arrangement and tranquility of the soul, between confusion and nervousness, between harmony of color and harmony of mind, between honesty of form and directness of thought,—then she will have realized the essential meaning of art in daily life." The words "tranquility," "harmony," and "calm" reflected the religious and moral responsibilities of nineteenth-century women, while "order," "organization," and "discipline" reflected the new twentieth-century interest in modern efficiency and activity.[3]

Young was writing of home planning and decoration, but her beliefs were shared by the Dress Doctors. Beautiful, efficient, and thrifty dress was the natural extension of a calm, well-ordered mind and promoted such qualities. And it improved a woman's chances at success. As one Dress Doctor explained in 1931, "the consciousness of being well dressed strengthens self[-]confidence, gives poise and courage to do greater things, [and] provides a keener wit, tact and resourcefulness."[4]

The Dress Doctors had great ambitions for their well-dressed sex in the modern age. Most of their students would marry and devote their lives to raising children, yet home economics textbooks stressed that the "the average woman" proved her good citizenship by looking after her family *and* paying attention to civic life. A book put out in 1936 by a team of home economists working in the Cleveland public schools featured pictures of prominent women, including Jane Addams, who worked to improve the lives of the poor and change the politics of Chicago, and Ruth Bryan Owen, who, having come into the public eye by being the daughter of the famous politician William Jennings Bryan, in 1928 became the first woman sent to Congress by a southern state. The final words of the 1936 textbook were taken from one of the most popular poems written during World War I, "In Flanders Field," by John McCrae, a Canadian doctor. The Cleveland authors sent off their students with a call to action.

"To you . . . we throw
The Torch: Be yours to hold it high!"[5]

Go, girl!

In a book for junior-high home economics courses put out the same year, a chic woman in a fur-trimmed coat is pictured standing in a voting booth, pondering her choices. Style and civic engagement, the authors seemed to say, are never at odds. This theme continued to be emphasized in later student texts. One book, published in 1963, explained that by dressing well, a woman could gain "a basic sense of security and self-respect" that would release her "from the tensions caused by concern about her appearance." She would then be free "to give her full attention to more vital matters, for herself and for the welfare of others." Dressing beautifully was satisfying in itself, because the human soul and eye craved beauty, but it was also a means to a more work-a-day end.[6]

And what of that squabble over whether colored underwear should be marked down if it showed up in a clothing club contest? The Bureau of Home Economics declared that such apparel was acceptable so long as it was "dainty, serviceable, and forms an in-conspicuous foundation for the outer clothing." The USDA rule on underwear is just one example of the art principles applied to dress. And the two women who distilled these principles into one handy and influential volume could be found teaching at the University of Minnesota.[7]

WHEN *TIME* MAGAZINE SENT A REPORTER to Minneapolis to inter-view Harriet and Vetta Goldstein in 1941, he treated them like a pair of dotty great aunts. No wonder. The sisters were white-haired spinsters who lived with their mother. Their appearance wasn't going to inspire any fashion trends. Harriet, the older and taller of the two, always wore dark maroon, Vetta navy blue. Their dresses were high at the neck and decorated with a pin at the throat. They wore sturdy, sensible oxfords and large black hats that looked a little too big on them.

For some three decades, however, the sisters had lectured together at the University of Minnesota on the decorative arts. They were so close a pair that they finished each other's sentences. Whenever Vetta got excited while talking about a painting during class, she would do a little dance back and forth in front of her desk without even knowing it. When they traveled to Europe, the sisters jotted every expense down in a book, even the price of the postcards they sent home to Mother. So it is not surprising that the magazine reporter who met them in their apartment was a little patronizing. "To University of Minnesota home economists," he wrote "their prim, judicious maxims are cultured pearls of wisdom."[8]

The Goldsteins were actually astonishing. First-generation Americans born to a Jewish couple from Poland who ran a general store in a small town in Michigan, both sisters had earned degrees in art. Harriet first attended the Art Institute of Chicago, and then both sisters went to the New York School of Fine and Applied Art, which later became Parsons School of Design. Harriet started teaching at the Art Department at Minnesota in 1910, and Vetta joined her four years later.

Students said that they were never the same after studying with the Goldsteins. The sisters' enthusiasm was contagious. Their evident happiness with their lives and their work inspired wonder among the young women. The spiritual satisfaction the sisters took in a beautiful object also fascinated their students, who yearned to dedicate themselves to life in the same "whole-souled way."[9]

The *Time* reporter had come to see the sisters on the occasion of the publication of the third edition of their one and only book: *Art in Every Day Life*. It was the only book they ever wrote because it was the only book they ever had to write. Published in 1925, it made them, so the reporter admitted, "the Emily Posts of domestic art and decoration." The University of Chicago, which once boasted one of the country's finest home economics departments, recommended it as an excellent student text. Every decade, the sisters came out with a new edition—four in all, the last in 1954. Every textbook on dress that followed that first edition borrowed from *Art in Every Day Life*, and every generation of American girls growing up during this time had their ideas on color and design shaped by it. Their book was "a bible to home economics classes from Maine to the Middle West."[10]

The sisters took several ideas from the Arts and Crafts movement and turned them to their own use. Like John Ruskin, the nineteenth-century English art critic, they thought of art, spirituality, and nature as intertwined. They believed that good taste was based on the order and beauty found in God's creation and reflected our highest ideals. Everyone could see that God had created an ordered universe, the Goldstein sisters believed, but to fully appreciate and imitate its beauty through art, one needed a trained mind. They would train women's minds. In dress, for example, "honesty and sincerity" were "the outward expression of one's ethical standards," the Goldsteins taught. Good dress design was "genuineness, as against imitation," so not even the smallest note should be false. Buttons should actually button something shut, for example, not fool you into thinking they did.[11]

Honesty was a common theme in discussions about dress. An appreciation for a Dress Doctor who had written a best-selling book read: "She believes in sincerity in clothes as she does sincerity in conversation or in writing." This is why the Dress Doctors believed that dressing children properly—in simple, beautiful, and comfortable clothing—helped "to improve the disposition, to cultivate genuineness, and to establish ideals."[12]

The notion that the design of an item could affect the ideals of the people using them had played out throughout the history of fashion. Think of the American Revolution, when homespun clothing made by the Daughters of Liberty signaled their independence from Britain. American suffragettes on parade usually wore white, a color that symbolized purity and the argument that women—the morally superior sex—needed to clean up politics by gaining the vote. Young working women wore clothing—sometimes ladylike, sometimes something tougher, such as overalls—to express their self-respect and sisterly solidarity when they struck for higher wages.[13]

The link between design and ideals was being played out elsewhere in the early twentieth century as well. Modern furniture designers rejected the folderol of the eighteenth century, a time when inlays of rare colored woods had been used to make a table, for example, misleadingly appear to be festooned with tassels and garlands and seashells. The Shakers of the nineteenth century were rediscovered and praised for their simple, unadorned, honest designs. Modern architects pointed out the incongruity of putting up English Tudor homes in Chicago, and Frank Lloyd Wright came up with a truly American style, the Prairie Style. The modern ideal of good design was linked to honesty and authenticity whether the topic was buttons or bricks.

The Goldstein sisters were encouraged by Ruskin's argument for why people should "get rid" of the idea that decorative art was a degraded form of art. Was not the ceiling of the Sistine Chapel decorated by Michelangelo? The logic worked in both directions. A student must realize, explained Harriet Goldstein, that "the art of a fine painting . . . is just the same expression that she finds . . . in a beautiful dress." Think of the body as a canvas, the fabric as the oil paints, urged another pair of Dress Doctors, and the woman's personality as the idea "to be given visible form" through clothing.[14]

Mary Brooks Picken urged women in 1918 to "take the matter of dress seriously and conscientiously," just as we do "reading matter for the development of the intellect." Jane Loewen, a milliner who taught at the University of Chicago, made the same comparison in 1925: "It is just as stupid to dress your body in ugly clothes as it is to fill your mind with cheap and ugly literature."[15]

Like the Goldstein sisters, John Ruskin and fellow designer William Morris had held that art was necessary to a happy and fulfilling life. Ruskin and Morris preached that the hand (the worker) and the head (the designer) should be one and the same person. Morris lived what he preached. He mastered many hand techniques before he set to designing tapestries and fabrics in his workshop. Yet, as with so many movements started by men to free the world from some oppression, the Arts and Crafts movement did not do much to free women. Women were not really welcomed as designers; they were usually set to work making products designed by men.[16]

The Dress Doctors put both design and creation firmly into the hands of women by teaching the art of dress and the craft of sewing. Two Kansas State teachers echoed Morris in 1935, writing: "The average person of today is said to be shorn of the opportunity for creative artistic expression that characterized the age of the craftsman." Clothing was happily the one remaining opportunity for creativity available to women, they pointed out, even if men's clothing had become deadly dull. The Dress Doctors delighted in discovering and encouraging female talent. One told the story in 1913 of a young girl who appeared at school in a gingham dress "so beautifully cut and made" that her teacher asked her where it had come from. It turned out the girl herself had designed and made it. The teacher arranged for her to take a specialized course in dressmaking at a technical high school to prepare her for a career in dress design.[17]

Of course, not all women sew, and the Dress Doctors knew this. Early in American history, many women who did not have a talent for sewing had their clothing made by professional dressmakers. Men's ready-to-wear lines developed long before women's, however, because military uniforms drove the manufacture of men's clothing on a large scale. As women's ready-to-wear clothing improved—before the 1910s it was considered so awful that it was the last resort of the poor—it became clear that more women would be buying their clothing rather than sewing it themselves or hiring a dressmaker. The shift to ready-to-wear clothing was helped by changes in fashion. In the early 1900s, styles moved away from the tight Victorian hourglass gowns, which only fit properly when they were custom-made, to a looser silhouette. By 1914, women were buying more ready-to-wear than men.[18]

Choosing combinations from among the myriad offerings of America's great department stores still offered women an opportunity for artistry. Harriet and Vetta Goldstein wrote: "The clerk who chooses the right hat and dress for a customer has done a piece of work that calls for much the same kind of knowledge as the man who designs and paints a picture." Although sometimes Dress Doctors noted that some women seemed to have an "innate feeling" for design, their message was ultimately democratic: every woman could be an artist. Armed with knowledge, "whatever fad or fashion may come, we can at least select the best of what fashion offers us."[19]

All we have to do is learn the principles that artists have relied upon for centuries. Harriet and Vetta illustrated their books with fashions from the past in order to emphasize that neither time nor place can alter the principles governing beauty in dress. A floor-length medieval robe with sweeping sleeves may no longer be the fashion, but it remains beautiful if it follows the art principles.

THE DRESS DOCTORS DREW UPON THE WORK of two important American art teachers, Arthur Wesley Dow and Denman Waldo Ross. Dow taught at the Pratt Institute and then at the Teachers College at Columbia University. He was a founding member of the American Home Economics Association and spoke on the "Household Arts" at its first convention in 1908. Dow turned the art education program at Teachers College into the most important of its kind in the country. His book on composition, which came out in 1899 and went through twenty editions, clearly had an impact on the Dress Doctors. Like them, Dow thought of art as "a way of life, of doing, of thinking, of feeling, of making choices, of living in a fine way." He studied art from all over the world, especially Japan, and came up with his own system of principles.[20]

The other important art teacher, Ross, taught at Harvard University, where he worked out what he called a "theory of pure design" in 1907. Ross denied that he could define "the Beautiful," but he was sure that he knew where to find it: in the order found in pure design.[21]

The Dress Doctors took their ideas, reworked them into the Five Art Principles—harmony, rhythm, balance, proportion, and emphasis—and applied them to dress.

As a glance around any college campus will prove, studying the principles of art changes how a person dresses. While the law faculty members in their neat, dark suits appear ready to testify before Congress, and the Romance language professors dress with a certain *je ne sais quoi*, it is the art historians whose subtle color schemes, unusual accessories, and artfully groomed heads draw admiration. There is one exception to this rule: art historians who study ugly things. If a professor's specialty is the life and work of an old man from Alabama who made murals out of carburetors and teaspoons, no one looks to her for fashion tips. For the rest of us, there are the Five Art Principles.

The Dress Doctors' art principles restored what historians call "the unity of truth," an idea that took a blow in the nineteenth century. Once all of creation seemed to be ordered according to the same God-given rules; now modern science—Darwinian evolution, geology, archaeology—challenged those centuries-old beliefs. In the hands of the Dress Doctors, the biology of the eye, the psychology of the human mind, and the principles of art agreed on beauty in dress and appealed to something deep within the human spirit. The spiritual implications were muted but clear early on. The Goldstein sisters, for example, liked to tell their students that when they strove for good taste, they must remember that "good" is only one letter away from

"God." But such spiritual ideas disappeared over time, and the emphasis on science became more pronounced. As one Dress Doctor put it, "art is founded upon definite principles as understandable and applicable as the principles that govern the different forms of science."[22]

The art principles capture truths sensed even by people who have never heard of them. As one Dress Doctor put it, "most people are more discriminating than we give them credit for being; if they do not quite know how to describe the ideal they cherish . . . they know a monstrosity at sight." For any woman who has realized that a certain outfit looks terrific, the principles will tell her why it does. For anyone who has looked over a friend's outfit and thought, "It just doesn't go," the principles will help her figure out exactly what went wrong.[23]

The Goldstein sisters evaluated student outfits before the class as a whole during a lesson on "Becoming Costume." One day a young woman stood before them in an outfit that hurt their eyes and broke several of the rules set out in their book. They could educate the poor girl later; for now they were determined to say something nice: "The blue in your blouse exactly matches the blue in your eyes," Vetta told her sweetly. "You may sit down."[24]

HARRIET AND VETTA GOLDSTEIN LIKED TO SAY that harmony, the first art principle, was like a strong family resemblance. All the different parts of an outfit need to look as though they are related to one another. Harmony requires some consistency. Even someone who has not learned the art principles will be jarred by the lack of harmony in design, the Dress Doctors told us, because our desire for it is innate. "A unified harmonious whole . . . is insisted upon inexorably by the mind," explained one dress textbook in 1935. "Complete satisfaction is not possible without it." Another author added, "Nothing is superfluous in such a design," and "nothing could be omitted without destroying the effect." Harmony satisfies both the eye and the mind.[25]

A family resemblance does not mean uniformity, however. If every element repeats the same color or shape, the design will be monotonous, even a little strange. That is why women in the 1980s who thought they would look taller and thinner if they wore the same exact shade, be it pumpkin or plum, from head to foot ended up looking like flight attendants on a spaceship. In order to achieve harmony, the larger elements making up any design need to be alike, said the Dress Doctors, but the smaller elements should vary. A little variety prevents a harmonious design from becoming a boring design. Too much variety, and the family resemblance will be lost altogether.[26]

And harmony, they said, has four elements—shape, texture, idea, and color. Each of these elements needs both that family resemblance and a little variety.[27]

The shape of a garment expresses harmony by following the lines of a living, moving human body. The lines of the body are naturally beautiful and its movement naturally graceful, so any clothing that impedes that movement is, by definition, ugly. "No dress can be really beautiful which in any way hampers action," explained designer Elizabeth Hawes in 1942. Of course, shape must accommodate what a woman wants to do. "Tennis is one thing, and drinking cocktails is another," said Hawes. Hawes herself liked to design with her feet up on a table, so she preferred loose trousers when working in her studio. When clothing restrains the body or gets in the way, it requires its wearer to use up more psychic and physical energy, which amounts to as much as a 10 percent decrease in efficiency, according to one early calculation.[28]

The two important violations of the principle of harmony of shape in the early twentieth century were corsets and high, pointy shoes. Fashion had once asked women with 26-inch waists to squeeze themselves into 20-inch corsets. Dress reformers asked women to rethink this fashion. Elizabeth Stuart Phelps, a best-selling novelist and crusader for dress reform, asked in 1877: "Could your father or your husband live in your clothes? . . . Could he conduct his business and support his family in your corsets?" Like men, women should be able to move freely in their clothes, said the Dress Doctors.[29]

Reform and shifts in fashion brought welcome changes. The 1920s brought a far looser fashion silhouette than the Victorian hourglass, and with it much relief. The Dress Doctors celebrated an end to the days when the corset's tightly laced stays rendered woman a "weak, faint, and frail creature."[30]

Shoes continued to be a problem for the Dress Doctors, and they still are. World War I asked women to take on men's jobs in factories when men went off to war, and women went off to help as nurses, ambulance drivers, and canteen workers, all of which prompted talk of getting rid of high heels. The YWCA required its war workers to wear so-called walking shoes, shoes with flat heels. The Y's head of physical education explained that study had proven that "a woman couldn't work, or walk, or have perfect health or a happy, cheerful disposition and wear high heels."[31]

Helen Goodrich Buttrick, a University of Chicago home economics graduate who went to work at Michigan State, argued in 1923 that pointy shoes and high heels handicapped women. "Fashion has caused women to compress their feet into shoes having soles anywhere from one-quarter to three-quarters of an inch narrower than the foot. . . . Not only this, but the foot is tilted forward and the whole ankle and instep thrown into an abnormal position by a high, narrow heel, and the toes are compressed into a point." Pointy shoes produce bunions, corns, enlarged joints, and overriding toes. In fact, Leona Hope of the University of Illinois had estimated, in 1919, that half of the young women in her classes had "hopelessly enlarged big-toe joints" from wearing high heels. Armed with X rays, the Dress Doctors at the USDA explained that women were crippling themselves.[32]

As career women, they hated the idea of women teetering their way into the work world. Women wasted energy and made themselves

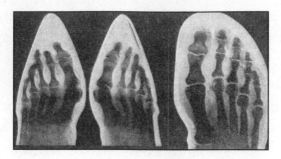

Fig. 1: The Dress Doctors from Kansas State
University used this USDA X-ray machine to prove
to women that "Toe Room Means Toe Health."
USDA

inefficient with such shoes. "If you want to be graceful, to work with
fine freedom and to stand without tiring," wrote an adviser in the Girl
Scout magazine in 1927, "don't mistreat your feet. Give them their
chance to carry your body well."[33]

Nine years later, two other home economists trained at Chicago
were wondering why women were still mincing along in high heels
with pointy toes. They decided it was because women misunderstood
the nature of beauty. "They say that the narrow, pointed shoe has
more slender lines and graceful proportion than the low-heeled,
broader-toed shoe," they wrote. "But what is the standard by which
we can judge true beauty in clothing design? The lines and proportion
of the human body are beautiful, and clothing must not contradict
those lines and proportions if it is to meet the first requirement of
well-designed clothing." A high, pointy shoe destroyed the grace and
freedom of a woman's stride. "If you watch closely you will see the
ankle wobble unsteadily as a step is taken," said the same authors.
Women wobbling unsteadily were unable to move confidently, and
they wasted effort staying upright that they could have used to get
something important done.[34]

Fashion editors agreed with the Dress Doctors. We think of
the 1950s as the decade of the stiletto heel, but *Vogue*'s longtime

editor-in-chief, Edna Woolman Chase, who helped to shape fashion tastes from her desk at *Vogue* from 1914 to 1952, advised against high heels or open-toed shoes on city streets. She spoke instead in favor of something "smart, comfortable, and with a medium heel."[35]

Yet today's fashion magazines are still giddy about shoes. The otherwise practical advice offered in *O* magazine—large bag, cropped jacket, gray trousers—is marred by insanely high heels on a platform pump. A feature on business wear in *Marie Claire* magazine in 2012 warns us, "When in doubt, stick to 3.5 inches or less." But television regularly features women running law firms, dissecting corpses, and chasing down bad guys in 4-inch heels.[36]

In a 2011 article for the *Wall Street Journal*, a fashion reporter condemned women for tottering tipsily down the street on high heels, then offered this strange solution: "I'm almost always in heels between 3 and 4 inches high—except when I have to walk more than a block." She changes into flats that she carries around in her purse when she has to walk more than a block.[37]

If you cannot walk more than a block in your shoes, they are not shoes; they are pretty sculptures that you happen to have attached to your feet. You could hang them from your wrists for all the good they are doing you in terms of locomotion. Better to put them on a shelf and admire them from afar. Remember Elizabeth Stuart Phelps, who asked, in 1877, "Could your father or your husband live in your clothes?" Well, could he live in your shoes?

Since hats are no longer fashionable, women's most frivolous urges have to be channeled somewhere, and shoes it is. But the idea behind a shoe for streetwear was support and protection, according to the Dress Doctors. It's a mean world out there; women need all the support and protection they can get. People will shoulder you on the sidewalk; sometimes you have to run for the bus.[38]

The most famous violation of the harmony of shape, however, was the "hobble skirt." It debuted in June 1910 and has been a byword for bad dress design ever since. A real hobble is a kind of soft handcuff used on horses to let them move around a bit but not roam. The hobble skirt did the same thing to women: it ballooned outward below the waist, narrowed at the knees, and was tightest at the ankle. "'The Hobble' Is the Latest Freak in Woman's Fashion," trumpeted a *New York Times* headline. The subtitle told the true story: "Skirts Are So Tight Around the Ankle That Locomotion Is Impeded and Speed Is Impossible." The paper printed pictures to accompany the story and declared: "These are not exaggerated at all. The skirts really look like this." Women were spotted in hobble skirts trying to hop across Fifth Avenue. Facing death by oncoming traffic, they yanked their fashionable skirts up to their knees (a shocking thing to do in 1910) and made a run for it. A Frenchman wrote a dance tune called "The Hobble Skirt Walk." A one-step, of course.[39]

The *Times* seemed pleased to report that summer that a hobble-skirted woman had fallen flat on her face in front of the casino at Newport while alighting from her electric runabout. A girl trying to hop over a mud puddle from a curb fell and broke her ankle. Then, the worst happened: a Miss Ida Goyette, eighteen years of age, wearing a hobble skirt, stumbled while crossing a bridge over the Erie Canal. She fell over the low railing and drowned.[40]

But death could not discourage the fashionable. By 1914, a similarly crippling number was dubbed the "eel skirt." According to one Dress Doctor, it, too, required "a piteous makeshift of walking." Slitting the skirt up the side made the tight, unyielding style ugly, but endurable, she said.[41]

Clothing this tight is "nothing short of disability," according to the Dress Doctors. No woman should allow her clothes to disable her, yet many did and do. Looking back from 1936, one author shook her head, writing, "It seems impossible that we should deliberately choose to wear clothing which makes it difficult to step into a street car, to dance, even to walk naturally, yet in 1913 we wore such skirts."

Another reminded her readers how they had laughed at women trying to move about in hobble skirts. "Do you suppose they gave a thought to design principles when selecting such garments?" No, they did not.[42]

But neither do we when we wear the hobble skirt's descendant— the straight skirt—as a short history of the skirt will show. In the 1920s, skirts were so straight and so loose that their sex appeal was limited to the lack of real underwear. With only camisoles and tap pants beneath, or a combination, called "step-ins," these dresses were most revealing when a woman moved and the fabric pressed against her body. Belts slipped down to the hipline, the only place where the dress was fitted to the body. Tight at the hips, the dress must have given a rhythmic "sha-boom" each time a woman took a step.

Typical 1920s skirts had only two virtues: they offered large, flat areas, which allowed for impressive beaded designs; and their loose fit, in fringed versions, made it possible to dance the Charleston with wild abandon. Elizabeth Hawes blamed these "shapeless bags" on the same "buncombe, hokum, and stupidity" that led to the Crash of 1929. But because 1920s dresses fell straight from the shoulder, often had pleats, and stopped at the knee, they left a woman's legs plenty of room to move.[43]

In the 1930s, skirts got longer for both day and night. Some say this illustrates that the fashion cycle and the stock market move in tandem. When times are good, hems go up; when times are bad, they drop. What the drop in skirt length in the 1930s really illustrates is that women can get tired of showing off their knees, especially when it requires wearing a shapeless sack.

French designer Jean Patou gave women a push in the new direction. After he looked around a drawing room of short-skirted women, he decided he could take no more and designed a collection with longer skirts. As the models showed the new designs within his spacious showrooms on the Place de Vendôme, he got the first reaction from his clients: "All the women are squirming about in their chairs tugging at their skirts. Already they feel démodée!" Skirts dropped to the lower calf and were always worn with a bit of a heel. Sometimes they were cut with a charming set of gores (a slice of fabric from the waist to the hem) that flared out around the lower edge and gave a flirty swish as a woman walked. Wealthy women lined up to buy Patou's creations, and the rest got tips from sewing books and women's magazines on how to add tiers of chiffon to their short dresses to lengthen them, and how to lop off the top of a dress and add a longer skirt in a new print fabric, with a tie-scarf and belt to match.[44]

The skirts of the 1930s were fitted through the hips, though they had some room to move, with flares below, but a version of the straight skirt did appear during the decade as an evening gown. Mary Brooks Picken disapproved of it heartily. It was "usually slashed to the knee to make walking possible," she said.[45]

By the late 1930s, skirts for daytime had shortened a bit again, moving to just below the knee. The new skirts were often gored and pleated. During World War II, the War Production Board froze American women's skirts at the then-fashionable length with its Order L-85. In order to limit the fabrics used by civilians, manufacturers were told that skirts for a woman with 38-inch hips could be no wider than 65½ inches around and no more than 28¼ inches in length. Soon home dressmakers were under the same order. As stultifying as it may seem, it was an optimal shape for the times. Gasoline and rubber were rationed during World War II, so more women did their errands on foot and by bus. Flared skirts hemmed just below the knee let them move easily.

It was Christian Dior who lengthened skirts 8 inches after World War II. France was free of the Germans, Americans were free of L-85, and Dior wanted to bask in the luxurious abundance of fabric. "We were leaving a period of war, of uniforms, of soldier-women with shoulders like boxers," he recalled of the old look. True enough. Take almost any women's suit pattern from the war years, do it up in dark blue, and you have a WAVE officer. Take almost any day dress pattern, do it up in white, and you have an army nurse. But Dior had something else in mind for women. "I turned them into flowers, with soft shoulders, blooming bosoms, waists slim as vine stems, and skirts opening up like blossoms," he later wrote.[46]

Dior's day dresses allowed a woman's legs plenty of room to move, but they were anything but serviceable. They flared as wide as 27 feet at the hem. His dinner dresses could take 40 feet of fabric. One remarkable concoction of a ball gown in 1950 was made out of layer upon layer of mauve and white silk netting—80 yards in all. Looking back at her own girlhood stints as a bridesmaid in New Look gowns, one historian of fashion celebrated the pleasure of wearing a dress spun from gossamer. Padding around the hips made the skirts flare wider and the models' waists look smaller. Waist-cinchers increased the effect.[47]

The New Look set off a panicked scramble across Europe and the United States as women tried to figure out what they could salvage from their now out-of-date closets. Some balked. A woman in Texas created an organization to freeze hemlines at a little below the knee; she led a demonstration in front of Neiman Marcus in Dallas. In California, young wives picketed a dress shop wearing bathing suits and holding placards that asked, "Do We Need Padding?" But they couldn't stop the New Look. "Hiplines, waistlines, hemlines so new you'll want them all," crowed Sears Roebuck in 1948 as it dropped the skirt length, nipped the waist, and rounded the hips of all its dresses. In 1952, McCall's Patterns boasted that one of its spring dresses was 7 yards wide at the hem.[48]

Still, there was no need to buy something new, if a woman was clever. Simplicity Pattern Company sold a pattern that showed how to take an old skirt and add either a yoke to the top or a flounce to the bottom. *Vogue Patterns* magazine suggested updating a tweed suit by adding a wide band of suede to the hem of the skirt, along with a suede collar and cuffs to match.[49]

But designers thrive on the new. In the fall of 1954, Dior launched what one editor called the "Flat Look." "Slithering through the couturier salons all over Paris," explained *Life* magazine, "some of the most striking and newest-looking designs were dead black, *femme fatale* outfits as skinny as shadows." These straight skirts still went down to the lower calf, causing the legs of the model wearing the Dior suit named "Conspiration" to strain against a tiny tube of a skirt narrower than her natural stride.[50]

By 1956, the straight-skirted sheath dress had tightened its grip on American women. Women were forced to run out to buy all-in-one corselettes and long-line bras that came down to the waist. A girdle sales manager boasted in 1956, "The sheath paid for my house in Westport." Women crowded into reducing salons in hopes of losing enough weight to fit into the new dresses. One Dress Doctor admitted that the necessarily "tight-fitting" sheaths were "difficult to wear, but excellent for the person with a good figure." And a good girdle, she could have added. Pattern companies nevertheless sold the same unforgiving sheath cuts for stout women up to size 22½, with a 41-inch bust, calling it "the slim look for five o-clock on . . . sure flattery for half sizes."[51]

Before the 1950s, dress design books pointed out that a skirt that dropped straight down from the hips was silly because it lacked "wearing ease." "Ease" is the term that designers use for the difference between the measurements of our bodies and the measurements of our clothes. Wearing ease allows a woman to move in her clothes. If she can squeeze into her jeans while lying flat on the floor, but can't sit down in them, they lack wearing ease. (Designers also speak of "design ease," which accounts for clothing that is much wider than necessary for easy movement, such as a coat that flares out dramatically from the shoulders.)

A skirt cut straight from the hip downward is a mistake, explained the Dress Doctors of Kansas State in 1935, because anything less

Fig. 2: Only a woman armed with the long-line corselette dared to wear the "little" dress in the mid-1950s. *BUTTERICK PATTERNS*, Fall 1954

than six inches wider at the hem than at the hips would miss the all-important "swing" that makes for graceful feminine movement. Pattern designer Harriet Pepin—who boasted a stylish French grandmother, studied at Parsons, and had her own Academy of Fashion—pointed out the drawbacks of a straight skirt in 1942: it might cover the legs enough to satisfy modesty, but it would not allow room for the legs to actually move. Hence, she showed how to add some flare.[52]

As Elizabeth Hawes pointed out in 1942, straight skirts pose a particular challenge for a woman's rear in action. Like Mary Brooks Picken, Hawes was a sewing prodigy. She could make clothes by the age of nine and was making and selling children's clothing in a small way by the time she was twelve. A Vassar College graduate who did a stint copying (i.e., stealing) designs from Paris fashion houses in the 1920s by posing as a legitimate customer, Hawes turned designer herself. Art museums now collect her creations. Hawes was marvelously opinionated, so much so that she got herself blacklisted for her support of workers' causes after World War II. Before then, she wrote several best-selling books on fashion that explained what designers of straight skirts still seem unwilling to admit: "When a woman sits down, the flesh around her buttocks and hips spreads." If a skirt is to avoid getting all kinds of ugly wrinkles, it either needs a hinge, where the body bends, such as a yoke across the top of the hip from which the skirt flares, or has to be full all around. "What you cannot do, and have a beautiful dress," Hawes wrote, "is to put a straight, flat back on a skirt."[53]

Designers have tried to cope with straight skirts by adding slits on the side, but the slit is the last resort of bad design. It's an admission that a garment doesn't actually allow the body to move. Some designers added a kick-pleat at the center back instead. Even so, a straight skirt must wrinkle across the hips and thighs if a woman is to engage in the simple act of walking. Straight skirts have no walking ease, much less running ease. Every woman who has had to hike up her skirt to sprint for a train knows this.

Even after the tight-fitting sheath arrived, the Dress Doctors continued to object. They pointed out that a gentle flare was kinder to the figure and avoids what they called the "cupped," or "seated," look in a skirt. These days, starlets' skirts are taken in at the seams in order to maximize the exposure of their rears. The Dress Doctors lived in wiser times.

The sheath remains a modern staple, and women don one (or two!) pairs of Spanx in order to wear it. And yet its flaws are obvious. Consider Michelle Obama's outfit on Inauguration Day 2009. The sheath dress looked great when she stood still, but she is not a woman to stand still. When she strode down Pennsylvania Avenue, her sheath did what they all do: pulled and wrinkled across the hips. The design flaw was apparent, though partly hidden by her matching coat.

So why are straight skirts still the default mode? Three reasons.

First, manufacturers know it is cheaper to make a straight skirt when it comes to fabric and labor. A straight skirt that hits just below the knee takes 1 yard of fabric and has two side seams. A six-gore skirt takes $1^5/_8$ yards and has six side seams. A circle skirt needs almost 3 yards and a great deal of hemming. Straight skirts are as much a matter of stinginess as they are of style.

Second, the dreaded Fear of Fat. FOF seems to guide all fashion choices today. Women hope that if they take all the wearing ease out of their clothes, they will reduce themselves to the tiniest silhouette possible. True. But this can also produce some appallingly bulbous shapes. Tight skirts also ignore the fact that a skirt with walking ease done up in a fabric that drapes well will make a woman's figure look more slender and infinitely more graceful than it appears in a straight skirt. The skirt will swing, ever so gently, as she walks. And when she sits down, she does not have to worry about it hiking up her thighs.

The third reason for straight skirts is that many of us have no idea how to dress attractively without squeezing ourselves into our clothing. Women seem to think that a garment fits if they have not yet burst a seam. We need a healthier alternative to the competition over whose dress is tightest and shortest. The Dress Doctors can give us one.

Modern fashion has also violated the principle of the harmony of shape in more flagrant ways. During the 1980s, women wore shoulder pads that made them look like linebackers for the Raiders. Then there was Rei Kawakubo, a Japanese clothing designer who got a lot of press in 1997 with her "Lumps and Bumps" collection: dresses that had giant lumps of stuffing stuck on them in random places.

The models looked like they were riddled with enormous tumors. Harriet and Vetta Goldstein would have furrowed their brows, told Ms. Kawakubo that she had picked some very nice colors, and then told her to sit down.

THE SECOND RULE OF HARMONY IS TEXTURE. A dress book from 1923 ended one chapter with a quiz: "Why should we not wear earrings with a middy blouse? Satin slippers with a sports skirt? Woolen sweater with a georgette dress? The answer: Harmony of texture requires that the different materials combined in an outfit all resemble one another.[54]

The idea is that all of the fabrics and leathers you are wearing have embarked with you upon the same activity, so they should have the same capacity to deal with the conditions that they are about to encounter, whether that be cold, heat, rough wear, or delicate handling. Earrings are shiny and delicate and liable to fall off, while a middy blouse is a tough, sporty number in cotton duck to be worn while playing tag. Satin slippers are fragile and prone to staining, so they should only be worn indoors; they should only have to endure dancing, while a sports skirt must make it through a hard game of tennis. A silk georgette dress is soft, fragile, and cool, best worn while floating across a dance floor or a garden party, but a wool sweater is rough and durable and meant for a chilly day. Wool and silk georgette cannot be worn together harmoniously.

The Dress Doctors would not be impressed with today's ensemble of silk blouse and blue jeans. "Silk, the fabric of luxury," wrote two Dress Doctors in 1935, "does not go well with cotton, the fabric of utility." They thought such a pairing "inharmonious," just as the Goldsteins did when they sighted the 1925 equivalent of silk and denim: hats made of golden lace worn with coarse wool sweaters. Tsk, tsk.[55]

Harmony in texture is also essential to success in sewing, which is why the Dress Doctors were particularly attuned to it. Because certain fabrics suit certain kinds of designs very well, we always see them together. If a tailored jacket with sharp lapels is going to keep its lines, it needs to be made of a fabric with some heft and crispness to it. Tightly woven wools and heavier silks will do. Try to make a tailored jacket in a soft rayon weave or a knit, and it will droop sadly. Take that same soft rayon or knit and make a dress fitted at the waist and flared below the hips, and the fabric will give the perfect swirl as a woman walks. To the dressmaker, harmony in texture has this second meaning.

True, today's fashion magazines throw all kinds of textures together, but they do that to make readers stop and stare. (People stop and stare at traffic accidents, too.) As a Dress Doctor explained in 1923, "such a combination outrages our common sense as well as our aesthetic sensibilities." The Dress Doctors recognized that the winds of fashion might throw two incongruous textures together for a time, but they were happy to observe that such "discordant" experiments were usually "short-lived."[56]

Harmony of texture mirrored their understanding of the difference between clothing for city life and country living. But a change of accessories allowed you to wear the same suit in either place if it "occupies a middle ground" in terms of texture. Take the casual tweed suit offered by the *Better Homes and Gardens Sewing Book* from 1961. In the city, people are surrounded by concrete and glass. They may have to run, but their running will be up and down stairs and in and out of buildings. They can wear finer fabrics and leathers without fear of ruining them. For a tweed suit to be worn while in town, the book suggested smooth and delicate textures: brown kidskin gloves, purse, and shoes; a silk scarf printed in a rusty brown; gold necklace and earrings; and a felt hat in yellow.[57]

In the country, people are walking among trees and grass and wooden fences, and may need to hop across mud puddles or skirt cow flop. For country wear, *Better Homes and Gardens* offered rougher and tougher textures: gloves, belt, and canister bag in heavy leather;

darker suede flats; and a wooly cardigan instead of the suit jacket. The difference between city and country seems less important now because so many Americans live in the suburbs, a place that splits the difference between the two. The suburbs manage to offer both office buildings and mud puddles, if not cow flop. Early suburbanites opted for slightly countrified wear, but today's suburbanites opt for no style in particular.

If suburbia split the difference between city and country, chemists who invented manmade fibers also undermined the logic of harmony of texture. Delicate fabrics of luxury were transformed into tough synthetics. Silk is a stunningly beautiful fabric laboriously made from threads gathered by unwinding the cocoons of silk moths. When dyed, the color seems to glow from within the fiber itself. However, because the quality of silk fabric is judged by weight, wily manufacturers of late nineteenth century took cheap silk and coated it with heavy metallic salts to make it pass as a better, weightier grade of fabric. Chemicals sometimes accounted for as much as half the weight of a cheap silk. Worse yet, the chemicals were known to make the fabric spontaneously combust. Women were advised not to store weighted silks in hot attics. One batch caught on fire simply sitting on a shelf in a Paris shop. Weighted silks burst into flame in the hold of a German steamship in mid-ocean in 1879, nearly sinking it. So, in the interests of shoppers and sea captains everywhere, the home economists convinced the Federal Trade Commission (FTC) to hold hearings on silk weighting in 1932 and to issue the first textile labeling rule to prevent anything less than 90 percent pure silk fiber from being labeled as silk.[58]

Silk makes up a velvet plush that is amazingly soft and beautiful, but extremely fragile. A drop of water will spot it. In an evening or two, a lovely velvet evening gown will become squashed in the rear from sitting. Designers in the 1920s suggested a solution: a dress made of two layers, one of tunic length. The wearer could sweep aside the tunic layer when she sat, and no one would ever see the squashed skirt layer when she was standing. Early textile manufacturers eliminated the problem by embracing it; they invented precrushed versions: *nacré* (pearlized) velvet, and *panné* (pressed) velvet.[59]

In contrast, stretch velvet, made out of polyester, first marketed by Dupont in 1953, seems almost indestructible. Figure skaters use it for costumes. Throw it in the washing machine and dryer, and it comes out fine. Only months of use can squash the plush slightly. The same is true of lace, which was once woven by hand, every thread interlaced by patient fingers. Now, most lace comes in machine-made nylon that can take a beating. Embroidery, too, once took many hours to make by hand and was done with silk; now, except in rare cases, embroidery is sewn by machine with rayon or polyester thread.

EMBROIDERY BRINGS US to the third element of harmony: idea, which requires that decoration not interfere with an object's purpose or distract from the lines of its structure. One of Harriet and Vetta Goldstein's favorite examples of bad design was a particular flyswatter that they brought to class on the day devoted to the harmony of idea. The flyswatter was embroidered with wooly flowers that definitely interfered with its purpose. It was, to quote the sisters, "manifestly absurd."[60]

Decoration on a dress can violate the principle of harmony of idea by distracting from the garment's structure. To use a humble phrase of the Dress Doctors, decoration on a garment should not look "stuck on." Jewelry, too, should be "subject to the rules which insist that the lines and colors of a costume be kept in mind and the decorations subservient to these."[61]

Some Dress Doctors would not tolerate any added decoration. Elizabeth Hawes considered her dresses complete as she designed them. If they needed any decoration, she had already put it on. When a woman trying on one of her creations made the mistake of asking,

"What kind of jewelry shall I wear with this?" Hawes had the urge to commit murder. The habit women had of "sticking extraneous objects on themselves"—pins shaped like Scottie dogs, birds, or arrows—was proof of the survival of "the primitive instinct" of decoration, an instinct that should please only children, thought Hawes. Grown women should learn "a more sophisticated appreciation of beauty that is to be achieved by fusing their clothes and their bodies, making one beautiful whole."

Hawes condemned Italian designer Elsa Schiaparelli for failing to achieve that fusion. "Schiaparelli's tendency was simply to put flat designs onto round bodies," Hawes complained. In truth, Schiaparelli was capable of cutting a suit for a round body with expertise, but Hawes was thinking of Schiaparelli's wackier creations, which were inspired by the paintings of Pablo Picasso and Salvador Dali. Schiaparelli covered the back of an evening jacket with embroidery that was either the silhouette of a vase of flowers, or two faces turned toward one another, depending on how you squinted at it. An enormous lobster by Dali sprawled across a white evening gown. The "Desk Suit" was spotted with pockets shaped to look like desk drawers, only some of which were usable as pockets. Amusing, but not good design, according to America's Dress Doctors. As Hawes put it, Schiaparelli "designed clothes for long flat boards and not for women." Indeed, the embroidery and the lobster would have done just as well hanging on a wall. And the Desk Suit? It would have made . . . a nice desk.[62]

Clothing most often violates this element of the harmony of idea through overdecoration, such as when innumerable bows, flowers, or buttons are stuck on without any regard for the overall structure of the garment. "Temperance is desirable in decoration as in life," opined a dress book in 1935, "and is, perhaps, as uncommon."[63]

The demand for simplicity in decoration places the Dress Doctors alongside other twentieth-century thinkers: architects, interior decorators, and even writers came to stress the importance of simplicity. The elaborate dress of earlier eras struck the Dress Doctors as silly.

One book used the eighteenth-century portrait of Doña Matilda Stoughton de Jaudenes by the artist Gilbert Stuart to "illustrate the period when woman's line was obliterated by the excessive decoration of her costume." In addition to a mystifyingly complicated belt around her waist, *La Doña* wears what appears to be a basket of feathers on her head from which hang golden stars or snowflakes, or something. She also appears to have emptied her jewelry box onto her person. Compare her, the book instructed, with the dramatically simple portrait of *Madame X* by John Singer Sargent. Her black dress is decorated with only its jeweled straps. The sparkle of a small ornament adorns her hair. (You can see both paintings at the Metropolitan Museum of Art in New York.) In the twentieth century, girls were taught that "overelaboration often causes the dress to smother the personality of the wearer."[64]

La Doña and Madame X had their clothes made for them. The rest of us rely on ready-to-wear where trimmings are often added in order to distract us from a poor design and a cheap fabric. But "a good pattern needs but simple decoration to accent its fine design," wrote two of the Dress Doctors. Laura I. Baldt of Teachers College featured in her 1929 volume a color sketch of a set of decorated undergarments that she praised for their simplicity. The camisole and tap pants were of pale turquoise silk crepe de chine trimmed with appliqués and binding of tan silk chiffon attached with hand-stitching. Simple decoration could be exquisite. But bad design tries to distract us with a frenetic assortment of decoration such as our shapeless acrylic Christmas sweaters covered in reindeer, snowflakes, penguins, and Santas.[65]

The last element of the principle of harmony of idea pertains to the style of the decoration itself. The subject landed the Dress Doctors smack in the middle of a tussle among nineteenth-century British decorative artists.[66] In one corner stood Owen Jones, one of the most influential designers of the mid-nineteenth century. Jones was the author of *Grammar of Ornament*, which summed up a lifetime of ideas in thirty-seven propositions. His Proposition 13 requires that any decoration inspired by nature be "conventionalized," or stylized. Instead of roses reproduced realistically down to the last detail, Jones called for the suggestion of a rose, such as the red and pink "Mackintosh Roses" that take shape with only a swirl of black outlining.

Charles Dickens mocked the conventionalizers in the weekly magazine *Household Words*. He has a Mr. Crumpet of Clump Lodge, who had recently acquired "correct principles of good taste," take tea at a friend's house. Suddenly, having spotted a realistic decoration, he drops his cup and saucer and falls back in his chair with a cry of agony:

"Papa, papa, what is the matter?" cries his child.

(The poor man is so overcome he can hardly speak).

"Butter-fly inside my cup! Horr—horr—horr-ri-ble!"

(He is taken home in a cab).[67]

John Ruskin called Proposition 13 "absurd" and stoutly defended realism in decoration. When the conventionalizers condemned a carpet covered with realistic images of roses as a misleading fraud, Ruskin pointed out that flowers were strewn during festivals, for weddings, or in the path of a hero returning home. So why not put realistic-looking flowers on a carpet?[68]

It was a romantic idea, but the Dress Doctors sided with Jones. They condemned realistic decoration as dishonest—those are not flowers on the rug; incongruous—for goodness' sake, why would we want flowers on the rug; boring—if we wanted flowers, we would go outside and find them; unimaginative—ditto; and ugly—those are ugly flowers on the rug. Stylized designs, they said, were preferred by "people of taste." The battle that began with Ruskin, Jones, and Dickens continued well into the twentieth century with the invention of new materials. Vetta Goldstein explained to the *Minneapolis Star Journal* in 1944 that it had erred in praising plastic furniture that mimicked mahogany. "Whereas an honest piece of molded plastic might be excellent for some purposes, an imitation of wood graining and carving in plastic is the height of insincerity."[69]

The Goldsteins offered an example of how to conventionalize an image for a dress. A grapevine should not be drawn in realistic detail as if it were growing up the side of a dress; better to run a mere suggestion of a grapevine around the border of a sleeve.

The modern equivalent of that literal grapevine design would be our printed T-shirts. So shapeless that they resemble the flat boards at which Elizabeth Hawes sneered, T-shirts bring out our primitive urge to stick things on ourselves. A T-shirt might have the exact image of a sea otter floating in a sea of kelp. Sea otters are adorable, but why float one across one's chest? As Harriet and Vetta Goldstein liked to say: a picture needs a frame.

COLOR IS THE LAST ELEMENT OF HARMONY. It can be as simple as using variations of the same color in an outfit, or as complicated as working out a three- or four-color harmony. Of course, artists have written and thought about color for centuries. But the systematic study of color dates back to Isaac Newton, famous not only for his theories about gravity and the laws of motion but also for his discoveries about optics and light. Much of the technical language of color and many of the basic principles of the effects of color were worked out long before the Dress Doctors through Newton's work and then through important new theories that appeared in the twentieth century. The Dress Doctors used this specialized vocabulary, but their main points about color are easy to understand. In fact, many will remember the basics from playing with paints in school.

The primary colors, or primary hues, as the Dress Doctors called them, are three in number: red, yellow, and blue. Mixing them together makes the secondary colors or hues: red and yellow make orange, yellow and blue make green, red and blue make violet.

As the Dress Doctors note, all of these colors have effects on the eye and on the mind. Red, yellow, and orange remind us of fire and the sun. They seem to give off heat, which is why they are called the warm colors. Margaret Story was a slightly loopy but popular author on dress and home decoration who did the rounds of women's clubs and radio programs during the 1920s and 1930s. She attributed enormous emotional powers to colors. In fact, emphasizing the psychological impact of color, she called herself a "consulting dress doctor," saying that her advice might do away with the need for a psychoanalyst.

The warm colors are stimulating and cheerful, but the color red is so powerful, warned Story, that "a headache or even an attack of nerves might be induced by the violent hue." Other Dress Doctors wrote, less dramatically, that bright, warm colors seem to advance toward the viewer, and so dresses made up in them appear larger than they really are. Therefore, the Dress Doctors advised, one should bring them into an everyday ensemble in limited quantities. Skip the orange day dress in favor of a brown dress trimmed with orange. Save the orange dress for a dramatic occasion.[70]

The cool colors—blue, green, and blue-green—are quiet, calming, and serene. They remind us of the heights of the sky and the depths of the ocean. Story went so far as to say, "A blue frock would increase spiritual emotions and induce the recalcitrant one to attend the Sunday morning church service!" But pale, cool colors can also seem so dreamy that they leave a woman hankering for a shot of espresso to get through the afternoon. Cool colors seem to recede from the eyes, which is why a dress in a blue-green looks smaller than it actually is. "The stout woman . . . if she wishes to conceal her size, . . . should select the most becoming of the receding colors," concluded the Goldsteins, "and leave the conspicuous, advancing hues to the small, slender figures."[71]

Warm and cool meet between red and blue. Their mixture produces shades of violet or purple that seem more serious than other colors, reminding us of the deep shades of evening. At their best, they are stately and mysterious, like the plush velvet robes of a queen. The ever-romantic Margaret Story wrote that purple "speaks of sleeping passions conquered and of suffering gallantly borne." At their worst, red-blues and blue-reds can seem depressing and dreary, like faded lavender flowers.[72]

Warm and cool also meet between yellow and green. Because yellow-greens remind us of the leaves of plants, the Dress Doctors said, they can make us feel cheerful and peaceful, like a walk in the park.

The Dress Doctors called the primary and the secondary colors "the principal colors" and advised that most of us cannot wear them. Only those of us with the richest complexions and the liveliest of personalities can wear them. Bright colors, to quote *Paris Frocks at Home* from 1930, "extinguish" the rest of us. People will notice and re-member the dress but overlook the woman wearing it. In short, never let your clothing make more of an impression than you do. Women can wear a red dress, insisted the slightly contrary Elizabeth Hawes, but only "if they are not afraid of it, if they can stand up to it."[73]

For those of us who are not in the mood to make the effort, many other colors are easier to wear. Mixing primary and secondary colors produces a few of them; such mixes "are more interesting, more refined, and more effective" than the obvious primary and secondary colors. Add blue to blue-green to produce a dark turquoise; add red to violet and amethyst results. Or we can mix the principal colors with the neutrals of white, black, and gray. Adding white to any hue creates a pastel, what the Goldsteins called a "tint." Add white to red and you have pink. Adding black to any principal color results in what the Goldsteins called a "shade." Add black to red, and you get burgundy. Those Dress Doctors who taught sewing pointed out that layering a transparent fabric—such as georgette or chiffon—of one color over another fabric, which was not transparent but that was too bright, was a wise method of toning down the latter: "The effect is similar to that produced in nature by mist, haze, frost or twilight," said one.[74]

Adding gray to any of the principal colors produces what the Dress Doctors called a "tone." Complicating (and beautifying) the notion of grayed tones is the fact that grays come in a wide range, from deepest charcoal to palest oyster. Grays can be laid out on a "Value Scale" that gives each variation a number according to how dark or light it is. Value 1 is pure black, value 2 is the darkest charcoal gray, and so on, with value 9 being the palest of grays and value 10 pure white. All colors fall somewhere on the Value Scale depending on whether they have had black, gray, or white added to them. The Dress Doctors taught that the darker values should come at the bottom of any outfit and the lighter ones at the top to keep the apparently heavier hue at the bottom. Such a design takes a tip from the beauty of nature: "The earth, grass, and trees near at hand are darkest, the distance is lighter, and the sky is lightest of all," wrote two of the Dress Doctors in 1936. And so the top of your dress should also be the lightest color used in your ensemble.[75]

The value of a given color is important. When in doubt, when combining different hues in an outfit, keep to the same value. A dark red and a dark blue, both of which are colors mixed with black, will combine well, while a dark red and a bright blue will probably be jarring. And as anyone who has dressed a baby in a combination of pale pinks, blues, and yellows knows, all the tints combine easily together. Colors also vary in intensity, which can overlap with value. A red tint, for example, is usually less intense than a pure red, but a screaming fuchsia pink may be much more intense than the pure red. The Dress Doctors advised using the most intense colors in the smallest amounts for two reasons. First, such colors can overwhelm the eye through their brilliance. Second, they have reflective power. Imagine several people gathered around a table during a committee meeting. One woman has very pale skin and has wound a neon yellow-green scarf around her neck. The scarf reflects on her face, tinting it the palest of greens. She looks ill. An older woman sits at the other end of the table looking perfectly healthy. She's wearing a suit the color of orange sherbet that casts a golden glow upon her face. This is the reflective power of color and the reason why the only creature that should be wearing bright yellow-green is a small poisonous tree frog living in the Amazon.

One of the simplest and most satisfying ways of combining colors, according to the Dress Doctors, is the one-color harmony, which takes a color and adds its tint, tone, or shade. College women studying home economics called it a "monochromatic" harmony, from the Greek words for "one" and "color." One-color harmonies may sound boring, but they made Dress Doctors swoon. One called them "symphonies" and thought there was no prettier dress for spring than one that combined the several shades found in the petals of violets, from the deepest shade at their middle to the palest tint on their edges. By 1930, the Sears Roebuck catalog was touting "harmonizing costumes," such as a dress in *Marron Glacé* (French for sugared chestnuts) to wear with dark brown shoes, hat, bag, and gloves.[76]

Jewelry can be part of a one-color harmony if it adds intense colors in small doses. A magazine writer mused over the perfect taste of an advertising executive named Helen Lansdowne Resor: "Henna flat crêpe . . . a Vionnet model . . . gorgeous color for her brown eyes and chestnut hair . . . simply heavenly lines . . . the topaz beads are a nice accent." Twinkling yellow topazes could "awaken" the somberness of a brown costume, pointed out Margaret Story. So would the purple-blue of lapis lazuli for an outfit of navy blue.[77]

Closely related to one-color harmonies are the neighboring color harmonies, also known as "analogous" harmonies, which combine colors found next to each other on the color wheel. Such combinations "create a rhythmic, vibrating effect very pleasing to the eye," wrote Grace Margaret Morton, who taught at the University of Nebraska.[78]

So a dress pictured in a high-school textbook, for example, came in a medium-brown shade and was paired with dark brown shoes, belt, and hat and a warm gold hat ribbon and scarf. The browns are shades of orange, and gold is a shade of yellow, which sits next to orange on the color wheel. A golden-brown cocker spaniel was even included as a harmonizing accessory!

It is no accident that the dress copied the colors of autumn. In keeping with their understanding that art merely copies God's creation, the Dress Doctors thought that nature was the ultimate color harmonist. Margaret Story relieved the anxiety of women from the western part of the country who feared they could not keep up with Gotham, much less Paris, when she wrote in 1925 that women on the coast, surrounded by nature, "unconsciously take color schemes that nature originates." While women from the East could get caught up in every passing fad, the blooms of the western landscape inspired women "to dress naturally and beautifully."[79]

Indeed, the Dress Doctors believed that nature supplied the most beautiful and inspiring of the neighboring color harmonies. They referred to color studies that listed the following:

the blue/violets of the skies,
the yellow/oranges of sunsets,
the green/yellows of plants,
the blue/greens of the ocean,
the red/oranges of fire.[80]

How can one go wrong following such lovely examples? There is only one way: if the two hues chosen are so similar that it looks like they were supposed to match exactly but don't.

More ambitious color harmonies take more thought. Colors lying opposite one another on the color wheel are "complements." The complement of blue is orange, so the Dress Doctors would show a brown dress—brown is a dark shade of orange—trimmed with a blue collar, cuffs, and hat. A "split complementary" is a combination of colors that form a "Y" on the color wheel. A blue dress worn with a violet hat form the top of the "Y," and the bottom of the "Y" is orange, which can be added with a scarf at the neck.

The triad combines colors that form a triangle on the color wheel. Some of the Dress Doctors suspected that a triad of the primary colors of red-yellow-blue satisfies some primal human need because it is so common in nature: "The evening sky often presents a glorious mingling of blue sky, golden sunlight, and red glow low on the horizon," noted one book. In a dress, this same beauty might be achieved with a print of red and yellow flowers on a pale blue background.[81]

For these kinds of color combinations, the Dress Doctors held that the "safe rule" is to combine one color in a large area, one color in a smaller area, and a third in even smaller areas. Bright colors are like spices: a pinch goes a long way. "Cultivated people"—and don't we all consider ourselves cultivated?—"do not like abruptness in any of the relations of life," wrote Kansas State Dress Doctors, quoting a specialist in interior decoration. "Suave curves and blended colors please in the same way that suave manners and carefully modulated voices please, and for the same reason."[82]

Color-blocking, which we see in the unfortunate modern practice of wearing a bright pink bodice with a bright orange skirt, came under attack. One Dress Doctor wrote that, in wearing such a dress, a woman declares: "Here I am; you are obliged to see me, for I am a blot on the landscape, an object that defies the canons of true art."[83]

The possibilities of color harmonies gave shivers of pleasure to Grace Margaret Morton, who considered centuries of cultures and their colors. "If we like, we may appropriate the earthy tones and lapis lazuli of old Egypt," she wrote, "or the rich glowing jewel tones of the aristocrats of the Renaissance with their costumes stitched stiff with sparkling gems. We may choose the refined and smoky tones of rose and green, fawn and blue violet of the late eighteenth century; or the joyous pomegranate reds, heavenly blue-greens and topaz of Chinese embroideries; or the strong magentas, rich, dark sunset oranges and brilliant greenish yellows of Mexican folk arts." A whole world of color from which to choose.

Imagine the world's colors multiplying and combining endlessly. Artists can do it with tubes of paint. Dressmakers search fabric stores and experiment with dyes to create the exact hue they are seeking. The rest of us have to sort through the offerings of stores to find what we want. But shopping counts as a creative effort, too. "The choosing, assembling, and wearing of costume which demonstrates art principles in a superior way can be for many a high form of original expression," Morton assures us, "bringing satisfactions comparable to that of the artist's original achievement."[84]

Mary Brooks Picken believed that a woman should learn color harmonies for herself, but the Woman's Institute produced a remarkable chart to help steer us. A glance reveals both the richness of the Dress Doctors' vocabulary of color—have you ever heard of "Gobelin"? "Quimper blue"? "Bois de rose"?—and the extraordinary subtlety of their understanding of color. After all, how many of us have thought to trim a black dress with a combination of pistachio green, the lightly grayed blue called "Copenhagen," and the pale orange of a honeydew melon? For the record, Gobelin is a greenish blue-gray, a color often seen in French tapestries of the Gobelin brothers made in the late fifteenth and sixteenth centuries. Quimper is the Anglicization of Kemper, a town in the province of Brittany in France, and the blue is a medium pure blue found on the region's famous pottery. Bois de rose is French for rosewood, a softly grayed red.

All of this can be a bit overwhelming. Emily Burbank, author of The Smartly Dressed Woman, wrote in 1925 that she realized that "the average woman, more often than not, stands stupefied before the infinite variety of materials and colors of our twentieth century."[85]

Fig. 3: Part of the Woman's Institute's remarkable chart of daytime color combinations.

	Black	Navy	Brown	Red	Green
Combinations in Large Quantities	White Copenhagen Reseda American beauty Champagne Putty	Pearl gray Beige Gobelin Scarlet Lacquer Old Gold	Beige Old gold Maple sugar Reseda Terra cotta *With red browns* Bois de rose	Gull Nude Ecru Black White	White Sand Champagne Silver Jasmine Old gold
Combinations in Small Quantities	Salmon Pink Turquoise Flesh Tangerine Emerald green Chartreuse Fuchsia Carmine	Maize Pink Spanish yellow Strawberry Emerald Chartreuse Hollyhock Carmine	Blue turquoise Coral blush Maize Gold Burnt orange Almond green Chartreuse	*With bright red* Navy *With wine shades* Peasant blue Amethyst Old rose	Mignon lavender Spanish yellow Amethyst Pablo Topaz Weigelia Grecian rose
Combinations For Trimmings	Violet Royal blue Cherry	Bisque Mahogany Burnt orange	Tarragon Pablo Crab apple	*With bright red* French gray Marine Black	Crane Amethyst Crab apple
	Pistache Copenhagen Honeydew	Spring green Old gold	Gold Olive Mulberry fruit	*With wine shades* Mignon lavender Quimper blue Raspberry	Gold Lacquer Leaf mold
	Chartreuse Nude	Strawberry Saxe blue Tarragon	Topaz Henna	*With wine shades* Pigeon Royal blue	Terrapin Tangerine
	Periwinkle Jade Jasmine	Magenta Bottle green Imperial purple	Mahogany New cocoa Peasant blue	*With rust or henna* Beige Quimper blue Mahogany	Mulberry fruit Raspberry Oakwood

WOMAN'S INSTITUTE OF DOMESTIC ARTS AND SCIENCES, *HARMONY IN DRESS: COLOR, ITS THEORY AND APPLICATION*, 1936

The Dress Doctors believed that any woman could learn to use color
harmonies if she put her mind to it, but they agreed on a list of the
universally flattering colors for those who wanted some guidance:

> Dark blue, like navy, and grayed blue
> Dark green
> Dark blue-green
> Dark red, violet-red, and orange-red (which includes
> 　　browns)
> Dark warm gray (i.e., taupe)
> Black
> Warm off-whites (i.e., whites with a little yellow in
> 　　them, such as ivory or cream)
> Lighter blue-greens
> Lighter orange-reds (i.e., coral or peach).[86]

Notice that there are no pure colors here. They are all shades,
tones, and tints and the neutrals of black, gray, and white. In 1914, an
early Dress Doctor advised using "vivid hues for pleasure, dim ones
for sobriety, and all the delicate shading taste and judgment can direct
for the ordinary circumstances of life." Laurene Hempstead, a retail
specialist who worked for Fairchild Publications and lectured at New
York University, concluded that certain bright, pure hues were almost
universally *un*flattering:

> Bright vivid blues
> Bright blue-violet, violet and red-violet
> Bright yellow and orange

Even a woman whose coloring and personality were strong
enough to handle these colors would look better if she wore something else, Hempstead said. The Dress Doctors were also of one mind

when it came to black on older women: don't, but that is a topic for Chapter 6.[87]

One caveat: these lists are for women whose ancestors came from Europe. Although the Dress Doctors studied fabrics and garments from across the globe, they did not view all lands equally. They often traveled to gather items for their personal collections of textiles, which later became the beginnings of their universities' textile museums. Elizabeth Tarpley of the University of Texas joined a group of home economists in 1937 to study the textiles of China and Japan. And the Dress Doctors brought their discoveries into their teaching. A woven Peruvian bag might illustrate the ideal of proportion. No lesson about informal balance was complete without a Japanese print. Persian miniatures were used to display color harmonies. And the American Indian provided "our country's most original contribution to the world's esthetic estate."[88]

But Africa was not a source of design ideas for the Dress Doctors. "The term primitive should be applied only to the instinctive work by the tribes of central Africa, certain Polynesian peoples of New Guinea, New Zealand, Hawaii, or Samoa," explained Elizabeth Burris-Meyer of New York University in 1938, in her historical guide to color. Kansas State authors implied that the penchant for abundant decoration found among such tribal peoples was proof of their barbarism.[89]

Perhaps we should not be surprised at the attitude of the Dress Doctors in this regard, as they lived in a world where retailers used the words "*Tête de Nègre*" and even "Negro" and "nigger brown" as names for a season's colors. There was no "Caucasian," but there was "Flesh," which meant only the pale pink-orange of the skin of white people.[90]

That the complexion charts in textbooks went as dark as a light-skinned Hispanic is testimony to the popularity of Hispanic stars in silent movies and the early talkies. Dolores Del Rio, whose skin was described as "palest café au lait," played elegant women and was described as Mexican, which she was, or as Spanish or Castilian.

Photoplay magazine dubbed her "the present leader of the Latin invasion whose sudden success has been equaled only by the Scandinavian Greta Garbo and the American Clara Bow." But no crossover African American stars darkened the complexion charts any further. Hollywood remained segregated, and so did the Dress Doctors' books.[91]

The Dress Doctors identified only "Five Types of Complexions" and the best color choices for people of each type.[92] The Goldsteins illustrated the Five Types by putting them into historical dress, in order to keep us focused on the colors, not the styles. All the complexions presented were essentially warm, as they ranged from pale pink to pale red-orange, but the Dress Doctors divided them into those that were paler, and thus cooler, and those that were redder, or warmer.

They put the woman with skin that falls in the cool color range with golden hair and blue eyes into a single-color harmony of blue, but noted that she can also wear blue-purples, purples, blue-greens, and greens.

The cool type, with blue-black hair, pale skin, and blue or gray eyes, can wear the same colors as the blonde, with the addition of the red-purples, which she was shown wearing in the Goldsteins' book.

Then there was the redhead, whose hair is really a shade of red-orange. Redheads are relatively rare, but the Dress Doctors had a weakness for them and discussed them at length. Her skin is a warm color, often peachy. The redhead can tone down her hair, as the Goldsteins did by illustrating one wearing a brown dress. Brown is a dark red-orange. To play up her hair by stressing its complement on the color wheel, she can choose soft greens, blue-greens, and brown-greens. The pale blue veil that the redhead wore in the Goldsteins' book aimed at a complementary color harmony.

Next was the brunette, a woman with a warm skin type and dark brown hair. Her strong coloring means she can choose much brighter, warmer hues than the others, because they won't overwhelm her. The

Goldsteins put her in an analogous color harmony of yellow-orange, orange, and red-orange. But she can also wear darker colors, they said, such as red-browns and bronze-greens, when she is feeling less aggressive.

The intermediate type is most people of European descent. She is neither strikingly warm nor strikingly cool. In fact, she is not striking at all. But the Dress Doctors assured their readers that this is no cause for lamentation. Intermediates have options. We can decide to play up our blue eyes with clothing of cool blues and greens, or our brown eyes with the warmer hues of gold and orange.

Having identified Five Types of Complexions, the Dress Doctors were happy to admit that human beings presented innumerable variations, people who could wear a large number of colors. "It would be impossible and useless to list all the thousands of hues which might possibly be worn by each group of individuals," wrote Elizabeth Burris-Meyer in 1935.[93]

This is where the Dress Doctors part company with the 1973 book *Color Me Beautiful* by Carole Jackson. Jackson's book said every woman could be identified as one of the four seasons and prescribed a palette of colors for each. (Later the number of types was raised to twelve.) Women were supposed to go out and buy clothes that matched their palette. The Dress Doctors would have found such limited palettes laughable. Besides, the Dress Doctors wanted to train women to use their own eyes to make judgments. And the *Color Me Beautiful* system did not work all that well in practice. As an experiment, one woman had her colors "done" by thirty-two color consultants. She was told that she was a Spring. And a Summer. And an Autumn. And a Winter.[94]

African Americans appear only once in Grace Margaret Morton's book, when she asks her students to "make of selection of colors to bring out the rich skin tones of a member of the negro race." Her students would have to figure this out for themselves, since nothing in the chapter actually dealt with the rich skin tones of the Negro race.[95]

Mary Brooks Picken was one of the only early Dress Doctors to acknowledge openly that her advice on color was useful only to Caucasians. So it is unsurprising that she was also the only one to admit that "savages" could attain "many excellent effects" with their brilliant color choices, even if she believed that civilization called for subtler, quieter colors. Elizabeth Hawes was unique in her wholehearted welcome of the contributions of African Americans to fashion. She wanted all American men to branch out into brighter colors, and she praised the black men of Harlem for "wearing wonderful colored suits" in "light blues, bright greens, stripes of orange and rust."[96]

So African American women were almost entirely on their own when it came to advice on choosing the best colors for their complexions. Black women earned home economics degrees in small numbers, but they tried to fill in the gap. Their books were few and short, thirty pages in one case. No big New York publisher would put them out. Their efforts are a testimony to the determination they had to provide black girls with information that every white girl took for granted.

"The peoples of dark skin have been forgotten," wrote Ella Mae Washington in 1949 in her *Color in Dress (For Dark-Skinned Peoples)*. And yet personal appearance was essential to their success. "They must look the part if they are to reach the height to which the race is aspiring," she noted. As a woman who taught at a black college, Washington felt a particular need to use her home economics training at the University of Iowa to do well by her people.[97]

Although black women had to fight against the racist presumption that they were all loose women, their advice for dressing wasn't all that different from that of the white Dress Doctors. Baptist women were taught to avoid "gaudy colors and conspicuous trimmings." At the time of the eel skirt, Baptist mothers were warned that any skirt that was so tight it needed a slit in it should not be found on their daughters. The Dress Well Club of the Detroit Urban League advised migrants from the South to avoid "carelessness in regards to dress" and "flashy clothes" in 1917. When a woman joined a Pentecostal church in the 1920s, the sewing circle helped with alterations to cover her cleavage and knees. Racism only made these recommendations for good taste more important.[98]

Another black author, Charleszine Wood Spears, had never seen her own coloring studied in the textbooks she was assigned in home economics classes. After teaching in the Kansas City public schools, she decided in 1937 to write a textbook that covered "the darker races." She dedicated her book to her mother, "one who symbolizes every beautiful ideal of womanhood."[99]

Spears came up with her own names for three general types of non-Caucasian complexions:

Negra, the Black woman
Brunegra, the Brown woman
Blonegra, the Yellow woman

Ella Mae Washington agreed with Spears's recommendations, although she was content to name her major types of dark complexions, more prosaically, I, II, and III.

The "Negra" woman with truly black skin and hair must avoid bright yellows and bright reds, according to Spears, yet looks lovely in the darker tones and shades of each. Spears acknowledged the long history of racial mixing in America when she called this type of woman "the full-blooded Negro woman."[100] Dusty colors, such as rose gray and sandalwood, make up the neutrals she can use.

The black woman with very dark brown skin looks well in the same colors as her darker sister, said Spears, but she can wear more intense and brighter versions of these colors. The black woman with brown skin has more of a red undertone in her complexion, so reds of all kinds look good on her, as do the warmer yellows and the grayed greens. She can also wear the paler neutrals, such as eggshell and cream. And all of these women can wear seal brown and black.

The "Brunegra" woman includes Mexican Americans, Native Americans, and African Americans who have skin a shade of medium brown paired with jet black or dark brown hair. The red or red-yellow undertones of her skin harmonize with the colors red and yellow, and she can wear a wide range of them, from the brightest hue of "American Beauty Rose" and canary to the quietest tint of champagne and shell pink. She can also pick from the palest eggshell to the darkest chocolate or black for neutrals.

The "Blonegra" woman came from Asia in Spears's schema, although Spears admitted that women of mixed white and black ancestry and the peoples of Spain and Portugal could have similar coloring. Within this category, Spears put the olive-skinned woman with black or brown hair, who can wear all the reds, from scarlet to maroon; all the oranges, from paprika to tangerine; and the duller yellows, such as maize. She must not wear pure blues or greens, only grayed or blackened blues and greens. Pastels are definitely out, and the only neutrals she can wear are the dark browns, such as seal and tobacco.

A woman with pale yellow skin and black or brown hair can go wild, said Spears, with intense reds, such as cherry, and intense oranges, such as Mandarin. Like her darker sister, she should stick to the duller yellows and greens, but her neutrals can be much more varied, with everything from cream and gray to brown and black. If she has auburn or red hair and dark eyes, then the yellows, browns, and grayed browns look good on her, and so do most blues and greens. If she has red hair and gray or blue eyes, then blues, greens, and purples are her colors.

The woman with yellow skin and yellow hair was Spears's last subtype. On her, purples of all kinds look good, and so do bright and dark blues, grayed greens and dark greens, and dark reds.

Spears's preference for warmer colors on African Americans was shared by many. A 1966 survey of African American girls from Detroit, who fell within the middle range of Spears's dark complexions, named red as their favorite color to wear. The white girls at the school liked blue best.[101]

THE SECOND ART PRINCIPLE IS RHYTHM. Rhythms surround us: they are in the turn of the seasons, the waves on the shore, the hours of the day, and the beat of our hearts. "Our response to rhythm is largely instinctive," wrote a Dress Doctor at Teachers College at Columbia University in 1916. Grace Margaret Morton asked her students to appreciate the rhythm found "in fields of waving grain, in smoke curling from a chimney, in the folds of the robe worn by 'Winged Victory.'" She was referring to the *Winged Victory of Samothrace*, a dramatic sculpture from ancient Greece that stands at the top of a staircase in the Louvre in Paris. Rhythms can be vigorous and exuberant, explained Morton, or they can be slow and stately, or exciting, or calm and dignified. The rhythm of a garment should suit its purpose and its wearer's personality. Whatever the type, rhythm creates order through repetition, yet it allows us to feel "the double pleasure of anticipation and realization" as our eyes follow its motion. Our eye is led along by rhythm, or it should be.[102]

The Goldsteins pronounced one strip of lace pleasing because the eye could follow the easy flow of its recurring curves, just as it follows the inner curves of the nautilus shell. They condemned another strip of lace because it asked the eye to go every which way, following at least three different rhythms, leaving its possessor a bit annoyed. The same is true of dresses.

Examples of good and bad rhythm were offered by Mabel B. Trilling, who taught at the University of Chicago in the 1910s before moving on to the Margaret Morrison Carnegie School for Women (founded by Andrew Carnegie in honor of his mother), and

Fig. 4: Far too many rhythms on the left and the correct use of rhythm on the right. MABEL B. TRILLING AND FLORENCE WILLIAMS, *ART IN HOME AND CLOTHING*, 1928

her colleague Florence Williams. "In order to put education upon a really sound and scientific basis," Trilling and Williams urged their fellow clothing teachers to come up with standardized tests. They combined this commitment to science with an equal devotion to art and wrote half a dozen books on art, home decoration, and dress.[103]

Trilling and Williams offered examples of good and bad rhythms in all their books. The good examples stuck to one rhythm that allowed the eye to travel easily from skirt to bodice, or bodice to sleeve, where it found the same soft curve or harder angle repeated again. The bad examples offered rhythms, but far too many of them. In one instance, rounded scallops showed up on the bodice front and cuffs, creating one rhythm, while zig-zags on the collar and cuffs created another. The triangle of a pocket created a third. Such a variety of rhythms annoyed all the Dress Doctors. The Goldsteins said that

when the eye is faced with too many rhythms, "the result is so confusing that it is tiring."[104]

Sticking to one rhythm is best, but it's no hardship, because
rhythms come in a great variety, each having its own psychological
effect. First, there's repetition, which reminds us of a picket fence
when stripes cover an entire garment. Repetition is orderly and tidy,
but it can get a little boring. Sequence, or progression, is a rhythm
with gradations, such as moving from large to small, from dark to
light, or from top to bottom. This is seen in *ombré* fabrics, for example,
which have gradations of color. Annette J. Warner, who organized the
teaching of the household arts at Cornell University, offered a sketch
of a coat by Erté, a Russian who went by a French name when he
began designing clothes and theater costumes in Paris in the 1910s.
The coat combined gradations of narrow to wide bands alternating
in white and black.

Alternation is another kind of rhythm. Here, a pattern alternates
between two or more series, as in, say, a print fabric that repeats a
row of circles, then a row of flowers, again and again. Plaids offer the
rhythm of opposition, where sets of lines and colors meet and repeat
at right angles to one another. Radiation is the rhythm found in a skirt
of sunburst pleats flaring out from the waist.

But not all rhythms are equally good. Margaret Story recounted
how a dignified woman appeared in a spotted silk dress. Her hat was
covered with round pinwheel cockades, and her slippers were trimmed
with round buckles. There is something inherently loopy about so
many spots, and "her most serious statements were met with laughter."
Of course, if she were a comic actress, the outfit would have worked
perfectly. The point is to choose a rhythm that suits your purpose.
Which brings us to the third art principle: balance.[105]

ALMOST EVERY DRESS BOOK FOR JUNIOR-HIGH GIRLS asked this question: What happens if you put a big kid on one end of a seesaw and

a little kid on the other end? Bang! The big kid whacks down on the ground and the little kid pops up into the air. A seesaw works better if the kids are about the same size. Design works better with balance, too. Balance is needed in art, explained the Dress Doctors, just as it is in "the social order, man's mind, his body, or his work." The eye seeks balance unconsciously. Without balance, it grows uneasy and fatigued. One Dress Doctor pointed out in 1930 that "sometimes in hectic modern lives" we need balance more than we realize. Since 1930, our lives have only become more hectic. An unbalanced design in a dress gives you the weird sense that the woman who is wearing it is lurching precariously to one side. Unbalanced design cheats the mind of its "sense of repose."[106]

There are two kinds of balance in dress. The simplest is formal balance—perfect symmetry. If you can cut a dress right down the middle and get a mirror image on each side, the dress has formal balance. Each half of the collar is the same, each pocket balances one on the other side. Formal balance gives "a sense of equilibrium, stability, permanence." A formally balanced dress can lend its wearer a stateliness and dignity precisely because of its static quality. Formal balance suits serious occasions and women of a certain age and power. But formal balance can also seem somewhat mechanical.[107]

The other kind of balance is informal, or "occult." It's the balance you get when you put two small kids on one end of the seesaw to balance one large kid on the other side. Together the small kids can lift the big kid off the ground. This is the balance a designer creates when she counters a draped gather on the left shoulder with a draped gather on the right hip.

Some early Dress Doctors did not like informal balance. Since the human body is formally balanced, they argued, so should our dress be. But the study of Japanese prints—a popular activity in American art schools from the late nineteenth century onward—convinced many that informal balance was both natural and beautiful. Laura

Fig. 5: Straight lines create a feeling of force, formality, and directness appropriate for work and travel, while diagonal lines create grace and elegance perfect for evenings out. ANNETTE J. WARNER, *ARTISTRY IN DRESS*, 1926

I. Baldt, who taught at Teachers College at Columbia, chose a print from Toyokuni, a Japanese artist, for the opening image of her 1916 dress book. Informal balance gives a dress or other outfit a feeling of movement, of spontaneity, because the eye follows the design from one side to another; yet it never creates a feeling of instability. Informal balance also gives the dress designer many more possibilities to explore. The potential for sophisticated, informally balanced dress designs explains why the Goldsteins admired it, and why it eventually became the Dress Doctors' favorite form of balance for women over the age of thirty.[108]

When the human body isn't naturally balanced, in fact, dress can help. Margaret Story told of a woman who was burdened with one hip higher than the other, along with a high shoulder and an arm that was two inches longer than the other. She wanted desperately to camouflage her figure. She "found a heavy drapery over one arm, balanced by a band of fur and slim pointed train, a dream of rare delight," said Story. No one could see the flaws.[109]

AT ITS SIMPLEST, the fourth of the Five Art Principles, proportion, requires that a woman avoid making her figure look out of scale. A large woman cannot carry a tiny handbag without looking like she swiped it from a child. A tiny woman cannot lug around an enormous handbag without reminding us of a little girl playing in her mother's closet. Retailers took such suggestions seriously: Lord and Taylor introduced proportioned handbags in small, medium, and large sizes around 1950.[110]

These are only the simple rules of proportion. In order to understand the more important ones, we need to travel to three places: the University of Minnesota in the 1940s; Pisa, Italy, in the twelfth century; and Greece in classical times.

First, to the University of Minnesota, and a story told by Esther Warner Dendel, a colleague and friend of the Goldstein sisters.[111]

An angry student stormed into Harriet Goldstein's office one afternoon. "I have to tell you, Miss Harriet, that I don't believe in your old art principles!" Note, this was the 1940s, when students were very well-behaved. This young woman, whom we shall call Greta, was way out of line.

Harriet flushed, but kept her temper. She asked the girl to sit down. Greta was a farm girl, big and muscled, a first-generation American born to German parents. In almost every class, she got angry about something. The cords on her neck would stand out, her jaw would twitch, and she would glare at people with her pale blue eyes.

The teachers found her so disturbing that some talked of throwing her out of the program. The Goldsteins wanted to let her stay. Harriet's theory was that Greta had found that she couldn't rebel against her father, who ruled his home with an iron fist, but that she could rebel against the teachers, and so she did. Vetta said, "We must try to teach her how to rebel in a gracious and creative way."

Greta sat down in a sulk in Harriet's office. She was ready to do battle, but Harriet was ready, too.

"These aren't my art principles, my dear, they belong to nature," Harriet said. "Now, why don't you like them?"

"The rules are too confining. Too limiting," the girl said. Her voice was high and nearly hysterical. "I want to be FREE!"

"The rules are limiting," Harriet admitted. Greta's jaw dropped. She had expected more of a fight, but Harriet went on. "That is precisely their value, their glory. The blessings of limitation are beyond our comprehension. One day we must talk about those blessings."

Harriet told Greta about Leonardo the Blockhead. Born in the twelfth century in Pisa, Italy, Leonardo earned his nickname because he was always daydreaming and preferred to play with his pet rabbit than with other children. Leonardo got a second rabbit and kept records as his rabbits multiplied, as rabbits will do. He noticed that each larger number of pairs of rabbits seemed to be the sum of the previous two: 1, 1, 2, 3, 5, 8, 13, 21, 34, 55, and so on. Leonardo Fibonacci grew up to become a mathematician. He is now remembered as a genius, not a blockhead. In *The Book of the Abacus*, he introduced the world to the Fibonacci Series, which is found not only in frisky rabbits, but in proportions throughout nature. The seeds in the head of a sunflower form two spirals that follow the Fibonacci Series, as do the compartments that spiral inside a nautilus shell. Divide one of the numbers in the series by the one that comes before it, and you get a number that becomes closer and closer to 1.618 as you proceed to the higher and higher numbers. This number has been given the Greek name Φ, or *Phi*. It is the Divine Proportion, the golden ratio, part of God's order in the universe, and it has been found to be especially associated with beauty. "This is nature's hidden, exciting geometry. We feel comfortable, pleased with it," said Harriet, and this is why people have so often organized a design around a two-to-three ratio—for example, by making an object 2 feet wide by 3 feet high, or by taking something 5 feet high and marking a break 3 feet from the ground to create two spaces: one 2 feet high and the other 3 feet high. The ancient Greeks used this two-to-three ratio to plan everything from the Parthenon to vases. Europeans relied upon it to build cathedrals. Moderns used it for homes, placemats, and dresses.[112]

Look at your little finger, Harriet told her student. If we call the length to the first joint one unit, then the length to the second joint is one as well, and the length from the second joint to the knuckle is two, and from the knuckle to the next joint is three. It's the beginning of the Fibonacci Series. The whole human body can be measured this way. The same ratios repeat from the foot to the waist, from the waist to the neck, from the neck to the head, from the hand to the lower arm, from the lower arm to the upper arm, and even in the divisions of the leg.

Other Dress Doctors followed Harriet Goldstein's example. "Nature has planned our bodies so as to express pleasing rhythm of line and proportion," wrote Trilling and Williams in 1936. "Should our clothing not emphasize the beauty of these lines and proportions?" Garments that acknowledged the body's divisions "will be beautiful and interesting in their proportions," and those that don't will be ugly and awkward.[113]

The Dress Doctors considered 1-to-1 ratios to be the ugliest kind in dress. They pointed to the short dresses of 1924 that belted at the hips and ended at the knees. "Of course, everybody looked hideous," wrote Mildred Graves Ryan, a former high-school home economics teacher, but everyone followed the fad anyway. Today very short skirts worn with a top that stops at the waist have the same effect. A 1-to-1 outfit is blocky. It proves that "monotony kills," to quote Leona Hope of the University of Illinois.[114]

All the obvious proportions—such as 1 to 1, 1 to 2, and 1 to 3—are bad, while the more subtle ones that follow the body's natural proportions—2 to 3, 3 to 5, and 5 to 8—are good. Faced with subtle divisions, "the mind does not detect the exact proportion at once," Leona Hope explained. "The attention is stimulated and held, and interest is the result."[115]

Yet the Divine Proportion is not a rigid formula, Harriet Goldstein insisted when talking to Greta. Instead, it is a feeling for space, a feeling that needs to be cultivated through study. Greta left Harriet's office with two things: a begonia, so that she could observe the Fibonacci Series as it appeared in the plant, and an assignment: use the Fibonacci series to create a set of quilt patterns. "Share them with the class," said Harriet. "Vetta and I would photograph them for you. Who knows what may come of it? Some magazine may even want to publish them." We don't know if they ever were published, but we do know that Greta was no longer angry.

Like Harriet Goldstein, the rest of the Dress Doctors held the ancient Greeks in high esteem because they had discovered some of the most fundamental elements of beauty. Laura I. Baldt at Columbia's Teachers College marveled, "How many centuries has the Greek drapery held first place in the realm of beauty!" Another teacher of design, at New York University, called the Greeks "ingenious" lovers of beauty.[116]

But the Dress Doctors failed to realize that when it came to ideals of human proportions, the Greeks also left us with a curse. Surviving Greek statues present an impossible ideal: the eight-head-high figure. A Greek statue's full height amounts to the length of her head multiplied by eight. The Dress Doctors were willing to admit that most high-school girls managed 6½ heads high at best, and that women averaged 7½ heads high. One Dress Doctor admitted that the Greek

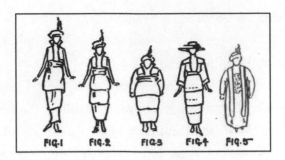

Fig. 6: First, the fashion plate twelve heads high;
second, the Greek eight heads high; third, a stout
woman who believed the fashion plate; fourth, her
taller neighbor; and fifth, what the stout woman
should wear. LEONA HOPE, *ARTISTIC DRESS*, 1919

ideal of 8 heads high was "seldom found in actual man or woman."
Yet it persisted as the ideal.[117]

Fashion illustrators only made it worse. Professor Hope explained
in 1919 how they mess with our heads by offering us impossibly
tall creatures not only 8 heads high, but even 12 heads high. The
Dress Doctors made a point of telling their students that fashion
illustrations were deceptive. Two professors at the Alabama College
for Women warned in 1932 that women in fashion illustrations were
always far thinner and taller than is physically possible. Any fashion illustration had to be reimagined on "the human figure" in all its
stubby splendor.[118]

Despite their insights into the deception, the Dress Doctors were
not immune to the siren call of the fashion illustration. Starting with
Leona Hope, the home economists at the University of Illinois were
some of the leaders among land-grant colleges in putting out dress
publications. They published their first circular on organizing a clothing club for girls in 1922 and followed it up with a second edition in
1924. Each edition featured girls in "middy blouses," named after the
midshipmen of the US Navy. American mothers had long expressed
their chaste love for sailors every spring by putting their offspring into

middy blouses with big square collars in combinations of red, white, and blue. So it was natural that clothing clubs taught girls how to make them. It was a project designated for fifteen-year-olds because it involved trimming the finished blouse with braid and proper insignia. The photo from the 1922 edition showed two grinning girls accessorized for the two occasions for which they would wear middies: school and sports. So far, so good.

The photo was captioned: "School Girls are Attractive in Middy Blouses." But apparently they weren't attractive enough, because they were replaced in the 1924 edition by fashion illustrations that had taken on the impossible proportions of Greek statues. One textbook on fashion illustration from 1930 offered pictures of women who were 8½ heads tall, and by 1953, they were 9½ heads tall. Fashion design students today are regularly assigned an illustration book called *9 Heads*. The Greek curse lives on.[119]

THE FIFTH AND FINAL ART PRINCIPLE, emphasis, is so important in both life and art, according to the Kansas State Dress Doctors, that failure to achieve it in either will lead to disaster. "Failure in life purpose or loss of the goal that dominates a life may lead to the disintegration of the personality," wrote the authors of one text, which is why people who have had a terrible disappointment may have a nervous breakdown. A dress can't have a nervous breakdown, but it can have the wrong kind of emphasis. Annette J. Warner of Cornell University wrote that "emphasis in dress design, like emphasis in reading or speaking, is more forceful when used sparingly and in the right places."[120]

Let's start with the wrong places.

A black satin evening gown sailed down the runway in the spring of 1934. Across one shoulder and the front bodice sprawled a seagull in full flight. A seagull in flight is a beautiful thing, but a fake one, stuffed and sewn across the bust line, is bizarre. If this were an event to raise money to save the seagulls, there would have been some excuse. At a dinner party, there was none at all. The seagull dress is an example of misplaced emphasis: nobody will pay any attention to the woman wearing it.[121]

There are plenty of other examples of goofy emphasis, some carefully preserved in museums of art. Italian designer Elsa Schiaparelli's famous Lobster Dress looks like an advertisement for a seafood place. A leotard with two dragonflies embroidered directly over the nipples is "incentive for exercising," according to *Cheap Chic*, a wonderfully awful book from 1976. Indeed, the generation of the 1970s seems to have harbored a yen for flying creatures perched on breasts. We find white birds tie-dyed over each breast on a leotard in one book, and two baby chicks appliqued over the breasts on an undershirt in another. The editors of *Mademoiselle* called the latter the "chick-shirt."[122]

Compare those monstrosities with a long, white silk jersey gown described by Grace Margaret Morton in 1943: "There is a beautiful movement of corded shirring across the shoulders, and the fullness of the garment is confined at the front with a simple tie belt. Played against this extreme simplicity is the owner's beautiful topaz jewelry—a necklace, brooch and earrings." The eye sweeps up the length of the gown to the shoulders, where the jewelry draws its attention, before it settles on the face.[123]

All good dress design moves the eye upward on a garment so that it can come to rest on the face—not the breasts, not the hips, not the seagull, not the lobster. The earliest Dress Doctors emphasized the spiritual element of the face. One pair writing in 1913 paraphrased a political scientist who expounded on the moral quality of a woman's hat: "Woman makes both a spiritual appeal and a sex appeal. The spiritual appeal is made through the expression of the face, while the sex appeal is augmented by bodily contrasts. Whatever thus features a woman's face, whether in art or in dress, gives her a spiritual impress."

It follows that a hat that brings attention to the face leads to moral uplift. Who knew?[124]

In 1925, another Dress Doctor would argue, less spiritually, that the face is the most important part of the body: "It is the part that most clearly conveys one's personality to strangers and impresses itself upon the memory of friends," she wrote. Later Dress Doctors did not bother arguing, they just said bluntly that the emphasis must be on the face.[125]

A corollary is that anything that draws attention from the face—be it elaborate cuffs, pockets, or buckles—is "poor design." Junior-high textbooks advised students to stand in front of a full-length mirror and ask themselves a question: "Is the face the center of interest in *your* design?" Or, God forbid, "Did you come to school to-day with a flower or bow in your hair, with a bright-colored sweater with pins, with a brilliant plaid skirt, gay ankle socks, dirty saddle shoes, and maybe a ring or bracelet?" asked Mildred Graves Ryan. "Did you by any chance have the idea that you looked charming? I hope not." The Goldsteins called such a look a three-ring circus. Even too many matching accessories—hat, gloves, shoes, scarf—all in the same lively color force the eye to jump from place to place without ever settling. Without a point of emphasis, "the eye grows weary and the mind confused." The Dress Doctors called such outfits "spotty."[126]

Notice that when Professor Morton described that beautiful white silk jersey gown worn with yellow topazes, she did not mention any shoes. Obviously, the woman was wearing shoes, but to Morton they were unimportant. The obsession that many of us have with shoes today may have grown, like weeds, from the abandonment of the Five Art Principles. If you don't think of your ensemble as a composition, you don't ponder yourself from head to toe. But it's easy to see the one part of you that is always visible to your eyes without the need of a mirror: your feet. Thinking of your appearance as a composition means imagining how others see you. Looking at your shoes is seeing yourself entirely from your own perspective.

AND FINALLY, A WORD ON PRINTS. Most prints did not please the Goldstein sisters, because they send the eye whizzing from place to place. The eye needs something to rest on (harmony) without boredom (variety). In fact, prints require almost everything that an entire ensemble needs. They need harmony, rhythm, proportion, and balance, but without too much emphasis on any one element. With so many requirements to meet, a good print is hard to find. The wildest ones approved by the Dress Doctors were paisley designs, but they much preferred subtle plaids, stripes, dots, and small florals. They feared prints that seemed to move or "vibrate unpleasantly." American women actually bought more of these small and subtle prints than they did large or vibrating prints. This preference, explains one book, was "partly due to many women instinctively knowing that a too-interesting material may interfere with their own personalities." One kind of print that we have today could be added to the list of subtle prints: the vague print that reminds you of a watercolor painting that has lost its focus. It offers no particular motif, but merely gentle swirls of color.[127]

The other reason why prints are a problem is that they need to suit the woman wearing them—the general rule is that larger prints are appropriate for larger women, and delicate prints work better for tiny women. But even that rule does not always work. There are "few women sure enough of themselves . . . to wear big, bold designs in material," wrote Elizabeth Hawes.[128]

And there is also a technical difficulty when it comes to sewing with large prints. The motifs cannot be matched easily, if at all, at the seams where the pieces of fabric are sewn together. So a lovely image of a giant flower, for example, may be cruelly lopped off on one side of a blouse only to appear again in full on the other side. This may mean little to most women today, because even expensive ready-to-wear clothing is often cut so carelessly that the print does not match at the most obvious point—the front seam. But dressmakers have always aimed for matching the motifs in order to allow the eye to travel smoothly across them without a hiccup. The most recent answer to the problem of large prints is what I call the tablecloth solution: a garment consisting of a rectangle with a hole for the neck and slits for the arms. Then, the large flower, sunburst, star, or other image remains intact. But a tablecloth is not much of a garment. And do you really want your face to compete with that large flower or sunburst?

Even if the images are not cut into pieces, prints can create un-intended effects. A McCall's shift dress from 1966 put a gigantic strawberry right across the model's crotch. Then there was the coat in a python print worn by a chunky professor of literature. A slender woman might have looked like a serpentess in the garden, a little dangerous but alluring, but this poor soul looked like a python digesting a goat.[129]

Fashion magazines today regularly run articles about how to mix prints. Beware. Mixing prints produces "a very inharmonious result," states a dress text from 1918. The eye gets tired and dizzy following the numerous patterns around. Of course, some people want us dizzy for their own reasons. Have you ever been in a casino? There are flashing lights, loud music, buzzers and bells, and the management, being the kind of host who wants to go through your wallet, offers you free drinks while you're playing at the tables. Mixing prints has the same effect. So, go ahead and wear a shirt in a black and white and red stripe, a jacket covered in black and white spots, and a pair of pants in a black, white, and red plaid. But don't think anyone can hear what you're saying. "The eye requires plain surfaces upon which to rest itself in the midst of intricate and exciting pattern," explained Helen Goodrich Buttrick of Michigan State. Wear a solid with a print if you would like people to listen to what you have to say.[130]

WE ARE OFTEN MORE AWARE of the burdens of beauty than its
pleasures. A dress book from 1913 tells us, "It is woman's duty to be
as beautiful as possible." That dutiful strain became even louder in
American culture as the beauty industry invented itself in the early
twentieth century in order to sell us all kinds of supposedly magic po-
tions. The bathing beauty contest for Miss America in Atlantic City,
invented in 1921, seems to capture an important shift for American
womanhood toward far too much concern about looks.[131]

Nineteenth-century America put woman on the side of the an-
gels, because she was supposed to be the more moral and spiritual of
the sexes. But whatever power a woman gains parading around in a
bathing suit, it ain't spiritual. The original beauty-pageant winners got
furs and a shot at a movie career, which at least made more sense than
the decision in 1944 to begin awarding college scholarship money to
women for parading around in their swimsuits. (The only men who
win college scholarships in swimsuits are on the swim team.)

Emily Burbank's 1917 book on dress was entitled *Woman as Dec-*
oration. Burbank's readers seem to have been members of the leisure
class (or women who wished they were). She wrote about choosing
garments to wear in the sunroom, in the boudoir, on the lawn, in a
motorcar . . . you get the idea. And she wrote as though her readers
had all the money in the world to make sure that their sunrooms and
boudoirs were decorated in the most flattering colors, and that their
gowns made them look especially lovely in those surroundings. Emily
Burbank could have called her book *Woman Dressed in Harmony with*
Her Surroundings, which is not all that far from what other Dress
Doctors would advise, but she didn't. The title *Woman as Decoration*
implies we are useless, if pretty, objects.

But Burbank would surprise you. She included in her book an
entire article from the *Philadelphia Ledger* about young women in
Britain who had taken jobs left open by men who had gone off to
fight in World War I. These women worked as mechanics and mu-

nitions makers, drove cabs and buses, planted crops and ran elevators. They made good money, and they did it in trousers. One explained that she wanted the war to end and the boys to come home, but added, "I should hate to go back to the old days of relying upon some one else for everything that really matters."

Burbank hardly wanted these women to go back to relying on someone else for everything, either. She thought the war had proven their unlimited potential. "Women," wrote Burbank, "like men, have untold untried abilities within them, women and men alike are marvelous under fire—capable of development in every direction. . . . The inexhaustible stock of her latent qualities . . . await the call of the hour." It hardly sounds like Burbank thought of women as mere decoration.[132]

And decoration, if well-chosen, required exercising the powers of the mind. Grace Margaret Morton wrote in 1943 that a neat appearance "more often" reflects a mind that is "clear and organized," while a sloppy appearance means it is "safe to assume the mind behind it is unorganized and ill-disciplined."[133]

Dress can help lead any girl or woman to success in life, according to the Dress Doctors. "Beautiful and becoming clothing that contributes to one's attractiveness gives poise and assurance and thus contributes to success," concluded Helen Goodrich Buttrick. In the 1920s, the Dress Doctors told the story of a ragged street urchin who was taken up by a welfare agency and then bathed and dressed in new clothes. Almost immediately, the once sad and listless child became "a self-respecting and well-mannered little lady." In the 1930s, the Dress Doctors quoted Judge Camille Kelly of the Juvenile Court of Memphis, Tennessee, who told a reporter, "I often do more with a delinquent girl by giving her a new dress than by preaching all the sermons in the world."[134]

Although the programs of the Dress Doctors began with formidable governmental help and were aimed at teaching Americans what to wear, they were very much at odds with, say, the ancient sumptuary laws of Renaissance Europe, which were designed to signal the differences of rank and wealth. The Five Art Principles were democratic principles. Beauty cannot be hoarded by the wealthy few who can afford fine paintings and sculptures. The plain people deserve beauty as well. Clothing gives women the chance to create and choose beauty. And the Dress Doctors taught them how to eliminate the distinctions in dress that reflected distinctions in wealth.

❈ 3 ❈

Occasions

The Duty and Pleasure of Dress

I N 1951, MORE THAN 10,000 YOUNGSTERS between the ages of
fourteen and sixteen were asked whether they agreed with the
statement, "I am an important person." Only 12 percent answered
that they did. This makes sense. After all, how many fourteen-year-
olds are VIPs? The Dalai Lama's next incarnation? A millionaire
singing sensation?

In 1989, the same question was asked, and the results were star-
tlingly different: 80 percent of girls and 77 percent of boys believed
they were important persons. Where did a bunch of kids get this inflated sense of self-worth? From grown-ups who worried that children
with poor self-esteem would not succeed in life. These people meant
well, but their fears were misplaced. The teenagers with the lowest
self-esteem today are the same ones who usually shine as the academic
stars of their schools: Asian Americans. Self-esteem has nothing to
do with the practice of actual virtues.[1]

This shift could not have happened if home economists had remained influential. They put self-esteem *way* down on their list of qualities that a student should cultivate. "Believing in her own ability" shows up at number twelve in a junior-high textbook from 1933. Instead, a girl first needs to work on "correcting mistakes if there is an opportunity," and must become good at "recognizing but not advertising her own shortcomings."[2]

Young egos need restraining, not encouragement. A fourteen-year-old does not have much time to think about herself when she is busy thinking about how she is treating others. The home economists' list of fourteen social habits started with courtesy and honesty went through sympathy and consideration before ending with the Golden Rule. Along the way it asked girls to be "sensible in choice of dress, companions, and forms of recreation." Mary Brooks Picken said that good taste in dress and good manners were equally important "to a child's future success and happiness." She explained, "Both should be acquired gradually so that they may become natural and permanent."[3]

Dress, the Dress Doctors said, is one of our social duties for two reasons. First, because the world has to look at us whether it wants to or not. Second, because the world has work to do, and an inappropriately dressed individual can be distracting. These two reasons explain why "making the most of your looks is not vanity." The effort "indicates proper self-regard and consideration of others." If a young woman follows the Five Art Principles, she will not be a public eyesore. If she learns how to "Dress for the Occasion," she will not distract from the task at hand. Lucy Rathbone and Elizabeth Tarpley at the University of Texas pointed to the story of Cinderella in 1931 to illustrate this principle. Cinderella's fairy godmother thoughtfully put her back into her drab work wear after the ball so that she would be ready for work in the morning. Indeed, a ball gown would have made it impossible to sweep cinders efficiently.[4]

Clothes help to make character.

Fig. 1: The girl on the left is too dressed up to play, and the girl on the right is too embarrassed to play—her mother having opted for the false economy of not bothering to renew her daughter's play wardrobe. The girl in the middle is just right, so she gets the jump rope. CORA IRENE LEIBY, *CLOTHES FOR LITTLE FOLKS*, 1925

The Dress Doctors at the Bureau of Home Economics tried to use dress to shape the character of Americans beginning with an effort in the 1920s directed at toddlers. Children, boys and girls, had resembled tiny women throughout the nineteenth century: they were put in little dresses with petticoats. The petticoats had disappeared by the early twentieth century, but the clothing remained complicated. A nursery school director described the difficulties in 1929: "In order to dress herself entirely one little girl had to be able to fasten three lengthwise buttons in her underwaist, pull in place elastic at [the] knee and waist of bloomers, fasten two snaps at the center back of her dress, tighten the draw string in the waist of her leggings, adjust three buttonhole loops in the front of the neck of her sweater and fasten four buckles on each overshoe."[5]

The Dress Doctors wanted change for three reasons. First, such complicated clothing discouraged self-reliance in little Americans. They needed to prepare themselves to become self-made men and women. Child experts advised that children should put on their own clothes as soon as they were able. They would get better at using their tiny hands, at focusing their tiny minds, and taking initiative. Look at poor Bobby, turned into a passive child by winter clothing that his two-year-old fingers cannot undo. He must wait for the teacher's help, while Betty is secure and confident because she wears a snowsuit that she can put on and off by herself.[6]

Second, the Dress Doctors worried about tight clothing causing a long list of bodily disorders: poor circulation, bad digestion, shallow breathing, round shoulders, weak muscles, lame feet, bad nerves, and "displacement of certain organs." They worried, just as reformers of women's clothing had for decades as they harped on the horrible things that tight corsets could do to women's insides.[7]

Hygiene was the third reason for change. Germs became something of an obsession early in the twentieth century because scientists had recently figured out how bacteria could spread disease. The Dress Doctors feared that long skirts sponged up whatever bacteria lurked in the dirt. If children's clothing was tight and made them sweat, bacteria multiplied in the moisture, and you were left with smelly kids covered in germs. Scientists advised that sunlight was "a tonic and a disinfectant in one"—it let the body produce Vitamin D, which builds strong bones and kills certain kinds of bacteria. Progressive thinkers therefore wanted children to wear clothing that would allow them to get some sun during the summer months.[8]

Then there was the bonus of teaching the little ones good taste. The daughter of Professor Wilbur O. Atwater (the man who had invented a way to measure calories), Helen Atwater, followed him into the USDA and soon specialized in explaining scientific ideas in popular terms. She wrote in 1929, "A child's clothing can be used to start his appreciation of color and design and thus lay the foundations for good taste and enjoyment, not only in matters of clothing but in other fields of art as well."[9]

The design specialists and dressmakers at the Division of Textiles and Clothing put their heads together. They did away with hooks, which are hard for little fingers to work; snaps, which come apart too easily; bows, which tie themselves into impossible knots; and elastic, which often loses its springiness.

The new models had loops, tabs, and buttons—BIG BUTTONS— and none of them down the back. The bureau's staff tested their models on the residents of orphanages around Washington. The tiny tykes donned bibs, sunsuits and sundresses, rainsuits and rompers, all in the name of scientific research.[10]

In 1927, the Bureau of Home Economics issued its first leaflet on children's clothing. Yes, federal tax dollars paid for the publication of *Children's Rompers*.

The bureau's traveling exhibits of children's clothing were ready to send out by 1930. Posters with photos illustrating self-help bibs and dresses traveled all over the country. Bureau head Ruth O'Brien was happy to report "a noticeable effect on children's clothing throughout the country." When Singer Sewing Company did up its *Style Digest* for 1939, it featured the offerings of six major pattern lines—Vogue, Butterick, DuBarry, Simplicity, McCall's, and Hollywood—under the headline, "The Modern Child Goes to a Party in 'Self-Help' Clothes." The toddler style revolution was complete.[11]

During this same period, the Dress Doctors were explaining that for older children and adults, there were six occasions that required their own kind of dress:

School	Spectator sports and active sports
Street, travel, or work	Afternoon affairs or tea
Housework	After-five or formal evenings

Every dress textbook taught the appropriate styles for each occasion and explained the logic behind them. The Dress Doctors spread the word in other ways, too. Across the countryside in the 1930s, women could submit their creations at competitive Dress Revues organized by rural extension agents of the USDA. The categories for submission were identified by occasion, so a woman could choose to show a "wash dress for home or work" or "ensembles for street or church." The "Correct Dress Contest" for 4-H girls in Augusta County, Virginia, offered the category of a dress worn "while at work, in the home, on the farm, or while milking." Winners received prizes, everything from sewing machines made by Singer to yardage from Peter Pan Cotton Fabrics. The extension office for what is now Oklahoma State University was pleased to report, "Both the clothing work involved in the style show and clothing outfits have done much to emphasize the principles of appropriate dress."[12]

Other organizations lent their support to training the young American woman in what to wear. The General Federation of Women's Clubs required that anyone competing in their "Junior Leadership Contest" demonstrate her leadership qualities, her public speaking skills, *and* her ability to choose the correct "street and evening clothes."[13]

These ideas were widespread. The largest mail-order retailer in the country explained in 1930 that "modern woman . . . dresses now for the *occasion*, even the *time of day*, where formerly she chose for the *season*." *Vogue*'s former editor in chief Edna Woolman Chase told readers of her autobiography in 1954 to "ask yourself always, Am I harmoniously put together, am I appropriately clad for the deed at hand, and am I free of nonessentials? If you can truthfully answer yes, you are a well-dressed woman."[14]

The Dress Doctors were aware that dressing for the occasion was a new phenomenon for a prosperous twentieth century. Many a junior-high-school girl had heard her grandmother or great aunt talk about

Fig. 2: USDA clothing clubs organized contests among their members. One winner poses with her prize—a Singer sewing machine—in Texas in 1938. PRAIRIE VIEW A&M UNIVERSITY

"her Sunday dress of black taffeta, which she wore as her best for a number of years." For the rest of the week, these women had had just one other dress to wear. It had not been hard for a nineteenth-century farmwoman to figure out what to wear on any given day, as she had few options. Her granddaughters faced a whole wardrobe of opportunities, and the Dress Doctors were determined to guide her choices.[15]

"THE PATTERN OF SCHOOL CLOTHES should be simple and semi-tailored with sensible sleeves and collar," wrote Lucretia Hunter in 1932 in *The Girl Today, the Woman Tomorrow*. "The dress should be long enough to cover the knees, and the neckline should be conservative." Anything else would prevent her from focusing on the task at hand.[16]

"Have you ever watched a girl who has on a fancy dress at school?" asked another Dress Doctor in 1942. "Does she act quite natural?

Of course not, because she really is afraid of spoiling it; moreover, she likes your admiring glances." A girl in party clothes at school is distracted and distracting. School is not a party. "We can think of school as a kind of workshop where we spend many hours working with other people," explained two other Dress Doctors.[17]

The work done at school was especially important to home economists in the early twentieth century for a couple of reasons. First, American children were staying in school longer than they had before in what was touted as better preparation for adulthood. The number of children enrolled in public high schools nearly doubled every decade from 1890 to 1930. Junior high schools were first carved out of elementary school systems around 1909. Home economics was one of the new fields, along with general science and manual training, whose courses multiplied rapidly. More education would prepare girls to play their full part as citizens, an idea that became all the more important in 1920 when women won the right to vote.[18]

A second idea, that women needed to be physically active to be healthy, had been gaining ground since the late nineteenth century. In the 1890s, women took to the greens for golf and girls began playing basketball. The first richly illustrated dress advice books for girls from the 1930s were peppered with sketches of young women leaping about in gym suits. Comfortable clothing allowed the girl of today to become the healthy, active woman of tomorrow. True, schoolgirls may not wrestle on the playground like schoolboys do, one book explained, but they will still enjoy playing tag and hide and seek, and the freedom of roller skating. Their clothing must be up for anything.[19]

Both of these ideas—of girls as future leaders and of girls as healthy bodies—guided the Dress Doctors' advice for school dresses. "Since the code of life of the modern girl includes an ideal of health and strength and an ideal of activity and leadership," explained Helen Goodrich Buttrick, who taught in the 1920s at Michigan Agricultural College, now Michigan State University, "her clothing must contribute to these ideals by giving her freedom of action and the chance to develop all the grace and strength of her body." Nothing in the schoolgirl's wardrobe should restrict her physically. No trailing sleeves that drooped into lab experiments, no complicated skirts that hampered her rush down the hallways, no tight sleeves or collars or waistbands. Energetic young people need "freedom of movement" to be happy.[20]

Comfortable school clothes did not mean dowdy school clothes. When Lucretia Hunter wrote "semi-tailored," she meant neat and trim, no ruffles, no frills, no excess. But she expected the colors to be bright and lively. Stripes, plaids, and cheerful prints were all welcome, and the spirit of youth demanded them. Beauty and utility were both required, explained a pair of authors, who wrote: "Indeed, the one is dependent upon the other."[21]

Professor Buttrick treated the possibility that girls might veer toward goofiness in their sartorial choices with good-natured indulgence. "The adolescent girl seeks to impress the world with the fact of her own existence. She yearns for self-expression, and uses clothes as a means to it as naturally as a bird expresses itself in song. Let her have her lovely and brilliant colors, her quaint and picturesque effects," wrote Buttrick. She went on to urge her teachers: "Lead her to desire modesty and comfort in her clothes and turn her away from the hideous exaggeration that hinders her young beauty." If health arguments against the wrong shoes did not work—what teenager cares if her shoes blister her heels, so long as they are cute?—the Dress Doctors advised that we argue against the wrong shoes in the name of an attractive outfit that both friends and boys will admire.[22]

The Dress Doctors criticized the girl who wore party clothes to school for yet another reason. In words that still ring true for every parent whose daughter's voice has reached a high whine during a shopping trip, a textbook from 1919 pointed out, "Every girl, especially of high school age, has seen unhappiness inflicted on the plainly dressed student by the supercilious attitude toward her of some better dressed classmate." An overdressed girl could ignite a competition in dress that would annoy everyone's parents and humiliate girls from poor families. "The girl of true American spirit will use her example and influence against such snobbishness," said the authors.[23]

The girls of North Central High School in Spokane, Washington, had that American spirit. In 1925, they adopted a dress code that banned "satin slippers, high heels, silk and velvet afternoon or party dresses." They were none too keen on sleeveless blouses, either. Girls should wear dresses of cotton or "tub silk," which were easy to have ready for daily wear because they could be washed.[24]

Teachers invented clever ways to enforce their message. One asked her high-school students to vote each morning for the girl who was most suitably dressed for school. "In every case," reported a writer smugly in 1914, "the girl with the trim sailor hat, tailored waist [blouse], serge skirt, sensible shoes, and tidily-arranged hair secured the popular vote." Soon, all the girls were aiming for that same neat look in hopes of winning the daily vote. And no one was worrying about the losers' self-esteem.[25]

As girls grew into young women and moved on to college campuses, the less formal look also ruled. College clothes are "casual, carefree, gay, and sporting, to be worn with nonchalance" befitting an active young woman, wrote Grace Margaret Morton in 1943. Suits were a normal part of a young woman's wardrobe through midcentury. The most useful thing for a first-year college woman to pack in her bags was a three-piece matching skirt, dress, and jacket in a sturdy tweed, plaid, or dark wool. "Any wise Junior knows to build her spring wardrobe around a suit, maybe two," said *Vogue Pattern Book* in 1946. The shift in women's fashion in the 1960s would make everyone, even grown women, appear childishly young, but in 1946 the pages of Vogue Patterns offered a variety of skirt suits and dress suits sized for juniors who wanted to look grown-up enough to join the more formal and privileged world of adulthood.[26]

Coats of tweed, camel hair, and leather suited the campus in the countryside. Flat shoes such as slip-on moccasins, and tied oxfords and ghillies, made it easier to run to class. These were especially practical for a wooded campus, where young women might find themselves sprinting across the grass or down gravel paths.

Easy hats, such as berets and cloches, also suited campus life. Some Dress Doctors suggested they might go so far as to approve "a total absence of head covering" for co-eds in college towns. The city college girl, however, must wear gloves and a hat. Her wardrobe was more tailored and formal because of her surroundings. The upside was that she could wear higher heels if she liked. The shift in geography warranted the shift in style.[27]

Then as now, a co-ed campus tended to prompt a little more effort on the part of young women. The women of Radcliffe, comparing all-female and co-ed classes in 1934, noticed that in the co-ed classes "heels are a little higher, tailored dresses take the place of skirts and sweaters and hats are worn on well curled heads." Students of the early twentieth century were convinced that dressing properly would help them through college. Radcliffe's student newspaper told its readers in 1928, "Your mental attitude depends a great deal on your personal appearance; as you feel sloppy or scatter-brained, or neat and methodical, what you are writing will take on a difference appearance." And so the Dress Doctors taught.[28]

IN 2007, *GLAMOUR* MAGAZINE MOCKINGLY CELEBRATED "Take Your Breasts to Work Day." Opposing opinion pieces took the pro- and anti-cleavage sides. Some women were mystified why other women came to work looking as though they were applying for jobs as wet nurses; those women, in turn, wondered how some women could be such God-awful prudes. This is not a new problem. "Some of the girls haven't decided whether they are going to the office to work," observed Elizabeth Hawes drily in 1942, "or to attract men."[29]

88

Fig. 3: The woman in the city in 1937 wore the precise and impersonal dress that suits business—in this case, a "man-tailored" suit in gray, navy, or brown topped by a swagger coat. MONTGOMERY WARD catalog, FALL-WINTER 1937–1938

There was no cleavage in daytime clothing until quite recently. The "Many-Way Dress" offered by Sears Roebuck in 1938 came with a choice of V-necklines. The high neckline ended at the base of the throat, while the low neckline was only 3 inches below that.

Why? Because the display of a pair of pretty breasts was not going to help women be taken seriously as wage workers. Since the whore was the most public working woman of the nineteenth century, respectable middle-class women had long avoided the styles she wore to advertise her wares: bright colors, exposed flesh, and uncovered hair. When women first appeared in offices in the late nineteenth century, more than one leering boss had made their lives miserable. Good behavior and modest dress did not guarantee decent treatment by men, but women hoped it might help. It certainly couldn't hurt.[30]

In the past, the Dress Doctors explained, women had dressed in order to catch a husband; after marriage, they dressed to show off their husband's wealth. Now, women enjoyed "a new freedom" that allowed them to work and travel for themselves, and they were able "to resort less and less in dress to what was designated as 'woman's wiles.'" Men had been wearing dark suits for almost a century, and the arrival of the women's suit was celebrated by *Harper's Weekly* in 1893 as "sensible dress" that "kept pace" with the increasing numbers of women attending college and going into work business.[31]

Some women had always worked for wages, but they were being hired increasingly in offices and stores as secretaries, typists, and salesclerks by the 1890s. Some 37 percent of young women between the ages of sixteen and twenty-four were employed in 1920. Department stores were one place that women could find work at all but the highest levels of management. One woman, who worked at Marshall Fields, testified in the 1920s that "a great many girls who aren't married, and a lot of those choosing not to be married, are having lives of their own that are more exciting and stimulating than anything they dreamed could ever happen to them." Of course, salesclerks worked for hours on sore feet, but there were thrilling possibilities. More than one-third of department store buyers, a job that often required annual trips to Paris, were women by 1924.[32]

Hollywood movies of the 1930s recounted the struggles of working girls trying to get a job, get ahead, or get married. The Dress Doctors wanted to eliminate one of their problems: getting dressed. "The number of women who are earning a living in occupations outside of the home is constantly growing," noted Helen Goodrich Buttrick in 1923. These "working women must appear at their best at all times."[33]

An ideal job candidate mirrored business itself. She looked precise, focused, practical, and rational. "The idea which distinguishes business from other activities—the idea of accuracy and correctness," wrote Margaret Story, is what should be found in business dress. And their vision of business was shaped by the ideas of the country's first efficiency expert.[34]

Frederick Winslow Taylor was an engineer turned industrial manager who published *The Principles of Scientific Management* in 1911. He had three aims: first, to show how the United States was suffering from inefficiency in almost everything its people did; second, to convince Americans that scientific management could eliminate inefficiency; and third, to prove that good management was a science. He would show that the principles of efficiency that he had uncovered could be applied to all kinds of activities. His book became the best-selling business book of the first half of the twentieth century.[35]

Efficiency became a watchword among Americans in all walks of life, the equivalent of today's obsession with productivity. Not only did businesses aim for it, but so did the farmwoman from Vermont who asked the USDA in 1914 for "information on how to make an old-fashioned kitchen into one where steps could be saved and the work done more efficiently."[36] Home economists were especially eager to prove that they used the most up-to-date ideas, whether in designing kitchens or in planning what to wear. They paid attention to both the women who worked in the kitchens and the women who ate breakfast in them and then left for the office. Even schoolgirls were not immune from the lessons of Taylorism; home economists set out schedules for them timed down to the quarter hour from daybreak until bedtime.

Business's reputation took a knock in 1929 when the stock market collapsed and the Great Depression hit the country hard, but the ideals of Taylorism still guided women in how to dress for the office. Mary Brooks Picken, who managed dozens of women at the Woman's Institute of Domestic Arts and Sciences in Scranton, Pennsylvania, insisted on "clothes that will make it possible for them to give a good full day of intelligent service."[37]

Clothing was supposed to make clear that women belonged in business while allowing them to remain women. "While distinctly feminine," women's business wear "properly avoids anything in color or design suggestive of the social occasion," wrote Laura I. Baldt, a professor at Columbia University's Department of Household Arts, and author of a column in *Good Housekeeping* in the 1920s. Serious occasions like business called for clothes marked by "severity of lines, restraint of curves and absence of decoration." They fit the formality of the office and the seriousness of work. Similarly, Helen Louise Johnson, a home economist who specialized in cooking and budgeting, told the *Atlanta Constitution*, "I do not want women to become masculine, and lose the distinction and charm of their femininity. . . . They have no right, however, to emphasize their femininity in the office, where they are employed—or should be if they aren't—for their merit and efficiency rather than their sex." This was the fear: that women would be thought of as sexual creatures first and rational businesswomen second, if at all. Joined to this fear was the worry that women themselves would try to use their sexuality to get ahead. "I believe with all my heart that it is essential for the business woman to be of the mode and as feminine as possible," declared advertising genius Helen Lansdowne Resor in 1930, "without in any way trading on sex."[38]

The danger existed because women's clothing often bared more flesh and form than men's. The Kansas State Dress Doctors even pondered whether psychologists were right to think that women are more eager than men "to combine displaced exhibitionism with actual exposure." Sleeveless blouses, for example, have never had an equivalent in men's business wear. No, do not take off your suit jacket except in the privacy of your own office, scolded a book from 1938, and "please don't make it worse by wearing a sleeveless blouse. That is the unforgivable sin." Another Dress Doctor, who wrote for the Girl Scouts, said that she was no prude, but a sleeveless dress on city streets, in offices, or at luncheons was "very naked-looking to me."[39] Indeed, women on today's television news programs in the ubiquitous sleeveless sheath dress do seem naked-looking when you compare them to the men in jackets and ties sitting next to them. And if the contrast doesn't give you pause, consider the fashion opportunity lost with a sleeveless dress; sleeves can be businesslike or flirtatious, stern or romantic, useful or languid, depending on whether they are trim or full, cuffed or frilled.

The first business clothing for young working women in the early 1900s had sleeves. It was the shirtwaist, our blouse, worn with a skirt. Unlike custom-made Victorian dresses that fit "like wall paper," the shirtwaist was cut so loosely that it became the great (and inexpensive) success of the ready-to-wear garment industry. Some Dress Doctors were still not convinced it was a good idea. Two from Mason City, Iowa, fretted in 1923 that a classical Greek statue would not be caught dead wearing a blouse. A dress is "more graceful, more artistic, and more becoming." Unlike a dress, the shirtwaist creates a sharp horizontal break, in clear violation of the principle that vertical lines make the figure appear taller and more slender.

The different varieties of shirtwaists all had their bad points. The Gibson shirtwaist was unfeminine, cut just like a man's shirt, with

Fig. 4: Although early Dress Doctors disapproved of the shirtwaist, or blouse, because it cut the figure in two, young American women, such as the author's great grandmother, considered them lovely enough to wear in formal portraits in the 1910s. AUTHOR'S COLLECTION

buttons up the front and worn with a tie. The peek-a-boo waist made of sheer fabric was simply indecent. The ultimate fashion authorities, Paris designers, agreed that "the waist" wasn't chic.

But it was all in vain. American girls were not interested in looking like Greek statues or listening to Paris designers. They thought shirtwaists were pretty, and they had been making and buying them for years. A variety of shirtwaists could be worn with the same skirt, and even those with tiny budgets could afford at least one. Wash out a cotton blouse at night, and it will be dry by morning. This can't be done with a dirty dress. The Iowa Dress Doctors resigned themselves to the shirtwaist, consoling themselves with the thought that "the practical has often pushed aside the artistic." Others pointed out that if stout women opted for the shirtwaist, they must follow at least this one rule: let the skirt and the blouse be the same color.[40]

Thousands of young American women had shirtwaists hanging in their closets. And they were found in the closets of young French women, too; in 1908, the United States was exporting nearly $1 million worth of shirtwaists to France. And the blouse and skirt remained a mainstay of women toiling in offices and factories for decades.[41]

Early on, the shirtwaist spawned a hybrid: the shirtwaist dress. It solved the problem of the break in color at the waist by making both the shirtwaist and the skirt out of the same fabric. Plus, you didn't have to worry about keeping the blouse tucked in. The shirtwaist dress evolved through the 1950s while remaining impressively detailed and sharp. It usually buttoned in the front only down to the waist; a snap placket at the side made it possible to pull it on over the head.

We make do today with only a few styles in ready-to-wear day dresses, but earlier generations of women could pick from an astonishing variety. Every decade had a certain silhouette and length of skirt, but the sleeves and necklines came in many variations to suit any taste and any figure. The skirt of a dress was almost never as dull as our straight skirt, but its lines remained relatively simple. Designers lavished attention on the upper part of dresses, in keeping with the art principle that emphasis should be placed on the face. Dress bodices were double-breasted, single-breasted, or lapped. Necklines were high or wide, squared or round. Collars varied from the large cap-like bertha to the small standing mandarin, from simple *revers* (turn-back collar) to the full flounces of a *jabot*. Belted, unbelted, pocketed, unpocketed, the modern dress offered a woman every possibility. And if a woman could sew, she could choose any color combination she liked. Department stores sold fabric by the yard as well as ready-to-wear dresses.

There were also two kinds of suits available for businesswomen. Some women's suits mimicked men's. These were called "tailored suits." They had sharp lapels and came in wool twills and worsteds. Such a suit was perfect for the city, according to Kansas State Dress Doctors Alpha Latzke and Beth Quinlan, because of "its incisive and remote effect." Women almost always bought tailored suits from shops instead of making them at home. Those sharp lapels required painstaking hand-stitching to attach the fabric to a stiff horsehair backing. (Nowadays, all but the priciest custom-made tailored clothes are made by attaching a synthetic backing with glue.)[42]

Fortunately, the softer, prettier, so-called dressmaker suit, in silk or wool crepe, was also appropriate for office work—and was far easier to make at home. Dressmaker suits might consist of a skirt and jacket or a dress and jacket. Usually both items were made of the same fabric; in some cases, there was a combination of two fabrics, where one served as the trimming on the other, as with a checked skirt that was paired with a solid jacket trimmed in the same check. In 1956, one etiquette book called a good suit "the backbone of most women's wardrobes." It could be worn in the city or in the country, for working or for shopping.[43] Either kind of suit—and any kind of dress—might be topped by a matching cape, an option unhappily missing from today's fashion vocabulary.

In the summertime, the same dresses and suits came in lightweight fabrics such as linen, rayon, and cotton. More feminine touches were welcome, so long as they were restrained. Jewelry "serves the purpose if it adds a bit of color or completes the costume," wrote Lucretia Hunter, who taught in the Cleveland public schools.[44]

If a woman had a luncheon scheduled or a public lecture in the afternoon, she was advised to change to fancier jewelry, or even a dressier hat or blouse, that she had stowed away in her handbag (those must have been capacious handbags). Those of us who sometimes head to a restaurant after work can still find comfort and glamour in the Dress Doctors' solution for the businesswoman headed out after dark to socialize: a bare dress with a matching jacket that completely camouflages the neck and shoulders when buttoned during the day, then comes off for the evening's festivities.

As for colors, darker is best for business wear, because it will not distract one's fellow workers and because dark colors cope better with city soot and dirt. New York City is still full of women in black who have made a fashion out of saving on their dry-cleaning bills. Department stores in the big cities at the turn of the twentieth century originally required their workers to wear black dresses, but salesclerks grew tired of the color and began insisting on more options. In 1930, the saleswomen of Filene's of Boston voted by a margin of twenty to one for a rule that required "business-like styles and neutral shades." They insisted that they could not sell well if they did not "look smart," and they could not look smart unless they were allowed choices other than black.[45]

Business clothes should reveal little either physically or psychologically, said the Dress Doctors. Unlike today, when so many of us are eager to spill our deepest secrets to everyone and anyone through social media, the society in which the Dress Doctors lived believed that much information about a person was privileged. A woman's "friends" were people who knew her well because she liked them enough to share intimacies with them. Nobody would have thought of calling every casual acquaintance a "friend." Store clerks and plumbers, dentists and colleagues called Mary Brooks Picken "Mrs. Picken"; only a lucky few were allowed the privilege of calling her "Mary." It followed that the professional woman's working clothes should strike "a note of dignity and formal reserve," as this will keep people at the proper, respectful distance. A woman should avoid loud colors in dress, just "as she would loud talking or boisterous behavior." The goal was to make clear that she was a considerate person who did not impose on others. (Cell yell—shouting into a cell phone—did not yet exist.)[46]

The formality of business and street clothing meant that even a printed fabric in a blouse was not supposed to reveal your inner thoughts. Crazy about Paris? Fine, but save that poodle-dog-and-Eiffel-Tower print for social occasions and weekends. The best prints for business clothes are simple and regularly spaced—think polka dots and foulard prints—and reveal little or nothing about their wearer. Still, Laura I. Baldt at Columbia University assured her readers that "a generous bit of femininity may enter into business attire," so long as it remained "dignified, not frivolous."[47]

A woman on the city streets without gloves was not fully dressed unless it was a summer day. The gloves came in kidskin, lambskin, suede, or chamois for cold days, and cotton and silk for warmer ones. As they covered the hand, "a very expressive member of the body," gloves needed to be well-fitted, flexible, and comfortable. Housewives in New York City owned, on average, 4.8 pairs of gloves, according to a 1943 survey. We may say "thank goodness" we don't have to wear gloves today, but gloves do prevent (and hide) age spots. Now we are free to go without gloves, and then we get to burn off our age spots with laser treatments. Lucky us.[48]

The disappearance of the Dress Doctors has left many women today confused about what to wear to work. The stories of young women who appear at interviews for office jobs in flip flops and tank tops are legion. Even some of those who get the job need help. Managers at one law firm told the *Wall Street Journal* in 2008 that it had brought in a personal shopper to re-wardrobe its younger women lawyers. It seems they were taking their style tips from actresses playing lawyers on TV. One partner explained that the skirts were so short that "they have trouble sitting and getting into taxis." He meant trouble sitting without flashing their underpants at the world.[49]

Fashion magazines are little help, since their editors love to feature the wardrobes of actresses who are trying to show off as much flesh as possible. The Dress Doctors thought that the theater and movies were a great place for designers to try out new ideas, but they also knew that dressing like a starlet was a mistake, unless you were a starlet. "While this kind of design may be smart on the actress," wrote one in 1935, "the average woman has no excuse for the sensational." Trying for the spectacular, we end up making spectacles of ourselves.[50]

The Dress Doctors loved to tell stories about women who had won or lost jobs because of how they dressed. There was one able teacher who applied for a post at an exclusive private school in 1914. Usually a smart dresser, she got a little giddy that day and "arrayed herself in a hat of startling size and adornments, a suit of very pronounced color, while several jingling ornaments added to the 'loud' effect of the costume." The pupils, the teachers, and the principal found her a bit much, and she did not get the job.[51]

Luckier was the teacher who arrived for her interview in an outfit "tailored not extravagant, nor yet slack." The members of the school board were so impressed that they hired her in short order, with the hope that her mere appearance might have a good influence on high-school girls who suffered from a "foolish desire for display." The girls who get the jobs and get the promotions, explained one Dress Doctor, are "the girls who are most quietly and tidily dressed." Department stores were known to make appearance part of their promotion criteria.[52]

Then there was the woman in the 1930s who refused to believe that moving from college to work required a wardrobe overhaul. Year after year, as secretary for the president of a large retail store, she wore sweaters and skirts that "emphasized her juvenile appearance." She was eventually fired.[53]

Mabel B. Trilling and Florence Williams offered the "Do's and Don'ts" of the working woman in each of their books. Every time, Miss Don't wore something that was too frivolous for business. In 1928, the Don't dress, in a dark solid, was trimmed in flounces made from a loopy, floral print. Ties created long bows at the wrists that

Fig. 5: Who gets the job? Hint: It is not the woman who looks ready to dance the can-can. MABEL B. TRILLING AND FLORENCE WILLIAMS, *ART IN HOME AND CLOTHING*, 1928

would have trailed into the typewriter keys. In 1936, the Don't dress was a more acceptable small print, but the skirt was so narrow that it restricted her natural stride. The sleeves were childishly puffy, yet tight enough where they hit her arms that she might have trouble raising them. And her dozen bangles would be constantly clanging. Not a practical outfit for work.[54]

Miss Do in every instance wore a more modest and precise outfit. In 1928, her dark, solid-colored dress had a single bow at the end of deep V-neck, a V-neck that was filled with an inset of the same dark color and outlined with scalloped trim in a paler hue that drew attention up to her face. The only other decoration was her matching scalloped cuffs. Miss Do of 1936 wore an oufit that was quieter both literally (no bangles) and figuratively (solid color with polka-dot trim) than her unemployable counterpart. Her skirt flared enough to let her stride freely. Her sleeves flared, too, so that her arms were not constrained. Her practical hat shielded her eyes from the sun and also harmonized with the solid color of her dress and the print of her tie and belt. Her clothes revealed more than a man's suit would have in 1936—he would have been in trousers and long sleeves—yet her outfit was the feminine equivalent of a man's suit down to the bowed scarf that mirrored his tie. In fact, a good rule for checking whether you can wear something at work is to ask yourself whether it has an equivalent in male business wear. Which would leave out cleavage, sleeveless looks, and other peculiarly feminine inventions, such as peep-toe shoes.

The 1936 sketch denied us so much as a peek at Miss Do's shoes precisely because the Dress Doctors thought work shoes were unimportant so long as they were neat and practical. "Shoes and stockings should be inconspicuous and comfortable so that the wearer may be unconscious of her feet." The shoes of Miss Don't broke both rules. They were high-heeled and elaborately trimmed.[55]

Women traveling or out shopping in the city were supposed to dress much like businesswomen. The Dress Doctors of the twentieth century celebrated the fact that women no longer had to travel as they did in the eighteenth century, swathed in veils and mantles in order to prevent male strangers from getting so much as a peek at them. "In modern times custom permits women to travel with the same straightforward appearance which has long been accepted as their brother's right," observed the Kansas State Dress Doctors. But that meant she didn't draw any more attention to herself through her clothes than her brother did through his; a straightforward appearance mirrored her "entirely impersonal" attitude. Among complete strangers, and needing to move efficiently through busy railroad stations, the traveler was advised to choose "no emotional colors, no revelatory designs or fabrics, no temperamental hats or shoes." Although women heading for the beach brought their swimsuits and slacks, they were supposed to wear suits en route to their destination. "Packing for seashore or mountains?" asked Pictorial Patterns in August 1933. "The first thing into your trunk should be a tailored suit of uncrushable linen." Texas Dress Doctors Lucy Rathbone and Elizabeth Tarpley gave similar advice for plane travel in 1962, noting that, "of course," women would not be wearing slacks and beat-up shoes. They did not live to see women shuffling down to the breakfast buffet at the Best Western in their jammies and slippers, rubbing the sleep from their eyes.[56]

Clothes worn on city streets by women who had come to the city not to work but to shop should also be "characterized by a certain impersonal or formal tailored smartness." The idea was "not to make the wearer conspicuous among strangers." And since even the shopper was doing a kind of work, she needed to be dressed for any kind of weather in order to do it well. "If she wears thin-soled satin slippers, a perishable hat, dresses and coats which spot easily, she has no right to feel that she is appropriately dressed for shopping," wrote Trilling and Williams. They added cattily that when a woman wears party clothes on the streets, she forces onlookers to conclude that she has "no other place to wear fine clothes."[57]

CHURCH CLOTHING FELL INTO THE SAME GENERAL CATEGORY as business and street clothing because of its serious purpose. "Perhaps, you like to get all dressed up and go to church in new clothes, because you think that a large number of people will have the opportunity of admiring you there," suggested Mildred Graves Ryan. Wrong. A former junior-high and high-school teacher, Ryan was the most cutting of the Dress Doctors. All her books remind young readers that they were much uglier than they imagined.

Ryan's crankiness belies her otherwise charmed life. Her father was the New York State commissioner of taxation and finance. Her engagement and marriage to a vice president at Chase National Bank rated three notices in the *New York Times*. She wed in Albany, honeymooned in Bermuda, lived in New York City, and summered in Suffern, which has a lovely view of the Manhattan skyline. According to one of her half-dozen book jackets, Ryan enjoyed "reading, watching sports, the theatre, music, sewing—and of course making herself attractive." She became director of the Educational Department at McCall's Patterns in 1959 and traveled the country giving seminars to home economists about how to put on a fashion show.[58]

As for what to wear to church, Ryan made clear that the task at hand was the worship of God, not the display of your latest outfit. "You should never think of showing off your clothes at church," she ordered. Conservative, quiet, and tailored is what suits religious services. She would not have approved of church ladies wearing fancy hats.

Dresses for special religious occasions are a different matter. Ryan advised, "If there is to be a church wedding with a large number witnessing the marriage, the gown should be elaborate." A bride needs to pay attention to the design of the back of her gown, because that is what most people will be looking at during the ceremony. Catholic tradition, some Protestant churches, and the Dress Doctors agreed that the importance of a religious occasion should be marked by clothing obtained just for that purpose.[59]

The Dress Doctors would not have approved of the strapless wedding dresses of today, which have become the standard for brides keen on looking "hot" at their weddings. Mildred Graves carried calla lilies and wore a veil of tulle and a gown of heirloom ivory satin when she married in 1935. No doubt, it had sleeves.[60]

Strapless wedding gowns first appeared in the 1950s, giving them some historical standing, but a strapless wedding dress remains an oxymoron. The point of a strapless dress is to make every man in the room hope to see it fall off. This is why the rumors of Rita Hayworth flinging up her arms and popping out of her dress during the filming of *Gilda* still make the rounds. The point of a wedding, however, is for two people to plight their troth, and their bodies, to each other alone. Even if a woman would like to say, "Nyah, nyah!" to certain men in the room, this is an urge to be stifled.

IF WORK, CITY SHOPPING, AND CHURCHGOING required a certain sobriety in dress, the home needed something warmer. "A house is not a home" is an old saying, and the home economists repeated it with fervor. A house is simply a place where people happen to live; "the home expresses the family life which is lived within the house," wrote two Dress Doctors in 1914. And the character of family life depends on the efforts of the homemaker. Father was supposed to cooperate, of course, but in a time when most women worked in the home, the responsibility for the life of the home fell into Mother's hands. With some help from the home economists, "she will understand the physical, religious, intellectual, and aesthetic needs of her family and will be able to minister to them." A house only becomes a home, added a book from 1935, when it is "a happy, healthful, restful, and attractive place in which to live."[61]

Home economists insisted that homemaking was not only a profession, but "the *greatest* of the professions—greatest in numbers and greatest in its effect on the individual and on society." They called these professionals "home women," a nice counterpart to "business women"—and some textbooks asked high-school girls to appreciate their mothers by having them calculate how much the cooking, housekeeping, and child care done by them would cost if it were paid for by the hour. Mother "earns" a large income.[62]

As professionals, home women needed clothing that suited their work. Yet the word "housedress" conjures up hopelessly frumpy images of shapeless sacks done up in vague floral prints. Not so when the Dress Doctors flourished. In 1937 Mary Brooks Picken defined a housedress as "suitable for morning wear at home. Usually of gaily printed, washable cotton fabric. Often perky in silhouette, smartly

A1669

A1668

A1668—Frock. Sizes 14 to 20 and 32 to 42. Size 16 requires 3 yards 39-inch fabric. Bertha is businesslike with the tradesmen, but people say she gets a bigger dollar's worth—she looks so cute.

A1671—Frock. Sizes 16 to 20 and 34 to 42. Size 16 requires 2⅞ yards 39-inch fabric and ⅝ yard contrasting. Call it a house frock, or something else . . . "a rose by any other name. . . ."

A1670—Frock. Sizes 14 to 20 and 32 to 40. Size 16 requires 3⅛ yards 36-inch fabric and ⅝ yard contrasting. On cool days she wears it in the house . . . on warm ones at the beach!

A1670

A1671

Fig. 6: The housedress of the 1930s was washable and short-sleeved for practicality, yet cut and trimmed for beauty. *Prairie Farmer Pattern Supplement*, 1934

made and trimmed." The housedress was supposed to combine practicality with beauty. And it did.

The Dress Doctors advocated efficiency in the house, and the
right clothing would help. On the practical side, housedresses usually
had short sleeves to make cooking and cleaning, and reaching and
bending, all the easier. The skirt length of housedresses varied with
the given daytime fashion—at the knee in the 1920s, at lower calf
in the 1930s, back up to just below the knee in the 1940s, and down
again in the 1950s. Women were not hobbled by a straight skirt in
housedresses, which always had some flare. When it came to style and
color, the variety was endless. But the fabric itself and any trimming
had to be durable in order to withstand "the rumpling and tousling"
of children and their "sticky fingers and grubby hands."[63]

Pattern companies, often staffed with home economists, made the
same distinction between the house and the home when selling their
dresses. "With homemaking, not house-keeping, the aim of home
women," explained the Woman's Institute magazine, "such frocks as
illustrated here, which help to create a cheerful atmosphere, will be a
good choice."[64]

Do not settle for the cheapest housedress, advised the Dress
Doctors. Hunt out the ones designed with "imagination and style."
Demand something that will keep its color and wear well. As Ella
Mae Washington wrote in *Color in Dress (For Dark Skinned People)*,
the rare text that addressed African Americans, a woman "should wear
flattering colors in the home since the home is the center from which
all lines of human endeavor radiate." Let the dress be tailored enough
so that a woman can cover it with a smock on days when she's doing
only light cleaning, then dash out to get a few errands done.[65]

These housedresses were so sharp that it is hard to imagine any
of them as unsuitable for wearing outside of the house today. They
were well cut, well trimmed, and came in a delightful variety. "The
modern home dress is colorful, dainty, and as pretty in its own way as

any afternoon frock," announced *Fashion Service* magazine in 1928, and they were not kidding. Mail-order catalog Sears Roebuck boasted of their "Sears-ette," a gingham wraparound housedress with white rick-rack trim at the square neckline and on the pockets. Aprons, too, came in a variety of colors, shapes, and styles.[66]

Made of cotton, housedresses were both washable and less expensive than business wear or clothing intended for social occasions. A woman could easily afford more than one. In fact, the average American middle-class woman in 1959 owned five housedresses, one for each weekday. "Nothing is more conducive to a right beginning for the day's activity than donning a fresh dainty house-dress for breakfast," declared Margaret Story in 1930. And for Sunday mornings, when there was more ceremony, but breakfast still had to be made, a flattering housecoat was described as a necessity, not a luxury. A housecoat was usually a cross between an evening-length dress and a bathrobe, though sometimes they were shorter and came with matching pants. Sometimes they wrapped in front, and sometimes they buttoned. So as not to be mistaken for the wispy robes that matched negligees, housecoats were always made of substantial fabrics, whether fine ones, such as taffeta or velveteen, or more casual fabrics, such as seersucker or gingham. In either case, they were appropriate to wear should intimate friends be dropping in for brunch or a casual evening.[67]

One dress for day, however, might not be enough. Since a housedress would get dirty during all that cooking and cleaning, two Dress Doctors from Teachers College at Columbia University explained in 1914 that a woman should "change her gown before the evening meal when the family is united."

If changing for dinner sounds like too much effort, consider this: these same authors made it clear that a homemaker should do *less* cleaning in order to make *more* time for herself. "The ideal mistress is in control and is not controlled by things," they concluded. The house is made for us to live in and be happy in, and the home woman does not have to work herself to the bone: "A rest may add to that happiness in a way an immaculately ordered room may not." If changing out of dirty clothes takes time away from cleaning, so be it.[68]

Not all homemakers took advantage of these perky cotton dresses. It was not uncommon for women to make a charming appearance in public, explained one Dress Doctor, yet become "frumps in the privacy of their own homes."[69] The Dress Doctors could not stomach the ill-dressed homemaker. It was bad enough when a woman turned her hand to housework in a skirt from a worn-out suit and a stained blouse, and even worse if she chose to don a ruined party dress, an apparently common practice. The life of an evening gown might be cut tragically short by a single encounter with a greasy *canapé*, but it was not proper economy to wear it while scrubbing the floor. Dorée Smedley, who authored a dress book for middle-aged women after undergoing her famous makeover in 1939, explained that such bad habits only got worse. The woman who shambled around her house in ragged slippers, stockings with runs, a tattered dress, an old golf sweater, and straggling hair was likely to get into the general habit of carelessness. Stop making an effort to dress while at home, and soon a woman will find herself out doing errands looking like a bag lady.

Wearing worn-out party shoes for housework was another misdirected economy. Smedley thought it was the greatest cause of foot problems for women. She recommended that home women buy what she called "occupational shoes," sturdy numbers of soft leather that covered most of the foot and had a short, broad heel. Soft leather meant no rubbing or blisters, a mostly covered foot meant more protection from accidents or spills, and a shorter heel meant less strain. For heaven's sake, Smedley warned, do not be seduced by images from Hollywood movies and don mules trimmed in marabou feathers—unless there is a maid to do the actual housework while the lady of the house drapes herself across her *chaise lounge* in leisure. Otherwise, you are likely to trip and break your neck while trying to look picturesque while working.[70]

Just as bad was the effect that sloppy habits had on married life. "How can a woman hope to keep the joyful respect and admiration of her loved one," Mary Brooks Picken fretted, "if she allows herself to generate into frowsiness, to wear curl papers, caps, and mussy negligees all day long?" Maybe Picken was unnerved by how much the frowsy housewife resembled a bleary-eyed lady of the evening shambling around the morning after a profitable night. Or maybe she was dismayed that such a woman was willing to put the opinions of the strangers she met in public (for whom she would bother to get well dressed) above the feelings of her nearest and dearest (for whom she would not).[71]

Helen Hall, a businesswoman who ran a correspondence sewing course and lectured at department stores from coast to coast, hinted darkly in 1931 at what might happen to the homemaker who neglected her appearance. It was a wiser choice in the long run, she explained, to spend a bit more of your husband's paycheck to buy a nicer dress. Otherwise, he might compare you unfavorably with the younger, chicer women he met through business. Such a comparison ended "in a broken heart and a broken home."[72]

There was no word on what happens to the happy home if the husband lets himself get frowsy.

THE DRESS DOCTORS LAVISHED unusual attention on outfits for sports. Partly, it was because they were happy that the young women of the twentieth century could launch themselves into an unlimited number of healthy activities after a hard-fought battle for a chance to play in something comfortable. As one historian has pointed out, nineteenth-century women who first ventured into sports "quite literally had nothing to wear."[73]

HEALTH IS WEALTH
If you would have pep and charm, take some form of exercise out-of-doors every day.

Fig. 7: The Dress Doctors allowed the modern girl all the clothes she needed for sports. DULCIE G. DONOVAN, *THE MODE IN DRESS AND HOME*, 1935

When they first took up croquet and skating in the 1850s, athletic women simply hiked up their floor-length skirts. Women turned to tennis in the 1880s, but when a young American woman named May Sutton appeared at Wimbledon in 1905, her opponents complained that her skirt was short enough to expose her ankles, to say nothing of her short-sleeved blouse. Sutton lengthened her skirt, then took the women's title anyway.

Bicycling and golfing became the rage in the 1890s, and bicycling to the golf course combined the two. The big innovation here was knickers worn *under* a slightly shorter skirt. Meanwhile, young women did gymnastics (very mild exercises by today's standards) in the privacy of women's colleges in similar outfits. The gym suit was not invented until the very end of the century, when a new sport for women took off in popularity: basketball. College women who found gymnastics deadly dull turned to basketball with enthusiasm, and the bloomer gym suit was born.

At first, the bloomers on a gym suit were long, wide, and woolen. They were long enough to hit the top of the calf and wide enough that the material used for each leg was enough to make up a separate skirt. The fabric, which varied neither by season nor by region, was wooly, warm, tough, and scratchy; it was available through the Sears catalog. A matching long-sleeved blouse finished the ensemble. As women's bare legs and arms became less of a shock to the system, the gym suit shrank in shape. Fortunately, it soon also came in cotton. By the 1930s, the bloomers were short; so were the sleeves, and a pleated shorts version had been added to the mix.[74]

By the 1930s, women were doing every kind of sport in a wonderful range of outfits. Alpha Laztke and Laura Baxter of Kansas State explained that "the vigorous strides of the hiker, the smashing swings of the tennis star, the movements of the rider, make demand for a marked degree of freedom that must be considered in the choice of clothes if one is to get the joy out of these sports." The sheer number of sporty ensembles described by the Dress Doctors betrays a giddiness among usually sober women. After all, how many of their students were likely to need to know what to wear yachting and riding as well as skating and hiking?[75]

The underlying message seems to be: Partake of a variety of sports, and you may indulge in a great many outfits guilt-free! Sports require special clothing out of both necessity and tradition. In tennis, for example, necessity dictates a simple design with room for swinging limbs, and tradition puts tennis players in white. The Dress Doctors did warn the amateur to remember that athletes had particularly good figures: "Some weekend enthusiasts need to train before they can appear as smart and trim." But who wouldn't be willing to train in order to wear all these adorable ensembles?[76]

Fig. 1: Hats were a necessary daytime accessory until the 1960s. Fashion decreed that women top their summer outfits with enormous hats in 1909. Maybe the idea was to make the hips look smaller? *McCall's*, August 1909

Fig. 2: Women's suits had become the fashionable alternative to a dress by 1900, especially for women who were working or shopping in the city, but they were far more detailed than men's suits. Recommendations for these patterns from 1910 had the elderberry suit trimmed with black chiffon, the brown suit with brown velvet, and the tea green with rows of machine stitching. *McCall's*, October 1910

Fig. 3: By 1918, the American woman had loosened her corset and lifted her skirts off the ground. *McCall's, April 1918*

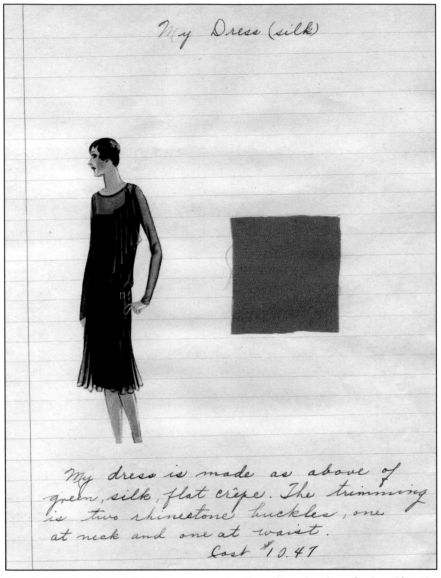

My Dress (silk)

My dress is made as above of green, silk, flat crêpe. The trimming is two rhinestone buckles, one at neck and one at waist.
Cost $10.47

Fig. 4: A high-school girl in home economics class planned a dress for herself in the 1920s at a cost of $141 in today's dollars. MARY ETHEL GUNDER NOTEBOOK, FROM THE COLLECTION OF HELEN LONG DEVITT

Fig. 5: Is it a skirt? A dress? No, it's beach pajamas!
These were the first pants that women did not wear
out of practical necessity. *Vogue Pattern Book,*
April-May 1931

Fig. 6: The easy-to-make dress in the 1930s was anything but a
T-shirt dress. This one in mulberry was a wrap dress with flared
sleeves and contrasting collar. *Vogue Pattern Book*, October-
November 1932

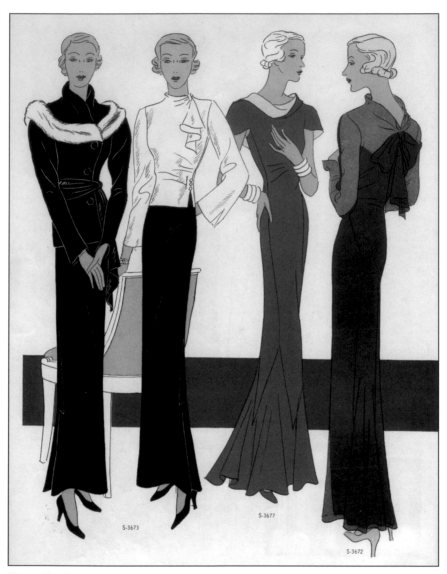

Fig. 7: For formal afternoons or informal evenings in 1934, Vogue Patterns offered a suit in black with its own white blouse, and dresses in lilac and red. *Vogue Pattern Book*, February-March 1934

Beginners' Patterns

■ MAKING a smart dress, even though you firmly believe you cannot sew a stitch, is actually a pretty simple matter when the dress has as many fashion points in its favor as this one has and when it is a Beginners' Pattern to boot. Notice the new look of its ruff collar and the low-placed fulness in its skirt. Now let's start putting the pieces together.

■ FIRST you add a strip of binding to the gathered edge of a collar that started out as merely a piece of velvet ribbon. The bow is ribbon, too, tied and tacked under the collar. Together they make this charming ruff neckline.

■ NEXT you divide your time between the two sleeves, gathering them at the elbow, as the perforations indicate, and sewing up the seams. Match the sleeve and armhole notches together, easing the tiny bit of fulness in between the notches, and then baste in the sleeve.

■ THE BODICE and skirt are just one long piece, making the making of the dress that much simpler for you. Merely make dart tucks at the waistline, darts under the arms and at the back of the neck, and, placing back and front together as indicated by the notches, sew up the side seams. The inverted pleats at each side of the skirt are already cut for you when you have cut out the pattern, and putting them in is really nothing more than continuing the side seams as the Deltor instructs you to do. The belt is a straight piece creased down the middle and stitched in a straight line.

■ IF, to 3⅛ yards of 39-inch silk crepe (which is all that is required to make this dress for 34 bust or size 16) you add 2⅝ yards of 4½-inch ribbon in a contrasting color the chic of the frock will be multiplied several times. Designed for sizes 12 to 20; 30 to 38 bust. Price, 45 Cents.

5485

Fig. 8: Butterick Patterns used exploded sketches of the pieces that made up beginner's sewing patterns to show how easy they were to make. The collar and bow on this dress from 1934 were made with wide velvet ribbon. *Butterick Fashion Book*, Early Spring 1934

6066   6054

Fig. 9: Unlike the shirtdresses based on men's shirts that appeared in the 1950s, the shirtwaist dresses of the 1930s offered variety to working women. BUTTERICK FASHION NEWS, MARCH 1935

Fig. 10: Using only two patterns from McCall's Patterns in 1935, a woman could make at least six dressmaker hats. *McCall's Fashion Book*, Midsummer 1935

9009   9006

Fig. 11: What the housewife in a small town fantasized about but did not need: an evening gown. The dinner dress on the left was trimmed with braid, while the one on the right featured a butterfly bodice. *McCall's Fashion Book*, Winter 1936–1937

Fig. 12: City living called for subdued colors and unrevealing clothing even on a hot summer day before the 1960s. *VOGUE PATTERN BOOK*, JUNE-JULY 1937

Fig. 13: A woman could create an entire wardrobe for day or for day into evening using only three sewing patterns from Vogue Patterns. *VOGUE PATTERN BOOK*, June-July 1937

SEWING WITH *Cotton Bags*

Fig. 14: Everything in the picture could be made from the cotton sacking that once held chicken feed. TEXTILE BAG MANUFACTURERS ASSOCIATION, *SEWING WITH COTTON BAGS*, 1937

Fig. 15: Spectator sportswear, or what to wear to watch the game in 1937: wool skirts, jackets, and hats to keep you warm or shaded. MONTGOMERY WARD CATALOG, 1937–1938

Fig. 16: Only the woman over thirty could claim the privilege to wear this afternoon dress in 1945. The draped bodice, the deep raisin color, the rayon jersey fabric, and the luxurious accessories all marked the style of the sophisticated woman. *Vogue Pattern Book*, October-November 1945

For horseback riding on the English saddle, there is the tailored coat of whipcord, breeches of twill, silk stock-collared shirt, and chamois gloves. But who needs a horse, if you have winter? "There is no better opportunity for a woman to look graceful" than while skating, wrote Margaret Story, as "the icy background helps her to make the most of her silhouette." Pick out a short fitted jacket, either brightened with embroidery or trimmed with fur. Add a short full skirt, heavy tights, and knitted gloves.[77]

Or wait for summer. The neat, pleated dress in cotton *piqué* for tennis was white, but a woman could always bring along a pretty, colored cardigan to wear in between sets. Golf in the fall calls for flannel skirts, pullover sweaters, felt fedoras, and pigskin gloves. With sports clothes, the fashion opportunities are legion and the colors can be bright, because all of these outfits are welcome at vacation spots, where the point is to look and feel playful. Sports clothing can have "an element of holiday gaiety about them."[78]

But pity the high-school girls who read Mildred Graves Ryan's advice on bathing suits in 1942. Remember her advice on dressing for church? She got meaner the fewer clothes you had on. "Have you noticed how few really attractive people you see on the beach?" she asked her junior-high-school readers. "This is due mainly to the fact that few people have nice figures which can appear in public practically nude." Most people were too fat or too thin, too bulgy or too bony. "So before you dash about in an abbreviated suit, I think you ought to do something about your figure, so that people will not snicker and stare as you go by."[79]

The Dress Doctors were not keen on pants for women, even for sports. Hiking, fishing, hunting, boating, or skiing seem to call for slacks, but the Dress Doctors were not convinced that trousers were necessary unless a woman was actually scrambling over boulders, riding horses, or on the ski slopes. They insisted that most sports can be played in a dress or a divided skirt.

Their hesitation about recommending pants even for sports was obvious and arose for several reasons. In the nineteenth century, any attempt by women to wear pants caused a hullabaloo. Amelia Bloomer tried out a puffy pair of pants in 1851 under a tunic so long that it would pass for a dress today. Cartoons mocked her experiment mercilessly with pictures of ugly, cigar-smoking, bloomer-wearing women who challenged the power of men. One cartoon shows a couple—the husband with bare legs—playing tug-of-war with a pair of pants to determine, literally, who will wear them. Their small son looks on and pleads, "Oh! Mamma, please leave my Papa his Pants!"[80]

Mrs. Bloomer gave up on trousers by 1859. She was tired of having the wind blow her tunics up over her head, and even more tired of everyone making such a fuss over what she was wearing. Besides, now that metal hoops could puff out a skirt, she could give up the traditional layers of petticoats that had made wearing a long dress so awkward. Yes, hoop skirts were an improvement, because they lifted petticoats away from the legs and allowed women to walk freely.[81]

Women first turned in large numbers to pants for purely practical purposes. During World War I, women in France and England, and some in America, took up many of the jobs and fashions that had formerly belonged to men. Women worked as cabbies, bus conductors, chauffeurs, elevator operators, and plumbers while wearing pants. British Land Girls, who took over farming jobs, wore breeches and boots.

Women in pants clearly made some people nervous. An account about Britain published in 1917 in the *Philadelphia Ledger* was designed to calm their fears. It described "a charming young plumber" in her "jaunty and attractive costume" marked with the dirt of her trade. The *Ledger* assured readers that "there has not been the faintest suspicion of an insult or an advance" made to any of the elevator girls. Apparently, revealing in public the fact that women had legs—a fact then camouflaged by ankle-length skirts—was so shocking that some feared men would forget all the rules of gentlemanly behavior when confronted with "an elevator girl."

Women opted for pants for these jobs because wearing them made life easier and safer. It was easier to get in and out of cars, buses, and wagons in pants than in long skirts. It was easier to kneel down and work on the plumbing in pants. A dress would have been constantly caught underfoot and might be caught up in machinery and cause an injury. A former stenographer working in a British munitions factory and wearing trousers in 1917 appreciated the change. She told a reporter, "I should hate to have to go back to work in the old long skirts." She had to go back to long skirts for a time, but skirts were up to the knee by the mid-1920s.[82]

The practicality of pants for certain kinds of work remained important to women after the war. Helen Louise Johnson sparked a bonfire of interest when she lectured on practical dress at Columbia University in 1920 and mentioned that she wore knee-length trousers specially designed for her whenever she was driving or gardening. Her female audience was eager to know where they could get a pair. Retailers took notice of the interest. Twill trousers and "woman-alls" cut with full legs were offered by the big mail-order catalogs by the 1920s for dirty jobs like gardening or painting the barn. By 1925, Emily Burbank wondered why anyone had worried in 1917 that women wearing trousers would make men insane, when women now wore pants for all kinds of sports. Meanwhile, Johnson had thrown her lot behind knickers as the perfect trousers for women for everyday wear—she also thought they looked good on men. Colors and cut were left entirely up to the individual, but she recommended wearing them with a jacket and a tailored shirt. Johnson, though, was a little ahead of her time.[83]

American women first wore pants as a fashion choice rather than for practicality in the 1930s, when they bought "beach pajamas," which had debuted in fancy resorts in France a decade earlier. These were charming, wide-legged pants of flowing silk or rayon meant to be worn at the beach or at home. Movie stars wanted to relax in something comfortable after being squeezed all day into girdles, and everyone wanted to dress like a star. The wide legs on beach pajamas—so wide that the garment could easily be mistaken for a dress—were part of their charm. Indeed, the playful swirl of fabric as you move is one of the pleasures of wearing beach pajamas. Trousers, cut full like men's trousers, also appeared in the 1930s—in illustrations of women on motoring vacations. Women wore trousers and shorts in the pages of *Butterick Fashion Magazine* while they lolled next to their campers or helped change a tire.[84]

Come World War II, Rosie the Riveter needed slacks or coveralls to stay safe on the factory assembly line, and there was a special effort to make sure they were attractive. A home economist visiting a war factory found the sight of women in overalls cut to fit men so depressing that she concluded "that it must be bad also for morale of the workers." So the USDA designed a woman's overall in pink and white striped cotton "suitable for the girl mechanic." One wonders if they imagined the effect of grease on such cheerful colors.[85]

But necessity did not make slacks popular with America's Rosies. Many of them changed back into a dress at the end of the day. "After a girl has worn trousers all day," explained a fabric designer in 1943, "when the whistle blows she wants to hustle into something soft and feminine." Sales of women's slacks actually dropped in towns near defense plants and army bases.[86]

Dress patterns almost always outnumbered pants patterns in depictions of vacation wear—whether the models were pictured on golf links, cruise ship decks, tennis courts, or beaches. According to Vogue Patterns, planning for a winter vacation at a warm resort in 1954 meant packing dresses: "For it is in dresses that you spend most of your time." Only an illustration of women spending their summer at a dude ranch offered more patterns for trousers than for dresses and divided skirts.[87]

Why this reluctance to put women in pants? There were at least three reasons.

First, the idea had persisted since the time of Mrs. Bloomer that a woman in pants threatened the social order. She was dressed like a man in a world where men controlled almost all large institutions. And men didn't like the competition.

Second, a woman in pants was dressed very casually by the standards of day. This remained true throughout the 1950s, when the line between casual wear and formal wear remained clear and important. Unless one was terribly sporty, there wasn't all that much reason for a woman to own a pair of pants. These first two reasons might blur together. An Englishwoman recalled that a village postal clerk had refused service to her and her sister—both clad in trousers—in 1939 because they were "improperly dressed." They had to go home, change into skirts, and come back in order to buy stamps.[88]

The third objection to women in pants, and possibly the most important one to the Dress Doctors, was their simple observation that pants are not terribly flattering to the female figure. When women first tried riding astride in breeches instead of sidesaddle in skirts in the 1890s, some objected that the change made women look broad in the beam. That objection echoed through the decades. In 1938, two Dress Doctors dismissed the idea that people were against women in pants because they challenged men's rights in some way: "We think that point of view would be exploded if a woman were given an opportunity to walk down the street behind herself." Harriet Pepin, who taught patternmaking and ran her own fashion academy, was happy to note four years later that many improvements had been made in pants designs for women, but she warned that Frontier Pants—what we call jeans—were not "for the plump figure." Only a woman who has "retained a slender hipline" can wear them. Slacks only flatter a woman "if they are faultlessly tailored," insisted two Dress Doctors in 1954, and they thought that achievement not at all likely to happen.

"A skirt is usually more attractive on the average figure than slacks," they concluded.[89]

American women must have agreed that they were neither sporty enough nor slim enough to wear pants, because they neither wore them nor owned them in great numbers. Eighty-nine percent of housewives in the New York City area wore dresses on any given day in 1943; for every fifteen dresses in their closets, there was only one pair of pants. Married women in Minneapolis/St. Paul in the late 1940s owned fewer than one pair of slacks each, despite the Twin Cities' notoriously frigid winters.[90]

The idea that women wore pants only for leisure, for dirty work, and for rough sports explains some of the hostility directed at women who decided to wear pants for every day in the 1960s. Women in pants in the city not only challenged the differences between men and women; they violated the rules of dress.

IF DRESSES DOMINATED ACTIVE SPORTSWEAR, they also dominated what was called "spectator sportswear." Yes, watching sports made up its own category of clothing, although some Dress Doctors lumped it in with campus clothing. Practicality drove their advice for spectator sportswear. Football crowds wore tweed woolen suits and coats with fur collars. These are rugged fabrics; if they get dirty in the crush of the crowd or during a raucous tailgate, they brush off easily. They will also keep you warm on a brisk fall afternoon. Such ensembles are best in rich mixtures of the browns, greens, and reds of autumn leaves. Gloves of tougher leathers, such as pigskin, suede, or deerskin, also suited the occasion. A casual felt hat, able to stand up to hard use, topped the outfit, kept the head warm, and shaded the eyes from the sun.

Today, when thousands of people descend upon universities in the fall to watch the football team on Saturday afternoons, there is a marked contrast to yesteryear. True, at some places, there is a tradition—followed even by the students—of dressing in polished spectator sportswear; at others, most fans dress as if they had been planning on cleaning their garages, but decided to come watch the game instead. The few dapper men and casually chic women stand out against a mass of rumpled T-shirts and lumpy cargo shorts.

For summer sports spectators, the Dress Doctors liked dresses or jacket/dress combinations out of linen or silk. Bright colors suited the summer sun, and cheerful prints were just as appropriate. Imagine the scene at a polo game: clusters of women in pretty silks looking out beneath the shade of their enormous hats. But the Dress Doctors were just as happy to see humbler fabrics, washable cotton ginghams and cotton *piqués*, in dresses with matching jackets, for women in the spectator stands. Again, a hat with a brim is a must to shade us from the sun. The burnt faces of today's crowds at a ball game prove that the Dress Doctors' prescription was a wise choice.[91]

THE END OF THE WORKDAY! Off with those tailored dresses and sober colors! Off with cottons and tub silks! It is time for clothing that is "impractical, glamorous, and seemingly unrelated alike to dish-washing, hose-mending, algebra, and science." Margaret Story described the spirit of the evening as a time for clothing of "make-believe, imagination, vivacity, glory, and splendor." No longer working among strangers and colleagues, but at leisure with a few chosen companions, a woman can wear clothing that expresses "the more or less intimate feelings of friendship and comradeship within a limited circle."[92]

Elizabeth Burris-Meyer, head of the department of costume design at the College of Fine Arts of New York University, explained that clothing for daytime reflected one's duties, while "evening clothes should give the greatest pleasure to every woman." Not only could a woman enjoy herself in the evenings, but she was able to wear "exactly what she wishes." A woman can choose any color that suits her—bright or pastel—and any fabric, too, from delicate ruffles and laces to layers of chiffons or slinky satins. Laura I. Baldt wrote that evening wear's "free use of broken lines and curves, repetition of pattern in design, and oft-repeated decoration bespeak festive occasions and joyous emotions." What makes no sense during a day of work, because it would get in the way—a full, flowing skirt of silk chiffon, for example—was perfect in the evening precisely because it added grace as a woman twirled on the dance floor.[93]

For women who worked as maids and wore uniforms or other plain and practical clothes during the day, changing for the evening was a special pleasure. "I would always go to work neat and clean," recalled one woman decades later. "But my dress up clothes, I didn't wear 'em to work. Because when I went out I wanted to change and I wanted to look different."[94]

But where was she headed when she went out? Outings in the afternoon—think tea, bridge club, lectures at women's clubs, and so on—came under the heading of informal affairs, while later and more elaborate occasions called for formal wear. (Notice that the word "informal" had nothing to do with the word "casual" the way we use it today.)

A page from the *Vogue Pattern Book* from the spring of 1934 offered afternoon dresses that would serve any woman attending a daytime wedding today. They had street-length skirts and sleeves, yet all of them had some special feature—bows, lace, gathers, folds—that put them worlds away from boring modern sheath dresses and shirt-dresses. Several were made from sheer fabrics with large, cape-like bertha collars, but they were sold to women as "afternoon frocks for the many times you are informal."[95]

These were also the kind of dresses college women called "date" dresses—not for a big party, but for dinner and a movie. The fabrics could be sophisticated. In fact, the same sewing pattern used to make a day dress made of navy crepe could be transformed into an afternoon dress if done up in a pale, blue-green sheer. A woman could wear a suit for these so-called informal events, too, if it was made up in a fine fabric, such as velvet, sequins, or lamé. Even wool crepe would do if the jacket was made of the same crepe but embroidered. Summer brought out silk and cotton dresses in floral prints. Pumps were still the standard shoe for afternoon events. Women's toes did not see the light of day, according to the Dress Doctors, unless it was the bright sunlight of a vacation resort.

It was possible for a clever woman to segue from the workday to an informal afternoon affair without changing her outfit entirely. "A smart, well-designed, well-cut wool dress can be worn anywhere," noted Grace Margaret Morton, "because it is easily converted by accessories and jewelry into a spectator sport frock, or the finest kind of town frock which will look equally well in an office or at an informal tea." It must be made up in a dark color in order to do work duty, Morton explained, and then the accessories can brighten it up for watching sports or dress it up for taking tea. In wool crepe, such a dress is comfortable three seasons of the year in most climates. Burris-Meyer praised designers in the 1930s for dressing "the business woman who is dining in town in the same dress or suit which she has been wearing all day" by adding "some ingenious contrivance," such as a collar, a scarf, or a blouse that could be removed or retied to make her outfit more formal.[96]

During the 1950s, designers often opted for having a woman take off a jacket or swap it for a matching stole. Butterick Patterns offered the louchely named "Peel-Off" pattern in 1957. It featured a solid fitted sheath dress, which was to be worn alone for dates. For casual wear, the sheath was covered with a short-sleeved print bolero. To make it business wear, over both sheath and bolero went a box jacket in the same solid fabric as the sheath dress, but lined in the print fabric of the bolero.[97]

The unveiling of a woman's neck and shoulders did not occur until the evening. Even then, the wiser choice than a shoulder-bearing dress alone was one that came with a matching jacket. A woman could keep the jacket on for a dinner date, then take it off should she go on to a dance. Anyone who has seen high-school girls shivering in their strapless frocks after winter formals can see the wisdom in the matching jacket.

Skirts were short even at night during the 1920s, but, in the decades that followed, evening dresses went long and stayed that way. Despite fabric shortages during World War II, the US government refused to outlaw the manufacture of floor-length dresses. Why? Because servicemen who came home on leave liked their evenings to be special, and only a long dress signaled a true celebration.

The other choice for semiformal evenings was the dinner suit, suits that were cut on simple lines but made up in fabrics that were "lustrous, sheer, and rich." According to Elizabeth Burris-Meyer, the idea of a dinner suit "originated with the clothes designed for wear in the speakeasies of Prohibition days." She does not tell us why. Maybe women did not like being too bare when buying drinks from gangsters? Or maybe a suit gave them more confidence when scrambling over tables during a police raid? With a suit pattern, a woman who sewed could take it any direction. For summer days, the suit could be made up in seersucker stripes. For evening, make it a floor-length skirt in velvet and the jacket in gold brocade. "Richly suited" worked for evening.[98]

For formal dinners, gowns could be made up in the most elaborate fabrics: satins, sequins, embroideries, laces, and chiffons. Then a woman added long gloves in white kid leather or black suede. Out came her toes in sandals, or she could hide them in slippers, perhaps of metallic kid leathers or in satin dyed to match her dress. By 1935, the Dress Doctors could complain that "shoes for formal evening wear are often impractical to the point of frivolity." However, fans, veils, fancy combs, and feather ornaments were all welcome, at least when Mary Brooks Picken wrote her first book in 1918. No one mentioned them after the 1920s.[99]

For a ball gown, a woman could shoot the works. The formal ball and the opera, wrote Grace Margaret Morton, "afford the greatest opportunity for women to dress up, to express through their clothes gaiety and romance, luxury and sophistication." A woman could choose from the most luxurious fabrics: layers of chiffon, draped silk jerseys, tulle embroidered with sequins, *panné* velvet, taffetas, or satins. These are all delicate fabrics that cannot survive the wear-and-tear of daily life, but do fine on the dance floor. Or at least they did when the cha-cha was as wild as things got. Top these long-stemmed beauties with real jewels, magnificent furs, and long white gloves. Our lives do not offer many such opportunities these days.

Owning some kind of evening gown was a necessity. The New Yorkers who came up with a young woman's $35 wardrobe budget in the 1940s made a point of including a long gown. So did Grace Margaret Morton when she drew up a college woman's wardrobe on a "minimum allowance." To Morton's mind, a college girl at a formal dance should not have to make do with her one cloth coat. Morton wanted her to top her evening gown with a velveteen evening cape warmed by a layer of flannel hidden beneath the lining. Morton wasn't dreaming. Capes are easy to make, so whipping one up would not have been beyond the skills of a young woman who had managed to pass her junior-high dressmaking class. Every working woman should draw a clear line between her working clothes and her evening clothes, argued Anne Rittenhouse, who wrote a fashion column for a living. "Life will be happier if she does not economize too sharply on the clothes which are least worn."[100]

Ever conscious of the importance of variety, the Dress Doctors figured out how to take that one evening gown that every woman should be able to squeeze into her budget and stretch its use. *Designing Women*, written by Margaretta Byers, an advertising whiz who worked at Lord and Taylor and Saks Fifth Avenue, and Consuelo Kamholz, an editor at Simon and Schuster (until World War II prompted her to devote her skills of persuasion to the Psychological Warfare Branch of the Allied Forces Headquarters[101]), explained the metamorphoses of a white evening gown:

1. Wear it with gold kidskin palm leaves in the hair, and add a belt, slippers, and bag, all in gold kidskin.
2. Don a sky-blue cape of ostrich feathers, a rhinestone tiara, and bracelets and bag trimmed in rhinestones.
3. Add a red velvet bolero, with a red and white velvet hair bow, white kidskin gloves, and red slippers.
4. Try a silver sequin jacket with a silver sequin cap, topped with a white gardenia and white gardenias pinned at the wrists.
5. Take a red chiffon scarf, 3 yards long, use a gold clip to attach it to the front of the dress, toss the ends over the shoulders, clip it again at the back of the dress, and let the ends flow down to the floor; add red slippers and white lace fingerless gloves.

The authors offered the same kind of transformations with a black evening gown, a black afternoon dress, a gray suit, and a brown suit.

The Dress Doctors wanted to stimulate a woman's mind so she could look over what was hanging in her own closet and dream up her own metamorphoses, not follow their ideas outfit by outfit. "Imagine our predicament," wrote Byers and Kamholz, "were reader to meet reader each wearing identical duplicates of these costumes." *Designing Women* became an instant best-seller in 1938, was excerpted in *Life* magazine, and earned a place in the time capsule buried in Flushing Meadows for the 1939 New York World's Fair. Its tips on versatility were not the only reasons for its success, but they certainly helped, and they can inspire us to rethink the possibilities of our own closets.[102]

Fig. 8: One doozy of a housecoat made of taffeta: the stripes are powder-blue and black, the solid powder-blue. *Singer Sewing Digest*, Fall-Winter 1941

ONCE A WOMAN WAS HOME FOR THE EVENING, the Dress Doctors believed, she should have something for that occasion, too. Individuality, gaiety, and bright colors then had free rein. "In the home where the most intimate human relations hold, there is an atmosphere of affection and confidence, permitting full self-expression," wrote two Dress Doctors in 1935.

By confidence, they meant the freedom to confide in one's intimates, those chosen few with whom one lives or who are invited into the home as friends. At work, a woman might wear a dark suit and an impersonal air, but at home she could choose silk pajamas in her favorite color, even if it was riotous or romantic. And strangers did not need to know what that color was. At home, a woman wore garments and colors that "reflect freedom, frankness, and enjoyment." If she was the shy type, she could opt for the daring colors and cuts that she would not have the nerve to don in public, but "for which her soul yearns." Byers and Kamholz confided of their friends who were nurses and had to wear uniforms all day: "Never have we seen giddier negligees" at night than theirs. And the home woman, especially one who had spent her whole day running after her kids, deserved something just as pretty and comfortable as the businesswoman who had spent a hard day at the office.[103]

The lounging wear of earlier eras puts us, in our velour tracksuits and yoga pants, to shame. Silk or rayon pajamas—little jackets over pants that were cut slim over the hips and flared into wonderfully wide legs—appeared in the 1930s. Tunics and trousers of various kinds evolved, some decorated with embroidery, fur, or lace. From Hollywood Patterns in 1940 came a stunningly pretty, full-length taffeta "house-coat"—the word does not do this creation justice—in black and powder-blue stripes with a softly gathered bodice in powder blue.[104]

This kind of housecoat was the descendant of the tea gown, which flourished around 1900. These were made up in lovely pastel shades of silk and lace, and a woman would wear one to pour tea for a few select friends who were allowed to see her in what was technically a state of undress. The loosely cut tea-gown did not require a corset, and without her corset, a woman was not dressed for public life. Tea gowns morphed into hostess gowns, always with long, flowing skirts. In the middle of a lesson on budgeting written during the Great Depression, Alpha Latzke and Laura Baxter of Kansas State stopped to make clear that "a professional woman in the city with uninterrupted evenings in the privacy of her apartment might have use for a velvet hostess gown."[105]

Being at home or among friends is no excuse for sloppiness. "So often we think, 'Oh! This is for every day, so it does not matter,'" wrote Mary Brooks Picken. "But it is our every-day clothes that mark our good taste in dress, that give our most intimate friends pleasure in seeing us. And is it not these friends, after all, who are the most important ones to consider?"[106]

EXCEPT AT HOME IN THE EVENING, hats were once a normal, often required, part of our wardrobes. The simple beret for the college girl, the casual felt for the young businesswoman, the veil for the bride. In fact, American girls marked their entry into womanhood by putting on hats. At the turn of the century, ten-year-old working-class girls wore braids and played on the sidewalks in front of their tenements. At fourteen, they put up their hair and donned the enormous hats then in style and went off to prepare themselves for a job. The girls captured on film entering the Manhattan Trade School for Girls in 1911 were all wearing hats. They were such tiny things, and the brims of their hats were so wide, that they looked like a group of midget waitresses who had decided to balance trays of flowers and ribbons on their heads. To us, they still look like kids, but hatted, they announced that they were young women ready to join the workforce.[107]

The big brims had disappeared by the 1920s. Women began wearing the *cloche* (French for "bell"), which nestled closely around the face, or the "helmet." Both covered the new bobbed haircuts and put a premium on big eyes and bee-stung lips. Anne Rittenhouse pointed out in 1924 that French women—"the world's most serious students of dress"—believed that it was often wise to pay more for a hat than for a dress.[108]

In the 1930s, hats grew to include proper brims again. The Great Depression actually encouraged hats. "Women reason as follows," a marketing whiz explained: "Times are hard, difficulties are great, our minds are depressed; we will relieve the mental gloom by going out and buying a new hat!" Margaret Story, the loopiest of the Dress Doctors, prescribed a hat as an "antidote for gloom" in 1930. A new hat had miraculous powers, according to Story: "A smart and becoming hat will buoy up a woman's spirits, give her confidence, increase her powers of repartee, and make her wit scintillate." Couldn't we all use some of that?[109]

Working girls wore sporty numbers in the 1930s, either casual felts that would shade the eyes, trimmed with a long feather in the band, or shaped berets that would stay on in a breeze. Trendy women wore so many wacky shapes in the late 1930s—Elsa Schiaparelli of Paris designed one that made a woman look like she was wearing a giant shoe upside down on her head—that comedian Danny Kaye's wife, Sylvia Fine, wrote him a silly song to sing as the character Anatole of Paris, a milliner: "I shriek with chic / My hat of the week / Causes six divorces, three runaway horses."

World War II brought more sober lines in hats, as war meant the end of Parisian imports and brought shortages of all kinds to the States, from silk to leather. War Production Board Order L-85 limited a hat to half a yard of material and its ribbon to a yard and a half. As one fashion writer put it, "both here and in Europe, 'dressing up' was not only out of keeping with the times, but to large degree, downright impossible." What milliners called "dressmaker hats," ones that were cut and sewn out of fabric, could be made by anyone with some time and patience. The beret and the turban were simple and popular. Milliner John Frederics offered an easy pattern for a scarf-hat that could be worn four different ways, including as a "Paris cycling hat."[110]

Women could make dressmaker hats themselves, but they could not make felt hats. Good hat felt is now made of rabbit fur, which comes from Europe, where the point of rabbits is a nice stew. (Wool felt hats are cheaper, but stiffer). Felt hats have always been the province of professionals because they are made by molding steamed felt over special wooden forms called "blocks," which sell for as high as $800 each today. (The Mad Hatter of *Alice in Wonderland* blocked hats—he was mad because the fur fibers were treated back then with mercury, which damages the human nervous system.) Felt hats could still have multiple lives. During World War II, milliner Robert Dudley came up with a felt hat that took on multiple personalities: its brim could be styled five different ways, and its veil could come off. It supported the Allied war effort by coming in the patriotic colors of navy blue, red, and French blue. Mid-war, the average American home woman owned 5.3 hats.[111]

After the war, some hats got bulkier and were fluffed with fabric and flowers, but the Paris designers also showed sleek, molded felt hats with a dramatic feather or two. Christian Dior covered small hats with hand-pleated fabric that combined design simplicity with the talents of his milliners. Throughout the 1950s, hats were an essential element of any elegant ensemble. Clothing budgets offered by the Dress Doctors made room for one new casual felt a year, and three dress hats every four years.[112]

Old movies can mislead us as to the necessity of hats before the 1960s. Actresses sometimes run around all tremulous and passionate and hatless on film, but their flowing locks were strikingly sexy precisely because no normal woman would appear hatless on a city street (any more than she would run around all tremulous and passionate). An English millinery book from 1957 pointed out that when the showgirls at the *Folies Bergère* took off their clothes, they kept on their hats. *Les demoiselles* could not be *chic* without them.[113]

Hats were more than essential; they were a style opportunity. They could be jaunty or sophisticated, sporty or dignified, innocent or mysterious, chic or businesslike. There was the cartwheel, with its extra wide brim; the skimmer, so flat it had to be held on with veiling; the profile hat, worn entirely on one side of the head; and the tricorne, reminiscent of a colonial gentleman. The French supplied the *chou*, named after the cabbage because of its crushed crown. American designers reworked the coolie hat out of straw from the Chinese and the tall and brimless Cossack hat of fur from the Russians. Milliners borrowed from sailors, equestrians, milkmaids, even Robin Hood in their quest to make fashionable women's hats.

A well-chosen hat can flatter any face. "The Hat is a Background for the Face," wrote Laurene Hempstead in 1931. Twenty years later, Bernice G. Chambers claimed that so many women had been "transformed by the selection of a new coiffure and a becoming hat that it is hard to believe any longer that there are ugly women." By balancing out flawed facial features, she argued, the right hat creates the illusion of perfect proportions.[114]

If a woman wanted a fur felt hat, she had to work with the basic shapes for sale that season. But there was a risk to shopping for hats, particularly on the spur of the moment. As one Dress Doctor pointed out, some women worked out their emotional crises by hat-shopping: "Where a man would get drunk, they relieve their pent-up feeling by buying a new hat." Inevitably, they wound up with some wacky model that tilted wildly over one eye.[115]

A more budget-minded woman could take stock of her old hats. (Today, we call this "shopping your closet," as if only the word "shopping" can focus our tiny minds.) If what she found wasn't exactly right, she could try a change of ribbon, an added feather, a tuft of veil, and . . . *Voila!* An entirely new hat.

Do hats still have appeal? Yes, they do. What would otherwise explain why college women today sigh at the idea of a hat trimmed with a veil? Or why there was so much excitement about the hats worn to royal weddings? How else to explain why two young Amish women in long dresses and white bonnets poked their heads into a hat workshop being given in 2009 in a brick Victorian rowhouse in downtown La Grange, Indiana, home of Judith M., a millinery supply house? They might have been Amish and officially devoted to all things plain and simple, yet they were drawn in by owner Judith Mishler's window display of fantasy hats made of warped 45 rpm records.

Laura Hubka, a woman of boundless enthusiasm, jet-black hair, mod rectangular glasses, and a tiny nose ring, was at Judith M. Millinery that day teaching some of the basics of her craft, using velvety felts in a rainbow of colors and two shapes: a hood (a kind of cone a bit longer than your head), and a capeline (which looks like a shapeless floppy hat with a very large brim). Once people steamed the felt in kettles, then in machines; Hubka wets it, wraps it in a damp towel, and pops it into a microwave for two minutes. It comes out piping hot. She pulls and stretches the felt over a block, and little bits of fur come off on her hands. She ties the felt in place with cords and set it under an old-fashioned hair-dryer, the kind women sit under to set their hair in the salon. After a few hours, the felt is dry. Then, the excess is trimmed off, a wire sewn along the edge of the brim, and a ribbon sewn inside the crown. The wire means the brim will keep its shape. The ribbon allows the hat to be fitted to the exact quarter inch.

Today, we have women obsessed with shoes instead of hats. We are willing to make ourselves painfully uncomfortable in order to attract attention . . . to our feet. "A costume that had striking footwear as its most conspicuous detail," wrote Laurene Hempstead at New York University, "detracts from the personality of the wearer because the observer doesn't notice her face." If a woman wants people to listen to what she says, she should not make her toes the center of attention. (Of course, if she is eager to attract men with a thing for toes, she should go right ahead.) Foot doctors have noticed that women with bunions have operations on their feet; men with bunions buy more comfortable shoes.[116]

Today, women go hatless in the summer sun so they won't mess up their hair, and hatless in the winter cold so they won't mess up their hair. As a result, women are sunburned and windblown when a good hat could have kept them shaded and sheltered. We spend much time fluffing or flattening our hair. Perhaps we would be better off spending that time choosing a hat to buy.

THE DRESS DOCTORS KNEW the pleasures of the rituals of dress. It isn't how much clothing you own, but how well your clothes suit each occasion in your life, whether that means school or housework or office work, a tea, a dinner, or a ball. "It is understandable," said Laurene Hempstead of New York University, "that a woman might wish to appear dignified while shopping or traveling, merely youthful in her own home of an afternoon, and to transform herself into a sophisticated creature for an evening at the theater."[117]

Under the Dress Doctors' guidance, the pursuit of novelty for its own sake was muted. Instead, the pleasure of novelty came from swapping out the sequin jacket for the chiffon scarf on the same evening gown. Or taking a brown suit and switching from one blouse, hat, pair of shoes, or bag to another. Novelty also came from changing out of the gray suit at the end of the workday. It came from slipping into a pair of silk lounging pajamas for a night at home or into a pretty wool crepe dress for a dinner out. Putting on those high heels only for a party would not only save your feet from bunions, it would make you appreciate their impractical charm all the more. Margaret Story advised daily clothing variety as a tonic. Otherwise, she warned, monotony would lead to melancholy, and disinterest to dementia. A bit extreme, to be sure, but marking the different occasions of our lives reminds us to savor them all.[118]

Thrift

Much for Little

T HE DRESS DOCTORS ATTACKED THE PROBLEM OF THRIFT from all angles. They taught women how to reuse and recycle patterns, garments, and buttons during wartime and through economic disasters. They taught sewing and budgeting in classrooms, through correspondence courses, and in extension programs sponsored by the USDA. Dressmaking allowed a woman to leverage her sweat equity into a beautiful wardrobe, or even into a career. And budgeting taught both girl and woman to make do with what she had. One quixotic home economist even tried to give women a way to opt out of the endless pursuit of what was fashionable by inventing a standard dress for everyone to wear.

Dress textbooks coached girls on the steps necessary to take control of their clothing budgets. First homework assignment: inventory your closet. Second, draw up a plan for the coming year, including enough clothing "to keep clean and avoid monotony."[1] Outfits for special events—are you expecting to attend the junior prom?—must be included. Last, figure out how much money you have to spend and how much you will spend for each item. Along the way, girls had to figure out whether it would pay to make what was needed or go out and purchase some of the items. Girls in 4-H clothing clubs were urged to keep records of how many hours they put into each garment in order to calculate the total cost, including labor.

So much was required for good wardrobe planning that Grace Margaret Morton, at the University of Nebraska, wrote, "It is not only a proof of our understanding of design and color and texture, of means of creating illusion and expressing temperament, but it also tests the real character of the person in discernment, in farsighted-ness, in self-discipline and in organization, and in ability to hold unswervingly to principle and purpose." And you thought you were just shopping.[2]

The number of garments the Dress Doctors thought sufficient for any woman was stunningly small. Margaret Story suggested that she needed "only three perfect outfits." Women like Story owned fewer clothes than we do, but spent more money for each item and then took good care of their clothing. Much has changed since then. Young women today may not know the meaning of the word "darn-ing," because they have never been asked to mend clothing. We are used to plenty, even to excess. Americans were buying clothing at the remarkable rate of one new item every five and a half days, on average, in 2005. This was possible because prices had dropped so low. Whereas Americans spent 13 percent of their incomes on clothing in 1901, they only had to spend 6 percent by 1997.[3]

Meanwhile, the garment industry shifted almost entirely from the United States to countries where wages are extremely low. Garments have also lost most of their fine detailing and are cheaper to make. Nevertheless, we can still learn much from the thrifty lessons of the Dress Doctors.

Let's travel back to the home front during World War I, when the home economists first proved their usefulness to the nation—not only by creating the Hoover apron, but by teaching American women how to conserve the nation's supply of fabric.

DURING WORLD WAR I, a prefabricated wooden "war hut" appeared on Boston Common. Its exhibits were organized by Mary Schenck Woolman, who was working for the US Department of Agriculture. She had noticed before the war that Americans earned high wages but saved hardly anything. (Sounds familiar, doesn't it?) Now it was time to break "the careless habits of a lifetime" and help the nation rise to the challenge.

Women stopped at the war hut to learn how to help the cause when it came to clothing. Woolman advised them first to use what they had. "Garments often lie forgotten for years in trunks, drawers and closets," she wrote. If something no longer fit, was worn out in places, or had fallen hopelessly out of fashion, it could be made over, perhaps into something entirely new. Woolman offered patterns to turn a woman's skirt into a dress for a girl, a man's shirt into a child's dress, and long silk gloves into children's stockings. She reminded women that planning a wardrobe was as essential as maintaining it. Most important of all, she reminded us: "Do all cheerfully!" Because there's nothing nice about a cranky patriot.

Other women joined the effort. The Junior League drew up thrifty designs that were put on sale at Wanamaker's department store in New York City and Filene's in Boston. Down south, the home economists who worked in rural counties set a good example, too, opting for tidy, washable dresses of blue-gray with white collars and cuffs. Like soldiers in the army, they had their uniforms.

Woolman was pleased that women signed onto the Thrift Movement so enthusiastically during the war, but what followed made her hair stand on end: "A riot of extravagance . . . and thoughtless buying" followed. Remembering the days when "women worked with intense enthusiasm that the home might do its share in saving for the government's need," she warned that "the lesson learned and the methods practiced should not be forgotten."[4]

Woolman was a crusader for thrift because she had lived its lessons. She was born the daughter of a brilliant and wealthy surgeon and had been sent to private schools, where she had studied literature and history. She expected to continue a life of ease when she married a leading attorney. Then her father died, and both her husband and her mother became chronically ill. Everything was in her hands, and she hadn't the faintest idea how to do anything practical.

She did have a well-trained mind, however, and she used it. She found a cook at a restaurant to teach her how to prepare food. She found a hospital where she could learn how to nurse the sick. She sat down for the first time in her life to work out a budget. How was she going to keep a roof over all of their heads? She sold their home and got a job in New York City correcting manuscripts for a publisher.

Then, she got a lucky break. An instructor at Teachers College at Columbia University, who happened to live in the same boardinghouse as Woolman, asked her to review a book on teaching girls how to sew. This was in 1891. The one practical thing Woolman had learned when she was little was how to sew, and she thought this book was awful.

It followed the English tradition. A teacher would make a little girl practice the same plain hand stitch over and over, and over and over again, until she had mastered it (and was bored out of her tiny skull). And then she could practice the basting stitch over and over again until she had mastered it. And then the overcast stitch . . . and so on. Only after a little girl had filled up dozens of little practice squares of cloth with perfect stitches would the teacher allow her to try to make anything. It was almost designed to make girls hate sewing, said Woolman. Nobody taught writing that way—teachers had children write out whole words long before they could form each letter perfectly—so why do it with sewing?

Both the instructor and the president of Teachers College were impressed with her critique. How would *she* teach sewing? She would have girls practice hand stitches until they could make something simple, explained Woolman, maybe a bookmark or pincushion. When they got better at their stitches, they could try something harder, such as a book bag or a stuffed animal. The girls would enjoy the sense of accomplishment they experienced with each project and would be encouraged to perfect their hand stitches as they went along.

Woolman's sewing manual was such a success that the Department of Domestic Science at Teachers College took her on as an assistant. She earned her bachelor's degree in 1897 and was a professor by 1903. By 1910, she was directing her own creation: the Department of Domestic Arts. Woolman was one of the leaders of the movement to bring sewing to the public schools and wrote the standard book on how to teach sewing. Her method became the American way. She also founded the Manhattan Trade School for Girls, which aimed at making young women into workers *and* into citizens by offering a combination of vocational training and general education. When not otherwise occupied, she found time to direct films on home economics.[5]

Thrift had a long history among domestically minded women. Sarah Hale, the nineteenth-century editor of *Godey's Lady Book*, advised her readers, "Economy is essential in a well-regulated household." She originally opposed her publisher's insistence on the colored fashion plates that her magazine made so famous. Forced to give in, Hale made the best of it: "We think it, on the whole, best to exhibit the syren [*sic*] Fashion in all her brilliant and changing costumes, offering at the same time reasons why she should not be worshiped as a divinity." The pious widow Hale wrote: "A *Christian* is the highest style of man." Or woman, one presumes.[6]

Too much interest in fashion and too much shopping also bothered Ellen S. Richards, the mother of modern home economics. Richards shook her head at the "large crowds of women seen daily on the shopping streets" at the turn of the century. She would prefer that they find "the delight of living" in their own homes, not in rifling the bargain counters at the department stores.

When a thrifty woman was called stingy, when frugality was confused with miserliness, Richards felt called upon to explain that such virtues were "essential to the preservation of the race." Ideally, she said, only 15 percent of a household income should be spent on clothing. A full 25 percent should go to what she called "Higher Living," which included books and travel, charity, savings, and insurance.[7]

Richards was not the only one to worry about consumerism gone wild. Historians, looking back, fret about the rise of consumption in American life and its effects on us today. They worry that Americans stopped thinking about the higher things in life, including spiritual life and civic duty, because they became obsessed with shopping. Women, in particular, wasted their time in chasing after fashion. And we struggle with the shallow materialism that resulted.[8]

Things may not have been as bad as they seemed. A sampling of actual middle-class families in 1911 spent only 8 to 12 percent of their household income on clothing, and they saved between 5 and 39 percent. The family that only saved 5 percent was spending some 25 percent of their income on their children's college education. So we might say they were investing 25 percent in the future. The virtues of thrift were not unappreciated in the early twentieth century, but some people still worried that Americans were not headed in the right direction.[9]

One of the Thrift Movement's most effective campaigners was Simon W. Straus, a poor boy who made good as a mortgage banker and then in 1914 organized the American Society for Thrift. Straus warned the National Education Association that "Babylonia, Greece and Rome fell because their people were pampered, because debauchery ran riot, and their substance was wasted." No wonder the US government threw its weight behind the Thrift Movement, especially after a thousand poor women rioted in Brooklyn in 1917 over the high price of food. With the support of the federal government during World War I, public schools began a Savings Stamp program that encouraged children to save their pennies. But it was the home economists who taught thrift most persistently over the decades.[10]

Mary Brooks Picken was not a home economist, yet she worked at the center of an endeavor that cham-

Fig. 1: The miserly hag wears rags, the party girl wears jewels, and the prudent woman dresses like a Grecian goddess. S. W. STRAUS, HISTORY OF THE THRIFT MOVEMENT IN AMERICA, 1920

pioned both thrift and enterprise: the Woman's Institute of Domestic Arts and Sciences in Scranton, Pennsylvania. To tell the story of the Woman's Institute, we need to start with the story of how a "shabby little stranger became the best dressed girl" in town, which appeared in *Good Housekeeping* and *Cosmopolitan* in 1919:

> Her real name was Enid, and I'll never forget how she looked that first morning! When she came in the door the whole office stopped and stared and—I'm ashamed to say it—we grinned. That dress—I supposed it had been stylish once, about five years before! Its tired out bronze color made her face look even paler than it was and it fitted her as if it had been made for a big sister. A faded old-rose toque sat dejectedly upon her mass of unruly yellow hair. She was a picture—so shabby and forlorn that I pitied her!

We all thought she'd gotten into the wrong place by mistake. But she hung up her hat and made herself at home at Sara Long's old desk. And there she quietly did her work for months—always the office mystery and always an object of pity among the rest of the girls at Warner's. Hartley, the office manager, told us all he knew about her—an orphan from a little town in Iowa—that was her story in a nutshell. She roomed alone, and in the office and out she kept to herself. The Truth was you just couldn't invite her out—in those clothes. And so we simply came to regard her as an office fixture that nobody quite understood. Then one morning, early in the fall, Enid gave the office its second shock—a more surprising one, if possible, than the first. Everybody was on time that morning—except Enid. We spent the first few minutes after the bell rang wondering where she could be. But by nine o'clock we had all nicely settled down to work and the typewriters were clicking like mad when the door opened and in walked a wonderfully radiant creature in the neatest, prettiest, and most becoming dress you ever saw and a charming hat that you just knew had been made for that little blonde head!

Every typewriter stopped as if by magic, and two dozen audible murmurs of admiration registered the effect on that office full of girls. Hartley looked up from a sheet of figures with a frown, then smoothed down what hair he had with one hand, yanked off his spectacles with the other, and rose to learn the caller's business. He was halfway between his desk and the door before the young lady who had caused all the commotion smilingly removed her hat, and we realized for the first time it was Enid! No one in the office could keep her mind on her work for the rest of that morning. After months of the shabby bronze dress, the old-rose toque, this was too much! And no one ever realized before how pretty Enid really was. But in her new attire she was simply a new creature. The transformation was so complete that even the old name didn't fit, and it just seemed natural that from that day we should call her "Cinderella."[11]

Now everyone wanted to have lunch with the beautiful Enid. She became the office expert to consult on questions of clothing, and a welcome sight at every party and dance in their small town. Before they knew it, the boss's son had fallen for her and whisked her away in a limousine. Cinderella had found her prince!

But before she left, Enid explained to the other girls how she had managed such a spectacular transformation. Each night, she had taken an hour to study the easy lessons from the Woman's Institute for Domestic Arts and Sciences. By her third lesson, she had made a little blouse. Soon she was making dresses and suits and could even copy the styles she saw in shop windows. Only when she had finished with her entire wardrobe, including the hats, did Enid unveil them to the wonder of all. Now she was getting married in a wedding costume that she had made entirely herself.

"So that's my confession," she told the girls. "The rest of my story you know—what a wonderful change this made in my life—how friends and happiness seem to follow close upon the change in my appearance that led you all to call me 'Cinderella.' . . . The whole thing is like a fairy story! But of one thing I am sure—I owe it all to the Woman's Institute." Enid went on: "And what I *did*—in saving hundreds of dollars on my clothes, having prettier, more stylish, better-made garments than I could have had any other way and attracting friends and happiness with them—*any woman or girl* can do!"[12]

"Cinderella's Confession" was one of dozens of stories of "fiction for fashion," a genre perfected by G. Lynn Sumner, who became one of the twentieth century's most famous names in the advertising business and the second husband of the widowed Mary Brooks Picken.

Sumner and Picken worked for the *Woman's* Institute because all women were supposed to possess certain qualities that belonged to

"Woman" with a capital "W." One of them was that women should be experts at the "housewifely arts," including dressmaking. The institute claimed that it filled "an urgent human need"—that of women who wanted training in these arts who could not attend school to learn them. "If they were to learn, the school must come to them," said one of the institute's catalogs. The dedication of the new Woman's Institute building in Scranton, Pennsylvania, in 1921 was so important that the governor presided over the ceremony.[13]

Every month, 50,000 American women sent away for a copy of the institute's catalog after reading stories about Enid and her fictional sisters in the pages of popular magazines. In five years, the fiction-for-fashion marketing campaign sold $12 million worth of courses (more than $30 million today). The institute enrolled 3,000 to 5,000 students every month. The oldest was seventy-three and the youngest was twelve, with the average age being twenty-six. More than half of the women who enrolled were married home women; the rest worked for a living. Some 17 percent were hoping to establish their own businesses.[14]

The Woman's Institute sold more than Cinderella stories. There was the tale of Eleanor, also fictional, which appeared in *Cosmopolitan*. Eleanor overheard her father confiding to her mother one night that they were practically broke, and she was determined to help. When her father gave her the extravagant sum of $50 to spend on a dress for her birthday, she used it not to buy a dress but to buy dressmaking lessons from the Woman's Institute. A few months later, she not only had a new dress that she had made with her own two hands, but she was able to give her father back the $50 out of what she had earned making dresses for her friends. "Wonderful!" her father said. "Why it's a modern miracle—and you've made me the proudest and happiest father in the world!" The Woman's Institute promised more than popularity and a good marriage. It promised a woman the skills to make her way in the world independently.[15]

G. Lynn Sumner and his staff made up the characters of Enid and Eleanor, but they were working from true tales from women all over the country. The institute received letters of thanks from many of its students with their own inspiring stories and was happy to print them. A mother from Utah was pleased to discover, after making a gingham dress for each of her two girls, that she had enough money left over to make a second dress for each. A stenographer from Pennsylvania spotted a skirt in a shop window and made it herself for less than half the price. A teenager took her white high-school graduation dress and remade it into a blue afternoon dress at the cost of only $1.10 in dye and satin ribbons. A Minnesota woman who did dressmaking out of her home wrote, "Best of all I have been able to take the first real vacation in ten years—three weeks without a care and with plenty for money for needed clothes and to have a good time."[16]

Most women expected to marry in the early twentieth century. Men were supposed to be the breadwinners, while women's skills as housewife or farmwife made it possible for a family to survive. But everyone knew that didn't always happen. Husbands died. Women discovered they had married hopeless drunks. Some women never married at all and preferred it that way. Women had to be able to take care of themselves. The Woman's Institute offered a way for them to do that. One magazine editor called the Woman's Institute "the Emancipation Proclamation, the Widow's Pension, the Declaration of Woman's Independence." By giving women skills they could put to work, the institute could save them from poverty.[17]

The widows' stories were perhaps the most powerful. A member of the institute from Pennsylvania explained that when her husband had died, "I was suddenly confronted with the fact that I had to support myself and three children. I was at my wits' end as to how I would be able to keep my little family together." She started the dressmaking course, and just a few months later she had a stack of sewing orders. Another widow, from New York, started sewing in her home and averaged $40 a week ($519 in today's dollars). Then she opened a shop, more than doubling her income by the second week. "If I added to my income what I have saved on our own clothes"—she had three children to dress—"I would be earning as good wages as nine out of ten men," she wrote. The eldest daughter of a third widow, from Hardinsburg, Kentucky—one of seven children—saw the advertisement featuring the fictional Eleanor and sent away for lessons. She figured that dressmaking would pay better than working for the telephone company. She figured right. She went from making $3 a week to averaging $18 to $25 a month as a dressmaker.[18]

Minnie from Georgia, Bertha from New York, Mildred from Missouri, and hundreds of others wrote to thank the Woman's Institute for what it had given them—skills, satisfaction, beautiful clothes, and cold, hard cash—at a time when there were few ways a woman could earn a living or continue her education. A book listing jobs that girls might hope to do in 1913 came up with only eleven: salesclerk, secretary, telephone operator, factory hand, cook, nurse, dressmaker, milliner, teacher, librarian, and maid. Dressmaker and milliner were the only ones that offered the possibility of a woman working for herself, and women knew this.[19]

Independence was especially important to black women, who were overwhelmingly stuck with jobs as maid and laundress because of racial prejudice. When 374 black schoolgirls in Atlanta, Georgia, were asked at the turn of the century what they would like to do when they grew up, the most popular choice was dressmaker or seamstress. An African American dressmaker could cater to the rising black middle class and run a sewing school on the side. American women who made custom dresses and hats were considered the "aristocrats among clothing makers." It was not until the 1930s that men, armed with the credit that banks would not offer to women, built ready-to-wear clothing factories and began the push that left most of these aristocrats out of business. In the meantime, the Woman's Institute trained those who hoped to join their ranks.[20]

The institute sent out lessons to thousands of American women for more than two decades on everything from "Underwear and Lingerie" to "Principles of Tailoring." In 1922, the total course in sewing, dressmaking, and tailoring amounted to 1,800 pages, with sketches and photographs guiding the students through thirty-eight lessons. The fashions pictured in the lessons changed from year to year, with lingerie blouses of the 1910s giving way to the jaunty bow blouses of the 1930s, and the once ankle-length skirts rising up to the knees—only to fall back down to mid-calf. The last lesson explained how to set up a dressmaking business, with advice on everything from how to choose a location for the shop and the style of stationery to how to cajole clients into ordering what actually looked good on them.

All the elements of a "real" school were in place. Students took exams (with questions such as, "What placket is best for a petticoat?" Flat-stitched, if you care to know). Between the pages of one copy of *Tailored and Lingerie Blouses* from 1923 is a graded exam for Mrs. Irwin Lauduer of Barrington, Illinois. It had been returned to her with check marks in red where she got the answer right and jotted corrections when she didn't. She earned a score of 97. Members also sent in samples of their sewing, and the staff of the Woman's Institute told them which skills still needed work. When a member of the Woman's Institute finished a course of study, she received a diploma signed by Mary Brooks Picken herself.

"Although I have never seen any of you, I consider you all as my friends," wrote a woman from Nebraska to the institute. "I feel as though you show personal interest in each lesson sent in and that has made me work doubly hard." The Woman's Institute was a business run to turn a profit, but learning dressmaking could change a woman's life.[21]

WHEN THE STOCK MARKET CRASHED IN 1929 and the Great Depression began, the Dress Doctors reminded women that they could save their families through thrift and sewing skill. Mary Brooks Picken was sure that "there is nothing a home woman can do that returns such big dividends as being able to sew—to take care of the family's clothes; to make new ones when they are needed, which fit into the wardrobe as well as into the budget."[22]

The USDA's public outreach—the extension programs—became especially useful to the rural population. Maryland farmwomen reported that they had spent $268 a year, on average, to clothe their families before the stock-market crash. Three years into the Depression, they only had $86 to spend.[23]

Extension clothing programs could help. In 1931, women agents conducted more than 91,000 demonstrations on clothing and sewing across the country. The farm girls who saw the demonstrations then went home and made more than 231,000 projects. Their mothers knew how to sew, but extension teachers still had some tricks to show them, and well over 175,000 women came to watch. Agents offered clothing clinics where farmwomen could bring in old coats and dresses to make over or cut down into children's wear. The USDA estimated that it saved rural women and girls $2,292,470 in 1935. That amounts to more than $36 million in today's dollars.[24]

Extension work was segregated. A white extension director explained in 1915 that there were "some things" that white women agents could not do, such as walk into a black woman's home and talk to her as though they were social equals. So black agents served black farm folk. Merely being included in the work was a victory for black women at that time, however. Once in, African Americans and their enthusiasm for the programs became one of the recurring themes of national reports on extension work. South Carolina black women called their agent a "Fairy God Mother" and "Magician." A Florida extension agent reported that clothing clubs were an instant hit with African American women in 1929, and she made them into a permanent feature of her program.[25]

Especially by the Depression, both black and white women could benefit from the thriftiest of projects, sack dresses. Extension agents demonstrated how to take the big cotton sacks that once held sugar, flour, and feed, wash them, dye them, and make "attractive garments" for pennies. Poor farmwomen had been using sacks out of necessity long before the agents came along, but extension sack-dress contests made the practice more appealing. One Louisiana mother declared that her daughter "ain't a bit ashamed to wear sack dresses now, and me and her together has made four." In 1933 alone, women in clothing clubs in Virginia made more than 10,000 garments out of sacks.[26]

Eventually the flour and feed companies figured out what women were up to and began to compete for sales by using pretty prints in their feed sacks. Their dealers found it rather odd. One feed dealer recalled that women used to ask him only for a certain kind of chicken feed, but now they asked if he carried a feed for laying chickens "in a flower percale." He complained, "It ain't natural."[27]

Feed sacks made an important difference when the graduate students studying home economics at the University of Alabama learned that the Farm Security Administration, a New Deal agency, had made the alarming discovery that families in the Deep South had only about $7.52 per person per year to spend on clothing, and that was supposed to cover everything from shoes to school clothes to underwear in what would be $116 in today's dollars. This was at a time when the annual cost of ready-to-wear clothing for a teenage girl in San Francisco was pegged at $58.32, or $905 if bought today.

The teacher of the Alabama students, Henrietta Mary Thompson, had come to the university in 1929 to organize its work in textiles and clothing and to help first-year college women plan their wardrobes. She had already noted how hard it was to guide the high-school girl through "the trying period" when "she is charmed by the alluring window displays, the persuasive arguments of advertisements, and the novelties and fads stressed in magazines and shops." Fads were all the more dangerous to the southern girl with little money. Thompson's graduate students decided to devise a homemade wardrobe for the high-school girl that would fit into the $7.52 annual budget. They knew there were precedents for the feat: USDA extension agents had been holding thrifty-dress competitions in their rural counties for more than a decade. At the start of the Great Depression, the winning entry at a "dollar dress contest" held in Virginia cost exactly 89 cents to make. Any woman who has ever looked into her overstuffed closet and moaned that she hasn't a thing to wear should prepare to feel ashamed.[28]

The Alabama students made it their goal to produce a three-year wardrobe, since three years was the usual length of time home economists expected a garment to last. They thought it would be fair to say that their imaginary southern girl did not have to buy all the sewing patterns with her own money. She could borrow some from a pattern lending library run by her church or school. They would limit themselves to blue as their basic color, and use red and white for accents. All the different pieces would have to go together.

The Alabama home economists managed to make three dresses of cotton, for starters. The first was a two-piece number made out of mattress ticking, an inexpensive fabric sold by the yard in country stores that usually came with blue and white stripes running down its length. The second dress was made from sugar sacks of cotton that were dyed blue, and it came with a matching bolero jacket trimmed in white. The third was made of new navy twill fabric. The Alabamans also made a long blue jacket out of sacks of jute, which they had also dyed, and which they lined with sacks of cotton. The jacket could be worn with any of the dresses. Of new fabrics they also made a pinafore, a red blouse, and a coat with a detachable hood that reversed from blue denim to corduroy. Amazingly, they sawed and painted wooden spools to make buttons, and recycled buckles from a pair of overalls. They finished off their sewing with four slips and a pair of shorts. Then they went shopping for shoes, gloves, stockings, and underwear.

Total cost for the three-year wardrobe? It was $22.50, and that assumed that their farm girl hadn't a stitch to wear before getting started. Professor Thompson explained it all in the pages of *Practical Home Economics*. She was clearly pleased that her graduate students had learned that what seemed impossible was not. They were headed toward jobs teaching southern girls who would need to make the most of what they had. Some were impressed. Elizabeth Todd, head of home economics education at the University of Georgia, said the wardrobe "beautifully illustrated" how planning required "the use of brains."[29]

Up North, a home economist at the University of Syracuse set out to prove that flour sacks, overall buckles, and sewing were all unnecessary because a three-year wardrobe, with careful shopping, could be bought ready-made for $34.96. The Dress Doctors always taught their students to ask, "Is the trouble or inconvenience of making a garment repaid by the saving in money?" For all their enthusiasm for sewing, they were more than willing to admit that not every junior-high-school girl was any good at sewing and not every girl enjoyed it. They never liked the idea of an unhappy woman bent over a sewing machine. "Busy, overworked mothers should not be further burdened with the task of making many garments," advised Laura I. Baldt of Teachers College in 1916. "Nor should the girl at school or college, nor the woman in business[,] be pressed with work of this sort in her leisure hours." Better that she get some "healthful recreation," a colleague of Baldt's chimed in, "even though it means a scanty wardrobe." Only if a working woman enjoys sewing as a "creative leisure experience" should she bother with it, according to the women of Kansas State.[30]

But the Syracuse wardrobe for $34.96 still didn't help the southern girl who lacked $34.96 and didn't live near a lot of department

Fig. 2: *Vogue* magazine showed off its sewing patterns
with photographs as beautiful as anything made by
a famous clothing designer. VOGUE, SEPTEMBER 15,
1944

stores. (The Syracuse wardrobe also *assumed* that their girl already
owned a winter coat, one dress, and a bathing suit.) If the southern
girl wanted a wardrobe, she would have to rely on her own labor and
ingenuity. Fortunately, such efforts could pay off. A University of Utah
instructor was surprised to learn in 1954 that junior-high-school girls
preferred a homemade wardrobe over one store-bought. They judged
both the materials and workmanship of the homemade wardrobe as
better quality.[31]

The sewing demonstrations and clothing clubs organized by extension work made a difference in women's lives. Take the case of
Helen Bailey, a teenager living in Monroe County, West Virginia,
during the Great Depression. Monroe County wasn't the easiest place
for an African American family like hers. After Abraham Lincoln
took office in 1861, the western part of Virginia refused to secede

from the Union and formed the new state of West Virginia. Not Monroe County. Its leaders insisted on siding with the Confederacy.

Helen had it even harder than most girls her color. Her mother died young, leaving the care of her brothers and sisters largely in her hands. When farm girls were so poor that they had no decent clothes, they simply stopped attending school. From 4-H clubs, Helen learned not only how to make the most of her garden crop by canning fruits and vegetables, but also how to sew well enough to make clothes for herself and for all her sisters. Extension clubs allowed her to stretch the dollars that her father brought home.[32]

The extension agents may have sounded a bit patronizing when they congratulated themselves (as they did in 1934) on raising "the standard of dress of farm people" by teaching them to wear "what is healthful, appropriate, and attractive." But they were also keen on reporting how farmwomen were gaining confidence as a result of learning new skills. Imagine the satisfaction of the woman from a rural parish in Louisiana who made a suit by recycling the fabric from a man's suit, wore it into a Shreveport city store, and found herself being stopped by a head clerk who wanted to know where she had bought it. It was exactly the kind that he wanted to get in stock. Or imagine the pride felt by the woman who wore a sack dress to a club meeting, and was asked where she had found such pretty "linen" fabric. The extension agents reported club members speaking up for the first time in public meetings and going on to work on community projects. A woman from Virginia recalled that her club leader had made the girls believe "that we could do anything we wanted to if we put everything we had into it." Looking back decades later, this former 4-H girl felt she owed everything she had accomplished in life to her club leader's encouragement.[33]

Besides the extension programs, starting in 1935 there were the more than 10,000 sewing rooms organized by the New Deal's Works Project Administration (WPA). Here, home economists helped women make clothing and household goods for themselves, while others earned wages making garments for the needy and got training for work in the garment industry. Sewing rooms became the largest WPA projects outside of construction work.[34]

Swings in fashion made it harder to cope with the Depression. Just a year before the stock market crashed and the economy took a nose dive, French designer Jean Patou had decided that every woman should be wearing longer skirts, and the trend caught on. "Fashion changed over night!" declared the Butterick Publishing Company. "Our nice modish two piece dresses with plaited [pleated] skirts barely reaching our knees (sometimes our bare knees) . . . all these perfectly wearable and hitherto undeniably chic clothes suddenly became discards." What to do? Not to worry. You could buy a new pattern and make a new dress, or you could do some recycling and remodeling of old clothes.[35]

With fashionable dresses now dipping down to the calf, it was necessary to figure out a way to lengthen skirts. One way was to treat a short dress as a tunic and wear a longer skirt underneath it. You made the longer skirt by taking an outmoded short skirt and adding a discrete piece of fabric high up where it wouldn't show. Or you could cut into the bottom of the skirt and add lengthy godets of a different fabric. Godets are flared inserts at the bottom of a skirt that give it swish. To keep the whole dress harmonious, you could use the same type of fabric and combine two different colors. Or you could stick to the same color and combine two contrasting textures, such as navy wool with navy silk, black crepe with black chiffon, or ivory chiffon with ivory lace.

Of course, one of the most effective ways of saving money on clothing would be to stop the churn of fashion, so that things never went out of style. It was tried, once, just a year before Mary Schenck Woolman set up her war hut on Boston Common.

On May 23, 1916, 20,000 conventioneers descended upon New York City. Unlike most conventioneers, who came to the big city for

154. Make these two new frocks from three old ones.

Fig. 3: When Paris dictated dropped hemlines in 1928, the Butterick Publishing Company came up with a solution that required cutting up old dresses to add length. *Paris Frocks at Home*, 1930

a good time, these were members of the General Federation of Women's Clubs. Men's clubs were wood-paneled retreats where members relaxed in leather chairs, smoked cigars, and had a drink. Clubwomen were far more ambitious. To quote one of their founders, clubwomen "must be synonyms for light, life and love. They must stand for all that is good and against all forms of evil. In these ways they can help to guide the great ship of Christian civilization out of the perilous storm of passion, ignorance and wickedness which threaten it, into the clear, deep calm waters of true wisdom." In short, they were do-gooders. Clubwomen were against child labor, impure drugs, and sweatshops. They were for women's suffrage, kindergartens, and "setting sensible and artistic standards in dress."[36]

Clubwomen had always objected to silly clothes. They pledged to give up their feathered headgear after ornithologist Frank Chapman of the American Museum of Natural History counted 542 dead birds on the hats of 700 fashionable women in New York City in 1886.

At that rate, he declared, the supply of songbirds in America would soon give out. Women and children joined the Audubon Society in unprecedented numbers to protect our feathered friends, and women lobbied for state and federal laws to end the plumage trade.[37]

In 1870, clubwomen condemned the day-dress with a long train that trailed behind it as "a germ collector." The Rainy Day Club of New York City was organized in 1896 in order to persuade women to raise their skirts at least 4 inches from the ground in inclement weather, "thereby freeing the wearer from the danger of spreading contagion by carrying into the home germs of disease." These were the days, rainy or not, when piles of steaming horse manure turned the streets into a daily obstacle course, so clubwomen clearly had good sense on their side. Nonetheless, it was a daring goal, since shorter skirts would expose "the whole foot" to the public eye. By 1922, fashion required shorter skirts, and club members now advocated skirts that were 7 inches from the pavement.[38]

It was no surprise then that dress reform became the subject of one of the most popular sessions at the New York convention in 1916. The discussion had started at the previous meeting, when the women of the federation had approved the following resolution: ". . . that this Convention, in full recognition of the rights and privileges of the individual, places itself on record as heartily in favor of the movement for simple, becoming, and modest designs in women's clothes."

The members put Helen Louise Johnson, the head of the federation's Home Economics Department, in charge of deciding what was to be done. Johnson had been writing cookbooks since the 1890s, and she had worked as an editor at *Good Housekeeping* and *Harper's Bazaar*, writing on home economics with a special emphasis on thrift. Johnson was tiny—not 5 feet tall—white haired, with the pure pink and white complexion of a Dresden figurine. But the resemblance to delicate china stopped at the end of her determined chin. "Were we," she asked, "the mere puppets of a mad thing called Fashion?"

Her committee surveyed club members and found hundreds of them "bitterly complaining," eager to rebel "against their unfortunate slavery to the vagaries of fashion and style." This "Pursuit of Dress" encouraged garment makers to produce novelties without end and forced women to keep buying or look hopelessly out of date. The Pursuit of Dress—notice it makes it sounds as though they were chasing and never catching it—also made life hard on the garment workers, whose lives were punctuated by overtime when each new trend took off, and idleness in between. "Our purpose," proclaimed Johnson, "is nothing less than a freedom from a kind of slavery."

Johnson thought that the trouble began in the nineteenth century when the American middle class had gained enough prosperity that its women no longer needed to make their own clothes or clean their own houses or do much of anything productive. Yet they were still not allowed to go to college, and women's clubs had yet to be invented. What were middle-class women supposed to do all day? "A round of social functions was devised, and for these functions women must dress, not merely becomingly, but competitively, each to outdo the other," she wrote.[39]

Johnson thought that many things had changed by 1914. Middle-class women now had much to do. They went to college. They joined women's clubs. Women, in fact, were as busy as men—yet they were still at the mercy of designers and manufacturers, unlike men, who never had to worry about the latest fads in clothing. "A man wears a suit without comment or feeling conspicuous until it is worn out," explained Mary Schenck Woolman. "A woman's suit often goes out of style in a few months."[40]

It was time for a mutual nonaggression pact among women regarding fashion. If women adopted standardized street dress, said Johnson, they would make themselves, not their clothes, the center of attention. Women would be remembered the same way people remembered men: by their faces. "If women wear standardized gowns," she said, "people who meet them in the street will look at their faces and not their frocks, and when they meet again they will remember them."[41]

Johnson's committee consulted men and women, designers, garment makers, and consumers. They were determined to invent a garment that would look good on any woman. Art must not be sacrificed, Johnson reminded the clubwomen. "It is our duty, as well as our privilege, to look as well as we possibly can." The ideal garment would not bind at the neck or chest or waist. It would have a "plain, close-fitting, and sensibly short skirt" that would be "sanitary, economical, and convenient." It would be made as either a two-piece suit or a one-piece dress, in any kind of fabric, from a lightweight silk crepe-de-chine to a heavier wool serge. And it should offer many possibilities for changing the details, such as the collar, the cuffs, and the trimming, so that there would be no need to fear the boredom of a uniform.[42]

In May 1916, Johnson's committee was finished with its consultations, its drawings, and its sewing. Women crowded into the session on Standardized Dress. Mrs. Thomas Alvah Edison was there to lend her support. Joining her was Lady Duff-Gordon, a once penniless English *divorcée* named Lucy Sutherland who had become a successful dressmaker and then married an aristocrat. She was renowned for bringing the graceful tea gown, once a boudoir-only confection, into social life. Yet even a lady who made her fortune catering to the whims of wealthy women was eager to prove her own thriftiness. Before the unveiling of the committee's handiwork, Lady Duff-Gordon displayed her own street costume to the crowd, boasting that she had been wearing it for the past six years.

It was now time for the committee to show its creation, the dress that would end "the constant and ridiculous, troublesome and costly, change of fashion." It would free women to spend their time and energy on higher things. It would achieve "a moral, an ethical

Fig. 4: Helen Louise Johnson hoped the Biennial Dress of 1916 would stop fashion trends forever. MARY SCHENCK WOOLMAN, *CLOTHING: CHOICE, CARE, COST*, 1920

ideal." The women waited eagerly. And then the Biennial Dress made its debut.[43]

Johnson and her committee had hit upon a style that captured the general fashion of the time. The silhouettes coming out of France were not so far from the Biennial Dress. Coco Chanel's collection for 1917—revealed just after the Biennial Dress's coming out—contained a cousin, if not a sister, to it. It had the same longer jacket or tunic, the same emphasis on the v-neckline, and the same not-too-full skirt.[44]

The Dress Doctors swung into action behind the idea of standardized dress, and they found followers. A student at the University of Missouri came up with her own variation with a Russian-style blouse. She inspired a club of thirty women, many of them faculty wives at Stanford University, to make a vow to wear her designs in order to "be relieved of the stress of the changing styles." A class of high-school girls and their mothers agreed that for graduation they would all wear a Peter Thompson dress in white linen with red ties. (Peter Thompson was a tailor in the navy who had taken the middy blouse and added a pleated skirt to it; many private schools for girls eventually adopted it as a uniform.) Lelia R. Gaddis, the head of home economics at Purdue University, reported, "These girls were the most wholesome, well dressed school girls I've ever seen." Businesswomen, who had their own federation of clubs, were especially keen on the idea of a simple but smart outfit for everyday wear. Variations of the Biennial Dress appeared both in sewing patterns and in stores as ready-to-wear items.[45]

Academics encouraged the standardized dress movement. A woman professor at the University of Chicago pointed out that standardized dress would help immigrant women who arrived from Europe and were faced with the bewildering range of novelties offered in American shops. A male psychology professor urged, in language that only a male psychology professor would use, further education so that men and women would "not respond impulsively to the stimuli of commercial establishments" and thus learn to subdue "the rivalrous impulse for superiority by display." A garment maker estimated that costs for clothing would go down 35 percent if style types were kept down to a reasonable number and if women were willing to wear them for several years.[46]

Helen Louise Johnson created her own wardrobe based on the Biennial Dress and took it on the road to show women how well it worked. She liked to demonstrate how easily her dress came on and off. If a man was in the audience that day, they had to take her word for it.

For Johnson, standardized dress was only for day wear. Evening was when women could shine in beautiful gowns and silks. She thought that men, too, ought to abandon their boring black suits for evening wear and make "a better showing themselves in the ballroom and the opera." She had an idea: Why don't men revive the satins and laces of the eighteenth-century dandy? Johnson was a big believer in gender equity.[47]

But the idea of standardized dress outraged some. "There could be no greater curse," said a French *modiste* working in Atlanta, going under the name Meri-Mee. Petite, black-haired, dark-eyed, and elegant, she told a newspaper reporter that American ready-to-wear was already standardized and atrocious. "The French girl knows her individual style—it is as much a part of her as her name." Every season *la Française* chose gowns and hats in only the designs and colors that flatter her. No freaks of fashion or sudden whims for her. Lily Daché, a milliner who immigrated to the United States in the 1920s, agreed. Mass-produced ready-to-wear apparel terrified her. Surveying the city streets, she thought that Americans seemed "stamped out of some gigantic machine."[48]

French immigrants were not the only ones who sung the beauties of individualized dress. A home-grown home economist at the College of Washington State argued that it was American taste, not dress, that needed to be standardized, or at least educated. If American women learned to apply art principles to dress, they wouldn't run after the spinning "tempo of style."[49]

Dorothy Dix, the "Dear Abby" of her generation, laughed at the whole idea of standardized dress. Who cares if it saves time, money, and energy? asked Dix. Standardized dress was boring. And it would do away with the easiest way to size up a woman. A neat, trim outfit told you that "the wearer has a tailor-made soul; that she runs her house on a budget; is conservative in politics, orthodox in religion and that everything in her linen closet is in neat labeled packages." A frowsy, messy outfit proved that a woman was "a thriftless and sloppy housekeeper, who lets her servants steal from her and her children run over her." Take away individual dress and every woman becomes a cipher.[50]

Besides, said Dix, women's dress cheers things up. Compare a women's club banquet with a men's club banquet. The women make up "a flower garden, masses of lovely color, or flashing jewels, or soft, alluring fabrics." The men? They are "a hideous picture in hard black and white, with blobs of bald heads making the high lights." Why in heaven's name be homely if you can be glamorous? Apparently Dix had not heard that Johnson wanted men to turn flower garden themselves in the evening hours.[51]

Other critics chimed in. An editor at the *Detroit Free Press* condemned the campaign as "a mean, under-handed attempt" to make women's clothes just as boring as men's. Leona Hope at the University of Illinois thought that "women are too fond of indulging their love of pretty things" for the plan to take hold. The best anyone could hope for was that they chose tailored suits for street wear. A New York merchant agreed that the average woman was "hardly prepared to go out on the street and see every other woman dressed just like her, any more than she would like to go to church on a Sunday and find every woman there wearing the same kind of bonnet." The *New York Times* proclaimed standardized dress doomed: "There is and ought to be in the heart of every woman, conscious of being well dressed, a triumphant satisfaction, not untinged, perhaps, with some rejoicing in the admiration, dissatisfaction, or envy stirred in the hearts of other women by the sight of her perfection." In short, women would not sign onto a mutual nonaggression fashion pact. They would rather dress at each other.[52]

When the United States entered World War I, both sides claimed that wartime would prove the wisdom of their arguments. The federation's members pointed out that standardized dress was a war measure, since it would prevent wasted fabric and labor. But a *New York Times* magazine editor answered that standardized dress was bad for morale: "When the boys come back they will want to see charm, and beauty and loveliness," not women in what amounted to a uniform.[53]

When women gained the vote in 1920, Johnson saw yet another reason to adopt Biennial Dress. Now that women were full citizens, and even more occupied with civic affairs, they would have even less time to chase fashion. Johnson died in 1926, still best remembered for her campaign for the Biennial Dress, but no standardized dress design had won over the masses of American women.[54]

The Biennial Dress may now be forgotten, but the idea behind it lives on. Mass production and our own tendency to fall into ruts seem to have achieved more than all of Johnson's urgings. Female students today are wearing "jeggings," the bastard child of jeans and leggings; working women are all wearing black pants; and retired women are seemingly all in crop pants. It's astonishing how often we see a herd of women coming down the street dressed uncannily alike. Maybe Meri-Mee was right when she said American women are cursed by standardized dress.

WHAT IF THERE WAS ANOTHER WAY to escape from the churn of fashion? A way to have variety without having to run out and buy something new every week?

Mary Brooks Picken wrote in 1918 that there was a woman who wore "one extremely well-tailored blue-serge" frock to work every day for two entire years. She topped it with a handsome coat and a good fur piece, and that was it. "I am sure that if you were to see this woman, no matter where, you would say she was smartly gowned," said Picken.[55]

Two objections come to mind. First, how do you prevent yourself from falling into a coma while wearing the same dress Monday through Friday for two years? Consider how a man wears the same suit day after day, week after week, with just a change of shirt and tie, and you begin to see how she did it. To avoid boredom, our thrifty businesswoman made numerous sets of collars and cuffs to change the look of her dress. She would baste them on at the neck and sleeves

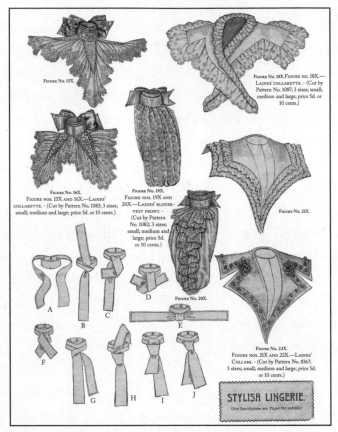

Fig. 5: Detachable collars added variety to the modern woman's wardrobe up through the 1950s. At the turn of the twentieth century, lace was the fashion. DELINEATOR, MAY 1896

every morning and snip them out every night. Clara Bow, playing the ultimate shop girl in the 1927 movie *It*, wears a dark dress trimmed with a collar and cuffs. ("It" means sex appeal, by the way.) And if a woman didn't know how to sew, stores sold collar and cuff sets through the mid-twentieth century.

Today, women make do with mostly boring collars that look like those found on men's shirts. Back then, women's collars came in an amazing assortment that would satisfy anyone's need for novelty. They were draped in every direction, tied with long bows, or short, squared off, rounded, triangular, flounced, or ruffled. Name a shape, and they came up with a collar.

Collar and cuff sets were a mainstay of fashion in the early twentieth century. Mabel D. Erwin, who ran the Department of Clothing and Textiles at Texas Technological College from 1926 to 1955, devoted entire chapters in her books on pattern designs for collars and cuffs. "No phase of dress designing is more intriguing or profitable than collar designing," she wrote, illustrating her point with dozens of variations. Detachable collars were a "boon" to the business professional, the young working woman, and the schoolgirl, so long as they were easy to take on and off. If it was too difficult, Erwin warned, a woman was tempted to leave them on even when they got dirty. Detachable collars were so important to a businesswoman's wardrobe that, as Harriet Pepin remarked, in 1942, "thousands of dollars are invested yearly for these dainty bits of lingerie that will give the up-to-the-minute look to some basic dress that is being mustered into service for a second season."[56]

The Dress Doctors did not approve of a white collar, because it was "trying" to all but the most perfect complexions. Yes, the white shirt—deemed essential by so many of today's fashion advisers—is a bad idea. A collar in one of the off-whites or pastels—eggshell, palest pink, pale coral, ivory, tan—would suit the complexion of any woman better.

Up through the early 1960s, the Dress Doctors preached "ringing the changes" on a basic dress not only by switching out collars and cuffs, but by using vests, sweaters, and capes; belts and purses; and necklaces and clips. Clips are the stepsisters of brooches, but they have a fanged hinge on the back instead of a pin. Alas, they have disappeared, and more's the pity—one or two clips on the neckline of a dress look terrific. Buttons could be switched out, too. A navy dress might sport red buttons for the classroom, heirloom brass buttons for tea, and hand-painted buttons for dinner. "A crisp, new collar will give you a feeling of a new dress," wrote Dulcie G. Donovan, the head of home economics at the Beverly Hills High School, in 1935. "Try it and see." Snaps on cuffs made the changes even easier.[57]

The perfect basic dress had to be simple, without any distinctive detail, explained the Dress Doctors. It should have a neckline that can be closed or opened up. The fabric must not wrinkle or stretch out. And a woman should be willing to pay a bit more for this wonder, especially when she realizes that she may "obtain the effect of perhaps six dresses for less than the price of two, and appear better dressed at the same time."[58]

The background dress became a staple in mail-order catalogs. A woman then picked out a week's worth of accessories: Monday, lace collar and cuffs; Tuesday, a rayon halter-scarf to tie over the dress; Wednesday, a wide suede belt; Thursday, a satin bib collar with pleats along the edge; Friday, a sash and matching flower; and Saturday night, gold belt, bracelet, and clip. Milo Anderson, a costume designer at Warner Brothers, did up a black background dress with seven changes, including a reversible, sleeveless coat, during World War II. Vogue Patterns explained in 1952 that "unmarked clothes are the clothes you sign your signature to by the look you give them, the mark you make on them with accessories."[59]

Valentina, a Russian émigré who made her fortune as a designer in America, was renowned for pulling off several such transformations during a single busy weekday. For work, she appeared in a black dress, pinned at the throat, with long sleeves. For luncheon, she pushed up the sleeves and replaced the pin with a jeweled one set a bit lower down. For an afternoon wedding the same day, she twisted a long white jersey scarf around her neck and let the ends fall freely. "Presto!" wrote Grace Margaret Morton in admiration. "She has three costumes in one." Valentina enforced thrift on some of her customers. "What? A new street outfit?" she responded to one request. "What's wrong with the navy one I made you four years ago?"[60]

Picken's thrifty businesswoman did not wear her one dress every minute of every day. She observed the happy ritual of dressing for the occasions of her life. She had a second silk dress for afternoons and evenings out. Changing clothing at the end of the workday makes a tiny wardrobe pleasurable by injecting variety. Picken does not tell us what her idol wore at home, but she would have had something special to put on. Perhaps one of those velvet hostess gowns?

But what about the smell? How could she possibly keep her work dress clean if she was wearing it every day of the week? Standards in the early twentieth century were probably lower than they are today, and people tolerated more than we do, but as far back as recorded history people have wanted to keep clean and smell good. Ancient Egyptians wrote of aromatic oils and bath oils that "will make the bodies of the males and females gold-like, beautiful, fragrant and lovely," while the ancient Greeks mocked men for smelling like goats.[61]

Even before germ theory was understood, cleanliness became especially important to Americans, starting with the Civil War, when "filth diseases" threatened soldiers' health and lives. Filth, whether in our clothes, our water, or our streets, prompted a national campaign for personal hygiene, citywide sewer systems, and municipal trash hauling. By the late nineteenth century, scientists were figuring out how bacteria spread diphtheria, dysentery, cholera, and the like, and in the twentieth century, cleaning off germs became an obsession. Ellen Swallow Richards, the mother of home economics, once warned that a "pin-point of dust" might contain 3,000 microbes![62]

But keeping clean took effort when not everyone owned a shiny bathroom with hot and cold running water, porcelain fittings, and electric lights. It wasn't until later in the century that they were found everywhere in America, from big cities to lonely farmsteads. Our 1918 businesswoman was probably better off than most, but many a young working woman rented an unheated room with access to only two baths a week. Mary Brooks Picken writes with admiration of a young woman who managed to give herself a daily sponge bath even in the winter. "She thought she would freeze the first few mornings," Picken tells us, "but after a little practice she could work so quickly that she soon had her skin stimulated and the little red blood corpuscles dancing." This creature seems extraordinarily brave. Indeed, Picken told her story in order to convince the working girls among her readers that they did not want to be one of those less brave salesclerks who gave off an odor "so offensive that much of the joy of shopping is lost."[63]

Americans in the early twentieth century did not wash their clothes as frequently as we do, either. A home economics textbook from 1935 advised junior-high-school girls on how to remove spots and wash out collars and cuffs, and then added, "If a dress is very dirty, washing may be best," as though washing a slightly dirty dress never occurred to anyone. When a book in home economics for boys and girls from 1936 declared that changing underwear daily was "an excellent habit," you can bet that it was a habit that a good number of people had yet to adopt. Advertisers cashed in on new worries about odor. A Lux soap ad featured a young woman who decided to chance wearing the same underwear for two days, only to notice that people she met that day—shop girl, bridge partners, boyfriend—were repulsed. She resolved to use Lux on her undies every day.[64]

Apparently, people much preferred to put off cleaning their clothes until they had to, because it was so much trouble. If bathing was hard for a young worker who rented a room in 1918, laundry was worse. It was done mostly by hand. There were fifteen steps to doing the household laundry in 1925, according to the Woman's Institute. The first step was "heat water." Women did dry cleaning at home with all sorts of chemicals, from gasoline to powdered "French chalk," a fancy word for ground soapstone. Remember, the books advised, do not rub a dress soaked in gasoline too hard—lest it explode.[65]

There were two ways to put off the washing of a dress: using dress shields, and using "airing closets." Dress shields are little crescent-shaped pieces of cloth that can be basted by hand into the underarm area, and then taken out at the end of the day and washed. Often they have a layer of rubber in them, which makes them stiff but impenetrable; the haute couture houses make them of much more comfortable cotton flannel. Dress shields once came in a wide assortment of styles, including demi-shields for sleeveless evening dresses, colored shields to match a dress, and deodorizing shields. One manufacturer promised that they would double the wear and assure "the freshness of your pretty new frocks." Dress shields show up as a basic item alongside soap in the budgets drawn up by the Dress Doctors. By the 1930s, an assortment of deodorants promised to help, too.[66]

USE EVERY PRE-CAUTION

Fig. 6: Women put off doing dry cleaning at home with gasoline because it was so dangerous. DULCIE G. DONOVAN, *THE MODE IN DRESS AND HOME*, 1935

Airing closets were based on the idea that fresh air deodorizes clothes. They're the reason why closets today still have louvered doors. If a woman had a backyard, she could hang her clothes outside. If she lived in an apartment, she could attach a swinging towel rack high up on a wooden window frame and hang her dress in the breeze all night. Most women aired their clothes, according to a 1943 survey: 46 percent of women aired them after each wearing, and 41 percent aired them every now and then. Only 7 percent of women never aired their clothes at all. These were probably the same people nobody wanted to sit next to on the bus.[67]

Although Mary Brooks Picken admired the one-dress woman, she was a little more generous when she described an ideal wardrobe. She thought that a businesswoman should have four or five dresses for office wear. Those, along with one afternoon dress, one evening dress, one blouse and one skirt, were all that a woman needed for

her public wardrobe. So, at most, she needed eight ensembles total
to wear both at work and out in the evening. Wardrobes this small
were considered normal in the past. When the editors of the *McCall's
Pattern Book* drew up what they called a perfect wardrobe in the winter
of 1936–1937, they listed one coat, one suit with a box-jacket, two
day dresses, an afternoon dress, an evening dress, and a ski suit. That
was it.[68]

Fashion magazines today have larger ambitions. *Glamour* magazine listed thirty-six garments in 2005 that made for a perfect work
wardrobe, but this was on the low side. Another stylebook identified
forty necessary garments in 2008. The most impressive suggestions
come from *Lucky*, a magazine proudly devoted to shopping. A regular
monthly feature, "A Month of Outfits," has a model wearing different
combinations of clothing for up to thirty-one days. The November
2007 segment offered three dresses, eight tops, three pairs of pants,
one skirt, five items of outerwear, and six pairs of footwear (only one
of which passed the more-than-a-block test), plus assorted accessories
and tights. The price for the month's outfits? Over $18,000. And they
ran this feature every month of the year.[69]

Such figures would have given heart palpitations to the Dress
Doctors, who offered thrifty ways to dress for even the most special
occasions. The only thriftier project than the single dress for work
was Vogue Patterns' wedding dress from 1938, which could be transformed into "an evening frock later on with little revision." The bride
would only need to cut off the train at the back of the dress. The dress
was sleeveless, so it was easy enough to take off the bolero jacket for
a dinner-dance. The magazine showed the bride in white and the
evening dress in a print, but readers would have understood that they
could dye the bridal gown.[70]

The Dress Doctors relished stories of the beautifully dressed
woman with the tiny wardrobe. She embodied all their ideals of art
and thrift. Florence Hull Winterburn admired a widow who came to

a resort in 1914 and impressed everyone with her lovely appearance. Yet she had only three dresses: a wool dress of black and white for the mornings, a dainty dress of violet silk for the afternoons, and a creamy satin gown for dances. If she had had a hundred outfits but all of them badly chosen, said Winterburn, she would never have made such an impression. And book from 1924 proclaimed that one of the best-dressed women in all of Paris bought only three ensembles a year.[71]

Margaret Sawyer, a bureau director at the American Red Cross, advised what she would do on a small income: "I would save up little by little until I could plunge on just two dresses, then with one good piece of jewelry, I would always be sure of presenting a smart appearance." Even during the prosperity of the 1950s, Mildred Graves Ryan and her coauthor reassured their readers that many of the career women in New York City who were noted for "their smart appearance" owned only two perfectly assembled street costumes.[72]

BUT THE SUPERIORITY OF THE SMALL, perfect wardrobe was a lesson that had to be learned. Take the dramatic and true story of Dorothy Moeller, who sat weeping in a jail in St. Louis one morning in 1933.

Her crime?

Trying to charge clothing to her father's account at a department store without his permission, according to the *New York Times*. A. C. Moeller, aka Dad, was a manager at a chemical company, so he could afford to pay off the bill when it came due, but he was tired of the way his twenty-three-year-old daughter spent his money. He was going to leave her in jail until she had learned her lesson.

"It's about the toughest lesson I've ever had," she told a reporter through her tears.

Her father told her friends they better not bail her out, but she had hopes her mother would come and save her.

"Mother called me up this morning," Dorothy said. "She would have come down and probably got me out but for father."

Mrs. Moeller, however, did not sound particularly sympathetic. "We warned her a number of times," said Mrs. Moeller. "But it went in one ear and out the other." So there Dorothy sat until her dad decided to have the charges dropped. Her mother declared simply: "Dorothy is just a spoiled child."[73]

How much had Dorothy charged? $27.15.

It doesn't sound like much, until you remember that this was 1933 during the midst of the Great Depression. In 1933, Sears Roebuck would sell you a simple gingham house dress for $1.39, or a fancy two-piece angora dress for a whopping $4.74. In today's dollars, Dorothy Moeller's shopping spree would have amounted to $452.66.

By 1933, American department stores had perfected ways of luring in customers. New kinds of dyes produced a stunning variety of colors. Plate glass made possible enormous windows and beautiful cases displaying tempting goods from every angle. Lighting was carefully arranged to make everything in the cases look all the more beautiful. And, if that wasn't enough, every season brought new displays, as well as shopping festivals organized around both familiar and exotic themes. Easter and Thanksgiving, of course, but also Parisian street scenes, Egyptian temples, and Japanese gardens. No wonder Dorothy lost it. "Buying isn't always a virtue," Hazel Rawson Cades warned readers of the Girl Scout magazine in 1927. "Sometimes it's a weakness. Frequently it's a mistake. Quite often it's a form of dissipation."[74]

Credit cards that you could use anyplace did not become widespread until much later, but store charge accounts were already common by 1933. After World War I, government and business cooperated to make credit easier to come by. State usury laws had long barred anyone from lending money for more than 13 to 20 percent, rates too low for any reputable business to risk charging in 1900 because there was no easy way to verify annual personal income. There were no Social Security numbers, for instance. So loan sharks took on the high risks of lending, charging interest at rates of between 60 and

480 percent a year. When reformers convinced the states to pass new laws to allow businesses to make small loans, some loan sharks were actually tempted into going straight.

Department stores, like the one where Dorothy went wrong, offered credit without interest as a convenience to their customers. Only in the 1950s did the department stores realize how much money they could make with charge cards. Not only could they charge interest, but, more importantly, they could sell more. Credit weaves a psychological charm: people holding a store's charge card are far more likely to go shopping at that particular store, and to buy more, than people who count out dollar bills from their wallets. Stores worked hard to get their charge cards into people's hands.[75]

The Dress Doctors would have grown pale in horror in the 1980s when credit cards offered by banks, once the prerogative of the wealthy, were peddled to everyone, even first-year college students. More credit created more debt. Between 1990 and 1996, credit-card debt doubled. A survey of one large company's employees revealed that close to 90 percent of them owed money, on average $13,700.[76]

As credit expanded over the decades, so did the Dress Doctors' warnings against its allure. Elizabeth Todd, head of home economics at the University of Georgia, emphasized in 1948: "*It is unwise to buy any garment for which the money is not already on hand.*" A girl should never pay interest, when she can save up and buy a dress for cash. Girls like Dorothy became cautionary tales.[77]

But the girls weren't really the problem, according to home economics textbooks. Parents were. Parents of girls like Dorothy had failed to train their children. Too often a girl hankered for the latest new outfit and her indulgent parents let her get it, even though it meant Father would go without a suit he needed for work, and Mother's worn winter coat could not be replaced. How could a child mature to adulthood if her parents encouraged her "to remain in the self-centeredness of childhood?" asked the Kansas State Dress Doctors. How would she ever learn to do justice to others? Parents could make their daughters "as incompetent in the use of money as a young child."[78]

What did *all* the Muellers of the world need? Training in home economics, of course. If only Dorothy had had the wisdom of the Dress Doctors set before her long before she was allowed to roam freely through a department store, she would not have gone wrong. She would have had to sharpen her pencil and solve such problems as these: "Mr. and Mrs. Abel have three children, a girl of sixteen, a boy of fourteen, and a girl of twelve. Mr. Abel, a clerk in a retail store, has an income of $175 per month. Their budget allows 12% to be spent for clothing the entire family. What proportion of this amount should the older girl spend?"[79]

The Dress Doctors worried about good family relations, because the tricky part about the family clothing budget came in divvying it up. What portion did each member of the family deserve? And this is where the Dress Doctors confronted head-on the selfishness of teenage girls.

"Do You Spend More Than Your Share of the Family Clothing Allowance?" asked one reading assignment from the University of Texas Dress Doctors. Big Sister went out socially more than her little sister and brother did, and she could not wear her school clothes to dances and teas, but what if you were the little sister? "Are you a good sport about your allowance, or do you tease and beg to spend as much as she does?" The Kansas State authors were displeased to learn from a study of Chicago families that for every $1 spent on Father's clothing, Mother, on average, spent 90 cents, while the older teenage daughter spent $1.20. Mother should not have to go around looking shabby. A girl could either play fair, to the benefit of her entire family, or she could become yet another one of her family's problems. Which would it be?[80]

The home economists hoped that their pupils would use what they had learned in class. Their dream was pictured in a book from 1928 coauthored by Kate W. Kinyon, who supervised home economics

Fig. 7: And a Child shall lead them. . . . The young home economist draws up a family budget. KATE W. KINYON AND L. THOMAS HOPKINS, *JUNIOR HOME PROBLEMS*, 1928

in the Denver public schools, and L. Thomas Hopkins at Teachers College. The family is gathered around a table: bespectacled Father in a suit and tie, Mother, Little Sister, Little Brother, and our heroine, a young home economist, who takes the lead in making a family budget. Pencil in hand, she shows them her calculations.

Far from quarreling over money, family members might take pleasure in budgeting. Or so the Dress Doctors hoped. Alpha Latzke and Laura Baxter hoped that "a clothing plan may be the means of enriching the relationship between the girl and her mother. Cooperation . . . may reveal to both the mother and the daughter abilities in the other that have been overlooked, and may lead to a very real joy in working together."[81]

The Dress Doctors would have clutched their hearts to learn the dollar amounts that modern fashion writers throw around for a clothing budget. A 1999 book on how to build a wardrobe suggested that women spend 25 percent of their take-home pay, and a 2003 volume devoted to making the most of your money whittled this down to 20 percent. These amounts are stunningly high compared to the figures the Dress Doctors recommended, and even more astonishing when one considers that many people in big cities today are spending 50 percent of their take-home pay on rent—How exactly are they supposed to pay the electric bill and still eat on the 25 percent or so that's left over? Maybe they can't. In 2012, most adults surveyed said they did not budget their spending, and 22 percent admitted they had no clear idea what they spent on housing and food. Eighty percent of adults said they could do with some advice on everyday financial questions. Perhaps that's because only fourteen states required students to take a class in personal finance in 2011.[82]

But we need not despair. The American Association of Retired Persons Foundation created a program with the Charles Schwab Foundation to teach people aged fifty and up what they should know about thrift. To help educate adults under thirty-five, the American Institute of Certified Public Accountants created a scary piggy bank and a website called FeedthePig.org. The Vanguard Group of mutual funds aimed even younger and started a program called "My Classroom Economy," with an award-winning teacher, who teaches students from kindergarten to high school how to budget, apply for jobs, earn paychecks, and sign up for mortgages.[83]

"What if all graduating students knew how to budget, how to save more than they spend, and how to resist impulse buying?" asks the Vanguard program on its website. "What if they truly had the skills to be smart with their money?"

Better yet, what if home economics hadn't been gutted in the 1970s?

If Dorothy Moeller had enrolled in a home economics course, she would have learned a number of things. The home economists ran what they called effectiveness studies to find out what stuck in their students' minds. One compared two groups of high-school girls in Kentucky in the 1940s: one group took home economic courses and the other did not. Girls who took home economics got better at sewing, made themselves more clothes, made a greater variety of clothes, and were better at reading labels and picking out quality in ready-to-wear garments.[84]

The Dress Doctors spoke of wise consumer choices based on "scientific knowledge." It was "scientific" because a girl who was trained in textiles could take in the quality of a fabric with a touch and a glance, and would not be swayed by seductive advertising or sneaky sales-clerks. Indeed, one mother, commenting in the early 1960s about how her daughter's attitude had changed after studying home economics, said: "Yesterday when we were looking for a skirt in the store, Alice examined each one carefully, noting workmanship, color in relation to other clothes she would wear with it, quality of material before deciding on a purchase." Alice was much better informed than the untutored New York City high-school girls who were asked about their latest clothing purchases in 1931, and touted their satisfaction with remarks such as, "It did not fall to pieces soon" and "It did not wear a hole the first time I wore it!"[85]

The Dress Doctors thought that girls would learn how to budget if they had an allowance. Have your parents take a look at *Parents, Children and Money*, one dress textbook suggested to its young readers in 1947, and they will see that you should have a clothing allowance. The Dress Doctors believed that "if the child is to learn to handle money, he must have money to handle."[86]

But would parents of the era really let their children have money to handle? Not really. Most of the Kentucky girls questioned in the effectiveness study did not have a clothing allowance and did not plan their own wardrobes. What little pocket money their parents gave them was spent on candy and soda, movie tickets, and cosmetics, in that order.

The Dress Doctors never did convince parents to hand over money to their daughters to spend on their wardrobes. One can see why. If a mother handed over enough cash to her daughter to buy a good winter coat and a pair of school shoes, then let her loose in a department store, her teen might come back with a stunning party dress and silver strap sandals. Most mothers were not willing to let their daughters learn a lesson by letting them freeze all winter in silver strap sandals. So Mother would have to return the dress and sandals and pick out the coat and school shoes herself. It would have been easier for her to buy the coat and shoes in the first place.

Parents may have been wary of giving children choices, but the lessons of home economics seem to have struck a loud chord with university women. A survey done by Grace Margaret Morton of twenty-nine women teaching at the University of Nebraska in 1928 found that they managed to save a whopping 27.7 percent of their income and spent only 14.7 percent on clothing. Morton was even prouder of a young home economics professor who spent a total of $97.46 on a complete professional wardrobe in the 1940s. Her outer garments, the dresses, jackets, and coats, were designed to last from two to four years. She managed to split the difference between the ways of the Alabamans and the New Yorkers of Syracuse. She bought some of her wardrobe and sewed some clothing herself, including her winter coat and two pairs of gloves. She always bought her fabric on sale. Perhaps she was the model for that picture of the young home economics prodigy, the one who taught budgeting to her family.[87]

The Woman's Institute once explained that budgeting is a topic much talked about, and like a person who is much talked about, is heartily disliked by some people. "But spending becomes even more enjoyable and infinitely more satisfying, when carried on systematically according to a prearranged plan." In fact, it can be "a fascinating game." A woman can win the game and have enough for what she really needs, or she can lose by indulging in an extravagance (pretty shoes, anyone?) that has her eating Ramen noodles for the rest of the month.[88]

Any woman who has had to live close to the bone knows that budgeting can be a grim game at times. But since almost all of us have to play it anyway, why not play to win?

The one thing you mustn't do is trade your virtue for a lavish wardrobe. The Dress Doctors worried particularly that hankering after finery would lead working-class girls into trouble.

One of those worrying was Grace H. Dodge, a New York City philanthropist whose money founded Teachers College at Columbia University at the very end of the nineteenth century, and who created clubs for working-class girls. Their "loving, weak natures, their fondness for dress, their difficulty finding lucrative employment, their lack of training, [and] their love of excitement," she said, left them "fearfully open to temptation, liable to lead directly to sin." Another woman worrying was Mary Brooks Picken. In the same book where she praised her thrifty businesswoman, she pointed out that a lavish wardrobe could raise suspicions. When people saw a girl who appeared in finery that cost far more than her father's income, they reacted one of two ways: either they pitied her poor judgment, or they wondered who besides Dad was funding her wardrobe. And the Vice Commission of Chicago worried that department store salesclerks, who were not all that well paid but were "surrounded by luxuries, which all of them crave," were likely to fall into prostitution.[89]

One clerk told a story in 1913 of how that downfall might begin. A fellow would notice a girl sighing over something in a store window and ask, "Like that dress?" Then, he would invite her to become his "sweetheart" in exchange for all the dresses he would buy for her. This woman told her story in disgust: "Sometimes the girl is fool enough to do it." A woman psychologist wrote in the 1930s that the temptation was real. "A considerable amount" of delinquency among teenage girls, she explained, was "directly traceable to the intense craving for the right clothes" and a willingness to do bad things in order to satisfy it.[90]

Screenwriter Preston Sturgis made this worry into the plot of his 1937 movie *Easy Living*. A millionaire, sore at his wife's free-spending ways, tosses a sable fur coat off the roof of his Park Avenue home, and it lands on our heroine, who is played by actress Jean Arthur. When she wears the fur to her job at the earnest publisher of *The*

Boy's Constant Companion, her boss promptly fires her. She could not have bought a fur coat on her salary, so, he concludes, some man must have bought it for her, and no man would buy a woman who was not his wife a fur coat unless she had done something truly wicked. Mary Brooks Picken would have shared his concern: "No woman," she wrote, "should place herself in a position where she will be the object of undeserved sympathy or suspicion." Nowadays we would simply conclude that she had maxed out her credit cards.[91]

Middle-class women tsk-tsked the gaudy choices of even those young working women who stayed virtuous in the early twentieth century. You might think they were just a bunch of snobs turning up their noses at the working-class fashion parade, but their objection was often the wasteful impracticality of young women trying to look like what they were not: wealthy women of leisure. A rich woman rode down the avenue in her snug limousine wearing a large, feathered hat; thin stockings; and fragile satin slippers. Poor working girls bought cheap versions of the same clothes and had to make their way around puddles and hop onto streetcars, hoping they wouldn't lose their hats or ruin their shoes. Some women will always wear impractical fashions while their chauffeurs drive them around town, but don't pretend you're riding in one if you aren't.[92]

MANY OF US DAYDREAM about what lovely things we might add to our wardrobes while window shopping and still not fear the smooth-tongued Romeo, but dreaming can lead us astray in another way.

Dorée Smedley asked one of her friends, let's call her Eileen, to think of her perfect wardrobe. This is what she came up with.

For home:

Satin negligee in apple-green, trimmed in lace
Dressing gown in a rich rose satin brocade to wear in
    the bedroom

Hostess gown in a shade of green turquoise trimmed
    in silver lamé for tea

For afternoon:

Black dressmaker suit with a fox scarf
Black silk dress for luncheons at the club
Silk satin dress in bottle-green for bridge

For evenings:

Black silk chiffon dress for dinner at a restaurant
Black silk satin dress with a scarlet jacket to wear to
    cocktail parties
Jade-green velvet dress with a silver jacket to wear to
    more cocktail parties
Gauzy silk and lace full-length dinner dress in a pink-
    ish lavender
Black velvet full-length dinner dress trimmed with a
    red rose at the waist
Sapphire velvet full-length dinner dress topped with a
    silver lamé jacket
Black velvet evening gown with a train
Slim, satin evening gown in pale yellow
White wrap in ermine fur
Three-quarter-length mink coat

It was a gorgeous, luxurious wardrobe that would have looked wonderful on Eileen, who had fair skin, black hair, and blue eyes.[93]

Here's the problem: Eileen's life had nothing to do with this wardrobe. She had forgotten to dress for the occasions in her life. As Grace Margaret Morton so nicely put it: "Clothes should be chosen for the places we go, the things we do all day, the people we are with—and not for the places we would like to go."[94]

Eileen would never wear the negligee, because she woke up early and made breakfast for her family, and that could not be done in satin and lace without courting disaster. After breakfast, Eileen drove the kids to school and her husband to work, and she could not do that in a hostess gown of rose satin brocade. She then did the grocery shopping for the day, an activity that did not work all that well in a black silk dress, a green satin dress, or a mink coat.

Eileen would have been well-prepared for any evening event (notice the dress with a train), but her life was not marked but many such events. On any given weekday evening, her husband fell asleep while reading the paper. Even if the man could be roused, there wasn't anywhere to go in her town (pop. 50,000). No one gave formal dinners or teas, and the few casual cocktail parties thrown during the holidays would have come to a screeching halt if Eileen had appeared in one of these stunning evening ensembles. Eileen had picked a glamorous evening wardrobe, but her life was completely lacking in glamorous evenings.

Such wardrobe fantasies would not matter if they did not creep into real life and spoil it. Eileen did buy herself a lovely black cocktail dress with a gold jacket. She wore it exactly once. She talked herself into buying a custom-made dressmaker suit to wear to Chicago, where her husband went for an annual business convention. It turned out to be too tightly fitted to be comfortable while running errands and climbing in and out of the car, so she never wore that outfit again, either. Meanwhile, she had blown her wardrobe budget for the year; she couldn't buy anything else all spring and summer, even things that she truly needed.

What Eileen's fevered imagination had concocted was the wardrobe of a Hollywood starlet circa 1941. What she needed were good-looking and comfortable clothes for a home woman who spent most of her time doing housework and running errands. Her friend

Dorée recommended "casual spectator sports clothes." The clothes in which a woman spends most of her time are the clothes upon which she should spend most of her money, time, and attention.[95]

Eileen is like the heroine in a 1958 book by Paul Gallico called *Mrs. 'Arris Goes to Paris*. Mrs. Harris, who does not pronounce the H that begins her name, is a scrubwoman who pines for a beautiful custom-made evening dress by Christian Dior. She decides to save up enough money to buy one. We are supposed to cheer her on as she walks to save bus fare, counts her pennies, and denies herself simple pleasures. We are supposed to cheer her on when the snotty saleslady at the couture house sneers at her, and when Christian Dior himself comes to her rescue and allows her to buy a dress.

But the whole effort seems an exercise in futility. Mrs. Harris should have bought herself a lovely, warm, wooly bathrobe and soft shearling slippers, and come home after a hard day to relax with a pot of tea and a pile of good pastries. Gallico seems to realize the pointlessness of her effort: he has Mrs. Harris loan the dress to a young woman, who ruins it. The fantasy wardrobe cannot survive even in the pages of a book.

The Dress Doctors had heard it all from women. The color was irresistible! The shoes were such a bargain! The hat was most becoming! They remained unmoved. They already knew that the color went with nothing else, the shoes would not be worn more than once, and the hat did not suit a single occasion in their life.[96]

They would have thought Mrs. 'Arris a silly ass.

When the Dress Doctors at Kansas State College put forth a case study in 1938 of a home woman whose husband was a college professor, a woman not unlike Eileen, they came up with a very different summer wardrobe:

A blue dress in cotton piqué
A grey-green knit dress

A colorful, printed chiffon hostess dress
A crisp organdy dress in eggshell
Six house dresses in cheerful colors

For winter, they added a few more formal things for evenings out:

An evening dress in blue-green with a jacket
A crepe dress in dark green
A dress-and-jacket suit in blue wool tweed[97]

Such a wardrobe expressed practicality, friendliness, and informal hospitality, they explained—exactly what suited the wife of a college professor and mother of three.

To drive the fantasy wardrobes from students' minds, the Kansas State Dress Doctors gave them an assignment: to come up with three wardrobes for three imaginary women who happened to represent the students' present condition and possible futures.

Their first wardrobe was for a young woman much like themselves: Sara Sewell, a college senior at a co-ed college in the Midwest who had two siblings, and whose father made $4,000 a year. The second was for Marie South, a recent college grad who was headed toward a teaching position at a rural high school in Nebraska, where she would make $90 a month during the school year. And the third was for Mrs. Brown, the wife of a college engineer in a small town who made $1,800 a year. The Browns had three children, and Mrs. Brown did all her own housework, but still found time to volunteer at the church and attend a literary club and a bridge club. Mrs. Brown needed snappy housedresses, but the students were going to have to make sure she had afternoon dresses for her clubs.

Dress Doctors clinched the argument for acquiring only regularly useful garments by asking students to do the calculations of the "real cost" of a garment: dividing its cost by the number of times it was worn, and taking into account the cost of repair and upkeep. A woman should inventory her closet before setting out to the stores. Then she would have a list of exactly what she needed in the colors that would harmonize with what she had. Such advice was heard far beyond the Home Economics classroom. "Mrs. Exeter," a *Vogue* magazine feature targeting women pushing sixty, offered a page in 1948 with three columns: "HAVE," "NEED," and "How *Much?*"[98]

The Dress Doctors advised women to stick to classic and simple lines. "Fad" stands for "For a Day," which is about how long you will find a passing style amusing. Choosing a fad may mean being stuck with a garment marked conspicuously as last season's style. But a simple style, explained a Dress Doctor in 1924, will protect a woman against "that bugbear" of fashion trends and allow her to continue to wear a dress for years.[99]

Pick a basic color, such as navy or brown, they advised, for all the important garments for the season, and then bring brighter accent colors in with smaller items. Edna Woolman Chase, former editor-in-chief at *Vogue*, writing with her daughter in 1954, agreed: "If your clothes are interchangeable, shoes and accessories doing duty with several dresses and suits instead of only one, you will achieve greater variety at less cost." Wardrobes "keyed" to particular colors—chestnut brown, golden brown, spruce green, cranberry red, peacock blue, carbon gray, and black—were offered up by Vogue Patterns in 1955. Each one featured a suit in the key color, with harmonizing dresses and separates to make up an entire fall wardrobe from no more than six sewing patterns. To add some variety, a woman can switch out accessories and ornaments. Blue outfits can have blue and wine accessories, for example. Brown or green coats and dresses can be worn with hats, gloves, and scarves in beige and brown.[100]

All of this may sound drearily dutiful, but budgeting did not stop the Dress Doctors from loving fashion and beautiful clothes. They considered a vivid interest in fashion a requirement for their job. "The teacher must be constantly on alert for new ideas," wrote Mildred Graves Ryan, "recognizing worth-while fashion trends. In other words, she must be an authority on clothes. She must know them, enjoy them, and look the part at all times." The Dress Doctors taught women to give up on the fantasy of infinite variety in favor of the reality of artistic single-mindedness.[101]

And they were not the only ones who recognized the advantages to a small wardrobe. Chase agreed that it was easier to be fashionable if one bought fewer things. "There is nothing to sap the morale and dull the appearance of a closet of half-worn, no-longer-at-their-peak clothes," she wrote. "Buy only what you need at the time, make it serve you well, and get rid of it." It was Chase who coined the slogan "More Taste Than Money" for *Vogue* magazine, which set it across the cover in the middle of the Great Depression. That the cover featured a photograph of an incredibly expensive ensemble made up of a stunning black cape lined in dark-red satin by Charles James over a white silk dress by Madeleine Vionnet appears to have struck no one as ironic.

Chase only approved of splurging—her word—in two cases. A woman should splurge for something if it will last several seasons. A cashmere sweater, a winter coat, a tailored suit, and street shoes all qualified. Or she should splurge if a purchase will change her life: "Obviously, if you sense that a certain ravishing garment will cause him to pop the question don't be a fool. Buy it." The home economists were rarely so romantic.[102]

THE GREAT DEPRESSION ENDED when World War II revved up industry in order to supply the armed forces. Jobs and prosperity came back to America. But war meant that consumer goods were in short supply, as it had during Mary Schenck Woolman's time. The government imposed War Production Board Order L-85, which put restrictions on every kind of garment sold to civilians. Even women sewing at home were subject to yardage restrictions. "Yesterday the

United States had the best dressed women in the world," wrote a Dress Doctor in 1942. "Today we have the best dressed army." Almost all silk, cotton, and wool fabrics were devoted to the war effort. Even Bakelite, an early form of plastic used to make buttons and bracelets, was rationed, because it was also used in antiaircraft shells. L-85 restrictions prompted one congressman to grouse, "They tell me they're taking the ruffles off women's lingerie. Who the —— thinks we're going to win a war that way?"[103]

The Dress Doctors did. They signed the Consumer's Victory Pledge and promised, "I will waste nothing—and I will take care to salvage everything needed to win the war." One Dress Doctor offered *200 Ways to Alter a Dress*, while the Bureau of Home Economics published pamphlets on how to mend clothes, reline coats, even re-cover old umbrellas. Mid-war, Grace Margaret Morton told the inspiring story of an enterprising young woman who wore "a good suit made by a good tailor" for seven years, then ripped it up and turned it into "a very smart" school dress trimmed with new velveteen.[104]

Prosperity continued after the war, yet the Dress Doctors never wavered from their devotion to thrift. The 1950s editions of their books still taught the same lessons of sewing, recycling, budgeting, planning, and ingenuity. They offered graphs of the Consumer Price Index, created charts on average annual expenditures, and defined the items that would make up a minimum budget for a working woman. The Dress Doctors ran experiments in the 1950s that proved that a woman who could sew could still save money over buying ready-to-wear.[105]

The Dress Doctors wanted to empower young women by giving them the financial tools they needed to survive as businesswomen or home women. Even in books on dress, home economists chided girls for placing too much importance on clothes and forcing themselves to cut down on food, rent, or savings as a result. This kind of spending was completely unnecessary to achieving beauty in dress. "Good taste

in dress cannot be bought with money," they explained. "Good taste requires knowledge, which sometimes we must work hard to acquire."[106]

Willpower was needed as well. Mildred Graves Ryan and Velma
Phillips wrote in 1954 that "a person who enjoys solving problems will
face a limited income with determination and soon a basic wardrobe
will be evolved." Without that determination, "she will throw up her
hands in horror and bemoan the lack of money, making herself and
her family most unhappy." But in the case of the determined young
woman who also possesses imagination, "her wardrobe will be a delight, filled with exciting innovations."[107]

Summoning up the willpower is harder today. Sometime in the
twentieth century, the word "save" underwent a perverse transformation at the hands of merchants. They started putting it into their
advertisements like this:

BUY 1 PAIR OF SHOES, SAVE 50% ON THE 2ND!

When what they are really saying is:

BUY 2 PAIRS OF SHOES, SPEND $150!

The perversion of the word "save" is so pervasive that it appears
even in the new statements required by the Credit Card Act of 2010,
which Congress passed when it became clear that many Americans
do not understand how compound interest works. There is a little box
spelling out the difference between your possible fate, if (A) you pay
only the monthly minimum payment required by the bank, or (B) you
pony up a bit more each month. The calculation of how much less
you will pay in interest by opting for Plan B is called "Savings."

If you look in the *Oxford English Dictionary*, you will find plenty of
meanings for the word "save," and none of them involve being in a bit
less debt. You can save your soul, save your skin, and save your breath.

You can save time or save face. You can say, "God save the King!" But what the word "save" really means is this: "To deliver or rescue from peril or hurt; to make safe, put in safety." Surely, we all should have known that bankers could be evil. We have all seen Mr. Potter make life hell for George Bailey every Christmas. Paying off the bank does not qualify as putting money in safety, even if paying off the bank will deliver you from the clutches of the Mr. Potters of this world.

Meanwhile, fashion magazines do what they have always done— display the luxurious goods that only a few can afford—but the Dress Doctors' favorite thrifty alternative—the sewing pattern—rarely, if ever, graces their pages these days. And the Dress Doctors' lessons on budgeting seem utterly lost.

When the recession that began in late 2007 arrived, it gave many households a jolt from which they have yet to recover, and fashion magazines did their best to make the constant churn of fashion more affordable. The month of outfits in *Lucky* for November 2008 cost only $16,252, and the one for May 2009 a mere $6,153. Finally, the feature disappeared, as did the petulantly entitled monthly article "What I Want NOW!" Perhaps several years of newspaper headlines on foreclosures, layoffs, and food stamps prompted a little more effort. The March 2009 issue offered a "Fashion Calculator" that discovered good designs at such everyday retailers as Target, Kohl's, and Walmart. The July 2009 issue offered nothing that cost more than $100, and the editor assured us that her staff had found the experience of identifying such items "pretty exhilarating." How nice for them.[108]

Other magazines made similar efforts in the name of "Style-O-Nomics" and "Recessionistas." Even a magazine of luxury goods took a shot at thrift. *Vogue* began a "Steal of the Month" feature, which presumes that most of us cannot find a blouse for less than $400 without its help.[109]

Glamour, a magazine that has always made more of an effort to present affordable clothing, took over the idea of a month of outfits, but with a twist. The articles offered five new garments each month for their editors to mix with what was already in their closets to create thirty days of entirely new looks. A thrifty idea, but one that resulted in random combinations of colors and shapes, violating all the principles of art.[110]

And all these efforts beg the question: If an outfit looks good on Day 2, why can't you wear it on Day 12 and Day 22? Isn't there a difference between mere novelty and beauty?

The Dress Doctors once acted as a counterweight to the temptations of fashion, even as they enjoyed its charms. Grace Margaret Morton prescribed with relish the perfect ensemble for each particular woman whom she discussed. Despite this enthusiasm, Morton put clothing in its place. She explained that some things were more important than stuff: "People who live richly, who have broad interests and activities, plan their expenditures so that they will have more for books and travel, leisure and hobbies, home improvements, entertaining, and giving." In short, they get on with living, not shopping.

At the same time, Morton believed that planning a wardrobe and sticking to it required skill, knowledge, and practicality. A thrifty and beautiful wardrobe proved that a young woman had not only mastered the Five Art Principles and understood the Six Occasions for Dress, but was also self-disciplined, organized, and determined. The qualities that allowed her to dress beautifully without spending a fortune were the same qualities that would allow her to take on a position of "trust and authority." Just as the art principles improved one's mind and one's appearance, so did the exercise of thrift.[111]

Morton wrote these words in 1943 on the eve of the phenomenon that would explode many of the Dress Doctors' dearest ideals: the Baby Boom. It began as the men came home at the end of World War II, and it meant that within twenty years, a new generation of young Americans, raised in prosperity, overwhelming in numbers, had arrived.

❊ 5 ❊

Revolt

The Fall of the Dress Doctors

M AGAZINE WRITER HAZEL RAWSON CADES explained to her
Girl Scout readers in 1927 that girls needed to choose the
right handkerchief when dressing for the occasion: large
squares for sports, and dainty ones for evening wear. Yes, they had
rules for handkerchiefs. Dressing well meant more than choosing a
dress; it required coming up with the right handkerchief, hat, shoes,
hose, gloves, purse, jewelry, umbrella, underwear, plus a coat or cape.
No wonder young people rebelled.[1]

Of course, the Dress Doctors had seen youthful revolts before. As
Alpha Latzke and her Kansas State colleague noted in 1935, "youth
is the age when mankind tends to rebel against all customs, clothing
customs included." The Dress Doctors from the Cleveland schools
wrote a year later that they sometimes had to reason with "young
people" who thought that their parents and teachers just made up
"manners and conventions" in order to keep them quiet or to create

snobby class distinctions. "Nothing could be further from the truth."
The 1960s were different because the enormous wave of Baby Boomers coincided with several movements against injustice, which threw
into doubt all customs and distinctions among people. Manners and
conventions looked more and more like oppression in disguise.[2]

The hardships of the Great Depression and World War II had
kept down birthrates. Afterward, when prosperity returned, American
women produced an unprecedented crop of children: 75 million of
them born between 1946 and 1964, which marked a doubling of the
birthrate. The country had never seen such a crowd of young people,
and their clamor was deafening. As one newspaperman put it in 1966,
millions of Baby Boomers had come to believe that being young was
an accomplishment in itself.[3]

And this bumper crop of young people coincided with the rise of
several mass movements that encouraged the questioning of all authority. Objections to the second-class status of black Americans had
long simmered under the surface. World War II brought the hypocri-
sies of the United States into sharp focus for African Americans—it
was a war waged against racist Nazis by American fighting men who
were segregated by race. The National Association for the Advancement of Colored People (NAACP) focused its legal strategy against
segregation in education first. After a series of victories targeting
colleges, the NAACP persuaded the United States Supreme Court
to rule segregation in the public schools unconstitutional in the land-
mark 1954 decision *Brown v. Board of Education*. Local campaigns,
such as the Montgomery Bus Boycott in 1957, and the national effort
to pass the Civil Rights Act of 1964 exposed ugly, racist opposition
among white Americans.

Alongside racist violence were the more casual acts of discrimination that permeated society, including dress textbooks and fashion
magazines peopled entirely by white girls and women. Excluding
black women became increasingly indefensible.

By challenging long-held beliefs about the distinct and inferior nature of black Americans, the civil rights movement also caused many to question the assumption that women were distinctly domestic creatures. The President's Commission on the Status of Women, created by John F. Kennedy in 1961, did not up-end the idea that women should work only in the home, but it recognized that many women did work for wages and deserved to be treated fairly. Still, opposition to federal legislation ending sex discrimination in hiring was rampant, and feminists had to work to have the laws enforced.

Feminists wanted to know why women were not allowed to take on positions of trust and authority except in a few limited fields, such as home economics, nursing, or teaching. The *Harvard Business Review* estimated in 1965 that out of 26 million working women, a little more than 5,000 held executive positions. Those who did consoled themselves that at least the *idea* of a women executive was no longer considered "ridiculous." But a woman executive still might feel guilty for working, a sentiment that prompted the writing of one of the best-selling books of the 1960s.[4]

In 1963, Betty Friedan's *The Feminine Mystique* hit the bookstores, arguing that young, college-educated mothers like herself were being driven quietly out of their minds by the boredom of domestic life. A graduate of Smith College, Friedan began with these words: "Gradually, without seeing it clearly for quite a while, I came to realize that something is very wrong with the way American women are trying to live their lives today." Friedan and women like her felt pressured into defining themselves solely as wives and mothers, unable to use their talents or education in any other kind of work without feeling guilty. Although the earliest home economists came out of the Progressive era, when reform was in the air, the feminist movement had quieted during the 1920s. The Great Depression had made many question whether married women should have jobs when so many men were out of work, and the end of World War II prompted a rush to domesticity. Out of it grew the "mystique," or myth, that all women found only domestic work satisfying—or if they didn't, they should. *The Feminine Mystique* sold more than 2 million copies by 1974, launching thousands of women into activism. A fellow feminist wrote, "Betty Friedan is to women what Martin Luther King was to blacks."[5]

The limitations built into the idea of home economics as the one reliable place at universities where women were welcome became glaringly apparent. Some had noted the drawbacks of women's segregation into home economics early on. When the president of Vassar College tried to create a program in the 1920s, alumnae were enthusiastic, but a psychology professor told him, "You are driving women back into the home, from the slavery of which education has helped us escape." A federal report on the land-grant colleges from 1930 objected that some home economics programs taught their students that women should be "submerged" within the family, something such programs would never do to men. And home economics was not always a haven at universities. Home economics faculty members were keen to demonstrate their scientific knowledge of nutrition and textile chemistry, but they were often expected to serve as caterers at college events. Their departments' reputation often hinged on the tastiness of what they dished up.[6]

As more women began to question strictly domestic notions of womanhood, the discipline of home economics came to seem unnecessary. If women were capable of earning degrees in chemistry, why couldn't they teach in the chemistry department? Why were they teaching only in home economics? If a young woman was interested in child development, why shouldn't she major in psychology instead of home economics? If she was interested in the design of houses, why not study at a school of architecture?

Dress came under criticism as a sexist ploy to waste women's time. As one feminist put it in 1972, "one of the best ways to keep a woman down is to keep her so involved with how she looks, she doesn't think of anything else." Although reporters noted regularly what feminist women were wearing, the women themselves were reluctant to talk about it, either because they realized that feminists were divided in their opinion of fashion—some saw pants as liberation, some still wore dresses—or because they didn't think they should take the topic seriously. Invited to join a group of designers and manufacturers to talk to the fashion press in 1970, a Los Angeles women's liberation group refused to go, telling a reporter, "We consider fashion too superficial to even comment on its importance to women." And yet there would have been much to say.[7]

Fashion mainstays like dresses and girdles came under attack during the 1960s as uncomfortable oppressions. Dress codes at colleges, which banned slacks on women and long hair on men, were targeted by the leftist group Students for a Democratic Society (SDS), which was better known for protesting against the Vietnam War. Vassar College graduates still tell with glee the story (or myth?) of what student Jane Fonda did when she was turned away from the Faculty Tea because she lacked the required gloves and pearls. She left and came back wearing ONLY gloves and pearls.[8]

The protest mentality trickled down to the younger set. One-third of all high-school principals had confronted student unrest over dress codes by 1969.[9] Of course, Americans have always had a constitutional right to petition their government for redress of grievances, but I suspect that the example of the social movements—civil rights, women's rights, antiwar—inspired a greater willingness to protest in both high schools and colleges.

Nor was that all. Other factors—including the rise of the suburbs, which blurred the once clear distinction between city wear and country clothing; new designers who wanted to dress the young; changes in the world of art; even inclement weather—combined to give a powerful push against the conventions of dress and everything the Dress

Doctors held dear. By the end of the 1960s, the Five Art Principles had become hopelessly square, and dressing for the occasion a plot by the establishment to stifle creativity.

WHAT WERE THE LEADERS of the American Home Economics Association expecting when they invited "militant women's lib advocate" Robin Morgan to speak at their annual meeting in 1972? They must have read about how she and a hundred other women had thrown bras, girdles, curlers, false eyelashes, and wigs into a Freedom Trash Can at the Anti–Miss America demonstration in Atlantic City in 1968. Morgan was scheduled to talk about women's liberation, and they got an earful: "I am here addressing the enemy," she announced.

Morgan accused home economists of turning young women into a "limp, jibbering mass of jelly waiting for marriage." She told them that marriage and the nuclear family were doomed. "It's your choice whether you're going to crumble with the system and stand in the way while history rolls over you," Morgan warned, "or whether you are going to move with it." And the only way home economists could move with history, according to Morgan, was to quit their jobs.

This was not exactly what they were hoping to hear.

Some of them booed.[10]

Morgan was not the first to go after home economics. University deans and presidents—all men—began their attack in the 1940s, for entirely different reasons. They coveted the buildings and funding controlled by home economists. To their eyes, only the hard sciences—and their ability to knock the Russian communists' Sputnik satellite out of the sky—were what the country needed during the Cold War. Deans of colleges of home economics, mostly older women, found themselves reaching out to their alumnae in frantic and sometimes fruitless efforts to save their programs.

The quality of a program was irrelevant. Agnes Fay Morgan, the chair of the Home Economics Department at Berkeley, had a PhD in organic chemistry and great fashion sense. She demonstrated her work on animal nutrition by wearing a fur stole to scientific meetings—the garment combined the dark, luxurious pelt of a fox fed a healthy diet with the pale, ratty pelt of a fox deficient in Vitamin B.[11] While other home economics departments were criticized for being scientifically lightweight, Morgan was criticized for demanding too much of her students. But when she retired in the summer of 1954, Berkeley's Home Economics Department disappeared. Its nutrition programs were sent over to food science, where men ran the show. Virtually the only place at the university that had welcomed women into science was gone.

Across the country, university women who retired were replaced by men, their resources scattered, their hard work forgotten. The prestigious home economics programs at Columbia University's Teachers College and the University of Chicago were dismantled in the 1950s. At the USDA, the Bureau of Home Economics' research programs, along with those of other bureaus, were combined in 1953 into the Agricultural Research Service. Research and publications in clothing and textiles were essentially ended. As one historian put it, the Bureau of Home Economics was "reorganized out of existence." The home economists were too "ladylike" to know how to dramatize their plight or to reach out to the women's movement for help. By the time Robin Morgan came along to jeer at them, the home economists were a beleaguered bunch trying to prove their relevance.[12]

So, after hearing Robin Morgan's tirade, what did the home economists do? Quit their jobs? Abandon marriage? No, they formed a committee.

The members chosen for the Women's Role Committee were all professional home economists, but tension ran through the committee's discussion. Morgan's attack shocked one member because she believed that home economics had been teaching "dual roles" for years. Another insisted that home economists must admit, "We teach one lifestyle"—homemaking—while practicing another as professional women.[13]

The task the home economists faced—defending both women who wanted to work only in the home and women who wanted to work outside it—was impossible, because women on each side felt insulted by the choices made by women on the other side. "If we could get women to accept the fact that some women can and want to have dual roles," lamented one committee member, "just as other women prefer only the domestic role."[14]

We are still getting women to accept that fact. To start with, what words do we use? Mothers without servants work. They do it by housekeeping, through child care, and by cooking, chauffeuring, and—last, but not least—sewing. So when people say "working mothers" and mean only mothers who earn wages, mothers with baby spittle on their shoulders who just put dinner on the table tend to bristle. With good reason. The home woman has never been part of the labor force officially. This was a problem for home economists from the beginning, and it only got worse over time.

When the Smith-Hughes National Vocational Education Act was up for debate in 1916, one congressman supported funding the study of home economics because, he said, "the greatest of all vocations is that of home making and motherhood." Indeed, many a woman had to work for wages, but only as a wife and mother could she "fulfill her manifest destiny." Other congressmen were for motherhood and apple pie, too, but argued that homemaking was not a job because home women did not earn wages. They lost the argument. Every vocational education act from that point on funded home economics, but by then, more and more people were having doubts.[15]

Before Congress next held hearings on funding for job training, in 1975, two important laws were passed. The first was the 1964 Civil Rights Act, which banned most racial and sexual discrimination in hiring. Unfortunately, the members of the Equal Employment Opportunity Commission (EEOC), which was created to enforce the law, found the idea of sex discrimination so ludicrous—Would

Playboy Clubs be forced to hire male bunnies?—that the law was gutted in action. A frustrated woman lawyer working for the EEOC met with Friedan and said, "We may never have another chance like this law again. Betty, you have to start an NAACP for women." And so Friedan and some two dozen other feminists organized the National Organization of Women (NOW), and she became its first president. The second important piece of legislation was the Educational Amendments of 1972, which banned sex discrimination in higher education for institutions receiving federal funds, with a few exceptions (such as beauty pageants). Patsy Mink, the first Japanese American woman to serve in Congress, drafted what became Title IX of that act, a section we know best for its effect on college athletics.[16]

In hearings in 1975 before a congressional committee on funding for vocational training, the testimony made clear what should have been obvious: training for jobs was skewed by sex, and the jobs young women trained for paid significantly less than the jobs for which young men trained. Ninety-two percent of the students in homemaking and consumer studies were female; so were 86 percent of those in "gainful home economics." By contrast, agricultural students were 94 percent male, and technical students were 90 percent male. The difference in what women and men did for a living helped to explain why the incomes of women with full-time jobs in 1972 averaged $5,903 a year, versus $10,202 a year for men.[17]

The hearings captured all the gender bizarreness of the 1970s. Well-intentioned congressmen complimented the women testifying on how pretty they were. Reports referenced during the hearings were equally appalling. A report on the public schools of Ann Arbor, Michigan, quoted a school principal on why girls could not be crossing guards: "I don't want girls to get in the habit of standing on street corners," he said. Crossing guards by day, hookers by night? A superintendent of a program that taught auto mechanics, carpentry, and electricity explained that there were no women in his programs because girls couldn't climb ladders while they were having their periods.[18]

Although homemaking classes were still the most popular vocational training courses for girls, witnesses at the congressional hearing fretted that homemaking classes encouraged "passivity, dependence and domesticity." Girls had better give up on the idea that they would marry "and live happily ever after," because divorce was becoming more common. But girls were not all that clueless. Only 22 percent of those surveyed believed that most of them would never work outside the home for wages. Robin Morgan was wrong; home economics might have steered young women into low-paying fields, but these were not quivering jellies waiting only for marriage.[19]

Why would they be? The culture of the 1950s is known for its domestic strain, a result of post–World War II nesting urges and a way of coping with the scary Cold War world, but it wasn't all June Cleaver. Magazines such as *Ladies' Home Journal* regularly printed stories praising women who had succeeded in business, politics, journalism, or medicine. Pattern magazines featured wardrobes for the young office worker and stories about businesswomen who did their own sewing. Working women were not unusual in the 1950s, although working mothers were unusual. More than 40 percent of women worked for wages before they had children during the 1950s. Then they dropped out of wage work. But over the next three decades, more and more mothers would keep their paying jobs.[20]

Whatever home economics had done for women in the past, the narrowness of the futures that it opened to girls had become painfully clear by the time of the hearings in 1975. Consider the home economics book series put out by McGraw-Hill in 1959. Along with *How You Look and Dress* came *How You Plan and Prepare Meals, Teen Guide to Homemaking, Child Growth and Development, Your Marriage and Family Living,* and *The Home and Its Furnishings.* The fields for which home economics graduates were trained left out an awful lot of the world's jobs.

SUBURBIA IN THE 1950S MAY HAVE STIFLED the many readers of *The Feminine Mystique*, but it also quietly started a fashion revolution that would forever change what American women wore.

The growth of the suburbs after World War II popularized casual dress for every day. Suburbia had traditionally fallen on the country side of the distinction between formal city wear and tweedy country clothes. Patios, backyard barbecues, and swimming pools were places where women had traditionally worn sporty clothing. Postwar prosperity in the suburbs gave more and more people this kind of outdoor living space and time to use it.[21]

California's population boomed during the war, and its sunny climate inspired new fashions that signaled playtime near the beach but were worn all over America. Marketing campaigns stressed how California fashion was less fitted, less traditional, and more colorful.[22]

More people took up boating, golf, and spectator sports, and they got used to wearing sportswear. When *Time* magazine featured designer Claire McCardell on its cover in May 1955, she was surrounded by fashion models in a swimsuit, a playsuit, shorts, a tunic, and a blouse and skirt. Only one garment was clearly a dress. The dress was the queen of fashion (with the suit close behind) until McCardell popularized the idea of "separates"—an idea so new that *Time* put the word in quotation marks.[23]

Separates actually went way back under other names. Think of the young women who opted for a wardrobe of shirtwaists and skirts at the turn of the century. And pattern books had long offered what they called "capsule wardrobes"—a set of garments made in harmonizing fabrics that could be worn together. "Capsule" meant "small and compact," a distinctly American use of the word.[24]

McCardell said she invented separates by creating two-piece dresses so she could switch out a modest top for a bare top, or a long skirt for a short skirt, but she wore the tops with dresses and shorts too. Mix-and-match separates became the mark of a suburban wardrobe. American women even preferred separates for afternoon teas and evenings out, although then they were made of dressier fabrics. For the holidays, a sporty woman might don slender slacks in dark velveteen with a sumptuous white silk blouse and red cummerbund to wear "by hearthside or television set." Velveteen may have made women's slacks suitable for a celebration, but they were still worn only at home. These "casual" clothes of the 1950s were still beautifully harmonious and detailed, a far cry from our printed T-shirt and jeans outfits, but they undermined more formal ways of dressing.[25]

A tongue-in-cheek guide to East Coast women's colleges written by the young men of Yale University in 1951 declared, "Blue jeans, pink shirts, and run-down shoes" to be the universal costume on women's college campuses. College women didn't actually possess all that many pairs of pants. A survey at Cornell University in 1960 revealed that they owned, on average, 8.7 dresses, 13.4 skirts, and only 2.9 pairs of pants. But young women probably wore pants more than they were supposed to. *Vogue Pattern Book* admitted, in 1955, "Nothing is more comfortable and warm than tapered pants" for studying, but reminded co-eds that their best choice for attending class was a good suit with a skirt. The fact that the Dress Doctors were forever reminding their students that slacks were for weenie roasts and not for the classroom proves that some of them needed reminding. Eventually, some of the students revolted.[26]

THE BERMUDA SHORTS AFFAIR OF 1960 began when the president of Columbia University noticed how the women from neighboring Barnard College were dressed when they came over to his campus. Columbia was all-male then; Barnard all-female. Barnard's president agreed to ban her students from wearing slacks and shorts. She noted that Barnard was one of the few women's colleges "within strolling distance of male students that had not already banned bare knees in classes."[27]

Barnard students were not pleased. "Everyone is screaming about it," said one sophomore." Another said the college administration was "just doing it to be nasty," and many of her sisters agreed. Someone printed a manifesto proclaiming the dress code "a contradiction of Barnard's liberal tradition." To show their opposition to the new rule, students wore shorts and slacks to a mass meeting even if they didn't own a pair and had to borrow one. Protest petitions appeared in elevators, and some four hundred students signed. Finally, a compromise was reached. When at Barnard, women students could wear Bermuda shorts, if they were "not too short, too bright or too tight," but when they crossed the street to the campus of Columbia University, they had to wear a coat over them.[28]

Why all this fuss? We tend to think of pants as freedom, partly because certain activities are easier to do while wearing them, and partly because men monopolized both power and pants until very recently. But there were other reasons why girls in slacks made Columbia's president so unhappy.

For one thing, women's slacks started to get really tight in the 1950s. The Jax brand perfected skinny slacks—Audrey Hepburn owned fifty pairs—but some customers worried about the pants being "a little too snug." Yet that was the whole point of Jax pants. A seamstress worked at the Jax shop to make them as tight as possible and give the customers the "courage" to wear them. You have only to see the young Lee Remick's hourglass figure packed into a pair of skin-tight slacks in *Anatomy of a Murder* from 1959 to understand why the Columbia University president feared for his men's virtue. Worries about female flesh ran through the Barnard discussion. One fine arts instructor at Barnard remarked, "Most of the girls wearing shorts look like third-rate Rubens." (Peter Paul Rubens is known for his paintings of large, mostly naked women.)[29]

Stretchy fabrics made tight pants possible, and women wore them as tight as possible. In her last dress textbook from 1968, Alpha Latzke and her coauthor pointed out that women were buying pants a size too small, so they were not buying them in order to be more comfortable. As one New York City school official put it that same year, slacks on girls were "erotic stimulants." Today's jeggings provoke similar worries. As an Indiana high-school principal said in 2012, "The one thing we don't want in our hallways, and I'd be lying if I said we don't have it, is Spandex."[30]

Pants on women also remained decidedly casual, leisure wear, but the fashion winds were shifting directions. By the mid-1960s, haute couture houses such as Valentino and Dior started selling "pantsuits" to wealthy American socialites.

There were holdouts. American designer Norman Norell told *Women's Wear Daily* in 1964 that he believed "no woman should run around the streets in pants," because they looked "lousy" in them. One spokesman for a New York City restaurant said in 1969 that it would not seat men in turtlenecks or women in pants; another said, "They do not belong in a restaurant like La Côte Basque any more than swimming suits or golf clothes." Other restaurants would seat women wearing pants only at dinnertime and only if their trousers were "elegant and dressy." But most fancy restaurants had given up.[31]

The arguments continued. Insurance companies and banks continued their ban on pants for women employees. In Chicago, Marshall Fields & Company still thought pants were too distracting on salesclerks in 1969, while Bonwit Teller allowed them on anyone who worked in the "youth-oriented" departments. Some women got tired of the ban. After a memo went out in 1970 informing the news department at CBS headquarters in New York that women could not wear slacks during business hours, thirty women employees organized a "pants-in."[32]

It helped that, one morning in January 1968, the fashion stars and the weather aligned. The temperature on the East Coast of the United States stood at a mere 3 degrees as children headed back to school after the Christmas holiday. More than five hundred parents sent their daughters out in pants, only to have school principals send them right back home again for not being properly dressed. The New York Civil Liberties Union swung into action. By the following winter, the superintendent of schools issued a letter saying that principals did not have the power to ban girls who wore pants. A school dress code could not require frostbite.[33]

The Dress Doctors were divided over the issue of pants on women. Harriet Tilden McJimsey, born in 1902, taught "Costume Selection" to every first-year home economics major at Iowa State University. She did not want them to select tight slacks in 1963. And heaven help the stout woman. "It takes hardly an ounce of good taste," wrote McJimsey, "to recognize the inappropriateness of slacks for the overweight figure. The indignity is compounded if the woman is over 40 as well as overweight."[34]

Other Dress Doctors were eager to get women into pants. Try culottes, suggested Adele P. Margolis in 1969 to readers who were hesitant. Margolis was called the Julia Child of sewing by some, so when she wrote a full-throated paean to pants in her next book in 1974, we should hear it as the equivalent of Child's coaxing the timid women of Middle America into trying coq au vin. She cataloged the types: "blue jeans, dungarees, clam diggers, pedal pushers, hot pants, Jamaica shorts, Bermuda shorts, deck pants, toreadors, jodhpurs, breeches, trunks, gaucho pants, frontier pants, Capri pants, classic trousers, palazzo pants, 'at homes' of lace, velvet, brocade, lamé, chiffon; even those hybrids known as culottes—part skirt, part pants. Skinny, straight, flared pants; long, short, in-between pants. Just so they are pants."[35]

As that amazing list makes clear, pants in all shapes and sizes were becoming enormously popular with American women. For fall 1967, McCall's Patterns offered everything from playful short suits in *faux* pony-skin to elegant black and white evening suits. By 1969, 45 million pairs of women's pants were being sold a year.[36] Women chose pantsuits by the millions in the 1960s for many reasons: sexiness, comfort, fashion, and because pants allowed them to avoid the anxieties of donning a minidress, an invention brought to America by an Englishwoman named Mary Quant.

LIKE THE BARNARD COLLEGE WOMEN who claimed the right to wear shorts, Mary Quant targeted the fashion oppression of young women. She predated the Baby Boom—she was born in 1934—but she invented the clothes that the young Boomers made popular. Quant said, "I had always wanted the young to have fashions of their own." She told a British journalist that she never wanted to become a grown woman like those in the 1950s who wore stiletto heels, corsets, and pointy bras. So instead, she gave the young the miniskirt, skinny ribbed sweaters, tights, and low-slung hipster pants.[37]

Before the 1960s, most new fashions had been dictated by the Paris couture houses, which catered to a privileged set of women. Styles usually trickled downward. American manufacturers and department stores bought authorized copies, or they sent in spies like Elizabeth Hawes to memorize styles. But during the 1960s, fashions often came from below, from the small boutiques.

Boutiques were groovy places where modern music played and young owners and customers collaborated on new looks that came only in small sizes. The aim was constant variety and frenetic excitement. By 1971, there were some 15,000 boutiques in England. If you have ever wandered into a department store and found yourself stunned by pulsating music, odd lighting, and a jumble of incoherent styles, you are in the Juniors section, a re-creation of the boutique experience.[38]

Quant's miniskirt was not without precedent. In the 1950s, mini-dresses with small waists and wide skirts were shown *over* matching shorts for beachwear. So it was no surprise that A-line minidresses were photographed as summer resort wear when they first showed up in 1965. But by the next fall, they were touted as everyday wear. *Vogue* magazine's editor Diana Vreeland wrote, "The mini-skirt will become more and more miniscule. . . . Let's not worry about it, let us just enjoy what suits us." Soon former First Lady Jacqueline Kennedy was wearing her skirts above the knee, joined by "cautious housewives over 30."[39]

The look spread, but many were not keen on it. Miniature skirts were banned in the Vatican and in the palace of a sultan in Malaysia in 1967. Dr. Ernest Dichter, an Austrian psychoanalyst turned American advertising guru, observed that "the dress industry" should be called "the undressed industry." But he advised the pope to be patient: "The more knees we see around, the less we're going to get excited." California's General Assembly banned miniskirts on the secretarial staff. Three hundred young women were arrested for wearing miniskirts in Brazzaville, Congo. The Arab world and much of Africa banned miniature skirts, but a court in Portugal ruled that a husband could not forbid his wife from wearing a skirt short enough to show her knees. Less amusingly, young men attacked girls for wearing short skirts in Zambia, and an Egyptian stabbed his sister to death for wearing one in public.[40]

Understand, these skirts shocked because they got *really* short. Hence, the need for new terms, such as "micro-mini" and "mini-mini." A photo from the races at Ascot in Britain in 1968 showed two young women wearing dresses falling about half an inch below the crotch. Standing next to them was a fellow in a dark cutaway coat, gray trousers, top hat, etc. They are so naked. He is so clothed. Are they freer? Or just chillier? After all, most political movements do not define freedom in terms of nakedness. Patrick Henry did not cry,

"Give me short-shorts or give me death!" (Short-shorts, by the way, arrived in the United States in 1971 and quickly became a favorite among prostitutes.)[41]

Certainly Quant had no greater political purpose in designing the mini than rejecting adulthood. When charged in 1967 with being frivolous, she replied, "If being frivolous is not getting involved in things like Vietnam then I'm all for it." She felt "entirely vindicated" by an American journalist who wrote that American women should realize that being a "Chelsea girl with a 'life is fabulous' philosophy . . . is a much more rewarding occupation than being a Lady Senator or even a Lady President." This wasn't very different from what generations of patronizing men had told women—not to worry their little heads about the state of the world—except that now their little heads sported a Vidal Sassoon haircut above a purple-and-white micro-mini while doing the Frug.[42]

Like the strapless gown, which promises to fall off, the miniskirt promised to ride up, and this launched innumerable and unapologetic accounts of men leering at women. A Boston businessman told *Time* magazine that he once walked into a wall while "relishing" the view of a secretary bending over to reach the bottom drawer of a file cabinet. "Sure it's a distraction," said a male college student of miniskirts, but "I can't think of a nicer one, and most of the professors feel the same way." A London boutique owner told a reporter how much he enjoyed "following a mini-skirt up the steep steps to the top of a double-decker bus." Men at one Chicago company went roaming from office to office looking for women wearing micro-minis, apparently just to get a look up their skirts. The *Chicago Tribune* sent a reporter and photographer down to North Michigan Avenue to interview "girl-watchers" and take pictures of women's legs, which the paper then rated. One photo caught a slice of a woman's legs and a row of five men in suits and ties grinning like idiots. It read: "Aficionados need little excuse for inspection sessions. A specimen passing in review draws approval." The American Society of Girl Watchers urged its members to approach women, rate them on a scorecard (lovely, feminine, refreshing, sexy, chic, and WOW!), and then endow the worthy woman with a sticker of approval. They frowned upon actual assault; their constitution commanded: "Don't pinch."[43]

For the Dress Doctors, the miniskirt was an artistic problem. Cutting across the widest part of the thigh, the mini skirt "was anything but flattering," according to the Kansas State Dress Doctors.[44] The miniskirt violates proportion by making a woman look both wider and shorter. As Elizabeth Hawes once explained, design should cut the body at a natural break: the neck, just below the knee, the ankle, et cetera. She was thinking of movement—she studied dancers when designing clothes—but the body tends to narrow at the places where it has a natural break.

More importantly, the miniskirt violated the principle of shape, because it prevented easy and confident movement. It was impossible to be fashionable and retain any dignity. Fashion writer Bernadine Morris of the *New York Times* explained the plight of the fashionable woman: "Getting on a bus or up from a table in a restaurant can mean a total loss of dignity; crossing one's legs in a friend's house a social disaster." A woman working at Macy's confided that she couldn't accept a dinner invitation while wearing her latest new cocktail dress because she could not sit down in it without flashing her underpants at the other dinner guests.[45]

Women found ways to cope. In the Ford Foundation's new all-glass offices, an enterprising secretary sewed a curtain for her typewriter pedestal, so she could stop worrying about men looking up her dress. Designer Anne Klein found business meetings a trial and solved the problem of sitting down by carrying a scarf to drape across her knees. Perhaps the most deranged solution was revealed when a male banker in Miami defined for *Time* what was acceptable office wear for women in 1968: "I talked it over with the woman in charge of our

office girls, and we agreed on miniskirts if the underpants matched."
And he'd know, because he could see them.[46]

When the women of Students for a Democratic Society grew sick
of making coffee while the men made policy, they drafted a statement
in 1967 challenging "their brothers" to root out "male chauvinism"
in the organization. The men agreed to print it—accompanied by a
sketch of a woman in a polka-dot minidress with matching polka-dot
underpants. The women of SDS were not amused. The men of SDS
were obnoxious, but they were right that it is hard to take women
seriously when the current fashion makes them look ridiculous.[47]

There was one group of females who had long worn thigh-high
dresses and matching underpants. They were called toddlers. In fact,
when asked about selling the miniskirt in 1967, a spokesman for Sears
vowed, "Our catalog will never have a thigh-high dress on any kid
over three years old."[48]

For decades little girls had worn short dresses with matching
bloomers so they would be free to scamper around playgrounds un-
hampered. The length of girls' skirts depended on their age. In the
mid-1930s, when women's day dresses hit around mid-calf, McCall's
Patterns showed skirts at mid-thigh for girls up to six years old and
skirts at the knee for girls from six to fourteen. Girls looked forward
to the day when they would be old enough to wear long skirts like
their mothers. But when fashionable dresses for grown-up women took
on the A-line, thigh-high shape of toddlers' clothes in the 1960s, the
distinctions of age were entirely lost.[49]

The similarity between the minidress and toddler-wear was apparent to everyone. Marylin Bender of the *New York Times* was
appalled to report, in 1966, that "7th Ave. Looks to Sandbox Set for
Summer Fashions." Designers offered adult-sized baby-doll dresses
with ruffles and puffed sleeves worn with large versions of children's
sunbonnets and sandals, or with tall white socks and Mary Jane shoes.
One twenty-year-old wailed, "But I don't want to be 12 so soon

again." A department director at the Mecklenburg County office in North Carolina required that his women workers wear skirts that stopped at mid-knee in order "to avoid the little girl appearance" of a higher hemline. A Dress Doctor dubbed the look "authentic kindergarten."[50]

Mary Quant cultivated the kiddy look. She and her husband and business partner, Alexander Plunket Green, appeared together in *Vogue* in 1963 when she was twenty-nine. He stands holding a cigar, wearing a double-breasted suit and a turtleneck. Clearly, he was dressed like a grown man, even if his turtleneck was too casual for eating at *La Côte Basque*. Quant sits at his feet sporting a bowl haircut, what may be a poncho, and a shirt with an oversized collar. She looks like "one of those wispy child heroines," as *Vogue* put it.[51]

When Quant came to the United States to show her collection for J. C. Penney in 1967, her baby-doll dresses came in pale pink, baby blue, and peach, and her models emphasized "the little kid look" by sucking their thumbs and walking pigeon-toed. She explained happily, "There was a time when every girl under twenty yearned to look like an experienced, sophisticated thirty. . . . Suddenly every girl with a hope of getting away with it is aiming to look not only under voting age but under the age of consent." Looking back decades later, Quant's husband mused, "I think there was a slightly sort of pedophile thing about it, wasn't there?"[52]

Many balked at the look. The skirts photographed for fashion magazines were actually shipped one inch longer to stores on the East and West Coasts, and three inches longer to stores in the South. And three inches of hem were included in every retail miniskirt "as insurance against the outraged strictures of square schools, parents and employers." Indeed, the knee test—if your hem doesn't touch the floor when you're kneeling, you are wearing a mini—was being used in public schools. Girls who failed could let down the hem of their skirts or go home and change.[53]

Nationwide polls done in the United States in 1970 revealed that only 51 percent of women in their twenties were willing to wear a miniskirt; 47 percent of women in their twenties preferred to wear their skirts at the knee. By the time they reached their thirties, women overwhelmingly preferred their skirts at the knee. It was men in their twenties—surprise, surprise—who preferred women to wear miniskirts, by a clear majority (64 percent). They lost their enthusiasm when they calmed down in their thirties.[54]

So women welcomed pants in the late 1960s in part because they were desperate for a fashionable alternative to the miniskirt. An executive at the *Chicago Tribune* noticed in 1969 that the office women were "much more at ease" when wearing pants than they were in miniskirts. Who could blame them? Miniskirts made crossing one's knees "an ordeal." Pants solved the problem.[55]

There was another way out of that ordeal: wearing tights with a miniskirt. Mary Quant explained, in 1966, "You must wear tights with short skirts so you can sit gracefully." But tights were too hot for every season in the United States, so women turned to a recent invention: pantyhose.[56]

In 1968, a reporter for the *Chicago Tribune* wrote: "These one-piece affairs protect the mini-skirted when the girls sit, bend, reach, or stretch, by preventing that patch of white look when the feminine form is a bit off balance. The patch of white glimpse, so familiar to the dedicated girl-watcher, was the despair of the mini-skirt set."[57]

He was lamenting that men could no longer look up women's miniskirts in order to catch a glimpse of their white underwear once women donned beige pantyhose.

Invented in 1959, pantyhose were the epitome of modern comfort because they liberated young women from the girdles whose metal clasps had held up old-fashioned stockings. When miniskirts shortened to the thigh, the tops of the stockings might show, especially when a woman sat down. Lower, smaller sports cars, and the lower, wider furniture that made for Mid-Century Modern style, compounded the problem, so young women turned to pantyhose. Production of pantyhose increased 523 percent between 1968 and 1970. By 1970, pantyhose made up 70 percent of the hosiery market. Young women had decided that girdles were uncomfortable and unnecessary. "All that hardware" put them off, explained one manufacturer.[58]

This was an enormous shift in behavior. Before the 1960s, donning a girdle and stockings was the way that a girl greeted puberty. In a 1944 book geared to high-school freshmen, Mildred Graves Ryan explained, "When you wear a girdle you will notice how much firmer and smoother your figure looks. You simply fail to jiggle and bounce in spots." Curves must be contained in "foundation garments," a term that suggests that women need some cement at the bottom to keep them steady. "Nobody is exempt from wearing one," warned Ryan, not even fashion models with perfect figures.[59]

Fitting a new corset or girdle was a tricky business that could take a forty-minute session with a specially trained saleswoman. To make sure she had the right size, a woman had to arrange herself in her girdle, tugging up and down, making sure she could walk and sit while wearing it. The athletic woman was advised to choose a flexible garment without any boning. The Sears Roebuck catalog sold a girdle "especially designed for dancing and athletic wear." But for the flabby figure, the stiffer, boned model was a necessity. When *Good Housekeeping* did more makeovers on middle-aged women following their experiment with Dorée Smedley in 1939, a "well-fitted all-in-one corset" was a crucial solution for each of them.[60]

When buying a girdle, a woman was supposed to choose one for a waist size two to four inches (!) smaller than her actual waist measurement. Before Dorée Smedley's makeover, she measured as follows:

Bust	38 inches
Waist	33 inches
Hips	42 inches

In her new all-in-one corselet, she became:

Bust	39 inches
Waist	30 inches
Hips	43 inches

The corset didn't shrink her. It rearranged her.[61]

Yet foundation garments were supposed to "mold" the figure, not squish it. If properly fitted, a corset would not leave "marks of constriction or pressure" when taken off, explained one Dress Doctor.[62]

The Dress Doctors expected foundation garments to avoid the exaggerated hourglass of the nineteenth century. They condemned tight corsets, writing: "Freedom of motion for all the muscles of the body is nature's requirement." Every advertisement for twentieth-century corsets boasts of their comfort and freedom with smiling models. (Don't laugh. Spanx catalogs today feature women dancing around, as if being squeezed by Lycra makes them so very happy.)[63]

Foundation garments had nearly magical powers. Advertisements for corsets and girdles in the 1920s and 1930s boasted that they reshaped a woman's body permanently. Their "gentle massage-like action removes flabby, disfiguring fat with every movement." This is scientific hooey, of course, the equivalent of those creams today that are supposed to rub out cellulite, but even the Kansas State Dress Doctors believed that a middle-aged figure "develops a tendency to thicken and become flabby" without a good girdle. Mrs. Ida Rosenthal, cofounder of the Maidenform company, claimed that women working in airplane factories during World War II wearing "good girdles and bras" suffered less from fatigue and got more done than other women.[64]

211

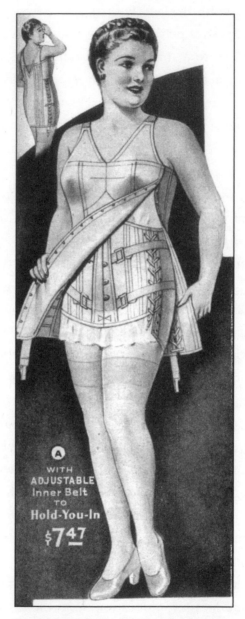

Fig. 1: The Dress Doctors expected all women to wear girdles of some kind, but the fabric, laces, boning, and clasps that held in stout women in 1946 were especially formidable. LANE BRYANT CATALOG, SPRING-SUMMER 1946

Here is one comforting fact: *American women often refused to wear their girdles*. Eighty-five percent of them did not wear a foundation garment, according to a study of more than 14,000 women published by the Bureau of Home Economics in 1941. City women and younger women were more likely to put them on (or more likely to fib to survey-takers?). Yet only 47 percent of housewives surveyed in the New York City area said they wore girdles on any given day in 1943. Twenty percent of eighteen-year-olds at a New Jersey high school said they wore girdles on schooldays in 1945, and 28 percent donned them for weekends, presumably for dates. Girdles may have seemed a necessity after Christian Dior's exaggerated hourglass silhouette took the country by storm in 1947. A survey found that women at Washington State College owned three girdles each, on average, in 1952.[65]

Fashion magazines still featured girdles in the 1960s, yet the fashionable A-line dresses seemed to make them unnecessary, especially for younger women whose figures didn't require much restricting. To keep customers, one company came out with a line of girdles called "Pop Pants" in 1965 which came in bright colors and swirly prints. The red, white, and blue "Stars 'n' Stripes" version ticked off the Daughters of the American Revolution, who forced it off the market. Du Pont came up with a kinder, gentler girdle called a "form persuasion garment" in 1968 and sent out 2.5 million brochures to high-school seniors and college students bearing the slogan "Every Girl Needs a Little Control."[66]

But girls preferred to be out of control.

There was an industry-wide slump in girdle sales by 1965. The *New York Times* could not resist a pun: "The industry sagged where its support had always been firmest." Between 1965 and 1975, girdle sales in the United States and Great Britain dropped by half. Du Pont, the company that had invented Lycra in order to put it into girdles, studied these young consumers in 1975 and concluded: "Women used to believe that there was a 'law' that they had to wear girdles and most believe that law has been repealed."[67]

The market for conventional brassieres also sagged. Before the invention of the foam cup, serious bras had lots of seams, padding, boning, and hardware. Watch any movie made in the 1950s, and you will notice the resulting twin missile-cone silhouette.

Then along came designer Rudi Gernreich. Gernreich, a Jewish refugee who left Vienna, Austria, in 1938 at the age of sixteen, ended up in California, where so many casual fashions started after the war. He invented the "no-bra bra" in 1964. Gloria Steinem, feminist and journalist, described it as "two wispy cups of molded nylon attached to shoulder straps and a narrow band of stretch fabric that encircles the rib cage." One department store buyer was happy to see that it made "women look like women again, instead of Sherman tanks." But Gernreich's creation "struck terror in the hearts of brassiere manufacturers everywhere," said the *New York Times*.[68]

Their terror was only partly justified. Going without a bra had become popular in Manhattan by 1970, but only among young, small-breasted women, and only on weekends. Marlo Thomas of the television series *That Girl* told *Good Housekeeping* that she was no longer wearing a bra on the show: "God created women to bounce, so be it. If I bounce, I'm glad to be a girl." Brassiere manufacturers warned darkly what would happen if you went ahead and bounced. Maidenform suggested we take a hard look "at pictures of women over 30 who live in primitive societies where bralessness has been a way of life." Even an ad for a minimalist bra warned that a bra was necessary while wearing heavy winter clothes or "you'll end up flat."[69]

Manufacturers rallied by designing their own minimalist bras, which were sold to that part of the market possessing minimalist bosoms. The "natural look" made up only 20 percent of the bra business in 1972, whereas Maidenform's "pointed bosom" look sold 25 percent. The biggest seller for Playtex was the 18 Hour Bra, which is a very serious bra indeed. Apparently, outside of very large cities, women kept wearing bras.[70]

None of the new fashion styles of the 1960s did any real harm to the Dress Doctors. After all, they had already lived through short skirts and long skirts, no waists and pinched waists, brisk lines and lavish lines, penury and plenty, wars and peace. They could have survived a few dresses that were ridiculously short, the advent of the women's pantsuit, and the end of the girdle.

What they couldn't survive was a wholesale rejection of the principles of good dress design at the very moment when political attacks threatened their authority to teach at all. It was the rejection of the art principles that did them in.

TRUE STORY: TWO TEACHING FELLOWS at Columbia University in the 1990s were surprised to notice that the seminar room in their building had a new, modern painting on the wall. It offered up a set of bold, black squiggles and circles. They rather liked it. Later, they noticed a blackboard leaning against the wall. They realized the modern art that they were admiring was actually the glue that had been holding up the blackboard.

This is the problem with modern art: art or glue?

The early twentieth century saw art movements that shook up traditional notions of the importance of composition. Jackson Pollock made his first drip paintings in the late 1940s. Art historians tell us that they were "the result of conscious ordering, technical control, and critical evaluation," but many members of the general public thought they were more like something a monkey splattered on canvas. A Baltimore newspaper made the point by running photos in 1957 of an abstract expressionist painting alongside paintings by a six-year-old girl and a chimpanzee named Betsy. A reporter in New York reviewed a gallery show of the paintings of a chimp named Beauty, explaining the different artistic "periods" that had marked her work. To be fair, a recent study has shown that people can distinguish between artists' splatters, children's splatters, and zoo animals' splatters. And, for all we know, the fellow who installed that blackboard was interested in conscious ordering, technical control, and critical evaluation, and thought of glue as his medium.[71]

Nevertheless, the rejection of the art principles was under way. The director of what was then called the Guggenheim Museum of Non-Objective Art explained, in 1951, that "no one is expected to 'understand' non-objective painting. One does not 'understand' beauty—one feels it!" Of course, anyone can understand the Five Art Principles that create beauty in dress, which is why the rise of abstract art posed a philosophical challenge to the Dress Doctors. True, almost any abstract form could be reduced and repeated as a print that worked for dresses. Butterick Patterns offered dresses in "Modern Master cotton prints" by Pablo Picasso and Paul Klee in 1957, but when art movements threw aside the traditional rules of composition, the rules of the Dress Doctors were in danger, too.[72]

Pollock's brand of abstract expressionism, which depicts nothing in particular, was followed by pop art, which does depict something, only nothing of any particular importance, such as *Campbell's Soup Cans* by Andy Warhol, or a panel from a cartoon by Roy Lichtenstein. Found objects—stuff you might find around your house—could become art when placed in a gallery. Robert Rauschenberg created *Bed* in 1955. It was an actual quilt and a pillow. Art critics championed pop art for its freedom, its inventiveness, its "cheekiness," and its commentary on consumer culture. Dress Doctor Marilyn J. Horn of the University of Nevada was less enthusiastic. She wrote, in 1968, "The essence of pop is to create an illusion that either fools or confuses the observer."[73]

In clothing, the illusion came in the form of a shift dress with a Campbell's soup can printed on the front, or a sheath dress with a Brillo Pad box printed around the hips.[74] Yves Saint Laurent's 1965 color-block dresses, based on Piet Mondrian's color-block paintings, qualified as a pop-art joke. The cartoonist Barney Tobey drew a little girl who cannot find her mother in an art museum because she is wearing a YSL Mondrian dress while standing in front of a Mondrian painting.

Op art, short for optical art, was even worse. It repeated undulating patterns of lines and spots that seemed to move. A delighted five-year-old said, "The paintings are playing with me!" But the overall effect was less benevolent. Epileptics were being thrown into fits, according to one writer; less vulnerable people merely became seasick. *Time* magazine published an article entitled "Op Art: Pictures That Attack the Eye." McCall's Patterns featured A-line dress designs done in "head-spinning pattern and eye-blinding color."[75]

Op-art does exactly what the Dress Doctors warned that a bad printed fabric could do: it vibrates unpleasantly. Instead of artistic repose, it creates optical disturbance. It is ugly by definition. But that did not stop it from being printed on fabric or made up into dresses. *Life* magazine featured op-art dresses worn in galleries of op-art paintings in 1965. The lost child in the cartoon would have found her mother only to be sick on her.[76]

Print dresses now came in previously "unthinkable" combinations of red, black, and purple, or pink, green, and purple, or yellow and purple. The "It" Dress of 1967—an A-line with large patch pockets—resembled nothing so much as a traffic cone in screaming yellow, green, or red. Jessica Daves, who had edited *Vogue* from 1952 until 1963, noted that "navy blue is sober, conforming, individual, sinking the wearer into the ranks of the conformers, therefore not for an era of domination." The "defiant colors" that defined the youthful look of the 1960s were actually some of the exact combinations that Florence Hull Winterburn had condemned in 1914 as "horrors" thrust upon the public eye "from caprice or stupidity." Such shocking combinations only appeared at masquerade parties in the 1920s, where the whole idea was to make a spectacle of yourself.[77]

Fashion photography also lost its interest in traditional rules of composition during the 1960s. In 1949, Carmel Snow, the editor of *Harper's Bazaar*, ordered photographer Lillian Bassman to retake a picture. In the original, the model, in a chiffon dress by Robert Piguet, is posed against a mirror, producing a fuzzy and utterly misleading image that resembles the outline of a butterfly. Snow complained, "The designer intended a column of chiffon, and you have given me a butterfly. . . . You are not here to make art, you are here to show the buttons and bows." Yet Snow's remark sold both herself and Bassman short. If midcentury fashion photographs were beautiful, it was because their makers followed the rules that govern the art of composition *while* showing the buttons and bows.[78]

The retake is beautiful. The column of chiffon is captured off-center between two rows of enormous stone columns that recede behind the model. She stands with her head turned up and away from the camera. The bodice of the dress is gathered chiffon that falls around her shoulders, leaving her bare at the neckline save for numerous loops of pearls, some of which circle high on her neck; the rest disappear down the front of her dress, where more gathers of chiffon divide the bodice. The fabric that flows downward is drawn in by a dark, wide belt at the waist before it falls softly to the ground. The model holds her arms behind her.

The pose brings our attention to how much the stone columns resemble the dress. But then the model's left hand catches up and lifts a portion of the full chiffon skirt so that light flows through it. We can glimpse the impression of her left knee as it presses against the soft fabric. The picture offers columns of stone, hard and cold, and a single column of chiffon, soft and light and filled with the warmth of living flesh. It is a beautiful composition and also allows the viewer to see exactly how the dress is cut. The 1940s saw many innovations, including the idea of taking photographs outside of the studio setting in order to capture women outdoors and in motion, and yet the art of composition remained. So did the desire to "Show the Dress."

Agnes de Mille, a dancer and choreographer, looked over the poses struck by fashion models in the mid-1960s and saw no such beauty. "Here we stalk, splay-legged, mouth wide, stiff-armed and stretching; here we stand feet spread, arms akimbo; there we lie waiting, knees up, knees parted, feet in air." She could not deny that the pictures were both "startling and new," but the models looked like prostitutes and drunks. Didn't the models realize what they looked like, asked De Mille. Didn't they mind? Or did they just do what the photographers wanted in order keep their jobs?[79]

Other forms of degradation crept into women's fashion, such as inserting pieces of clear plastic into garments to expose odd patches of female flesh. Betsey Johnson took this idea to the limit in 1966 with a kit made up of a dress that looked like a clear plastic shower-curtain and an assortment of sticky *appliqués* in opaque plastic. Model Lauren Hutton stands in the pages of *Life* magazine with her hands over her crotch until enough cut-outs are stuck to the dress to make her decent. "A girl" can now dress herself "by using the techniques of gift-wrapping," said the article, which was entitled "Dress for Non-Seamstresses: Glue-It-Yourself." But it's not an appreciation for Do-It-Yourself that runs through these pages; instead it's the cheap thrill of offering pictures of strippers to Middle America in the name of fashion.[80]

Women had admired the sophisticated and soigné models of haute couture, but De Mille did not see many women who were willing to follow the lead of the models of the 1960s, who lay sprawled on the floor in fashion shoots. "It seems unlikely that Mama, unless blind drunk, would lie on the floor at a cocktail party," she commented. The photos in sewing magazines were never quite so depraved—dressmakers demand clear images of the finished garment or they will not buy the pattern—but now the models' poses were decidedly awkward. They spread their legs wider than their shoulders, or they jutted their hip out to one side, or, for some strange reason, stood with their toes pointed skyward.

From the 1920s through the 1950s, *Vogue* magazine covers were invariably compositions that followed the art principles, save for a few experiments in surreal sketches. By 1965, they were all close-ups of the models' faces, often weirdly bonneted. A faint survival of the principle of harmony on *Vogue* covers appeared in the colors chosen for the article titles, which sometimes picked up the colors in the photo. What designer Betsey Johnson said about 1960s' fashions could have also been said about its photography: "The newer it was, the weirder—the better."[81]

Direct attacks on rules of dress were sometimes inspired by rebellion for its own sake. As a redheaded child, Mary Quant objected to being told to wear green. She decided that such rules were "invented for lazy people who don't want to think for themselves." Apparently, she never realized that people had figured out that the combination of red hair, which is really orange, and green clothing creates a pleasing harmony of color complements. Maybe there's a reason she flunked her art teacher exams. The fashion rebels' mindless logic could be summed up in her remark: "When you break a rule, you automatically arrive at something different and this is fun." A decade later, Clara Pierre, a self-proclaimed clothing liberationist, denounced the idea of good taste as "an arbitrary matter, a means of presenting the unadventurous consumer with a convenient measurement for choice, and a pat on the back for reassurance."[82]

Alas, if writers wanted to challenge good taste, it would have helped if they had known what it was or been willing to argue with the logic of the Five Art Principles or with the value of artistic repose, rather than denouncing all clothing advice as a plot by the Establishment.

Conventional   Picturesque   Dramatic

Artistic   Boyish   Modern

Fig. 2: The Dress Doctors aimed to advise all women, whatever their style. DULCIE G. DONOVAN, *THE MODE IN DRESS AND HOME*, 1935

For all their talk about breaking rules, the clothing rebels could be far less tolerant than the Dress Doctors were when/it came to questions of style. Pierre sneered at women on Park Avenue who bought trim little suits from Valentino. She foretold a utopian future in which everyone ended up dressed like her: in shapeless, unisex garments of handwoven fabrics made by Moroccan peasants (peasants work so cheap! she wrote).

The Dress Doctors embraced all types of women and styles. They liked the artistic woman who preferred peasant blouses just as much as the conventional woman who favored a tailored suit. "There are fascinating girls who sit at their desks in smart little Chanel frocks, with their hair waved just so, and talk to you in a cool, well-bred competent manner," wrote Hazel Rawson Cades in 1927, and "there are delightful girls you meet on the links, with brown hands, steady eyes, and dependable muscles under their casual tweeds." She liked them both. The Dress Doctors assumed that a variety of women could appear in a variety of beautiful clothes. They didn't care if a woman preferred tweed over silk, or silk over tweed. And they would have found it incredibly boring if we all had to dress exactly alike. Especially in handwoven fabrics made by underpaid Moroccan peasants.[83]

THE ONE TYPE OF WOMAN that the Dress Doctors overlooked almost completely was the African American. They thereby implied, even if they never actually wrote it down, that she could not be beautiful. When the civil rights movement and the women's liberation movement crossed paths, she found herself in an odd situation.

Consider Atlantic City in August 1968, when Robin Morgan and other women's rights activists were picketing the Miss America Pageant at the convention center. A reporter asked: Did they know that the first Miss Black America Pageant, sponsored by the National Association for the Advancement of Colored People, was also being held in Atlantic City, over at the Ritz Carlton Hotel? What did they think of it?

A black feminist from the Bronx named Bonnie Allen seemed torn. "I'm for beauty contests," she began. "But then again maybe I'm against them. I think black people have a right to protest." Robin Morgan would have no such shilly-shallying. "Basically, we're against all beauty contests," she said. "We deplore Miss Black America as much as Miss White America but we understand the black issue involved."[84]

Morgan thought beauty was a burden, but Bonnie Allen and other black women realized that beauty was also a privilege long denied to their race.

Long before the Miss America protest in 1968, black Americans had created their own beauty pageants, but the prejudices of white society took their toll. The black judges favored lighter-skinned contestants and always demanded straightened hair. Some African Americans turned to face bleaches that promised to lighten their skin, though these products often burned their skin. Some pioneering beauty tycoons, such as Madame C. J. Walker, a black woman who became a self-made millionaire, refused to sell such products. Black models could find jobs in the United States after World War II if they were paler skinned, but they often earned lower pay than white models. They found a warmer welcome abroad.[85]

Civil rights workers during the 1960s began to question their society's beauty standards as well as its sense of justice. One of them told *Ebony* magazine in 1966, "We, as black women, must realize there is beauty in what we are." Hair left natural, once a sign of slovenliness among African Americans, became a sign of political and fashionable militancy that divided generations. A young woman who called herself "the only black chick" wearing natural hair in Cincinnati recounted how a fellow bus passenger had wacked her over the head with an umbrella, so incensed was she at her Afro. But the style soon became

Fig. 17: Detachable collars and cuffs made it possible for a woman to take one basic dress and turn it into an entire workweek wardrobe. SIMPLICITY 4582, c. 1947

Fig. 18: The wartime dress in the 1940s, perfect for saving gas rations by doing errands on foot. Done up in white, it made a good uniform for nursing soldiers. DUBARRY 6059, 1945

Fig. 19: American women learned in 1947 that Christian Dior's New Look dictated a tiny waist and a luxurious skirt. This swirling skirt of brown wool was topped with a leopard peplum jacket trimmed in skunk. *LADIES HOME JOURNAL® MAGAZINE*, NOVEMBER 1947

NO. 545

Vogue
COUTURIER DESIGN

EXCLUSIVE DESIGN CREATED BY VOGUE

Fig. 20: Notice that only the bridesmaids of this 1951 wedding party appeared without the lace bolero to cover their bare shoulders. Vogue 545, 1951

Fig. 21: Even the woman headed to the mountains on vacation wore a suit on her way there in 1952. *Vogue Pattern Book*, June-July 1952

Fig. 22: A monochromatic harmony of orange suited the woman of the 1950s. VOGUE
PATTERN BOOK, AUGUST-SEPTEMBER, 1952

Fig. 23: By day, a businesswoman in 1952. By night, oh my! *VOGUE PATTERN BOOK*, JUNE-JULY 1952

Fig. 24: Vogue Patterns put out this housecoat in 1952, perfect for evenings at home, whether alone or entertaining a few close friends. They recommended taffeta, moiré, and shantung as well as the plainer cotton broadcloth and chambray. *VOGUE PATTERNS* CATALOG, SEPTEMBER 1952

Fig. 25: It took an older woman, one who moved at a leisurely pace, to wear dinner dresses with a draped bodice or skirt. *Vogue Pattern Book*, August–September 1952

S-4339–S1

Fig. 26: The sophisticated suit of the 1950s boasted velvet collar and cuffs, two-piece sleeves, and working pockets—all features largely lost by the mid-1960s. *Vogue Patterns* catalog, September 1952

Fig. 27: The sophisticated woman was not twenty and not worried about it in 1955. She wore grayed colors and finer details. *VOGUE PATTERN BOOK*, AUGUST-SEPTEMBER 1955

holiday seasoning...

7557B

7390—

7557A

7490

7462D

7462A, B

Fig. 28: Until the 1960s, women's pants were only for sports and casual at-home wear. *BUTTERICK FASHION BOOK*, FALL-WINTER 1955

Fig. 29: These perky suits on perky young women in the spring of 1958 show how girls longed to dress in ways that anticipated their future status as grown women. *McCall's Pattern Book*, Spring 1958

Fig. 30: Women's suits lost their shape by 1962, which may have made them more comfortable, but they also lost their collars and their pockets, leaving them with only vestigial and misleading pocket flaps. *SIMPLICITY* CATALOG, 1962

Fig. 31: This looks like something worn by a toddler, but this minidress came in sizes to fit a 38-inch bust in 1969. *Butterick Vogue* catalog, June 1969

Fig. 32: By the late 1960s, African American women were included in pictures of the latest fashion. Unfortunately, the latest fashion was a dress shaped like a sack. *Butterick Vogue catalog*, June 1969

so popular that 1968 went down as the year the "natural hair style took over in black America."[86]

The Miss Black America Pageant of 1968 was created in order to challenge the monopoly that white women had upon claims to beauty. The first winner, Saundra Williams, was part of the civil rights movement in body and spirit. Williams wore her hair natural and had led a student protest to integrate a restaurant. (And she made her own gown, sewing on the hundreds of sequins by hand.) "Miss America does not represent us," she explained to the *New York Times*, "because there has never been a black girl in the pageant. With my title, I can show black women that they too are beautiful even though they do have large noses and thick lips. There is a need to keep saying this over and over because for so long none of us believed it. But now we're finally coming around." By 1969, mainstream women's fashion magazines were using black models, and *Life* magazine put Naomi Sims on its cover. By 1970, the phrase "black is beautiful" was on the lips of all black Americans and some whites.[87]

Some dress textbooks did their best to make up for their neglect. By 1974, Mabel D. Erwin of Texas Tech had added a full complexion chart to the fifth edition of her coauthored book. Only white girls smile out of the pages of the 1962 edition to *Guide to Modern Clothing*, authored by two Chicago high-school teachers, and its cover features a blonde in blue. By the 1968 edition, a brunette, an African American, an Asian, and a Pacific Islander with a flower tucked behind her ear appear on the cover, each accompanied by fabric swatches of the most flattering colors. The 1973 edition is so groovy that the group on the cover is colored green and orange, as though race itself has disappeared in favor of bell-bottom pants and minidresses.[88]

But not everyone got the message. Alpha Latzke's last coauthored book from 1968 still only offered the Five Complexions. The first *Color Me Beautiful* book from 1973 lumped most women of color— whether black, Asian, or Indian—into the single seasonal category of "Winter." It advised most Japanese Americans with ivory skin to wear the same colors as most African Americans with dark brown skin. White women came in at least three other varieties. It's hard to say which was worse: completely ignoring African American women, as the early Dress Doctors had, or thinking that most people of color looked alike.[89]

THE FASHION REVOLUTION OF THE 1960s brought some welcome changes to women's clothing. Girls no longer had to shop for girdles as soon as they went through puberty. High-school principals allowed them into school if they were wearing slacks. The country opened up to the fashions and beauties from a continent it had hitherto shunned. This, along with the more casual looks, broke the spell of patrician beauty in the pages of high-end fashion magazines. Fashion trends came from the street, not just the haute couture houses. "It was the week of long yawns," wrote one bored reporter looking over the Spring/Summer haute couture collections of 1968. Even the French couldn't keep up "the old and precious pretense" that Paris dictated what women would wear.[90]

The outcry in 1970 against the "midi"—the A-line skirt that hit at mid-calf—is usually offered as the moment the designers' monopoly on what to wear was broken. When Bonwit Teller told its Fifth Avenue salesclerks that they had better start wearing midis, one twenty-year-old refused, saying, "It's the ugliest thing I've ever seen." A group dubbed FADD—Fight Against Dictating Designers—picketed stores and gathered signatures on petitions. Less excitable types just wore their skirts somewhere around the knee as they had for years.[91]

But the idea that the 1960s had broken the hold of the fashion designer over the marketplace may be underestimating the power of the woman shopper before then. Unless a woman liked a new style well enough to buy it, no garment maker, not even the house of Dior, was going to be able to sell it. Dior himself was amazed that the New

Look was taken up by French women from all walks of life in 1947. They took it up because, as his biographer put it, the New Look fulfilled their longings for "a return to a normal, happy, healthy, and romantic existence." *Les Françaises* could have copied looks from any of the Paris houses, but that year they copied from Dior. The customer has always had the power to make or break a designer.[92]

And the street has always generated fashions that made it up to the top. Paul H. Nystrom, retailing pioneer and Columbia University instructor, complained in 1928 that styles started in the United States and got snapped up by Parisian designers, who then sent them back as the new French models. These included shorter skirts as well as the Egyptian styles that were inspired by news of the discovery of the tomb of King Tut. Not to mention the rage for suntans, which Coco Chanel of Paris is supposed to have started after a yachting vacation, but which really began in the United States under the name "beach complexions."[93]

But for all the good the fashion revolution of the 1960s brought, it also did a great deal of damage. Foolish consumption peaked in the boutiques, whose owners created a constant churn of fashion to satisfy the short attention spans of teenagers. Working-class Londoners were willing to spend half of their weekly paychecks on clothing, because a new dress would become an "antique" after only a month. Novelty, not beauty, was their goal. And novelty for its own sake is a task for Sisyphus; it has no end.[94]

This giddy spending was only possible because of the prosperity of the decade. Jessica Daves attributed the youthful fashion rebellion in the United States to "permissiveness, easy money, lack of early discipline and a consequent need to identify as a group." If she was right, it was their parents' generosity, their childrearing practices, and the usual teenage eagerness to fit in that produced the Youthquake, not some unusual creativity found in people born between 1945 and 1960. Daves also pointed out that when retail giant J. C. Penney sponsored Mary Quant's first visit to forty-four American cities in 1962, it became pretty clear that the notion of nonconformity through youthful fashion was delusional.[95]

Under attack and eager to prove their worth, the home economists became uncomfortable with their own name. "Economics" was too limiting. What about their work in sociology and psychology, not to mention the art principles? "Home" seemed too limiting. What about all those young women who went on to do work outside the home, such as the nutritionists? The home economists renamed their colleges as "Family and Consumer Science" or "Human Ecology." But the changes didn't stop young women from increasingly choosing other majors. The number of college students training to teach home economics dropped by almost half between 1972 and 1979.[96]

Some Dress Doctors lost the courage of their convictions in the face of the many attacks. Teachers of clothing design could now be found speaking not of "principles," but of "guidelines." Some volumes didn't even bother with that. The very title of the 1977 book *Clothing—Your Way* signaled a readiness to pander to teenage delusions of self-importance.

One of the last of the Dress Doctors, Marilyn J. Horn, explained in 1975 how the world of fashion was working: "The bad was beautiful and the beautiful was worthless." But Horn had no intention of giving in. "Let us recognize," she argued, "that we live in a period in which aesthetic values are unfashionable." Not to worry. This was "not the first time in fashion history that this has occurred." The principles were transcendent. And they would survive, even if the Dress Doctors did not.[97]

Aftermath

Tyrannies of Age and Size

THE OWNER OF A LONDON BOUTIQUE in the 1960s once re-called the day her clerks caught a shoplifter. She was "really old," the clerks explained, "quite a middle-aged woman." So how old was this criminal? Twenty-seven.[1]

Actual old people were just as likely as the young to be influenced by what Agnes de Mille called the decade's "worship of perpetual childishness." When asked to describe themselves in the late 1960s, only 38 percent of people over sixty years of age were willing to call themselves old or elderly. Another 60 percent preferred to think of themselves as middle-aged. Which meant they were planning on living to one hundred and twenty.[2]

This loss of perspective was propelled by two shifts in the nature of the American population. The less obvious of the two was that more people were living longer. In the first census of 1790, fewer than 20 percent of Americans made it to the age of seventy. Being old was a remarkable feat, and older people were assumed to be rare fonts of knowledge and wisdom. By 1970, more than 80 percent of Americans were living to seventy. The elderly no longer seemed all that remarkable, or valuable.[3]

The more obvious shift was the arrival of the Baby Boomers and their influence on our culture. During the Youthquake, growing up no longer seemed a worthwhile goal. "Middle age has been abolished by the new fashions," Mary Quant assured us in 1967. "Provided you're prepared to take trouble about it, you just suddenly get old somewhere between 65 and 80, and until then you can stay looking young."[4]

Quant was thirty-two when she made this announcement. She was still being photographed in childish jumpers, and already wearing the hairstyle that became a necessity among designers who profited from the Youthquake: bangs halfway over the eyes. This coiffure covers as much of the face as possible in order to hide the lines that mark the no longer young.

The Baby Boomers and their favorite designers couldn't avoid middle-age any more than anyone else. Their problem was that they turned it into a tragedy, while discarding all the styles that their elders had claimed the privilege of wearing.

Once, clothing styles clearly distinguished between a young woman and a woman past her twenties. Sophisticated styles of dress were reserved for the older woman. The Dress Doctors liked to point out that the Paris fashion houses aimed at dressing the woman over thirty, for only with maturity could a woman wear clothes "with an air of smartness and chic." One magazine pushed the age even later. "The French say that all perfectly dressed women are over forty," explained the *Woman's Home Companion* in 1937. "That is because they know that a smart appearance is the result of study and experience." Butterick's pattern magazine assured its readers, "Often It Is the Older Woman Who is Truly Chic."[5]

The fashion photography of the 1950s reflected this belief. Of course, there were young models, but some models worked into their thirties and forties. You may object to their impossibly polished appearance and their girdled silhouette, but notice their superior attitude, their knowing glance. The older models of the 1950s looked like they could handle the world. By the 1960s, the idea was to look young and fun! Can you imagine asking Twiggy for advice?

Instead of sophisticated style, the Youthquake designers touted disposable and forgettable fads. They made supposedly "unexpected" and "amusing" fabric choices because they knew no better. They used oilcloth tablecloths to make raincoats, and cotton sheets to make dresses. Dressmakers had long ago figured out that these fabrics did not serve the purpose. The one is stiff, clammy, and awkward, the other too thin to endure wear and washings. To dressmakers, these were wasted efforts. To boutique shoppers, who clamored for the next new thing, they were weird and exciting. Andy Warhol said, of the Paraphernalia boutique in New York, "Almost everything in that store would disintegrate within a couple of weeks, so that was really Pop." The book jacket for a volume by an American boutique designer boasted: "She doesn't believe in mistakes—she says, 'Every mistake is a new design.'"[6]

Fads such as paper dresses and sweaters that lit up with batteries could not take the place of good design. Mainbocher, who first made his name as a designer in the 1930s, explained the problem at the showing of his spring collection in 1967: "As amusing as slang fashion is, it is not a complete language. I think women should dress as they talk: a basis of grammar, lightened here and there with a sprinkling of argot." But it was almost all slang by then. In the pursuit of novelty, a rich vocabulary of dress design was lost to later generations.[7]

As the teenage figure became the new cultural ideal, the styles meant for womanly figures were largely forgotten. The Dress Doctors' lessons on the colors that suited the mature woman, and the hats that could flatter an elderly face, were gone. Like every generation, the Boomers passed into adulthood, but they had to do it without the insights of the Dress Doctors on how to flatter a maturing and aging body. The dress revolt would come back to haunt them.

PATTERN COMPANIES HAD BEEN FEATURING "easy-to-make" dresses designed for the woman new to dressmaking for decades. But something different happened in the 1960s: almost everything became easy-to-make. The Dress Doctors had always touted design simplicity, but the very meaning of the word took on new meaning as almost every detail of early dress design was eliminated. By the 1970s, simplicity had slid into stupidity.

Mary Brooks Picken invented the most famous easy-to-make dress for the Woman's Institute in 1923: the One Hour Dress. Women crowded department stores to watch a dressmaker work on a platform underneath a ticking clock. A snowstorm couldn't keep 800 women away from a demonstration in Pittsburgh. When the department-store shows overflowed in San Francisco, 10,000 women turned out to watch a One Hour Dress being made at the Civic Auditorium. Buy a length of fabric from the department store, and the booklet on making the One Hour Dress is yours![8]

Making a dress in an hour was only possible because, in true 1920s style, the One Hour Dress fitted only at the hips. But patterns called "easy-to-make" were a standby in every decade. In 1932, waistlines had come back into fashion, and skirts had already dropped, when Vogue Patterns issued an easy-to-make afternoon dress that came in a rich mulberry with a draped collar in cream and a matching cream toque. The flared sleeves echoed the flare of the skirt. Easy-to-make dresses remained worthy designs through the 1950s. Strip them of their chic accessories—brooch, hat, gloves, matching pumps—and you still find harmonious details and attention to fit.

Absolute beginners usually started with easier projects than dresses. Junior-high girls worked on bloomers and slips in the 1920s, but aprons eventually became the project of choice. For its February 14, 1963, issue, a magazine for students at Catholic schools had Patsy Planner suggest, "WHY NOT MAKE AN APRON AND TRIM IT WITH LACE. . . . JUST LIKE A VALENTINE!" Patsy was very enthusiastic about aprons. Perhaps because aprons can be easily decorated in all kinds of ways because they are perfectly flat.[9]

It wasn't until the 1960s that anyone championed flat items as clothing. At least two groups of people made virtue out of their inability to sew. One was boutique owners. Mary Quant claimed that she loved to sew, but one wonders. She told a reporter in 1967 that she thought that chemicals—nylon, polyester, acrylic—should be shaped directly to the human body in the future instead of being woven into fabrics. "It's ridiculous that fabric should be cut up to make a flat thing to go round a round person."[10]

Some 1970s clothing rebels taught themselves to sew. They lived in communes, dedicated their books to their swamis, and were so mellow that one suspects that they smoked a lot of weed. Otherwise it's hard to understand their cheerful enthusiasm for garments that resembled a pillowcase.

(Inhale). *Hey, man, you don't have to fall for plastic fashions. Just like you build your own house, grow your own food, deliver your own babies, you can make your own clothes with that down-home funkiness. Groovy clothing is easy to make, so don't get uptight. Make something you really dig without spending a lot of bread. Remember that sewing isn't just a chick-thing. Men can make stuff for their old ladies too with no hassle.* (Exhale).

Out of a rectangle of fabric, you made a skirt by inserting elastic at the waist. Tops and dresses were made by laying the fabric flat and tracing the outline of the body, rather like cutting out a dress for a paper doll. The poncho, a rectangle with a hole in the middle, came in several variations. Only a pair of pants required that pesky third dimension called "depth." "The crotch measurement is pretty important if you want the pants to fit good," wrote the authors of *The Illustrated Hassle-Free Make Your Own Clothes Book*. Zippers were optional—too much of a hassle, apparently—so you closed your skirt with a safety pin, an item normally reserved for diapers.[11]

Bad taste and poor design abounded in the 1970s. A crowd of people in fringe and denim smile from the cover of *Clothing Liberation*, which assured its readers that they needed "no special skills" to follow its hundreds of suggestions, only the willingness to take a pair of scissors "to your formerly best dress and just hack it up." To make a piece that could serve as a cape or a skirt—the "cape/skirt"—you needed twenty-five men's ties. Urban legend has it that the wearer got a tie from each man she slept with. The book suggests more straight-forwardly that you visit a thrift store to collect them. You simply sew them together along the edges—all but the last two, and put on two pairs of hooks and eyes. Then you fit it around your waist and it's a skirt. Or throw it over your shoulder and it's a cape. Tip: any garment with a slash or hyphen in its name is probably a bad idea.[12]

But the *pièce de resistance* of *Clothing Liberation* consisted of six dish towels sewn together to create a dress. Don't forget to hack a hole for your head. Now you can walk the streets and everyone will want to wipe their hands on you. It is a waste of good dish towels.

Counterculture clothing went mainstream. The editors of *Mademoiselle* boasted in 1973 that their staff had worn every one of the "Things You Never Thought Of." These included the dish-towel smock, the dish-towel shirt, and the dishrag bag, which made the poor model look like a hobo traveling the rails. Time-Life Books joined the fashion rebel movement with an Art of Sewing series in the mid-1970s, which declared, "Breaking old rules and setting up new, personal ones is what makes boutique fashions fun to produce."[13]

The volume on *Shortcuts to Elegance* announced a new form of elegance. Not the complex colors and patterns of the Victorian age, when a dress would be closely fitted to a corseted body and decorated with a web of ribbons and lace. Not the molded wool suit of the 1950s, cut to the shape of the body and marked by magnificent couture details. The new elegance was young, comfortable, and simple. Very, very simple. "Never sew if you can glue," boutique designer Vivienne Colle advised in 1967.[14]

Like the clothing rebels, the authors of *Shortcuts to Elegance* took a three-dimensional dress pattern and turned it into a paper-doll pattern. Who needs "the trouble" of making and sewing a collar? Or darts, the slices of fabric pinched out to shape fabric around the bust, waist, and hips? Or separate sleeve pattern pieces? Or seams at the waist? Instead, we got a sack, a common and celebrated 1970s design. In contrast, the Dress Doctors had declared early on: "A perfectly plain sack dress is, of course, stupid."[15]

Dresses began to resemble sacks more and more. The T-shirt dress is a prime example. The T-shirt dress actually had a refined beginning. The 1950s saw a swell of innovations with knitting machines. A young *Vogue* fashion editor urged a manufacturer to create a T-shirt dress, which it featured in the April 1954 issue. The slim-fitting navy and white dress, with stripes that ran up and down, had a higher, dark-blue collar knitted into it and a tight matching belt. The model was also fitted out with the usual complement of 1950s accessories: a beige straw hat, a straw bag with leather trim, pretty beige gloves, and a couple of bangles. Inexpensive to make, the T-shirt dress in its original form increased sales for the whole dress industry.[16]

Crew necklines on dresses were rare in earlier decades, yet they had become the default on both sheaths and T-shirt dresses by the late 1960s. The name for the style came from the sweaters worn by college men rowing for their crew teams, and the crewneck is the only neckline illustrated with a drawing of a man in Mary Brooks Picken's 1937 fashion dictionary. Apparently, she could not imagine a woman wanting to wear one—which is hardly surprising, when you consider that Harriet Pepin would describe the crewneck in 1942 as utilitarian, characterless, monotonous, and badly proportioned. It does "nothing for the wearer," she said. *Any* other neckline was preferred.[17]

Over time, the T-shirt dress lost its shape and its accessories. Instead of separate patterns for the collar, sleeves, and pockets, it became a paper-doll pattern of only two pieces—front and back. Confronted with such a dress today, students deem it "a Mom dress" because it is "so frumpy."

The shirtwaist dress also evolved into something unrecognizable. For decades, the shirtwaist dress resembled a carefully detailed blouse on top and a flared or gored skirt. But the shirtdress of the late 1960s was a much simpler affair. The entire dress looked like the plainest of men's shirts, the only accommodation for womanly curves being two darts at the bust and a flare over the hips. Perhaps the shirtdress grew out of impromptu beachwear, when teenage girls in the 1950s threw their dads' old shirts over their bathing suits as cover-ups, but it soon became standard women's wear. This theory would explain the button-down collars on women's shirtdresses, vestiges of their original purpose of helping keep down a collar pushed up by a man's tie.[18]

By opting for the styling of men's shirts, with all their limitations, women's blouses also lost an amazing variety of design possibilities. A man's shirt always opens down the front with buttons, but women's blouses had often opened on the side and closed with snaps on a hidden placket. Side openings made possible all shapes and sizes of collars, yokes, ties, cowls, ruffles, drapes, and bows without having to work around a row of buttons marching through the middle of it all. Such variety made it possible to bring the emphasis up toward the face while countering any figure worries and suiting any mood. Widen a thin neck with a bow, fluff up a small bust with a flounce—the list was endless. Feeling romantic? Try the cape-like Bertha collar. Feeling dramatic? How about a deep cowl-neck? Plus, the side opening

Fig. 1: By moving the opening to a blouse to the side seam, designers freed themselves from the tyranny of a front row of buttons. *Vogue Pattern Book*, August–September 1934

meant that women were not stuck with today's alternative to a row of buttons down *the front* of a blouse: a row of buttons down *the back* of a blouse—a solution only a contortionist can love.

Women's suits degenerated as well. In the 1950s, suits were usually fitted to the body and carefully detailed. Pattern books from the early 1950s reveal how many ways a fitted suit can be cut. Beginning in the early 1960s, suit jackets turned boxy and lost their fit. This might seem a welcome move toward comfort, but the jackets also lost their buttons, collars, cuffs, and welt pockets. Sometimes they gained fake pockets, hardly a step toward convenience. Sleeves on suits had usually been made of two shaped pattern pieces to accommodate the slight natural bend of the arm at rest. Now, they were often reduced to a single pattern piece, which turned them into straight tubes.

But the true abyss of design was reached in the 1970s by a tube of knit fabric ten inches wide by 11 feet long. Hand it to students today and they come up with three possibilities: a belt, a scarf, or a turban. Oh, ye of little imagination. The Time-Life Art of Sewing's

Scarf-Tube can also be a top: Drape it around the back of your neck, crisscross the two ends so that each covers a breast, bring both ends back behind you, then to the front at your waist, and finally tie them at the back of the waist. Today's students laugh. They can see that the odds of the wearer's breasts popping out are very good. The Scarf-Tube was advertised as a good clothing separate for travel. Heaven knows where you were supposed to be headed.

ALL FASHION TRENDS COME TO AN END, and the pendulum did swing back toward greater formality in dress in the mid-1970s. "Kooky has been deemphasized," a J. C. Penney manager said of teenage clothing in 1974. "The look is neater." But the teenage fashion transformation was not always of the consumer's own free will.[19]

When the US Supreme Court allowed three high-school students to wear black armbands to protest the Vietnam War in 1969, school principals were frightened into thinking that all dress codes violated civil rights and loosened their restrictions. But by the late 1980s, violence by street gangs with their own dress codes had prompted principals to demand school uniforms, the most stringent and the easiest-to-enforce of dress codes. Uniforms may not have changed student behavior that much, but impressive claims, such as that of a 36 percent decrease in crime following the adoption of a dress code in a California school district, encouraged other districts to follow. Resistance was futile. When parents objected that uniforms cost more than jeans, or violated their parental rights, or that the Bible was against uniforms, the courts ruled against them. More than half of American schools had a strict dress code by 2005.[20]

Colleges had a slightly different trajectory. Of the hundreds of colleges that still had dress codes in the 1980s, most of their names included the words Baptist, Bible, Bethany, Aquinas, Assumption, or Yeshiva. Religious modesty aside, technical colleges, who want their graduates dressed for immediate employability, round out the list today. Historically black colleges recently reintroduced dress codes after male students adopted the droopy-pants-plus-boxers look. This was a style popularized by former prison convicts, who liked the fact that their prison duds did not actually fit. Unsurprisingly, college faculty were not amused at their students mimicking criminals. An administrator at Savannah State University told a reporter in 2009 that he sometimes would roll down his car window to yell out, "Hey, young man, pull up your pants!" It's a thought that a good many middle-aged Americans share.[21]

And grown women eventually grew tired of dressing like children. Reporting on the latest collections in 1972, Bernadine Morris of the *New York Times* celebrated the fact that there was finally something to wear for women old enough to vote. An interest in more feminine styles produced many a dress made of Qiana, a silky knit created by Dupont. Celebrities and socialites draped themselves in long knit creations by Halston that clung to the body.[22]

A soon-to-be famous V-neck knit dress, wrapped and tied, made up in a printed and washable jersey, debuted in 1970 and appealed to many women as a feminine alternative to pantsuits. Diane Von Fürstenberg sold more than 1.3 million wrap dresses within eight years.[23] People praised the dress for being easy to put on. Since pulling up a zipper is not all that difficult, they may have really been intrigued at how easy the dress was to take off. One pull at the ties and, oh, my! Dress Doctors of earlier eras had pointed out in disapproval that a wrapped dress tends to flap open when you walk, but that may have been part of its appeal by the 1970s. An inherently louche design, the wrapped and tied dress went well with the popular illusion of sex without consequences.

Men had experimented with the colorful peacock look of the 1960s and the hippie look of the 1970s, but by 1974 store buyers had "retreated" to the "relative safety of the classics"—the usual navy blue jacket, gray trousers, and button-down shirt. This made the timing of John Molloy's first *Dress for Success* book in 1975 perfect.

John T. Molloy, a high-school teacher turned "wardrobe engineer," used social surveys and observations to determine which garments could gain a man more respect. While France had Pierre Bourdieu, a sociologist who mapped the intricacies of the class system of his country in all things cultural, from movies to music, we got Molloy, and a quasi-shoving match. He sent testers dressed in various styles to bump into unsuspecting workers at a building's entrance. Would the workers be more likely to give way to the fellow wearing a black trench coat like those preferred by working class Italian-Americans? Or to the fellow dressed in a beige trench coat like the ones worn by middle-manager WASPs who shopped at Brooks Brothers? No and yes.[24]

Feel free to wear the hipper, tighter Pierre Cardin suit "for swinging," Molloy told men, but, for business, it had better be the traditional sack suit.[25] Young men who had never worn a tie found instructions for wearing the classic suit, while middle-aged men who had aimed for hipness by donning leisure suits, a kind of safari jacket made of polyester, were told how silly they looked.

Molloy also turned his eyes toward women who were entering the business world in the 1970s with greater ambitions than the secretarial pool. Fashion offered them nothing, he complained. European designers, who were peddling a haute peasant/hippie look, were trying to keep women barefoot and pregnant. The current fashions made women look sexy or weak, Molloy wrote, and women who aped menswear too closely—fedora, pinstriped trouser-suit, tie—simply frightened people. Neither style of dress was going to get women into the corporate boardroom.[26]

Molloy's answer was a female version of the men's suit, what the Dress Doctors knew as the tailored suit, with a long blazer cut along men's lines and a plain skirt. Only this type "tested" well with businessmen of a certain age, the same men who controlled almost all of corporate America. As the Dress Doctors had decades earlier, Molloy recommended that businesswomen limit their suit colors to shades and tones. But, he warned, if you can only buy one suit, it had better be medium gray. Never mind that gray had never been recommended as a flattering color by the Dress Doctors. The idea was not to look good, but to look acceptable. This book became a best-seller, too. Thousands of women wrote Molloy thanking him for helping them up the career ladder by putting them in suits.

Unfortunately, Molloy's advice meant there would be no concerted attempt to recover the rich tradition of women's suit or blouse designs. One writer called the dress-for-success women "the little gray mice." Their tailored suits, cut like men's blazers, came with man-collared blouses and relied on the sad, floppy tie, a degenerate descendant of the graceful Windsor tie. Any page of patterns from the 1930s, 1940s, or 1950s would have offered a far more beautiful and inventive assortment of suits, blouses, and ties.[27]

By the 1980s, the gray mice had scampered under the first barriers to corporate success, though, so the next group of women going into business "could allow themselves the luxury of dressing differently." Working mostly in black, Donna Karan created big-shouldered suits feminized with draped details, bodysuits, and substantial gold jewelry. Having grown tired of gray, many women shot directly toward suits in bright colors, which they called "jewel tones": cobalt blue, fuchsia, and fire-engine red. With the changeable collar and cuffs forgotten, scarves became a means to add some variety. Teaching ways to wear a scarf took up entire booklets. It's a turban! It's a halter! It's hanging out of your shirt! It's stuck on your shoulder with a pin! Stop![28]

Meanwhile, personal shoppers and image consultants taught women what any junior-high girl would have learned from the Dress Doctors in 1925: plan a wardrobe, value quality over quantity, get a good fit, and adapt an outfit from day to night.[29]

But several things were never recovered, and one was the Dress Doctors' far healthier attitude toward growing old.

"YOUTH IS ASCENDANT" wrote Helen L. Brockman in her 1965 book, *Theory of Fashion Design*. She was training young designers at New York's Fashion Institute of Technology, where she spent nine years before heading off to Kansas State University. Brockman explained that manufacturers now offered Young Styling and Youthful Styling and had largely abandoned Sophisticated Styling.

In 1965, Young Styling meant clothing that followed the latest fads in silhouette, fabric, and color, trimmed with something bright, cut along the simplest of lines. Youthful meant calming down a bit. The colors had to flatter the woman wearing them, which meant tones, shades, or tints. The silhouette had to flatter her, too, so either a modified hourglass or an A-line. The trimmings were more subtle and more expensive.

And what was Sophisticated Styling? Brockman didn't say. In 1965, Sophisticated Style didn't matter anymore. Not in an era when "women shop in misses departments along with their daughters and granddaughters." Future American dress designers were told not to bother learning how to design for the sophisticated woman. Apparently, no woman wanted to appear sophisticated. Not if she could pass for her daughter. Or her granddaughter.[30]

By the 1960s a significant shift had taken place in attitudes toward age and fashion. Harriet T. McJimsey at Iowa State wrote in 1963 that when a woman asks, "Does this make me look older?" she does it "fearfully rather than hopefully." Agnes de Mille, the choreographer and writer who was appalled at how models were posed in the 1960s, commented, "Recognition of age is an insult, assumption of youth the highest flattery . . . as though sexual attraction and enjoyment terminated at forty. Both are untrue, we know."[31]

Of course, women feared growing old before the 1960s, but earlier Dress Doctors, as well as many others, had insisted that women gained something valuable by growing older. The nineteenth century had been particularly hard on unmarried older women, creating the stereotype of the crabby spinster, but the New Woman who appeared at the very end of the nineteenth century was educated, dynamic, civic-minded, and very often older. Menopause ended years of relentless and dangerous childbearing, freeing women to turn their minds to other concerns. The early twentieth century saw a dispute between doctors who thought menopause made women generally crazy, or crazy to have sex with much younger men, or crazy to have sex with anything that moved; and doctors who thought older women became more beautiful. Wrote one doctor in the latter camp: "In many women, there is for long after the change of life an autumnal majesty so blended with amiability that it fascinates all who approach within its magic circle." Autumnal majesty: not a bad goal. Florence Hull Winterburn chimed in on the style that suited each age: "Simplicity for early youth, added luxury for the girl or woman in the twenties, splendor for maturity, and suitability with stately magnificence for age."[32]

But the 1920s, with its tubular silhouette, rendered the curves of grown women unfashionable. Even when dresses gained waists again in the 1930s, older women were urged to stay young through diet, exercise, and girdles. In fact, a ragged girdle was the center of the Dorée Smedley story, the most famous midlife makeover by the fashion editors at *Good Housekeeping* in 1939. They described her as "a drab, middle-aged woman, carelessly dressed, apathetic about her appearance." A housewife and magazine writer from Bronxville, New York, Smedley had given up on her looks, in part because it seemed wicked to spend money on vanities like a new girdle during the Great Depression.[33]

Smedley's "Before" photographs are hideous. Like every "Before" picture ever taken, they capture an expressionless face and a pose like that of a cow standing in a field. In the best pictures, she looks drab and dumpy. In the worst, she looks like a guy in drag. Even in her girdle, she has rolls around her middle. Her wrinkled brown tweed suit manages to be both baggy and too tight. "Exactly the kind of suit," remembered one retailer, that "a matron would wear until it dropped off her." She wore a tailored brown hat that "you could slam on your head as you rushed out the door" for a day of shopping in the city, plus a plain blouse and brown shoes, gloves, and bag—all battered. Smedley admitted that her "Before" pictures were a fair likeness of her "tubby figure." When she showed them to her dentist, he remarked that they weren't that bad: "I've seen you plenty of times when you looked a lot worse." *Good Housekeeping*'s photographer said Mrs. Smedley had the shoulders of a Fifth Avenue cop and that he didn't think he could ever take a good picture of her, no matter what they did to her.[34]

But Smedley's "After" pictures are charming. She looks prettier, shapelier, and "Ten years younger!" The photographer did his magic, after all, and she is posed with more grace, makeup, and a hint of a smile. But the real accomplishment was an entirely new wardrobe, including girdles and a new hairdo. In the "Before" shots, her hair is parted down the middle and drawn back into an ugly knot; in the "After" pictures, it is parted on the side, fluffed up, and curled with a permanent. Readers complained that her "Before" pictures were faked, so *Good Housekeeping* sent Smedley on the road to department stores from New York to Seattle, where she appeared in her "Before" and "After" clothes, wowing the middle-aged women who filled the audiences to see her and a fashion show staged just for them. When she came out dressed like her "After" photographs, she held aloft her ten-year-old girdle. This sad, saggy item always made her audience laugh.[35]

If giving up, as Dorée Smedley had done, was one way that women coped with the onset of middle age, the other was "emotional panic," according to the Dress Doctors. Bernice Chambers may have written an entire guide on how women should dress at different ages, but when it came to filling in her date of birth on her personnel file at New York University, she answered, "No, thank you." That was when she was in her early forties; ten years later, she wrote, then scratched out: "I object to having my age a subject of office gossip."[36]

Yet the Dress Doctors, on the whole, were generally impatient with the middle-aged woman who refused to acknowledge her age. Mary Brooks Picken asked her readers over forty to "take a vow" to never wear anything "appropriate for the girl of eighteen." Bad hair dye, unlikely beauty treatments, teenage clothing, and other desperate efforts were once understandable, wrote the Kansas State Dress Doctors. Once, a "woman's worth" was wrapped up almost solely in "her appeal to the opposite sex" and her ability to bear children, so the "span of joyous living was for her indeed short." But in 1935, civic causes of all kinds clamored for attention, and interesting, paid work was open to women in their fifties and beyond.[37]

Theirs may have been an overly rosy view of the employment possibilities for older women, but there were cases of just that. *Good Housekeeping* sent Smedley on a coast-to-coast tour, appearing at department stores before more than 70,000 women. Her talks proved so popular that she wrote *You're Only Young Twice.* Once established as an author, she wrote several guides to business careers for women. Smedley enjoyed telling tales of second careers: her forty-five-year-old friend who joined a drama club, got discovered by a theater agent, and ended up on Broadway; a woman who took singing lessons at forty and became so good that she was a featured soloist at church and civic events.[38]

In addition to second careers, there was the comforting thought that the Dress Doctors often expressed: something valuable is gained with age. The young face is fresh and unsophisticated, wrote Anne Rittenhouse, whose fashion columns appeared in the *New York Tribune* and the *Atlanta Constitution* in the teens and twenties, while the mature face expresses strength and thoughtfulness as well as the marks of worries.[39]

Perhaps because the Dress Doctors taught the young, they knew both their virtues and their weaknesses. It's hard to idealize youth as perfect when you watch young students caper all over campus shrieking at each other. You can admire their enthusiasm while recognizing their goofiness. Charla Krupp stumbled upon this truth in her 2008 book on dressing to look young. She noted that in some professions—high corporate, high finance, and universities—women can let their hair go gray without damaging their careers.[40]

Gray hair and old age do not cast doubt on women's competence at universities because so much time is required to master their fields of study. Women scholars hope to become what the French call an *éminence grise*—literally, a gray eminence—an elder of wisdom and distinction. But you can't become an *éminence* unless you are willing to let your hair go *grise*. Indeed, Mary Brooks Picken, Grace Margaret Morton, Alpha Latzke, and other Dress Doctors left lovely images of themselves taken when they had achieved the status of *éminences grise*s.

The Dress Doctors asked their readers to embrace age. "If her mind has kept pace with the years and is now a storehouse of inspiring thought," wrote Margaret Story of the middle-aged woman, "she is at the most interesting time of her life."[41]

Surely there are worse things than becoming one of the old women whom Laurene Hempstead, a retail specialist at New York University, described in 1936: "Such women, who have had the grace and wisdom to acknowledge, and thus minimize, the ravages of time and to accent their remaining points of beauty." Grace and wisdom are exactly what a woman should gain with time and experience.[42]

MILDRED GRAVES RYAN told junior-high girls in 1944 that they "may be going through a stage where you want to look older."[43] In eras past, girls put their hair up as soon as they could, because they knew that pigtails and braids marked them as kids. They were eager to be seen as women. But girls, said the Dress Doctors, should wear styles that mirror their blooming youth, their boundless energy, and the simplicity of their minds and characters.

Mary Brooks Picken pointed out in 1923 that these were the reasons why a dress for high-school graduation did not have to be fancy. "Youth, combined with health and budding intelligence, is in itself such a wonderful and glorious spectacle," she wrote, "that a young girl really does not require elaborate clothes to attract and please." Or, to quote the more succinct Florence Hull Winterburn: "The more nature does the less has art to do." Clothing sized for juniors followed the fashion trends of adult women during the first half of the twentieth century, but junior clothes were simpler in cut and marked by perky colors and playful details.[44]

A dress for a high-school girl was often so simple in cut that it resembled what dressmakers call the "sloper," the basic flat pattern pieces—bodice, skirt, and sleeves—from which almost every dress design grows. Darts at the bust and the flare of a skirt were about all that acknowledged the femininity of the junior's figure, a figure much less curvy than that of the woman who wore misses' sizes.

The young woman can wear bright colors to match her vivid complexion and her energy, advised the Dress Doctors. Mildred Graves Ryan barred black as too sober a color even for a college student of twenty. And styles have to suit the natural, energetic movement of the young woman's body. The athletic high-school girl especially should never have her swinging stride hampered by a tight skirt. Anything that makes a girl fuss with her clothing—retying, retucking, readjusting—annoys her no end and destroys "the simple naturalness of her manner." Skirts with trains, aprons, or "flying, dangling parts" are no match for a young woman on the move. The skirt will "fly out awkwardly with her brisk, vigorous movements." Her clothes must stand up to her "vigorous, unthinking activity." The best choices for the energetic young woman "who darts here and there in awkward fashion" are loose blouses and short, flared skirts. The floppy hat with a big brim is for the young woman, too, because it looks careless and matches "the irresponsibility of youth." Unthinking, awkward, irresponsible—the Dress Doctors recognized the drawbacks of youth even as they appreciated its bloom.[45]

At the same time, because young women's clothing followed the trends found in women's clothing, their clothing seemed to anticipate their growing older. In the same issue where *Good Housekeeping* urged middle-aged women to try the secrets revealed by Mrs. Smedley's make-over, the magazine offered more than a dozen suits for young women, all with fashionable just-below-the-knee flared skirts accessorized with hats, gloves, and bags. They were posed with more jauntiness than their middle-aged counterparts, but they looked like women in the making. Pattern books from the 1950s put juniors in boxy plaid coats perfect for fall on a Big Ten campus, and also in trim suits that would easily see them into an office job. By rejecting both women's clothing and womanhood, the 1960s Youthquake jettisoned this practice of junior wear anticipating women's wear. Suits are not even a category in juniors' sizes today at some of the largest clothing retailers.[46]

The Dress Doctors barred young women from wearing sophisti-cated designs in part because such styles cling to the body. Women's clothes should mirror their greater knowledge of the world, the in-creased sophistication of their minds, and—although the Dress Doc-tors did not actually mention it—their sexual experience. Sex was one of the privileges of age. Sophisticated dressing was for the woman who was old enough and responsible enough to earn or handle money, to have sex, and to feed the children and run the household in which they all lived.

The Dress Doctors insisted on modest clothing for girls, although they noticed that definitions of modesty evolved over time. In 1924, fashion reporter Anne Rittenhouse called for dress codes for high-school girls that would be as strict as the tests they took for English class. "Paint," she wrote—referring to what we call makeup—"should be abolished with slang, ridiculous coiffures should be suppressed along with the split infinitive, willfully transparent clothes should be barred as well as incorrect spelling." Rittenhouse wanted jewelry utterly forbidden to schoolgirls, save for a single semiprecious stone strung on a silk neck-cord.[47]

Evening posed a special problem. High-school girls have no business wearing "the extreme, formal evening dress with the low-cut neckline," explained the principal of Beverly Hills High School in 1935. Leona Hope at the University of Illinois said in 1919 that mothers need to draw the line for daughters who do not appreciate that girlhood is a "wonderful and beautiful" stage in their lives, a stage that should not be shortened "prematurely." Mothers of today, you are not the first to yank your daughters back into the house to change clothes.[48]

In the midst of World War I, Dr. Jeannette Throckmorton wrote an article that revealed how Americans thought fashions affected morality and health. She was worried about the spread of venereal disease, which had wiped whole battalions of American soldiers off the duty lists, and the way the infections were being carried back home from the war. (The prudish President Woodrow Wilson refused to have condoms issued, so the more practical commanders issued them on their own.) Throckmorton thought that teenage fashions in the summer of 1917—short skirts, "shoes designed to attract the eye," and sheer, low-cut blouses—encouraged the spread of disease by arousing the passions of men. Girls did not understand the "instincts and impulses" that drove them to long for male attention, explained the doctor. They needed parents who realized that "the mating instinct is strong" at this age and offered their children "wise guidance and sympathetic help."[49]

A guide for judging 4-H clothing-club contests put out in 1929 by home economists from Oklahoma Agricultural and Mechanical College (now Oklahoma State University) made it clear that judges would mark down any dress worn so tight that it called "attention to the figure." They had a category called Ethics of the Costume, which broke down into 5 points for Modesty and 5 points for Social Influence.[50]

A story told by Jessie E. Gibson in 1927, then dean of girls at a Spokane high school, illustrates what they meant by Social Influence. (Gibson was recommended for her next job, as dean of women at Pomona College, because of her religiosity, her charm, *and* her good taste in dress.) It seems that a famous artist and his young daughter moved to a small town for a year's stay. The local high-school girls were wearing elaborate dresses to school, dresses more suitable for parties than for running to English class, and they were using quantities of rouge, lipstick, and eyebrow pencil. But this new girl dressed simply. She wore no makeup. There she was, well traveled, well educated, well mannered, and nice to everyone. She never spoke a word of criticism about the clothing or makeup of the other girls, yet her lovely example prompted them to follow her lead. Soon, party dresses were reserved for parties, and eyebrow pencil was gone. It seems that dressing in good taste is contagious. "Just walking through the halls at school, or passing people on the street," Dean Gibson reminded her readers, "we have a lasting effect through our influence."

It could be a bad influence, though, if a girl dressed "immodestly." Dean Gibson had studied modern languages in college, not home economics, yet she defined immodesty in dress just as the Dress Doctors did: "If her dress attracts attention to some part of her body instead of helping to make a harmonious whole." If a girl dressed this way, Dean Gibson warned, "then she is hindering the world's progress." Not merely her own progress, but the *world's progress*—could be forwarded or hindered by what she wore. It was a tremendous burden to put on a teenage girl, even if it also seemed to promise her tremendous power.[51]

The Dress Doctors presumed that the junior-high and high-school girls they taught were virgins, although they used words such as "innocent" and "wholesome" instead. And the Dress Doctors did what they could to make sure they stayed that way. Throckmorton, Gibson, and the clothing-club leaders worried that young women would lose their moral compass, their virginity, and their health in an era when venereal disease had no cure and the penalties for an out-of-wedlock birth were heavy.

Across history, almost every effort to stifle young women's sexual activities has been part of a double standard that let young men off the hook for doing the exact same thing. So it seems particularly hard that the fashions of the 1920s launched what one historian has called an unparalleled "unveiling" of woman's body—bare arms, bare legs, bare neck. In order to make sure this unveiled body was ready for public display, women had to resort to shaving, painting, and so on. At the same time, the 1920s witnessed the first sexual revolution, which was made all the easier by the shift that took place from courting on the front porch of a girl's house to petting in the boy's automobile, a move that may have undercut a girl's control over her fate. Although skirts would drop in the 1930s, fashion designers have thought up new ways every decade to render women much more naked, while men's clothing, outside of beachwear, rarely uncovers more than their elbows. The Dress Doctors tried to act as a brake on this ever-greater unveiling of young women's bodies.[52]

Only after a girl had gotten through that tricky stage of life called adolescence, and through the young womanhood of her twenties, was she allowed to wear sophisticated styles according to the Dress Doctors. By the age of thirty, most women were married, held jobs, or both. And they were presumed able to handle the eroticism embodied in the draped designs that made for the most sophisticated styles.

Such designs were often many steps away from the basic sloper used to make dresses for the young woman. Sophisticated styles like this were usually designed in one of two ways: either by cutting and slashing the flat pattern pieces through clever manipulation, or by draping fabric directly on the body through a process of experimentation.

Either method will create the graceful folds of a draped dress. Such creations take more thought, more skill, and more time on the part of the designer. The kinds of fabric that drape well are not the crisp wash-and-wear cottons of the schoolgirl, but the softer, more expensive, and fragile crepes of wool and silk. Draped dresses look especially well on women who are old enough to have filled out their curves. For all these reasons, a draped dress is to be worn by a woman of a certain age and means.

Draping puts more fabric into a dress while at the same time drawing attention to how that fabric caresses the curves of a woman's body. It offers a more subtle eroticism than our usual bare fashions. There are still draped designs around, but they tend to favor a tight fit over the graceful fluidity prized by the Dress Doctors.

Elizabeth Hawes thought a designer should never "expose or make prominent all the lines of the female figure in any dress." Only by balancing revealment with concealment, as she put it, can you design a dress that will have sex appeal. Draped design covers a lot more flesh, but implies the promise of undress. A dressmaker once remarked to me that draped designs suggest that you were caught someplace naked and had to make a dress out of a bed sheet. No matter how well made the dress is, you can't shake the impression that the whole thing may slide off and land at your feet. Which is part of its appeal, of course. And why the Dress Doctors reserved the draped design for a woman old enough to handle the attention it would attract.[53]

More complicated designs, draped and otherwise, require their wearer to move in a certain way. Young people think old people slow down. We do, but we also calm down. The mature woman with poise, experience, and self-confidence can handle garments that are too complicated for the giddy young woman. "Intricate and regal styles" require what Laurene Hempstead called "a studied carriage." Only the woman who moves "with rhythmic, graceful movements, can wear floating drapes and intricate details," she explained in 1931. Loose panels, aprons, and the like add a "graceful flutter" so long as a woman walks with a leisurely gait. Indeed, the *directrice* of the salons at Nina Ricci, Madame Genviève Antoine Dariaux, explained in 1964 that it was hard for a young fashion model to show off a sophisticated ensemble to advantage. Only an older woman knew how to move in it.[54]

Yet reaching thirty may not qualify a woman to wear more complicated styles. It depends entirely on her temperament. "The woman who is forceful and energetic, with even quick motions, needs apparel that will express her force and vigor without interfering with her freedom of movement," wrote Hempstead. Such women require simple, tailored clothing. Their energy no longer expresses itself in the frenetic energy of youth, but they need their clothes to stay out of their way.[55]

Fig. 2: Only the woman over thirty could handle both the draped dress and the attention it would attract, according to the Dress Doctors. Lanvin-Castillo designed this sleeveless dress and bolero jacket offered by Vogue Patterns in 1957. The jacket and bodice of the dress were raspberry chiffon, while the skirt layered raspberry chiffon over violet chiffon. *VOGUE PATTERN BOOK*, MARCH–APRIL 1957

Fortunately, the fabrics required for draped designs are also the most flattering as a woman reaches the third stage: middle age. As the figure and skin of the face softens, so should the lines of clothing and the textures of the fabrics, according to the Dress Doctors. Crisp and tightly woven fabrics make older skin look ragged by comparison, while fabrics such as crepes, which have a crinkle to their threads, or soft wool jersey or velour, offer a texture similar to skin that is past the first bloom of youth. This is why the hard, brilliant surface of nylon spandex bathing suits can be particularly trying, and why suits in softer textures, with gathers, are designed for older women.[56]

The most flattering colors change, too. More complex colors express the more complex character of the woman who has lived

decades. They also flatter skin that is losing its natural color. Mildred
Graves Ryan, writing with Velma Phillips, the dean of home economics at Washington State, noted, "Aging usually produces a mellowing
of character." With toned-down colors, "the costume does not seem
more dominant than the person." A young woman who wore red
or pink should turn to russet-wine in maturity; instead of the light
blue she wore in her twenties, she should opt for blue-green or blue-
violet in her forties. The Dress Doctors explained that darker colors
also reflect the more restrained nature of the older woman. Only if a
woman retains "a vivacious manner and definite physical beauty" can
she continue to wear striking lines in dress and the vivid colors she
wore in youth.[57]

Grace Margaret Morton described an afternoon ensemble for
a matron as "a scheme to express stateliness, refinement, and feminine grace." The dress and matching coat were in dark wedgewood
(a grayed blue-purple), topped by a hat of purplish-red trimmed in
brighter hues of red and blue-purple. The virtues of this ensemble are
threefold, according to Morton: the brighter colors on the hat bring
attention to the face; the subdued colors "express the dignity and maturity of the wearer"; and the colors also cause "the wearer's full figure
to recede." Morton herself was remembered by her colleagues this
way: "She possessed the rare combination of dignity and overflowing
enthusiasm, and kindled something of her own fire in others."[58]

And with grace, dignity, and distinction as her goal, the mature
woman is no longer interested in faddish costume jewelry. She not
only values good jewelry, as Laurene Hempstead noted, but may have
the means to buy it.[59]

WHEN MORTON WAS WRITING IN THE 1940s, a hat was a crucial part
of an ensemble. But the hat was already on the wane by the 1950s.
Suburban American women, freed from "city living" and its more
formal standards of dress, began to go hatless in the local supermarket

or at the PTA meeting. But the trend was international. A French fashion writer sniffed in 1954 that many young women "go out bare-headed in Paris as in the country; and all they do in bad weather is to tie a handkerchief under their chins, like so many Russian peasant women."[60]

New hairdos—the beehive, the bouffant, the haystack—were at war with hats. Hair-spray sales increased by 280 percent between 1954 and 1957. As Geneviève Antoine Dariaux pointed out, "a hairdo that has been whipped to a froth like a meringue and carefully arranged in a hollow pyramid will fall to pieces at the slightest contact." A woman didn't dare put a hat on it. A textbook by Mabel D. Erwin of Texas Tech offers photos of a Texas beauty queen from the era, Miss Wool of 1967, whose hair was teased so high that she seemed to have a second head on top of the first. The General Federation of Women's Clubs had to admit in 1956 that "the hat is fighting a losing battle in this country," and that "a great many smart and impeccably dressed women (particularly young ones) don't own a hat of any kind, except the one they wear to church." Young women increasingly thought of hats as something only worn for special occasions. Between 1947 and 1967, more than half of America's hat makers went out of business.[61]

Some designers did put out groovy space-helmet hats in the 1960s, but they were photographed more than they were worn. Even Jacqueline Kennedy's pageboy, teased to within an inch of its life, was anti-hat. True, Jackie often wore a pillbox, but it clung desperately to the back of her head. Eventually, it fell off. When young women who loved inflated hair gave up on hats in the 1960s, older women were left wearing them, so hats became hopelessly old-fashioned. John P. John, who created hats for Greta Garbo and Vivien Leigh, retired in 1970 and announced, "Women are no longer chic. They have 'sold out' to hairdressers."[62]

It was hard to go back to hats because they were now offered in only one size. The bouffant hairdo meant a hat did not fit so much

as perched, and manufacturers opted to only produce 22-inch hats.[63]
"One-size-fits-all" hats put women off by either squeezing or sloshing
around. So the only women in America still in hats were those who
belonged to religious groups that worried about the erotic appeal of
women's hair, old women who felt the need to cut loose after years
of good behavior, and actresses/models whose job it was to make a
spectacle of themselves. (There was, and still is, the Kentucky Derby,
but that only happens once a year.)

American women were left largely hatless after the 1960s. As a
result, we have lost all the charms that the right hat can lend us as we
age. The middle-aged woman's hat was often more complicated and
thus more fragile than those of young women who raced around in
berets, kerchiefs, and casual felts. Her calmer movements also meant
that she was only likely to lose her hat in a brisk wind. Jane Loewen
taught millinery at the University of Chicago and designed dozens of
dressmaker's hat patterns that were sold through newspapers during
the 1920s. She advised the matron who opted for a turban to choose
one with a rolled or mushroom brim. A hard line across the forehead
was too severe for a woman over thirty.[64]

But what good a hat could do! "Hats that defy age are the mas-
terpieces of the milliner's art," wrote Bernice G. Chambers, who, you
may remember, had a little bit of a spasm about reaching her forties.
"Seemingly simple, they are really skillfully and subtly designed, and
just as subtley they give the wearer a psychological lift—a lilt that is
unmistakable."[65]

THE ONE COLOR that the Dress Doctors advised older women not
to wear was black, now the default color for practically any women's
clothing sold in America. Sometime in the 1980s, a color plague broke
out in New York City. Rumor has it that some hip advertising agency
ordered its staff to wear only black, and soon all the hip people caught
the germ, and then all the not-so-hip people caught it, too. Manu-

facturers helped to spread the epidemic. The only place now where black is not the rule is in the sunny South, where women cannot bear to put on a color that will only make them feel warmer on a hot day.[66]

There was too much black worn before the 1980s, too. The authors of the best-selling dress book of 1938 declared themselves sick of black dresses crowding out all the brilliant colors that women could only wear at night. "Men's fashions have cut the pageantry of the ballroom in half," they wrote. "It seems stupid for women to dispense with the rest of it." A woman looking around a New York City cocktail party in 1956 exclaimed how refreshing it was to spot a red dress in a sea of boring black.[67] The Little Black Dress had already become the Little Boring Dress by the 1950s. These writers were all talking about evening events—but the current plague of black has struck during the daytime, too.

Black's popularity is propelled by the belief that anything black looks smaller than it would in another color. Fear of Fat drives the rage. The Dress Doctors knew that black may make a woman look thinner in silhouette, but they warned that it also makes her look heavier in weight. Imagine a large, pale, shimmering yellow vase. It seems to almost float. Now, imagine the same vase in black, and it will sink solidly to the ground. So, unless a woman is standing against a black background (not exactly a common wall color in most offices), she looks particularly weighty wearing black. Gives one pause, doesn't it?

The Dress Doctors were of one mind when it came to black on older women: Don't. Through the decades, they have the same warnings:

> *Black is so somber and unbecoming at the neck that even widows wear a band of white at the throat.*
>
> —Mary L. McIntyre, *The Complete Dressmaker* (1912)

It is a mistake to confine the older woman to
black as a color suitable for her years.
—Elizabeth Burris-Meyer, *Color and Design in the Decorative Arts* (1935)

The French have a saying that no woman
over thirty should wear black.
    —Kay Hardy, *Costume Design* (1948)

WORN NEAR THE FACE, black deepens the appearance of shadows and lines, the Dress Doctors warned. In fact, the practice of wearing black may be one factor encouraging all the pulling, filling, and freezing of the faces of middle-aged actresses today. The Dress Doctors advised any woman who persisted in wearing black day dresses to at least throw strings of pearls around her neck to take advantage of the soft light they would reflect. Most argued that a pale collar could save a black dress, but Dorée Smedley shook her head: they are "the last straw," she said, "for those of us who are sallow or wrinkled." Smedley's "Before" wardrobe was made up of three black day dresses and a black evening dress. After her transformation, she wore dark greens, brown, navy, or wine. Elizabeth Burris-Meyer, a color expert who taught costume design at New York University and wrote books analyzing historical and contemporary color schemes, agreed with Smedley's choices, writing: "Dark blues, dark red, warm browns, and dark blue-greens would be far more becoming in the majority of cases."[68]

Some of you may be thinking, But I look wonderful in my black evening dresses. You may actually look wonderful *despite* the blackness of your evening dresses. Because it is dark out, the dress fades into the background, as does its apparent weight. If your gown is cut low, the color reflecting in your face is really the paler or warmer color of the skin of your neck and shoulders. "Décolleté softens unbecoming colors," explained a Dress Doctor in 1936, because it moves them away from the face. Black may also do you less harm in the evening when you wear jewelry that brings lighter hues closer to your face, and more makeup, which counteracts the shadows thrown by black. If you look wonderful in black, it's because black isn't able to mar your appearance, not because it's doing your face any favors.[69]

Because black is so ubiquitous today, we've lost it as the color for mourning wear, which is a pity. Victorian women turned to black clothing to signal that they had lost a loved one. Queen Victoria wore only black after the death of her beloved Prince Albert. Wearing black was a quiet way of telling people to be careful, because someone was in pain.[70]

The mourning tradition explains why black is missing from a list of colors for evening wear drawn up by Mary Brooks Picken in 1924. She was living in the decade after World War I, when Europe destroyed so many of its young men that millions of wives, sweethearts, mothers, and sisters were left wearing black to mourn them. If a woman did not have to wear black in 1924, she probably did not want to. It was such a depressing reminder of the horror of war. Picken offered color harmonies to go with evening dresses of white, blue, yellow, pink, and green.

Try the Dress Doctors' prescription. If going cold turkey on the color black is too hard, give it up for a week. Find a smoky blue that plays off your eyes, a rich burgundy that throws warmth into your face, a golden brown just a shade darker or lighter than your hair. See if you don't feel better.

AND WHAT OF THE OLD WOMAN? Again, colors and textures and lines should be softer. Laurene Hempstead wrote of a charming seventy-year-old who was usually mistaken for a fifty-year-old. Part of her secret was her palette. She always wore soft rose—the lighter shades for her dresses, and the slightly darker *bois de rose*, rosewood, for her coats and hats. Perhaps our charming septuagenarian had read Mary Brooks Picken's first book, which explained that vivid colors make old skin look pale and dull in comparison. Colors becoming to a woman in her youth need to be grayed from:

> Red to soft rose or henna
> Blue to steel-blue
> Yellow to beige
> Orange to citron
> Golden brown to taupe
> Green to olive[71]

Hats, once again, had amazing powers. After discussing clothing for the old woman, Bernice Chambers added, "When we add the right hat to the list, we have the picture of a woman with the wisdom and patience of age and the charm of youth."[72] Stiff sailor hats, so popular early in the twentieth century, were not for older women. "Much too harsh," explained the Woman's Institute magazine. "Some irregularity of brimline is essential for her." Older faces need shading and background, advised Laurene Hempstead, so their hats should be worn forward over the forehead with a good-sized brim. But not a brim that droops at the sides. A drooping brim will emphasize lines around the mouth by repeating them. Chambers liked a swept-up brim, too.

As in a dress, subdued color combinations and more complex textures are best for the older woman's hats. Fabrics such as brocade and velvet or soft fur are best, trimmed with veils, flowers, feathers, jewels, or embroidery. When nothing suitable was available that season—no grayed colors or soft lines—older women were likely to make mistakes, said one fashion writer, and "buy the absurd headwear intended for their daughters and granddaughters."[73]

Fabrics for an older woman's dresses should have textures "as soft as smoke," wrote a pair of Dress Doctors. For day dresses, this means heavier crepes, silk chiffon, georgette, or, for fancier daytime occasions, crepe de chine. And for evening, avoid fabrics with shiny surfaces. "To the older woman . . . lustrous fabrics would be unkind," wrote two others. Bright fabrics throw shadows on aging skin, while softer, duller surfaces do not. Annette J. Warner of Cornell University noted how becoming lace was to "elderly ladies," not unlike "moss to venerable trees or haze to the autumn landscape."[74]

Laurene Hempstead recommended furs, especially longer, softer ones at the neck—a great design argument for a little self-indulgence—or scarves and scarf-collars made out of soft fabrics that drape well. Almost any dress could be good looking on an older woman, said Hempstead, if she adds the right scarf, which offers "a splendid opportunity to place softening, becoming colors near the face." Long before Nora Ephron felt bad about her neck, the Dress Doctors advised what to do.[75]

Especially for the woman who thins out with age, the Dress Doctors had more advice: "The best disguise to wrinkles, hollows and bones are necklaces," according to Anne Rittenhouse. Three or more strands of pearls or some other softly colored jewel would be best. But chubby women had better try something else: tall, standing collars or wing collars, high at the back and sides, open narrowly in the front, to cover up the ravages of time. When low-cut or sleeveless gowns become too bare to be flattering, the Dress Doctors said, add jackets of velvet on cool nights or of double chiffon on warm ones.[76]

In short, the Dress Doctors advised covering up what can no longer be flattered. Edna Woolman Chase, former editor in chief at *Vogue*, put it bluntly: "Aging flesh is not appealing. . . . Too much revelation of a figure that is too thin, too fat, or too old can be lamentable." Because contemporary fashion for women is far barer than anything offered to men, we aren't allowed to age as gracefully. The world isn't longing for most sixty-year-old men to show off their chests or legs either, but fashion doesn't ask them to.[77]

Chase took her own advice. For her eightieth birthday portrait in 1957, she wore a long-sleeved, dark dress with a winged collar; the collar is close at the sides and open at the front, showing no less than five strands of pearls and jewels around her throat. A lavish silk bow trimmed with a sparkling jeweled brooch covers the lower edge of the V-neckline. She looks positively regal.[78]

In 1948, when Chase was seventy-one, *Vogue* first introduced the fictional Mrs. Exeter to demonstrate how to age with grace and style. "Approaching sixty," the magazine recounted, "she doesn't look a day younger, a fact which she accepts with perfect good-humour and reasonableness." People say that she looks young, but the article took pains to correct them. "She isn't young-looking. She is *good*-looking." The two are not the same.[79]

Vogue did use what one historian criticized as "fetchingly slim" illustrations of Mrs. Exeter, but her first fashion problem was real enough: how to avoid bulging on the beach with her thirty-three-inch waist, a problem solved with a suit made of a firm sharkskin (remember, bathing suits had zippers back then). Mrs. Exeter appeared in Vogue Patterns a few years later, where "her friends envy her silver hair when she plays it up with soft blue." Her patterns came in bust sizes up to 44 inches.[80]

The wide hips and softer shoulders of the New Look had debuted only a year earlier and were perfect for an older woman, even if the wasp waist required a girdle to achieve. Most importantly, the New Look—unlike the wartime look of upright, energetic, big-shouldered, businesslike competence—exuded the sophistication, poise, and grace only possessed by older women.

After appearing hundreds of times in *Vogue* in the 1950s, Mrs. Exeter spoke her last words of advice in 1962. Apparently, the miniskirt killed her off. She was resurrected in 2001, but, like most of the undead, she had lost some of her original personality.[81]

Western society has always had a mixed view of older women. They have been queens and duchesses, powerful and wise, and they have been witches and hags, ugly and vile. But the 1960s introduced a new difficulty by forgetting that age brings its rewards and by discarding the styles that best suited the older woman. Helen L. Brockman may have stopped explaining Sophisticated Style to her students in the 1960s, but she would live to be one hundred, long enough to take up the most venerable of draped designs: the Indian sari.[82]

Our culture is harder on older women than it is on older men. Formal evening wear for men covers the entire body, and a good tailor can even hide a paunch. Formal evening wear for women has brought the unveiling of our bodies to new extremes. Once sleeved gowns and bare gowns under matching jackets were abundant; now we must search for them. Many a middle-aged Hollywood actor who passes for handsome would be called an old cow if he put on a dress. Women would likely be as eager to sneer as men. How much better-natured are the members of the American Sewing Guild, a group of sewers who take on many charitable projects. They applaud enthusiastically whenever a white-haired woman shows off an elegant little suit made by her own expert hands during their annual fashion show. The applause increases tenfold if this *éminence grise* walks with the slightest of limps.

The Dress Doctors knew that youth is not always a happy age. One of Dorée Smedley's friends saw her book title (*You're Only Young Twice*) and flinched at the idea of being young once more. "Do we have to go through all that again?" she asked. "I couldn't bear it." The friend had been lonely and miserable, a bookish, plain-looking young woman. By age forty, she had blossomed. She was now a glamorous creature with more men to choose from than she had imagined possible. Another example: The photo of Alpha Latzke of Kansas State as a young professional woman makes her look a little haggard, a little unsure of herself, with her hair up in an awkward braid. The photo taken near her retirement is of a lovely old woman, with abundant, soft white hair arranged beautifully, and a general air of satisfaction. Her accomplishments seemed to have polished her. Smedley realized that it may take thirty or forty years to gain skill in "the art of living." A truth we seem to forget.[83]

THE 1957 ADVERTISEMENT for the Acme Dress Form in the back of the Butterick pattern magazine introduces us to the women of the Marsh family. There's Joan Marsh, a thin teenager weighing only 103 pounds; her older, taller sister, Ruth, who fills out the womanly curves of an evening dress at 122 pounds; and their white-haired mother, wearing a fitted suit she made herself, who "has a more matronly figure," weighing in at 139 pounds. Very different sizes, but never fear, all of them can use the same Acme Dress Form, because it expands and contracts.[84]

Today, some middle-aged women make it their great ambition to diet down to the weight they were in college or high school. In contrast, the Dress Doctors took it for granted that a woman would gain weight as she reached adulthood and middle age. Helen Goodrich Buttrick's 1925 dress book for high-school girls spelled out in pictures and words exactly that. "The greatest change in proportions" from a fifteen-year-old girl's figure to a woman's figure, Buttrick explained matter-of-factly, "takes place at the hips, the bust and the shoulders." While the hips of the teenager are narrower than her shoulders, the hips of a woman are wider than her shoulders.

Buttrick offered a sketch of the ideal womanly proportions based on her study of Greek statues, fine paintings, and "actual measurements of beautiful adult proportions." Through all the absurdities and abnormalities that fashion has decreed at various times, wrote Buttrick, "an ideal persists" of the beautiful body, and good design acknowledges that ideal. The pendulum of fashion swung from one extreme to the other, but by the 1960s, it had swung toward Joan Marsh, the skinny teenager. Where it got stuck.[85]

To be fair, women have worried too much about big hips at least since the 1920s, when a boyish look came into style, and breasts and

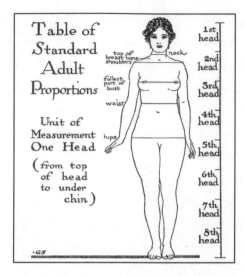

Fig. 3: Girls learned from the Dress Doctors that this was the ideal of a beautifully
proportioned figure. HELEN GOODRICH BUTT-
RICK, *PRINCIPLES OF CLOTHING SELECTION*,
1925

hips were out. Anne Rittenhouse thought the look started in 1918
with the end of World War I. After four years of fighting and hardship, Paris felt that "a well-nourished face was not patriotic." Suddenly,
the anemic, flat-chested woman, "once considered a failure," became
the darling of the fashion-makers.[86]

Another explanation for the appeal of a flat-chested look is political. Since being a woman in the 1920s meant not getting to do a lot
of things that men could do, some girls preferred to opt out of looking
like women as much as possible. If they weren't women, they weren't
doomed to give up their girlish freedoms. So flapper dresses dropped
straight from the shoulder, ignoring any curves, and belts were located
at the hips. Vogue Patterns called the look "frankly boyish."[87]

Flat-chested women must have been thrilled. We may celebrate
the end of corsets that squeezed women into that breathless hourglass
shape, but the boyish figure required things that were just as bad. First,

there was constant dieting and exercise. American college women in the 1890s had boasted of gaining weight and height, thus defying the skeptics, who said their weak female minds and bodies would break under the stress of serious study. But women students had so taken to dieting by the 1920s that the Smith College cafeteria staff had to buy fewer potatoes and more lettuce, tomatoes, and celery.[88]

And if exercise and dieting didn't eliminate all your curves, there was always a corset that squeezed what was left of your hips, as well as your breasts. Below an announcement of "The New Freedom in Corsetry," the Sears Roebuck catalog in 1925 offered an amazingly complex tube encasing the model from bust to thigh. It was guaranteed "to impart that straight slim beauty of line which the fashionable ensemble demands." Made of pink rayon, it crisscrossed the body with webbings of elastic and hidden boning.[89]

Fashions returned to a more feminine figure in the 1930s. The shift came from Paris fashion houses, but Elizabeth Hawes thought that it really expressed a new outlook on female independence: women had come around to the idea that "freedom and masculinity were no longer one and the same thing." They no longer had to copy men's shapes to have men's freedoms.[90]

Dresses had waists again, and no one was denying that women had busts and hips. The Woman's Institute magazine celebrated "the kindness of the new mode to feminine curves" in 1930. Many women were still wearing corsets, but retailers offered new styles that were meant to "indent" waistlines. As one magazine explained, "once more, flat chests are unbeautiful." The company that made the flattening bra called "Boyshform," which had sold so well during the early 1920s, went bankrupt, and its owner committed suicide. A fashion victim if ever there was one.[91]

Although the fashion plates remained unusually lean, the Dress Doctors of the 1930s liked curves and taught their students that a healthy woman had them. (Keep in mind that they still thought curves should be restrained by foundation garments.) The *Designing Women* authors shook their heads over "the modern goal" of possessing "a figure as slender as is humanly possible without actually baring one's bones." Kansas State Dress Doctors blamed Hollywood for "the vogue for unnatural slimness." One writer who denied in 1930 that there was such a thing as an ideal figure, then went on to describe it as a bust of 36.5 inches, a waist of 26 or 28 inches, and hips of 40 inches. This was for a nineteen-year-old. We're still talking a mild hourglass that was definitely bottom heavy, just like Buttrick's sketch of the ideal woman.[92]

American women were not all that far off the mark, according to a study from the USDA in 1941. This study, of almost 15,000 women, was part of a Works Progress Administration project during the New Deal and the culmination of a dream of Ruth O'Brien's at the Bureau of Home Economics. She had long wanted to rationalize clothing sizes the scientific way: by measuring people. *Life* magazine had one of its writers take a look at the report. She came to the "deplorable conclusion" that American women were short (5 foot 3 inches, on average) and chunky (133 pounds). This was when twenty-three-year-old fashion models averaged 120 pounds and stood nearly 5'8."[93]

The magazine decided to rub it in by offering a photograph of what it called a Glamour Girl standing next to the Average American Woman. You notice two things about this picture. First, the Average American Woman looks like she might be thinking of finding the guy who talked her into posing for this picture and belting him one in the face. Second, the Glamour Girl is meaty compared to today's fashion models. She's got thighs.[94]

Thighs were still a good thing in the 1950s, which brought back the hourglass ideal. Christian Dior's famous New Look suits were actually padded at the hips to make the waist look smaller. Directions for sewing hip-pads appeared in *The Singer Dressmaking Course* as late as 1961. Cut out two squared-off crescents of fabric, gather them at the top, sew them together to make a little pillow, and then stuff it. Attach two pillows to a ribbon-belt that closes at the waist. Wear it under your dress. You now have hips.[95]

Then the 1960s brought back the childish figure and launched our current Fear of Fat. An American newspaperwoman noted in 1967 that new British modeling sensation Twiggy measured 31"–21"–32" and resembled her nine-year-old daughter. Twiggy was not the result of a British population weaned on wartime and postwar food rations, as some people suppose. The switch to whole-wheat bread and vegetables, combined with limited meat, under a system that made sure the poorest Britons were not priced out of the market, meant that everyone there was eating healthier. Efforts to protect the most vulnerable, including pregnant women, meant that the "fitness of babies and school children was particularly striking." Britons had never been better fed.[96]

Twiggy was picked up by fashion magazines not because she looked like other postwar British teenagers, but because she looked really weird. As she put it, "I'm called Twiggy cos my legs are all peculiar and thin. Like twigs, see." In some photos, the bony knobs of her limbs make you flinch.[97]

The word "cellulite" was introduced to the United States in the late 1960s, when curvaceous women were passed over in favor of underweight teenagers. *Vogue* magazine wrote of a young woman who had not undertaken an exercise regimen as a teenager, had waited too long to be "diagnosed" for cellulite, and feared it was "too late" to do anything about the disease at the ripe age of twenty-two. Fortunately, she had managed to reduce her 39-inch hips down to 34 inches through exercise, "standing correctly," and using "a special rolling pin." If you didn't want to rub your butt yourself, you hired a masseuse to do it for you.[98]

And don't forget to diet. Here is *Vogue*'s suggestion for breakfast on 1200 calories a day: tea or coffee, no sugar. You get an apple at

10 A.M. Best-selling books promised they would reveal the secrets—diet, massage, Saran Wrap, creams—to removing what they identified as water, wastes, and fat trapped inside women's hips and thighs. For the record, it's just fat, and it isn't trapped. It lives there.[99]

American doctors squared off with French doctors over whether cellulite was different from other kinds of fat. Americans: No! French: *Mais, oui!* The French noticed that cellulite occurred first at puberty, then during pregnancy and menopause; it was found almost exclusively in women, and not necessarily overweight women. So they theorized its cause as "estrogen excess."[100]

In short, the diagnosis could be made at birth: "Congratulations, it's a girl!"

Diagnosing womanhood itself as a disease had some astonishing effects. Even naked ladies lost some of their curves over the course of the next decades. Psychologists, who actually get paid to study such things, noticed that the weight of a Playboy model was about 91 percent of that of other women in 1960. By 1978, they weighed only 84 percent of what other women weighed. This was also true of the young women who made up the more wholesome population of contestants for the Miss America Pageant. And Miss America herself was always thinner than the average contestant.[101]

Yet more enterprising psychologists estimated the bust-to-waist and waist-to-hip ratios of women pictured in the pages of *Vogue* and *Ladies Home Journal* from 1900 until 1981. They found the correlation between the two ratios to be so close that they only graphed the bust-to-waist ratio. When the line lurched downward, as it did during the 1920s, women's curves disappeared in favor of a figure like a popsicle stick. When it lurched upward, as it did in the 1950s, we're talking va-va-voom. There was not a lot of va-va-voom by 1981.[102]

Perhaps we can console ourselves with the thought that some of those curves were replaced by muscle. The 1970s saw an explosion of athleticism in women. Title IX made it easier for many of them

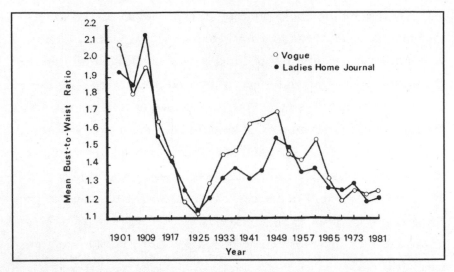

Fig. 4: When the line drops, the angular figure was in vogue. When it rises, women could have curves again. SILVERSTEIN ET AL., "ROLE OF MASS MEDIA IN PROMOTING A THIN STANDARD OF BODILY ATTRACTIVENESS FOR WOMEN," *SEX ROLES*, 1986

to be athletic by outlawing discrimination against young women in higher education, including sports. By the early 1980s, aerobics classes were becoming an obsession. Lycra, once used for girdles, was now blended with nylon to make brightly colored leotards that women wore while hopping around to pulsating music in a dance studio walled with mirrors. Aerobics were so popular that the Mattel toy company put out Workout Barbie in a leotard and leg warmers.[103]

Younger women may have turned against girdles, but they remained committed to what a girdle produced: a flat stomach. A secretary told a *Chicago Tribune* reporter in 1968, "I've learned to hold my stomach in myself, rather than depend on a girdle." Women were now free to work on their bodies, but they were also told that they had better work on their bodies.[104]

"Nobody knows better than you what you should wear or how you should look," proclaimed the authors of *Cheap Chic*. Then they made it clear that you don't look so great. Check yourself out in a mirror, they order. "Are you content with what you see?" Apparently, you shouldn't be. "Could the muscle tone of your stomach, upper arms and thighs be firmed up with a little jogging, swimming, or a ten-block walk each morning?" Skin-tight bodysuits cannot be worn with "the sagging contour or the ever-so-diminutive body bulge," scolded a Simplicity pattern magazine. Buy the book by the exercise guru at the Elizabeth Arden Salon, or the one by a Russian gymnast. She offers a twenty-one-day shape-up program, and he's got three hundred exercises.[105]

Clara Pierre's book on fashion liberation announced that there was a new, liberated body type in 1976: "the athletic mesomorph," who "laughs at underclothes and lives in leotards." The liberated woman had a gymnasium in her house, a bike in her hallway, and spent her lunch hour on a slant board doing sit-ups or on a court playing tennis. Pierre, a self-proclaimed athletic mesomorph, boasted on her book jacket that she skied and skated, hiked and jogged, and rode bicycles and horses. When she wasn't busy laughing at underwear. In a chapter entitled, "Better Fit Than Fat," she announced that "everyone" in the 1970s was playing tennis, doing cross-country skiing, or training for wilderness survival.[106]

Everyone? Really? Why not spend your lunch hour eating your lunch? Reading about this frenzy of activity can make a person want to lie down and nap.

But the shift to thin was complete. Once, models showing off designs at the haute couture houses came in an assortment of body types. Designers knew that the short women and the big women sitting in their salons were looking for garments that suited their physiques and needed to see the garments on women built more like themselves. But very tall, very thin young women took over the jobs in the 1970s. Their body type had become the ideal. Although the 1980s saw a handful of womanly supermodels, we have been dealing with some pretty skinny hips for the past three decades.[107]

As a result, girls in the late twentieth century became obsessed with dieting. The diaries of teenagers reveal an enormous shift in their understanding of what it means to be good. Before the 1920s, teenagers worried about becoming better people. Remember the long lists of mental and social habits that the home economists encouraged in junior-high-school girls? They were supposed to work on becoming courteous, honest, trustworthy, loyal, kind to animals, respectful to elders, and the like. And that's what they worried about becoming in their diaries. By the late twentieth century, teenagers worried almost entirely about their looks. Working on their bodies was their idea of being good. Weight loss became the primary obsession in the 1960s. The 1970s added on exercise as another requirement.[108]

Open any fashion magazine today and you will find ample evidence that girls are told to exercise or else. "Get Your Best Bikini Body: The Ultimate Secret to a Great Butt, Flat Abs & *Major* Confidence," reads a summer issue of a teen magazine. Apparently, major confidence can only be the result of a great butt and flat abs, all of which must be achieved through dieting and exercise. And if that didn't work, the next issue has a helpful pull-out guide entitled "Get Your Best Body for Back-to-School," which offers a six-week diet and exercise plan to make it all possible. There are no pull-out guides on honing your courtesy, honesty, or loyalty.[109]

Grown women feel the same pressures. An article from 1980 captures the way in which an opportunity for women to gain physical strength became yet another way to worry about their looks. Weight training, it said, meant "women taking control of their bodies and their lives" *and* ensuring that "they won't be saggy or flabby." But taking control over our bodies seems to take an enormous amount of time and effort.[110]

A fashion magazine's recent issue devoted to the body offered helpful tips from an Olympic swimmer for getting into shape after giving birth. Try two and a half hours of swimming six days a week, and ninety minutes of weight-lifting three days a week. This amounts to nineteen and a half hours of exercise a week, a possibility only for women who sweat for a living. Add a Paleo diet designed to get in touch with your inner Neanderthal. All this, and the magazine's editor still managed to bemoan the number of women who worry too much about "body-fat percentage." As if any of us had ever heard of a body-fat percentage before women's magazines told us to worry about it.[111]

How are young women to appreciate the natural roundness of the female body when they read that one pop singer has been on a diet since the sixth grade (she would have been eleven years old), or that another eats only 1400 calories a day? Ask an online calorie calculator what a 125-pound, 5'5" woman of twenty-five years of age with a very physically active life—like a pop singer—would need on a daily basis, and you don't get 1400 calories but 2270. Our young, female pop singers must be perpetually hungry.[112]

Fashion magazine editors have been fretting lately about models getting too thin, but then imply that it is not their fault that the average model is 5'10" and 124 pounds and beautiful. But who decided that 5'10" and 124 pounds is beautiful? In 1960, the 5'10" fashion model was supposed to be 150 pounds and beautiful. Fashion editors do not call that beautiful today. They call it fat.[113]

The figure now required to model clothing was once called "under-developed and awkward," because it lacked the curves that signal womanhood. "This person has no curves," wrote Grace Margaret Morton of the angular figure. "She is flat front and back; she has prominent shoulder blades and a bony neck; her arms and legs are thin and her posture is far from good." You've probably seen her on fashion runways.[114]

Dress books identified "Too Tall and Thin" as a problem that needed well-chosen designs for camouflage. The authors of *Designing Women* noted that a décolleté style is "cruel" to such women, because it exposes so much of their bony chests. They suggested that tall, thin women wear high bows, cowls, scarves, and large, rolled collars. To fill in under low-cut dresses, there were "guimpes"—sheer blouses with

Fig. 5: Fashions that
emphasized the hips
were popular before the
1960s. The plan for this
easy-to-make evening
skirt also described
how to add a peplum.
ISABELLE STEVENSON,
GIFTS YOU CAN MAKE
YOURSELF, 1947

high standing collars, a lost style of flirty modesty. Angular women
should add bulk to their "emaciated" figures with layers, tiers, ruffles,
gathers, blousing, or a peplum—a short extra layer of fabric added to
a dress that falls from the waist and flares over the hips.[115]

But much has changed since then. Today's young women gasp in
horror at a pattern from the 1940s sporting a peplum. Why would
anyone want "her butt to look big"? They have no idea that a peplum
adds a fetching swish to a woman's walk.

Of course, not all womanly curves are rejected today. The psychologists' graph ends in 1981, before the rise of the breast implant. Over
the past few decades, hundreds of thousands of American women have
had breast implants for cosmetic purposes. The number increased 39
percent between 2000 and 2010 alone.[116] Maybe if young women saw
Helen Goodrich Buttrick's idea of beautiful adult proportions, fewer
of them would worry about the size of their bosoms, and even fewer

would conclude that they ought to go under the knife to fix them. And the rest of us wouldn't be stuck choosing from an assortment of foam-padded brassieres promising to push our breasts ever onward and upward.

The Dress Doctors had never seen modern plastic surgery and associated "the disproportionately large bust" with a "decidedly mature appearance." They assumed that it was a "figure defect" that made a woman "unhappily top-heavy," a problem most often found in older women, mothers who had birthed and nursed an abundance of children. They felt rather sorry for the young woman who had to cope with such a problem. Even in 1954, in the midst of the popularity of the New Look hourglass figure, Edna Woolman Chase thought there was such a thing as too much bosom. While explaining that women should play down their bad points, she reminded her readers of the French saying, "*Beaucoup de monde au balcon*." Translation: "Lots of people in the balcony."[117]

THERE HAS BEEN A CERTAIN CRAZINESS in our ideas about women's body size for most of the past century. Vanity sizing already existed by the 1930s with the rise of large-scale ready-to-wear manufacturing. Butterick Pattern Company warned women to make sure to check their actual measurements against the pattern size chart and not simply go by the size they usually bought in a dress. "You may have some delusions possibly acquired by the size marked on your last ready-to-wear dress," explained a Butterick sewing book. A kindhearted manufacturer made you a size or two smaller "as a bit of subtle flattery." Ruth O'Brien began her measuring survey in hopes of rationalizing the sizing system for women's clothing. Bernice Chambers, who taught future department-store buyers at New York University, predicted that O'Brien's study would finally standardize sizes, so that salesclerks would no longer need to show a customer five different sizes. But it didn't help.[118]

A woman with a 36" bust in the 1930s would have worn a size 18 sewing pattern; now she wears a size 14. Measurements for sizes on sewing patterns have been increased over the decades, the last time in the 1960s, but measurements of ready-to-wear sizes have continued to increase since then. As a result, a woman who wears a size 14 in a pattern today is either a size 6 or a size 8 in ready-to-wear. A catalog peddling an "Italian super premium cotton blouse" for $238 calls a 36" bust a size 6, while the cotton-poly-spandex blouse with French cuffs at J. C. Penney for a 36" bust is called a size 8 and sells for $30. Vanity has its price.

But we like it. Researchers have found that if a woman tries on two pairs of jeans, she will conclude that the one marked a size 8 fits much better than the one marked size 10, not realizing that she has been handed jeans cut *from the same exact pattern*. Poor Ruth O'Brien. It is hard to rationalize a sizing system when people are so irrational.[119]

The Dress Doctors once acted as a calming influence. They taught sewing, and no woman armed with a tape measure can be fooled by vanity sizing. They also knew that fashion illustrations were already strangely lean and elongated. They pointed out that fashions change wildly from decade to decade and counseled American women to choose what fit their lives and their bodies. Instead of urging middle-aged women to lose thirty pounds in the 1920s in order to become fashionably thin, Mary Brooks Picken wrote a book on how to dress to *look* thirty pounds thinner.[120]

Elizabeth Hawes wrote "in favor of woman's natural tendency to roundness—fat and muscle—hips, stomach, and breasts," in 1942, but she was tired of women worrying about whatever size they were, tired as only a small designer who spent time listening to her clients could be. "Let them be fat. Let them be thin. Let their legs be short or long, their chests be flat or curved—but, oh, heaven, let the day come fast when the women of America will stand up straight!" Instead of size, the Dress Doctors worried about posture.[121]

Why did posture become so important to Americans? historians ask. They have a few theories. People could have become more self-conscious once they owned full-length mirrors. They could have begun focusing on self-disciplined posture to distract themselves from their self-indulgent shopping. Or it could be that the doctors who insisted on good posture, such as Joseph Pilates (yes, that Pilates), were simply worried that the modern life made people too sedentary, too hunched over, to the detriment of their health. World War I clearly encouraged a concern with posture, as "poor body mechanics" was named in more than 40 percent of the cases of men being rejected by the US military.[122]

Dress books and 4-H clothing-club manuals explained that "good posture is necessary to good health and good looks." The Dress Doctors were impressed by the confidence that good posture conferred, and referred to the work of contemporary psychologists for support. Standing erect "not only conveys an idea of courage to the observer, but literally tends to curtail despondency and banish fear in the individual who bears himself in that manner."[123]

Modern psychologists have confirmed all this. Test subjects who were asked to sit with their shoulders hunched felt powerless, while those who were asked to hold their shoulders back felt powerful. Those who held themselves erect and put out their chests felt confident, while those who slouched felt doubtful. *The Economist* summed it up: "Those who walk around with their heads held high not only get the respect of others, they seem also to respect themselves." It's nice to know today's scientists have just proven something that the Dress Doctors taught for decades.[124]

So perhaps it would be best to stop worrying about whether we fit the current fashion silhouette, whether we fit into clothes called a size 10, 6, or 2, and simply throw back our shoulders and lift up our heads. As a home economist from Cornell University declared in *The Woman and Her Posture* in 1942: "It's never too late to begin. BEGIN NOW."[125]

Eve Merriam, a poet and playwright, wrote a send-up of the fashion industry in 1960, entitled *Figleaf*, in which she suggested that the young Baby Boomers were already having an effect on their elders. She noticed how many adult women were trying to dress as if they were still teenagers: "Patterns from the adult world that can be striven for have disappeared. What can children look up to and try to emulate? What are the goals to be attained when they reach majority age?" asked Merriam. "When the word 'mature' in dress is taken for a pejorative, it also has an effect in fields far beyond fashion—reaching into all the spiritual values we consider worthy." The shift put both older women and younger women in a bind.[126]

In 1968, Mrs. Loel Guinness, a wealthy socialite known for her style, lamented the fate of the grown woman. "Ten years ago women dressed well and looked dignified," she said. "Today if you dress like a decent person, you are made to feel you are a million years old. If you dress young, you look like an idiot. What choice is there?" And 1968 was also the year a minor crisis occurred in determining the Best Dressed List, a list officially described on the voting ballot as "Women of Distinguished Taste." One of the judges, or "Fashion Authorities," complained that there weren't any teenagers on the list, when they were the only people with any style. "They are the real dynamos and everybody else is just plodding along," she told a reporter.[127]

In 1980 a writer for the *Los Angeles Times* called the two decades a woman lives between the ages of forty and sixty her "invisible years." The writer, a woman who was not looking forward to these decades, protested that a man could aim to look handsome his whole life, but middle-aged women must give up trying to look pretty or cute. "The best she can do is take refuge in looking 'chic.'" But looking chic was something the author didn't seem to think was worth the effort.[128]

Even those who appreciate the distinguished, old women of today have trouble finding a language in which to express it. In 2012, Ari

Seth Cohen published his admiring photos of old women of "advanced style," and then he praised them as "youthful in mind and spirit," thus committing a common mistake: confusing creativity with youth. The Dress Doctors knew that not all young women were creative. They found the Baby Boomers a hopelessly conformist set of teenagers who were only happy when they were dressed exactly alike.[129]

The Dress Doctors had once been there to advise women about a way to age with style. That said, efforts to defy time do appear in their books. Laurene Hempstead expected her readers to be eager to know how that seventy-year-old woman passed for fifty. But defying time was a minor theme, and the attempts of the middle-aged to dress like much younger women was looked upon with pity, if not contempt. Mildred Graves Ryan was more than a little impatient with women who answered coyly, "over twenty-one," when asked their age. When asked your age, "State your age," she ordered.[130]

The main reason anyone talks about middle-aged actresses today is to marvel over those who remain "hot," something that can only be accomplished by wearing your clothes really tight. In contrast, the Dress Doctors thought only a small group of women "pursue the art of dressing wholly to attract men," and they didn't think much of them. Such "an absorption," they believed, leaves a woman "vain and shallow." She forgets that clothing should suit the occasion and instead dons "alluring" garments regardless of the hour or the place.[131]

Now that the art principles have been lost, has luring men become our only standard for beauty in dress? Young women may imagine that sex appeal is the single most important public identity a woman can attain. Living in an age when the only standard of female attractiveness is hotness, and when every detail of life is offered up on Facebook, young women find it normal that the whole world, not just their sweetheart, their gynecologist, and their mother, should know the exact shape of their bodies.

But if men do not feel compelled to have the world pass judgment on every inch, why should we? The early Dress Doctors were so pleased at the thought that the modern woman faced such a world of possibilities. No longer did she have to dress solely to attract a husband. If the Dress Doctors looked around at womankind today, they would wonder why so many of us are determined to appear ready to seduce at all hours of the day. Don't we have anything else to do?

Today's culture seems to have little appreciation for what years of living can do for you. We all know that growing older usually makes you less of an idiot. But there's little sense today that age might endow you with sophistication, dignity, grace, stateliness, and wisdom. Or that we might aspire to dress in a way that expresses all these qualities.

Epilogue

Legacies

T HE ART OF DRESS DID NOT DISAPPEAR ENTIRELY.
Although some home economics programs were organized out of existence, programs at the land-grant colleges
usually survived, though many lost their independence. From 1938
until 1961, Velma Phillips, Mildred Graves Ryan's coauthor, served
as the dean of the College of Home Economics at what is now called
Washington State University, but her college was eventually swal-
lowed by the College of Agricultural, Human, and Natural Resource
Sciences. This kind of treatment left some members of the American
Association of Family and Consumer Sciences, formerly the American Home Economics Association—it changed its name in 1994
after much debate—a little anxious. Must you call it "Home Ec"?—a
scholar asked me. She feared that the shorthand signaled a sneer. College faculty members and students regularly refer to political science

as "poli sci," and sociology as "soc," and nobody worries about that. But then, those departments rarely worry about their survival.[1]

The Dress Doctors are remembered in small but significant ways. Alpha Latzke and her colleagues inspired a former student to endow a professorship at Kansas State in clothing and textiles. Mabel D. Erwin at Texas Tech donated money to create a student scholarship that is still awarded each year. Cornell University created HEARTH—an online archive of early home economics writings—making rare books and magazines available to anyone. And those of us who haunt used bookstores still occasionally come across the Dress Doctors' books and learn from them how to live "more richly and more beautifully," as a colleague of Grace Margaret Morton's once said of the students who had profited from knowing her.[2]

The art of dress and the craft of dressmaking have recently won new admirers. An exhibit on fashion in film broke all attendance records at the Taft Museum of Art in Cincinnati in 2009. The crush of visitors streaming in to see the work of designer Alexander McQueen in 2011 at the Metropolitan Museum of Art prompted the curators to extend the exhibit. The award-winning TV series *Mad Men*, which debuted in 2007, introduced young Americans to the styles and formality of the early 1960s. Women began searching for vintage clothing, and designers started creating new clothing with the silhouettes and details that marked vintage styles. Formality in dress intrigues both the men and the women of a generation whose parents abandoned it.[3]

And it is the sight of dressmaking, as much as the fun of watching the contestants shriek, weep, and swear, that earned another TV series, *Project Runway*, its many fans starting in late 2004. A host of other design shows followed in its wake. Students started showing up in courses on fashion design who lacked even the most basic sewing skills but possessed a strong desire to create. That same urge explains the proliferation of sellers on Etsy and the popularity of online lessons in sewing and other crafts.[4]

CREATIVITY HAS ALWAYS FUELED DRESSMAKING. In the late 1920s, Ruth O'Brien organized a survey of women who owned sewing machines to ask them all sorts of questions. How much did they sew? What kinds of garments did they make? What fabrics did they use? When asked whether they sewed in order to save money or because they were dissatisfied with the clothing found in stores, many women offered an answer that wasn't one of the options: they sewed because they enjoyed it. O'Brien made a note that she should have asked about that in the first place. The editor of the Woman's Institute magazine in 1930 tried to capture what a dressmaker feels upon completing a project: "a bubbling-over sense of happiness in the discovery of a new talent and the anticipation of future conquests." The pleasure of creation could give a woman a sense of satisfaction even when poverty made sewing a necessity. An Englishwoman from a poor family remembered how her mother had spotted a dressing gown of good gray wool flannel in a secondhand shop: she bought it, took it apart, and, as her daughter recalled, "made me the most wonderful frock I ever had for Sunday." By the late twentieth century, ready-to-wear prices had hit historic lows, and saving money no longer loomed large as a reason for home sewing; most American women who sewed did so because they enjoyed it.[5]

Dressmaking offers worlds of creation and imagination. Mary Ethel Gunder was an Ohio high-school student taking home economics classes in the 1920s. One of her assignments was to imagine a dress for herself. She cut a picture of a wine-colored dress out of a magazine, glued it to the page, and explained that she would like to make it up in green silk, which she estimated would cost $10.47, or $141 in today's dollars.

Did she ever get to make it? I don't know. Mary started nursing school, but stopped her studies to marry John Long in 1933. She lived in rural Ohio, where women and girls made cotton dresses regularly, but only half ever tried a silk dress, if we follow O'Brien's survey results. I do know that Mary passed on her love of dressmaking, as well as her school notebooks, to her daughter Helen Ann Long, who studied home economics in high school and spent years as a member of 4-H clothing clubs. Helen went on to get a college degree to teach home economics before she married Jack Devitt in 1958 and had four children. Helen Long Devitt was still judging 4-H contests when her grandson put us in touch, and she generously shared her family's collection of home economics notebooks with me.[6]

Like home economics, dressmaking is a traditionally womanly endeavor that can explode gender stereotypes.[7] Scientists say that the average man has a better capacity to imagine a three-dimensional object than the average woman, but how can this be true of the dressmaker starting from scratch? She not only imagines the dress, she also makes a blueprint of the pieces to achieve the shape she wants and figures out the steps to put the whole thing together. Dressmaking is a form of engineering. And in order to make the final product look good from the outside, a dress is put together *inside out*. Show me a bridge builder who's been asked to do that.

Home economics always made it clear that women could handle all kinds of machinery. Women enrolled in the Iowa State College program in Household Equipment studied physics, math, and electrical circuitry. Some answered a call to work for General Electric during World War II. One student was assigned to a high-security autopilot project for the US Navy, where the men thought her a joke until they saw her at work. "I made those test engineers swallow their guffaws about Home Ec majors!" she remembered.[8]

I thought of her satisfaction when the American Association of University Women issued a report in 2010 about how to get more women to succeed in fields of study that were traditionally dominated by men: science, technology, engineering, and mathematics—the STEM subjects. One of their recommendations was to teach girls to work with their hands in grade school and junior high. They suggested encouraging them to draw and play with construction toys.[9]

Why not sewing? Mary Brooks Picken could sew and weave by the time she was five. Even a little child can make things like pillows, mittens, or totes. The key is to indulge children's impatience, wrote Constance Talbot in 1943: let them "concentrate on speed in making the first garment." And let the child do it all herself. She will learn the pleasure of accomplishment. Who knows what she might be able to make? "Youthful talent is sometimes clearly marked," Talbot wrote, "but often it is deeply hidden; and unless it is given free and natural expression, it cannot develop." Talbot herself lectured on the radio, worked for Butterick Patterns, then Simplicity Patterns, and had her book on sewing chosen for the Book of the Month Club. She knew that sewing could open up a range of professional possibilities. So did Mabel B. Trilling at the Carnegie Institute of Technology. When she was asked in 1944 what her alumnae were doing, she listed textile research, radio announcer on fashions, and winner of a contest for the best-designed Victory suit.[10]

Talbot and Trilling were excited at the idea that some girls would discover they had the talent to become a designer, an artist, or a fashion writer, but those are only the most obvious ways in which learning to sew can train the hands, the eyes, and the mind.

The future probably does not hold a great number of physicists who will wear elegant gowns they made themselves. The fact remains that a sewing machine can teach a girl about motors and the practical elements of electricity, belts, cams, and lubrication. And once you've used one machine, others don't intimidate you. After learning to follow sewing patterns, any blueprint is easier to read. The Dress Doctors did more than teach girls to produce artistic dresses; they taught them skills to put to use throughout their lives. In 1936, the *McCall's Fashion Book* offered directions for an impressive lace blouse, "simply" made with braid and thread. The woman who managed to create this marvel could master the material world.[11]

Fig. 1: A blouse "simply" made from *peau d'ange* braid (skin-of-an-angel braid) and heavy thread. *McCall's Fashion Book*, Winter 1936–1937

One Saturday afternoon, I invited over two little girls, both named Margaret, to play with the fashion design kits sold by the Metropolitan Museum of Art. I was curious what they would do with them. The color wheel came with no explanation and was quickly passed over. The dolls came with the equivalent of long, satin hospital gowns that tied at the back, exposing their rears. The two girls stuck sparkly trims on their little gowns while we chatted. One Margaret made what we called "a stunning creation" in black and white decorated with rhinestones. We sorted through the fabrics provided in another kit, and they worked for a while on stitching Barbie-doll-sized purses. Then came the moment of real excitement. The older of the two Margarets asked if she could make a purse big enough to hold a cell phone. The younger Margaret gasped. Both girls were too little to own a cell phone, but the idea of having a purse to put one in thrilled them. We set to work on a small black bag that seemed to capture much of the wisdom of the Dress Doctors. It was simple, and useful, and it promised bigger things to come.

NO BOOK BY THE DRESS DOCTORS FAILED TO INCLUDE a passage on
the importance of bigger things than what to wear. By linking the art
of dress to spiritual purposes, the Dress Doctors turned the clothing
we make and buy into something more than thread and cloth. The
home economists always insisted that they wanted to help women
to master the stuff of life in order to give them time to think about
higher things. Summing up their principles in 1904, they declared at
their annual conference:

HOME ECONOMICS STANDS FOR . . .

> The simplicity in material surroundings which will most free the
> spirit for the more important and permanent interests of home and
> society.[12]

Annette J. Warner, who organized the teaching of the household
arts at Cornell University, ended a talk at the 1914 annual meeting
with a rapturous prayer. When art was truly made part of both our
homes and home economics, she proclaimed, then we could pray
like Moses did, knowing our prayer would be answered: "And let the
beauty of the Lord our God be upon us; and establish thou the work
of our hands upon us; yea the work of our hands establish thou it." In
a less biblical mood, she explained that the difference between mere
clothing and well-designed dress "is not one of the quantity, or outlay
or even of degree, but a subtle and important quality which lifts them
from the realm of mere physical necessity into one where the spirit
also is refreshed."[13]

Remember Mildred Graves Ryan, the woman who told junior-
high girls that they were public eyesores at the beach? For all her
hard-edged advice, Ryan managed to write with her coauthor Velma
Phillips that the practical need to have on something durable or
warm should not solely determine what you wear. Dress is more

than practicality, they said: "It is the means of expressing your love of beauty and of life."[14]

The Dress Doctors bridged the gap between our values and our appearance. By doing so, they collapsed into one the nineteenth century's interest in character and the twentieth century's invention of personality. Nineteenth-century notions of character were linked to solid ideals of duty, honor, morality, and integrity. But personality was all about outward charm. Personality makes people fascinating, attractive, and forceful.[15]

Some of the Dress Doctors saw character and personality as distinctly different from each other while arguing that *both* were needed for success in life. The home economists in the Cleveland schools taught their students, "We can at any age be improved in those personal traits that build up sterling character *and* make us congenial, interesting, and pleasing companions." Grace Margaret Morton thought only someone who appreciated beauty *and* had high ideals of character could teach clothing design through fine art. Other Dress Doctors used the word "personality" in ways that conjured up all the solid virtues of character. Mary Brooks Picken wrote, "Our clothes, like our faces, tell what we are. They tell our taste, our appreciation of the beautiful, our self-restraint, excessive modesty, naturalness or boldness—our characters, in fact." It was the rare Dress Doctor who realized that some sneaky person might consciously create "the wrong impression" by dressing with honesty and beauty in order to hide their weaselly soul.[16]

But you don't need to buy the argument that art in daily life, or art worn on your back, can be spiritually uplifting in order to appreciate the need to attend to the way you dress. If you still think that anything having to do with dress is superficial, let's just admit that we live in the superficial world, and heed the words of Jane Loewen, the millinery instructor. Since the Golden Age is not yet come, and everyone we meet is not going to have time to plumb the depths of our honest souls, we'd better "improve our externals," if we want to improve our destiny. Most of the people we bump into on a given day are going to judge us on those externals, Loewen reminds us. "In all casual and momentary meetings, we have the same status as package goods," and no one will pick out a package "mussily and carelessly wrapped" if there are others "done up carefully and neatly."[17]

The home economists who worked in Cleveland reminded their young readers that dressing attractively could not make up "for lack of sterling worth of character." The foreword to their book told teachers to make no mistake about their young charges: "The girl should never be allowed to feel that the only object of personal regimen is to make her prettier or more charming, but rather to make her a more desirable member of society and to help her bring out that which is best in her own character and personality."[18]

The last thing students read in their 1935 workbook coauthored by Mabel Trilling and Florence Williams of the Carnegie Institute of Technology was the cautionary tale of Alberta, whose obsessive interest in clothing interfered "with happy and successful living." Alberta spent her time window shopping, leafing through fashion magazines, watching movies to see what the actresses wore, and planning her wardrobe. She never read a book, played sports, listened to music, or went to the theater. She only cared for parties if she had just the "right clothes," and nothing seemed to satisfy her craving for new clothes. Were there many girls like Alberta? "Let us hope not!"[19]

Two decades later, Mildred Graves Ryan and Velma Phillips made clear their ambitions for the young college woman who read their book on dress: "It is hoped that through its study she will gain that inner confidence which will allow her to think about something besides herself—to see herself in relation to the family, the community, and the world." If she stopped at dressing well, they would have been disappointed in her.[20]

The Wisdom of the Dress Doctors

◇ Practice the art of dress. You may be self-conscious because you are far better dressed than the people around you, but maybe you can inspire them.

◇ Mark your day by the pleasures of dress. Change in some small way for a dinner out. Own something comfortable and beautiful to slip on at the end of a hard day's work.

◇ Less is more. So long as you value beauty over novelty, five outfits is all you need for work. Or maybe just one!

◇ Dress for the people you love. Yes, the people who love you will forgive those torn gym shorts, but don't ask them to if you can help it.

◇ Balance concealment with revealment. Flesh exposed all the time has far less effect than flesh revealed on special occasions and for a privileged few. People who receive privileges should be appropriately grateful.

◇ Celebrate girlhood *and* womanhood, and the difference between them.

ACKNOWLEDGMENTS

WRITING A BOOK IS IMPOSSIBLE WITHOUT HELP. I want to thank the History Department and the Institute for Studies in the Liberal Arts at the University of Notre Dame for the funding that made much of the work on this book possible, including the original purchases that began my collection of dress textbooks and the hiring of research assistants over the years. I am especially grateful for the research assistance of Catherine Bentzen, Allyson Lopshire, Jordyn Smith, Lauren Walas, Emily Hutchens, Michelle Gaseor, and Brendan Devitt. Notre Dame's Institute for Studies in the Liberal Arts also funded the creation of my College Seminar on dress and the garment industry called "A Nation of Slobs," where I first tried out some of the ideas in this book. I am grateful for the stimulating curiosity of my College Seminar students over the past few years.

The librarians and staff at the Hesburgh Library at the University of Notre Dame have done much to help my research, especially those working in the Interlibrary Loan office who responded gamely to hundreds of requests. I also owe thanks to Denise Massa, the curator of the Visual Resources Center at the University of Notre Dame, and her staff for their help in scanning a massive amount of material.

Several individuals and the staffs of several other libraries helped me in gathering biographical and research materials on the Dress

Doctors and their students. I want to thank Helen Long Devitt for sharing her and her mother's collection of home economics material; Professors Michael F. James and Joan Laughlin at the Department of Textiles, Clothing & Design at the University of Nebraska at Lincoln; Archives and Special Collections at the University of Nebraska at Lincoln; the New York University Archives in the Esther Holmes Bobst Library; the Pomona College Archives; Special Collections / University Archives at the University of Nevada, Reno; University Archives at the University Libraries at Carnegie Mellon University; Special Collections / Archives at the John B. Coleman Library at Prairie View A&M University; Special Collections and University Archives at the Iowa State University Library; and Morse Department of Special Collections at the Kansas State University Libraries. One particular online collection was a godsend: the Home Economics Archive: Research, Tradition and History (HEARTH) at the Albert R. Mann Library at Cornell University.

A number of scholars have given me useful comments on portions of this work. I want to thank the participants at the State of the Art Conference, "Home Economics: Classroom, Corporate and Cultural Interpretations Revisited," hosted at the University of Georgia at Athens in 2013, especially Rima Apple, Gwen Kay, and Sharon Nickols, our organizer. I also profited from presenting my work at the Great Lakes History Conference held at Grand Valley State University in Grand Rapids, Michigan, in 2011, with special thanks for comments by Charlene Boyer Lewis, and at the US Intellectual History Conference sponsored by the City University of New York's Graduate Center in 2010, with thanks especially for comments by Hilary Hallett. I have gained from discussions about this work with friends and fellow scholars Sarah Barringer Gordon, Hendrik Hartog, and Wayne K. Durrill. I want to thank also Catherine Stephenson of the Association of Sewing and Design Professionals for her willingness to share her knowledge with me, and Susan Guibert, formerly assistant director of public relations at Notre Dame, for her cheerful support.

I created a kind of cross-country women's reading club—Mary Jo Adams, Nancy Lucid, and Chantelle Snyder—who read drafts. My brother Victor Adams, though not part of the club officially, put in his two cents, too. They helped me figure out how to write this book so that somebody besides a professor would enjoy reading it. If I have succeeded, it is because of them. I want to thank Geri Thoma, my agent, for her enthusiastic and savvy help. I knew after two minutes' conversation that I could do no better than to put this project into the hands of my editor Lara Heimert at Basic Books.

And finally, I must thank my husband John Soares. He has put up with growing stacks of dress books and sewing patterns, supported my decision to take this swerve in my career trajectory, and looked after my care and feeding. This book is dedicated to him for those reasons and about a thousand more.

ILLUSTRATION CREDITS

Introduction

Fig. 1: Mary Brooks Picken, *The Secrets of Distinctive Dress* (Scranton, PA: International Textbook, 1918).

Chapter 1

Fig. 1: Dulcie G. Donovan, *The Mode in Dress and Home* (Boston: Allyn and Bacon, 1935).

Chapter 2

Fig. 1: Foot X-ray, US Department of Agriculture.

Fig. 2: *Butterick Patterns*, Fall 1954; Butterick® B7068, image courtesy of the McCall Pattern Company. Copyright © 1954 All rights reserved.

Fig. 3: Woman's Institute of Domestic Arts and Sciences, *Harmony in Dress: Color Its Theory and Application* (Scranton, PA: International Educational Textbook, 1936).

Fig. 4: Mabel B. Trilling and Florence Williams, *Art in Home and Clothing* (Philadelphia: J. B. Lippincott, 1928).

Fig. 5: Annette J. Warner, *Artistry in Dress*, Cornell Bulletin for Homemakers (New York: New York State College of Home Economics at Cornell University, 1926). Courtesy of Division of Rare and Manuscript Collections, Cornell University Library.

Fig. 6: Leona Hope, *Artistic Dress*, Extension Circular no. 34 (Urbana: University of Illinois, College of Agriculture, Extension Service in Agriculture and Home Economics, 1919).

Chapter 3

Fig. 1: Cora Irene Leiby, *Clothes for Little Folks* (reprint: Ames: Iowa State College of Agriculture and Mechanic Arts, Extension Service, 1925). Courtesy of Iowa State University Extension and Outreach.

Fig. 2: Clothing and dress winner of Singer Sewing Machine 1938. Courtesy of Special Collections / Archives, John B. Coleman Library, Prairie View A&M University, Prairie View, Texas.

Fig. 3: Montgomery Ward catalog, Fall Winter 1937–1938. Courtesy of Montgomery Ward.

Fig. 4: Shirtwaist, author's collection.

Fig. 5: Mabel B. Trilling and Florence Williams, *Art in Home and Clothing* (Philadelphia: J.B. Lippincott, 1928).

Fig. 6: *Prairie Farmer Pattern Supplement*, 1934. Courtesy of Farm Progress Companies.

Fig. 7: Dulcie G. Donovan, *The Mode in Dress and Home* (Boston: Allyn and Bacon, 1935).

Fig. 8: *Singer Sewing Digest*, Fall Winter 1941. Courtesy of the Singer Sewing Company.

Chapter 4

Fig. 1: S. W. Straus, *History of the Thrift Movement in America* (Philadelphia: J. B. Lippincott, 1920).

Fig. 2: Copyright © 1944 All rights reserved. Originally published in *Vogue*. Reprinted by permission.

Fig. 3: *Paris Frocks at Home* (New York: Butterick, 1930). McCall's®, image courtesy of the McCall Pattern Company.

Fig. 4: Mary Schenck Woolman, *Clothing: Choice, Care, Cost* (Philadelphia: J. B. Lippincott, 1920)

Fig. 5: *Delineator*, May 1896, 499.

Fig. 6: Dulcie G. Donovan, *The Mode in Dress and Home* (Boston: Allyn and Bacon, 1935).

Fig. 7: Kate W. Kinyon and L. Thomas Hopkins, *Junior Home Problems* (Chicago: Benjamin H. Sanborn, 1928).

Chapter 5

Fig. 1: Lane Bryant catalog, Spring Summer 1946.

Fig. 2: Dulcie G. Donovan, *The Mode in Dress and Home* (Boston: Allyn and Bacon, 1935).

Chapter 6

Fig. 1: *Vogue Pattern Book*, August–September 1934. Vogue® V6620, Vogue® V6015, Vogue® V5868, Vogue® V5969, Vogue® V6574. Copyright © 1934. All rights reserved. Images courtesy of the McCall Pattern Company.

Fig. 2: *Vogue Pattern Book*, March-April 1957. Vogue® V1366. Copyright © 1957. All rights reserved. Image courtesy of the McCall Pattern Company.

Fig. 3: Helen Goodrich Buttrick, *Principles of Clothing Selection* (New York: Macmillan, 1925).

Fig. 4: Brett Silverstein, Lauren Perdue, Barbara Peterson, and Eileen Kelly, "Role of Mass Media in Promoting a Thin Standard of Bodily Attractiveness for Women," *Sex Roles* 14, nos. 9–10 (1986).

Fig. 5: Isabelle Stevenson, *Gifts You Can Make Yourself* (New York: Greystone Press, 1947).

Epilogue

Fig. 1: *McCall's Fashion Book*, Winter 1936–1937. McCall's® M421. Copyright © 1936. All rights reserved. Image courtesy of the McCall Pattern Company.

Color Plates

Fig. 1: *McCall's*, August 1909.

Fig. 2: *McCall's*, October 1910.

Fig. 3: *McCall's*, April 1918.

Fig. 4: Mary Ethel Gunder notebook, courtesy of Helen Long Devitt.

Fig. 5: *Vogue Pattern Book*, April-May 1931. Vogue® V5572, Vogue® V5545. Copyright © 1931. All rights reserved. Images courtesy of the McCall Pattern Company.

Fig. 6: *Vogue Pattern Book*, October–November 1932. Vogue® V6059. Copyright © 1932. All rights reserved. Image courtesy of the McCall Pattern Company.

Fig. 7: *Vogue Pattern Book*, February–March 1934. Vogue® V3673, Vogue® V3677, Vogue® V3672. Copyright © 1934. All rights reserved. Images courtesy of the McCall Pattern Company.

Fig. 8: *Butterick Fashion Book*, Early Spring 1934. Butterick® B5485. Copyright © 1934. All rights reserved. Image courtesy of the McCall Pattern Company.

Fig. 9: *Butterick Fashion News*, March 1935. Butterick® B6066, Butterick® B6054. Copyright © 1935. All rights reserved. Image courtesy of the McCall Pattern Company.

Fig. 10: *McCall's Fashion Book*, Midsummer 1935. McCall's® M289, McCall's® M296. Copyright © 1935. All rights reserved. Images courtesy of the McCall Pattern Company.

Fig. 11: *McCall's Fashion Book*, Winter 1936–1937. McCall's® M9009, McCall's® M9006. Copyright © 1936. All rights reserved. Images courtesy of the McCall Pattern Company.

Fig. 12: *Vogue Pattern Book*, June-July 1937. Vogue® V7689, Vogue® V7690, Vogue® V7669. Copyright © 1937. All rights reserved. Images courtesy of the McCall Pattern Company.

Fig. 13: *Vogue Pattern Book*, June-July 1937. Vogue® V7477, Vogue® V7542, Vogue® V3938. Copyright © 1937 All rights reserved. Images courtesy of the McCall Pattern Company.

Fig. 14: Textile Bag Manufacturers Association, *Sewing with Cotton Bags*, 1937.

Fig. 15: Montgomery Ward catalog, 1937–1938. Courtesy of Montgomery Ward.

Fig. 16: *Vogue Pattern Book*, October-November 1945. Vogue® V263. Copyright © 1945. All rights reserved. Image courtesy of the McCall Pattern Company.

Fig. 17: Simplicity pattern 4582, circa 1947.

Fig. 18: Dubarry pattern 6059, 1945.

Fig. 19: Originally published in the November 1947 issue of *Ladies Home Journal® Magazine*.

Fig. 20: Vogue pattern 545, 1951. Vogue® V545. Copyright © 1951 All rights reserved. Image courtesy of the McCall Pattern Company.

Fig. 21: *Vogue Pattern Book*, June-July 1952. Vogue® V7698. Copyright © 1952. All rights reserved. Image courtesy of the McCall Pattern Company.

Fig. 22: *Vogue Pattern Book*, August-September, 1952. Vogue® V696. Copyright © 1952. All rights reserved. Image courtesy of the McCall Pattern Company.

Fig. 23: *Vogue Pattern Book*, June-July 1952. Vogue® V686. Copyright © 1952. All rights reserved. Image courtesy of the McCall Pattern Company.

Fig. 24: *Vogue Patterns* catalog, September 1952. Vogue® V7712. Copyright © 1952. All rights reserved. Image courtesy of the McCall Pattern Company.

Fig. 25: *Vogue Pattern Book*, August–September 1952. McCall's® M9009. Copyright © 1952. All rights reserved. Image courtesy of the McCall Pattern Company.

Fig. 26: *Vogue Patterns* catalog, September 1952. Vogue® V4339. Copyright © 1952. All rights reserved. Image courtesy of the McCall Pattern Company.

Fig. 27: *Vogue Pattern Book*, August-September 1955. Vogue® V4625. Copyright © 1955. All rights reserved. Image courtesy of the McCall Pattern Company.

Fig. 28: *Butterick Fashion Book*, Fall–Winter 1955. Butterick® B7490. Copyright © 1955. All rights reserved. Image courtesy of the McCall Pattern Company.

Fig. 29: *McCall's Pattern Book*, Spring 1958. McCall's® M4304, McCall's® M4402. Copyright © 1958. All rights reserved. Images courtesy of the McCall Pattern Company.

Fig. 30: *Simplicity* catalog, 1962.

Fig. 31: *Butterick Vogue* catalog, June 1969. Butterick® B4681. Copyright © 1969. All rights reserved. Image courtesy of the McCall Pattern Company.

Fig. 32: *Butterick Vogue* catalog, June 1969. Butterick® B5122. Copyright © 1969. All rights reserved. Image courtesy of the McCall Pattern Company.

NOTES

Introduction

1. Mary Brooks Picken, *The Mary Brooks Picken Method of Modern Dressmaking* (New York: Pictorial Review Company, 1925), 5.

2. Helen G. Buttrick, *Principles of Clothing Selection* (New York: Macmillan, 1925), 7.

3. For historians of sewing overlooking the art of dress, see Sally I. Helvenston and Margaret M. Bubolz, "Home Economics and Home Sewing in the United States, 1870–1940," in Barbara Burman, ed., *The Culture of Sewing: Gender, Consumption and Home Dressmaking* (Oxford, UK: Berg, 1997), 303–325; Sarah A. Gordon, *"Make It Yourself": Home Sewing, Gender, and Culture, 1890–1930* (New York: Columbia University Press, 2009). Historians of home economics largely ignore dress. The champions of dress reform in the nineteenth century, however, shared the Dress Doctors' interest in beauty. See Stella Mary Newton, *Health, Art and Reason: Dress Reformers of the 19th Century* (London: John Murray, 1974); Patricia A. Cunningham, *Reforming Women's Fashion, 1850–1920: Politics, Health, and Art* (Kent, OH: Kent State University Press, 2003). For nineteenth-century dress advisers stressing simplicity, modesty, and thrift, see Sally Helveston, "Popular Advice for the Well-Dressed Woman in the 19th Century," *Dress* 6 (1980): 31–46. Jenna Weissman Joseli notices the work of home economists in *A Perfect Fit: Clothes, Character, and the Promise of America* (New York: Metropolitan Books, 2001), 29–30.

4. Jessica Daves, *Ready-Made Miracle: The American Story of Fashion for the Millions* (New York: G. P. Putnam's Sons, 1967), 220.

5. Bea Danville, *Dress Well on $1 a Day* (New York: Wilfred Funk, 1956), ix.

Chapter 1: Introducing the Dress Doctors

1. Quoted in Kendrick A. Clements, *The Presidency of Woodrow Wilson* (Lawrence: University Press of Kansas, 1992), 56.

2. US Department of Agriculture, *Domestic Needs of Farm Women*, Report 104 (Washington, DC: US Government Printing Office, 1915), 53, 56.

3. Paul V. Betters, *The Bureau of Home Economics: Its History, Activities and Organization* (Washington, DC: Brookings Institution, 1930), 5.

4. *The Profession of Home Making: A Condensed Home Study Course* (Chicago: American School of Home Economics, 1911), 8; Herbert Kleibard, *Schooled to Work: Vocationalism and the American Curriculum, 1878–1946* (New York: Teachers College Press, 1999), 135–137.

5. "In Memoriam, Lucy Rathbone," n.d., University of Texas at Austin, www.utexas.

edu/faculty/council/2000–2001/memorials/SCANNED/rathbone.pdf; Rima D. Apple, "Liberal Arts or Vocational Training," in Sarah Stage and Virginia B. Vincenti, eds., *Rethinking Home Economics: Women and the History of a Profession* (Ithaca, NY: Cornell University Press, 1997), 79–95, esp. 84–85; quoted in Sarah Stage, "Ellen Richards and the Social Significance of the Home Economics Movement," in Sarah Stage and Virginia B. Vincenti, eds., *Rethinking Home Economics: Women and the History of a Profession* (Ithaca, NY: Cornell University Press, 1997), 17–33, esp. 21. Richards opposed women's suffrage, but far more home economists put themselves on record as supporters than as opponents of the vote for women; see Carolyn M. Goldstein, *Creating Consumers: Home Economists in Twentieth-Century America* (Chapel Hill: University of North Carolina Press, 2012), 31.

6. Ellen H. Richards, *The Cost of Living as Modified by Sanitary Science*, 2nd ed. (New York: Wiley and Sons, 1900), 13; Beverly Bartow, "Isabel Bevier at the University of Illinois and the Home Economics Movement," *Journal of the Illinois State Historical Society* 72, no. 1 (1979): 21–38; Margaret Rossiter, *Women Scientists in America: Before Affirmative Action, 1940–1972* (Baltimore: Johns Hopkins University Press, 1995), 129 (Table 6.1).

7. Joan L. Sullivan, "In Pursuit of Legitimacy: Home Economists and the Hoover Apron in World War I," *Dress* 26 (1999): 31–46; Goldstein, *Creating Consumers*, 46–60.

8. Betters, *Bureau of Home Economics*, 76; Kathleen M'Laughlin, "Sidelines Stressed for Girl Chemists," *New York Times*, April 16, 1939, 25.

9. Nick Cullather, "The Foreign Policy of the Calorie," *American Historical Review* 112, no. 2 (2007): 340–341.

10. Betters, *Bureau of Home Economics*, 34–35.

11. Marguerite A. Connolly, "The Transformation of Home Sewing and the Sewing Machine in America, 1850–1929" (PhD diss., University of Delaware, 1994), 75, 77; Anna Hope, Letter to the Editor, *The American Agriculturalist* 16 (1857): 223–224; Mabel Hastie and Geraldine Gorton, "What Shall We Teach Regarding Clothing and Laundry Problems," *Journal of Home Economics* 18, no. 3 (1926): 129.

12. Lillian C. W. Baker, *Clothing Selection and Purchase* (New York: Macmillan, 1931; printed 1932), xv.

13. Neil Harris, *The Artist in American Society: The Formative Years, 1790–1860* (New York: George Braziller, 1966), 300ff; quoted in Mary Ann Stankiewicz, "The Creative Sister: An Historical Look at Women, the Arts, and Higher Education," *Studies in Art Education* 24, no. 1 (1982): 48–56, esp. 54.

14. "Painless," *Chicago Daily Tribune*, June 14, 1919.

15. Diana Korzenik, *Drawn to Art: A Nineteenth Century American Dream* (Hanover: University Press of New England, 1985); quoted in Minna McLeod Beck, "Foreword," *Better Citizenship Through Art Training* (Chicago: A. C. McClurg, 1921).

16. US Department of Agriculture (USDA), *Report of Extension Work in Agriculture and Home Economics in the United States* (Washington, DC: USDA, 1933), 48; Edith J. Webb, *Boys' and Girls' 4-H Club Work in the United States: A Selected List of References* (Washington, DC: US Department of Agriculture, Office of Cooperative Extension Work, 1932), 162–203; US Department of Agriculture, *Bureau of Home Economics in Wartime* (Washington, DC: Bureau of Home Economics, 1942), 23.

17. Louis McCliame Converse, *Let's Sew*, 4-H Circular 151 (Columbus: Ohio State University Extension Service, 1945).

18. Elisa Miller, "In the Name of the Home: Women, Domestic Science, and American Higher Education, 1865–1930" (PhD diss., University of Illinois at Urbana-Champaign, 2003), 108; *Girl Scout Handbook*, rev. ed. (New York: Girl Scouts, 1929), 439, 425, 451.

19. Sally I. Helvenston and Margaret M. Bubolz, "Home Economics and Home Sewing in the United States, 1870–1940," in Barbara Burman, ed., *The Culture of Sewing: Gender, Consumption and Home Dressmaking* (Oxford, UK: Berg, 1997), 303–325, esp. 313.

20. Quoted in Marie Clifford, "Working with Fashion: The Role of Art, Taste, and Consumerism in Women's Professional Culture, 1920–1940," *American Studies* 44, no. 1–2 (2003): 59–84, esp. 61.

21. "Fellowships for 1938–1939," *Journal of Home Economics* 30, no. 2 (1938): 110; "Home Ec Staff Adds New Prof," *Daily Collegian*, State College, Pennsylvania, January 9, 1953, 8.

22. Only 16 percent of home economics faculty members were married, according to *Survey of Land-Grant Colleges and Universities*, 2 vols. (Washington, DC: US Department of the Interior, Office of Education, 1930), 1:869–870; Alison Cornish Thorne, *Visible and Invisible Women in Land-Grant Colleges, 1890–1940* (Logan: Utah State University Press, 1985), 5–6.

23. Eleanor Roosevelt, *It's Up to the Women* (New York: Frederick A. Stokes, 1933), 46.

Chapter 2: Art: Principles for Beauty

1. Ruth O'Brien, Maude Campbell, and Mary Aleen Davis, "Preface," *Score Cards for Judging Clothing Selection and Construction*, USDA Miscellaneous Circular no. 90 (1927). The scorecards used to judge commercial competitions were picked up by textbooks and were still being applied in 1965.

2. US Department of Agriculture, *Domestic Needs of Farm Women*, Report 104 (Washington, DC: US Government Printing Office, 1915), 55–56.

3. Sara Johnson, "A Pioneering Woman: Helen Binkerd Young," *Historic Ithaca's Preservation Quarterly* 40 (Winter 2008): 13–14; Helen Binkerd Young, "The Arrangements of Household Furnishings," *Cornell Reading-Courses* 4, no. 85, Farmhouse Series no. 7 (New York State College of Agriculture at Cornell University, April 1, 1915), 150.

4. Helen Hall, *Correct Styles for the Individual: Pattern Making* (St. Louis, MO: Sye Foundation, 1931), 9.

5. Adelaide Laura Van Duzer, Edna M. Andrix, Ethelwyn L. Bobenmyer, et al., *Everyday Living for Girls: A Textbook in Personal Regimen* (Chicago: J. B. Lippincott, 1936), 512. The poem itself is a call from the war dead to the living to take up the fight.

6. Nora A. Talbot, Florence L. Lytle, Millie V. Pearson, and Anna May Johnson, *Practical Problems in Home Life for Boys and Girls* (New York: American Book Company, 1936), 54; Harriet T. McJimsey, *Art in Clothing Selection* (New York: Harper and Row, 1963), 3–5.

7. O'Brien et al., *Score Cards for Judging*, 8.

8. Confession: I am guessing that the reporter was a "he"—but it may have been a clueless woman. "Art: Taste Without Tears," *Time*, February 3, 1941, 50.

9. My information about the Goldsteins is drawn from Esther Warner Dendel, *Beauty and the Human Spirit: The Legacy of Harriet and Vetta Goldstein* (Minneapolis: Goldstein Gallery, University of Minnesota, 1993), 6.

10. Katarine Blune, ed., *Art in Home Economics* (Chicago: University of Chicago Press, 1925), 3; "Art: Taste Without Tears," 50.

11. Harriet Goldstein and Vetta Goldstein, *Art in Every Day Life* (New York: Macmillan, 1925), 251. On the spread of such ideas, see Beverly Gordon, "Art in Everyday Life: Women, Taste and Aesthetic Education," unpublished paper given at the Goldstein Gallery, University of Minnesota, 1993; Mary Ann Stankiewicz, "'The Eye Is a Nobler Organ': Ruskin and American Art Education," *Journal of Aesthetic Education* 18, no. 2 (1984): 51–64.

12. Alice Hughes, in Margaretta Byers and Consuelo Kamholz, *Designing Women: The Art, Technique, and Cost of Being Beautiful* (New York: Simon and Schuster, 1938), viii; Cora Irene Leiby, *Clothes for Little Folks* (reprint: Ames: Iowa State College of Agriculture and Mechanic Arts, Extension Service, 1925), 3.

13. Margaret Finnegan, *Selling Suffrage: Consumer Culture and Votes for Women* (New York: Columbia University Press), 93; Nan Enstad, *Ladies of Labor, Girls of Adventure: Working Women, Popular Culture, and Labor Politics at the Turn of the Twentieth Century* (New York: Columbia University Press, 1999); Deirdre Clemente, "Striking Ensembles: The Importance of Clothing on the Picket Line," *Labor Studies Journal* 30, no. 4 (2006): 1–15.

14. John Ruskin, "Modern Manufacture and Design," in *The Two Paths: Being Lectures on Art, and Its Application to Decoration and Manufacture, Delivered in 1858–9* (New York: John Wiley, 1859), 80; Harriet Goldstein, "Related Art for Home Economics Courses in Smith-Hughes Schools," *Journal of Home Economics* 11, no. 7 (1919): 300; Alpha Latzke and Beth Quinlan, *Clothing: An Introductory College Course* (Chicago: J. B. Lippincott, 1935), 3.

15. Mary Brooks Picken, *The Secrets of Distinctive Dress* (Scranton, PA: International Textbook, 1918), 54; Jane Loewen, *Millinery* (New York: Macmillan, 1925), 179.

16. See Anthea Callen, "Sexual Division of Labor in the Arts and Crafts Movement," *Woman's Art Journal* 5, no. 2 (1984–1985): 1–6. For clothing not being central to the movement, see Sally Buchanan Kinsey, "A More Reasonable Way to Dress," in Wendy Kaplan, ed., *"The Art That Is Life": The Arts and Crafts Movement in America, 1875–1920* (Boston: Little, Brown, 1987), 358–371.

17. Latzke and Quinlan, *Clothing*, 1; Mary A. LaSelle and Katherine E. Wiley, *Vocations for Girls* (Boston: Houghton Mifflin, 1913), 50.

18. Claudia Kidwell and Margaret C. Christman, *Suiting Everyone: The Democratization of Clothing in America* (Washington, DC: Smithsonian Institution Press, 1974), 47ff; Susan Strasser, *Never Done: A History of American Housework* (New York: Pantheon Books, 1982), 143.

19. Goldstein and Goldstein, *Art in Every Day Life*, 4; Annette J. Warner, *Artistry in Dress*, Cornell Bulletin for Homemakers (New York: New York State College of Home Economics at Cornell University, 1926), 3; Mabel B. Trilling and Florence Williams, *Art in Home and Clothing* (Chicago: J. B. Lippincott, 1936), 354.

20. Foster Wygant, *School Art in American Culture, 1820–1970* (Cincinnati: Interwood Press, 1993), 27; Nancy E. Green, "Arthur Welsey Dow, Artist and Educator," in Nancy E. Green and Jessie Poesch, eds., *Arthur Wesley Dow and American Arts and Crafts* (New York: American Federation of Arts, in association with Harry N. Abrams, 1999), 55–58; quoted in Mable Russell and Elsie Pearl Wilson, *Art Training Through Home Problems* (Peoria, IL: Manual Arts Press, 1933), 13.

21. Denman W. Ross, *A Theory of Pure Design: Harmony, Balance, Rhythm* (Boston: Houghton Mifflin, 1907), 4.

22. Dendel, *Beauty and the Human Spirit*, 26; Helen Goodrich Buttrick, *Principles of Clothing Selection* (New York: Macmillan, 1925), 10.

23. Florence Hull Winterburn, with chapters by Jean Worth and Paul Poiret, *Principles of Correct Dress* (New York: Harper and Brothers, 1914), 167.

24. Quoted in Dendel, *Beauty and the Human Spirit*, 27.

25. Latzke and Quinlan, *Clothing*, 4; Bernice G. Chambers, *Color and Design: Fashion in Men's and Women's Clothing and Home Furnishings* (New York: Prentice-Hall, 1951), 45.

26. Goldstein and Goldstein, *Art in Every Day Life*, 21.

27. The Goldsteins included a fifth element, size, under harmony, and then told their readers to read the chapter on proportion in order to understand it.

28. Elizabeth Hawes, *Why Is a Dress: Who? What? When? Where?* (New York: Viking Press, 1942), 118–119; George Van Ness Dearborn, *Psychology of Clothing*, vol. 26 of *Psychological Monographs*, James Rowland Angell, Howard C. Warren, John B. Watson, Shepherd I. Franz, and Madison Bentley, eds. (Princeton, NJ: Psychological Review Company, 1918), 68.

29. Helene E. Roberts, "The Exquisite Slave: The Role of Clothes in the Making of the Victorian Woman," *Signs* 2, no. 3 (1977): 554–569; Vicki Lynn Dirksen, "Health Problems Associated with Women's Fashionable Shoes, 1870–1930" (master's thesis, Iowa State University, 1998); Elizabeth Stuart Phelps, *What to Wear?* (Boston: James R. Osgood, 1873), 19.

30. Laura Baxter and Alpha Latzke, *Modern Clothing: A Text for the High School Girl* (Philadelphia: J. B. Lippincott, 1938), 24.

31. Quoted in Arthur Halland, "Will the Horrid High Heel Actually Go 'at Last'?" *Montgomery Advertiser*, June 6, 1919.

32. Buttrick, *Principles of Clothing Selection*, 124; Warner, *Artistry in Dress*, 67; Leona Hope, *Fashion: Its Use and Abuse*, Extension Circular no. 33 (Urbana: University of Illinois, College of Agriculture, Extension Service in Agriculture and Home Economics, 1919), 7.

33. Hazel Rawson Cades, *Any Girl Can Be Good Looking* (New York: D. Appleton, 1927), 143.

34. Trilling and Williams, *Art in Home and Clothing*, 363, 365.

35. Edna Woolman Chase and Ilka Chase, *Always In Vogue* (New York: Doubleday, 1954), 216.

36. "Perfect Pairs," *Marie Claire*, November 2012, 130.

37. Teri Agins, "Ask Teri," *Wall Street Journal*, February 10, 2011.

38. Margaret Story, *Individuality and Clothes: The Blue Book of Personal Attire* (New York: Funk and Wagnalls, 1930), 325.

39. "'The Hobble' Is the Latest Freak in Woman's Fashion," *New York Times*, June 12, 1910; Anne Tyrell, *Classic Fashion Patterns of the 20th Century* (Hollywood, CA: Costume and Fashion Press, 1988), 30.

40. "Injured in 'Hobble' Skirt: Mrs. E. Van Cutzen, While Alighting from Runabout, Falls on Pavement," *New York Times*, August 5, 1910; Trilling and Williams, *Art in Home and Clothing*, 366; "Hobble Skirt Caused Her Death," *New York Times*, September 1, 1911.

41. Winterburn, *Principles of Correct Dress*, 197.

42. Hope, *Fashion*, 5; Trilling and Williams, *Art in Home and Clothing*, 366; Lillian C. W. Baker, *Clothing Selection and Purchase* (1931; printed, New York: Macmillan, 1932), 21.

43. Susan L. Hannel, "The Influence of American Jazz on Fashion," in Linda Welters and Patricia A. Cunningham, eds., *Twentieth-Century American Fashion* (Oxford, UK: Berg, 2005), 57–77; Hawes, *Why Is a Dress*, 62.

44. Quoted in Chase and Chase, *Always In Vogue*, 239; Margaret Murrin, "Rejuvenating Old Frocks," *Fashion Service*, Spring 1930, 11.

45. Mary Brooks Picken, "Sheath Gown," in *The Language of Fashion: Dictionary and Digest of Fabric, Sewing, and Dress* (New York: Funk and Wagnalls, 1939), 46.

46. "FRANCE: Dictator by Demand," *Time*, March 4, 1957.

47. "In the Grand Manner," *New York Times*, November 5, 1950; Anne Summers, "On Begging to Be a Bridesmaid in a Ballerina Dress: Some Meanings of British Fashion in the 1950s," *History Workshop Journal* 44 (Autumn 1997): 226–232.

48. Bobbie Woodward, "Manners and Morals," *Time*, September 1, 1947, 16; JoAnne Olian, ed., *Everyday Fashion of the Forties as Pictured in Sears and Other Catalogs* (New York: Dover, 1992), 99; "The Biggest Skirt of All," *McCall's Pattern Book*, Spring 1952, 38.

49. "Seven Ways to Add Length," *Vogue Pattern Book*, December-January 1947–1948, 66.

50. Marie-France Pochna, *Christian Dior: The Man Who Made the World Look New*, trans. Joanna Savill (New York: Arcade, 1996), 245. In truth, Dior had done straight skirts for the New Look in 1947, but they are forgotten. "Lurking Lady Spies Slink into Spotlight," *Life*, September 6, 1954, 14.

51. Geraldine Sheehan, "Pleaters Hate It, but the Sheath Delights Milliners and Corsetieres," *New York Times*, November 12, 1956; Chambers, *Color and Design*, 124; *McCall's Pattern Book*, Spring 1957, 76–79, esp. 76.

52. Latzke and Quinlan, *Clothing*, 90; Harriet Pepin, *Modern Pattern Design* (New York: Funk and Wagnalls, 1942), 171.

53. Hawes, *Why Is a Dress*, 119–120.

54. Buttrick, *Principles of Clothing Selection*, 119.

55. Latzke and Quinlan, *Clothing*, 73; Goldstein and Goldstein, *Art in Every Day Life*, 49.

56. Buttrick, *Principles of Clothing Selection*, 79; Latzke and Quinlan, *Clothing*, 73.

57. Goldstein and Goldstein, *Art in Every Day Life*, 48; *Better Homes and Gardens Sewing Book* (New York: Meredith, 1961), 287.

58. "Silk as an Incendiary," *New York Times*, October 20, 1879; Ruth O'Brien, "The Contribution of Home Economists to Textile Research," *Journal of Home Economics* 34, no. 7 (1942): 433–435; Margaret B. Hays, "What We Learn from Serviceability Studies," *Journal of Home Economics* 31, no. 3 (1939): 170–172.

59. "How to Handle Velvet," *Fashion Service*, October 1928, 11.

60. Goldstein and Goldstein, *Art in Every Day Life*, 9.

61. Emily Burbank, *The Smartly Dressed Woman: How She Does It* (New York: Dodd, Mead, 1925), 90.

62. Hawes, *Why Is a Dress*, 140, 101–102, 111.

63. Latzke and Quinlan, *Clothing*, 136.

64. Burbank, *Smartly Dressed Woman*, 169, 218; Baxter and Latzke, *Modern Clothing*, 79.

65. Trilling and Williams, *Art in Home and Clothing*, 388; Laura I. Baldt, *Clothing for Women: Selection and Construction* (Philadelphia: J. B. Lippincott, 1929), Plate IV.

66. Catherine Lynn, "Decorating Surfaces: Aesthetic Delight, Theoretical Dilemma," in Amy Horbar, ed., *Pursuit of Beauty, Americans and the Aesthetic Movement* (New York: Metropolitan Museum of Art and Rizzoli, 1987): 53–63.

67. Charles Dickens, *Household Words: A Weekly Journal* 6, no. 141 (1852): 270.

68. Jules Lubbock, *The Tyranny of Taste: The Politics of Architecture and Design in Britain, 1550–1960* (New Haven, CT: Yale University Press, 1995), 280–281.

69. McJimsey, *Art in Clothing Selection*, 128–129; letter reproduced in Dendel, *Beauty and the Human Spirit*, 28.

70. "Woman Is 'Costume Doctor'—Tells Best Dress to Wear," *Seattle Daily Times*, June 3, 1926; Story, *Individuality and Clothes*, 154; Milton B. Jensen, Mildred R. Jensen, and Louisa Ziller, *Fundamentals of Home Economics* (New York: Macmillan, 1935), 56–57.

71. Story, *Individuality and Clothes*, 154; Goldstein and Goldstein, *Art in Every Day Life*, 189.

72. Story, *Individuality and Clothes*, 155.

73. *Paris Frocks at Home* (New York: Butterick, 1930), 13; Hawes, *Why Is a Dress*, 136.

74. Warner, *Artistry in Dress*, 5, 12.

75. Trilling and Williams, *Art in Home and Clothing*, 16, 49.

76. Winterburn, *Principles of Correct Dress*, 140; Stella Blum, ed., *Everyday Fashion of the Twenties as Pictured in Sears and Other Catalogs* (New York: Dover, 1981), 139, 142.

77. Story, *Individuality and Clothes*, 338–339; Lucile Babcock, "What Should the Business Woman Wear?" *Delineator*, April 1930, 36, 48.

78. Grace Margaret Morton, *The Arts of Costume and Personal Appearance* (New York: John Wiley and Sons, 1943), 156.

79. "America's Best Dressed Women," *Morning Oregonian*, January 3, 1925.

80. See Ogden N. Rood, *Students' Text-book of Color, or Modern Chromatics, with Applications to Art and Industry*, vol. 26 of *The International Scientific Series* (New York: D. Appleton, 1881), 274.

81. Trilling and Williams, *Art in Home and Clothing*, 27.

82. Quoted in Latzke and Quinlan, *Clothing*, 138.

83. Winterburn, *Principles of Correct Dress*, 135.

84. Morton, *Arts of Costume and Personal Appearance*, 95.

85. Burbank, *Smartly Dressed Woman*, 263.

86. Laurene Hempstead, *Color and Line in Dress* (New York: Prentice-Hall, 1936), 62–63. This list is almost identical to the one offered by the Goldsteins in *Art in Every Day Life*, 299–300.

87. Winterburn, *Principles of Correct Dress*, 135; Hempstead, *Color and Line in Dress*, 63.

88. "To Visit Europe," *Seattle Daily Times*, June 19, 1937, 16; quoted in Elizabeth Burris-Meyer, *Historical Color Guide: Primitive to Modern Times* (New York: William Helburn, 1938), 1.

89. Burris-Meyer, *Historical Color Guide*, 1; Latzke and Quinlan, *Clothing*, 222.

90. See Story, *Individuality and Clothes*, 163; Picken, *Secrets of Distinctive Dress*, 125; Byers and Kamholz, *Designing Women*, 75.

91. *Photoplay* is quoted in Joanne Hershfield, *The Invention of Dolores del Rio* (Minneapolis: University of Minnesota Press, 2000), 13. Other details about Dolores Del Rio are from the same work, p. 10, and Mary C. Beltrán, *Latina/o Stars in U.S. Eyes: The Making and Meanings of Film and TV Stardom* (Urbana: University of Illinois Press, 2009), 21, 24.

92. Pattern companies did the same; see "How to Find Your Most Flattering Colors," *McCall's Pattern Book*, Spring 1958, 34–35.

93. Elizabeth Burris-Meyer, *Color and Design in the Decorative Arts* (New York: Prentice-Hall, 1935), 124.

94. Judith Rasband, "Questions: Swatches for Color Draping," *Threads*, January 1996, 10.

95. Morton, *Arts of Costume and Personal Appearance*, 328.

96. Picken, *Secrets of Distinctive Dress*, 127; Elizabeth Hawes, *Fashion Is Spinach* (New York: Random House, 1938), 325. For a rare reference to African Americans, see Elizabeth Todd, *Clothes for Girls: Their Selection, Construction, and Design* (Boston: Little, Brown, 1935), 254.

97. Ella Mae Washington, *Color in Dress (For Dark-Skinned Peoples)* (Langston, OK: Ella Mae Washington, 1949), 11.

98. Quoted in Evelyn Brooks Higginbotham, *Righteous Discontent: The Women's Movement in the Black Baptist Church, 1880–1920* (Cambridge, MA: Harvard University Press, 1993), 200; quoted in Victoria W. Wolcott, *Remaking Respectability: African American Women in Interwar Detroit* (Chapel Hill: University of North Carolina Press, 2001), 57; Anthea Butler, *Women in the Church of God in Christ: Making a Sanctified World* (Chapel Hill: University of North Carolina Press, 2007), 81.

99. Charleszine Wood Spears, *"How to Wear Colors": With Emphasis on Dark Skins* (Minneapolis: Burgess, 1937), 8.

100. Ibid., 8.

101. Isabelle Mushka Lott, "Self-Concept of Appearance and Related Adornment Behavior of Negro and White Adolescent Girls" (master's thesis, Michigan State University, 1966), 90.

102. Laura I. Baldt, *Clothing for Women: Selection, Design, Construction* (Philadelphia: J. B. Lippincott, 1916), 79; Grace Margaret Morton, "A Course in Costume Design," *Journal of Home Economics* 15 (1923): 191; Morton, *Arts of Costume and Personal Appearance*, 88; Latzke and Quinlan, *Clothing*, 14.

103. Mabel B. Trilling and Florence Williams, "Standardized Tests in Textiles and Clothing," *Journal of Home Economics* 12, no. 11 (1920): 486–491, esp. 486.

104. Ibid.; Goldstein and Goldstein, *Art in Every Day Life*, 135.

105. Story, *Individuality and Clothes*, 179.

106. Latzke and Quinlan, *Clothing*, 10; Buttrick, *Principles of Clothing Selection*, 16; Goldstein and Goldstein, *Art in Every Day Life*, 83; Story, *Individuality and Clothes*, 181; quoted in Latzke and Quinlan, *Clothing*, 11.

107. Morton, *Arts of Costume and Personal Appearance*, 76.

108. Baldt, *Clothing for Women* (1916), frontispiece, 61.

109. Story, *Individuality and Clothes*, 182.

110. Chambers, *Color and Design*, 42.

111. Dendel, *Beauty and the Human Spirit*, 16–19.

112. Mario Livio has pointed out that the Parthenon does not follow the Golden Ratio. See Mario Livio, *The Golden Ratio: The Story of Phi, the World's Most Astonishing Number* (New York: Broadway Books, 2002), Chapter 5.

113. Trilling and Williams, *Art in Home and Clothing*, 356.

114. Mildred Graves Ryan, *Your Clothes and Personality* (New York: D. Appleton-Century, 1937), 35; Leona Hope, *Artistic Dress*, Extension Circular no. 34 (Urbana: University of Illinois, College of Agriculture, Extension Service in Agriculture and Home Economics, 1919), 4.

115. Hope, *Artistic Dress*, 4.

116. Baldt, *Clothing for Women* (1916), 63; Burris-Meyer, *Color and Design in the Decorative Arts*, 459.

117. The Goldsteins measured 350 women and found the average was 7.5 heads high. Goldstein and Goldstein, *Art in Every Day Life*, 302. Quotation in Burris-Meyer, *Color and Design in the Decorative Arts*, 386.

118. Hope, *Artistic Dress*, 7.

119. Harriet M. Phillips, Fairie Mallory, and Margia Haugh, *Organization and Direction of Clothing Clubs*, Circular 280 (Urbana: University of Illinois Agricultural College and Experiment Station, 1924), 19; and *Organization and Direction of Clothing Clubs*, Circular 263 (Urbana: University of Illinois Agricultural College and Experiment Station, 1922), 29. Walter T. Foster started in 1920 with a figure of 7¼ to 8 heads tall and reached 8 to 8½ heads tall by 1930. Walter T. Foster, *Fashion Illustration, 1920–1950: Techniques and Examples* (1930; reprint, Mineola, NY: Dover, 2010), 5; Hazel R. Doten and Constance Boulard, *Fashion Drawing: How to Do It*, rev. ed. (New York: Harper and Brothers, 1953), 19.

120. Latzke and Quinlan, *Clothing*, 5; Warner, *Artistry in Dress*, 52.

121. Burris-Meyer, *Color and Design in the Decorative Arts*, 339.

122. Caterine Millinare and Carol Troy, *Cheap Chic* (New York: Harmony Books, 1975), 27; Editors of *Mademoiselle*, *You Make It!* (New York: Lancer Books, 1973), 195.

123. Morton, *Arts of Costume and Personal Appearance*, 91.

124. Simon N. Patten, "The Standardization of Family Life," *Annals of the American Academy of Political and Social Science* 48 (1913): 81–90, 88; noted in Ellen Beers McGowan and Charlotte A. Waite, *Textiles and Clothing* (New York: Macmillan, 1919), 229.

125. Buttrick, *Principles of Clothing Selection*, 85.

126. Baxter and Latzke, *Modern Clothing*, 50; Jensen et al., *Fundamentals of Home Economics*, 57; Mildred Graves Ryan, *Junior Fashion* (New York: D. Appleton-Century, 1944), 53; Goldstein and Goldstein, *Art in Every Day Life*, 142; Margaret Story, *How to Dress Well* (New York: Funk and Wagnalls, 1924), 133.

127. Latzke and Quinlan, *Clothing*, 207; Hawes, *Why Is a Dress*, 131.

128. Hawes, *Why Is a Dress*, 130.

129. McCall's Pattern 8190 (1966).

130. Picken, *Secrets of Distinctive Dress*, 183; Buttrick, *Principles of Clothing Selection*, 83.

131. Helen Kinne and Anna M. Cooley, *Shelter and Clothing: A Textbook of the Household Arts* (New York: Macmillan, 1914), 288; Lois W. Banner, *American Beauty* (New York: Knopf, 1983), 264.

132. Emily Burbank, *Woman as Decoration* (New York: Dodd, Mead, 1917), 322, 323.

133. Morton, *Arts of Costume and Personal Appearance*, 17.

134. Buttrick, *Principles of Clothing Selection*, 162; Grace Margaret Morton, "Psychology of Dress," *Journal of Home Economics* 18, no.10 (1926): 584–586; James Street, "Dixie's Mother Confesses," *American Magazine*, July 1938, 128.

Chapter 3: Occasions: The Duty and Pleasure of Dress

1. Jean M. Twenge and W. Keith Campbell, *The Narcissism Epidemic: Living in the Age of Entitlement* (New York: Simon and Schuster, 2009), 35.

2. Kate W. Kinyon and L. Thomas Hopkins, *Junior Home Problems* (Chicago: Benj. H. Sanborn, 1933), 26.

3. Laura Baxter and Alpha Laztke, *Modern Clothing: A Text for High School Girls* (Philadelphia: J. B. Lippincott, 1938), 94; Kinyon and Hopkins, *Junior Home Problems*, 28; Mary Brooks Picken, *The Mary Brooks Picken Method of Modern Dressmaking* (New York: Pictorial Review Company, 1925), 89. For a list of social virtues, see Dulcie G. Donovan, *The Mode in Dress and Home* (Boston: Allyn and Bacon, 1935), 415.

4. Mary Mark Sturm and Edwina Hefley Grieser, *Guide to Modern Clothing* (New York: McGraw-Hill, 1962), 2; Lucy Rathbone and Elizabeth Tarpley, *Fabrics and Dress* (Boston: Houghton Mifflin, 1931), 102.

5. From Josephine C. Foster and Marion L. Mattson, *Nursery School Procedure* (New York: D. Appleton, 1929), 175.

6. Katherine H. Read, "Clothes Build Personality," *Journal of Home Economics* 42, no. 5 (1950): 348–350.

7. Cora Irene Leiby, *Clothes for Little Folks* (Ames: Iowa State College of Agriculture and Mechanic Arts, 1925), 4.

8. Nancy Tomes, *Gospel of Germs: Men, Women and the Microbe in American Life* (Cambridge, MA: Harvard University Press, 1998), 145; Marion Harland, *Homemaking* (Boston: Hall and Locker, [c. 1911]), 254.

9. Helen W. Atwater, *Home Economics: The Art and Science of Home Making* (Chicago: American Library Association, 1929), 36.

10. Paul V. Betters, *Bureau of Home Economics: Its History, Activities and Organization* (Washington, DC: Brookings Institution, 1930), 54.

11. Ruth O'Brien, "The Program of Textile Research in the Bureau of Home Economics," *Journal of Home Economics* 22, no. 4 (1930): 281–287, esp. 285.

12. Quoted in Ann Elizabeth McCleary, "Shaping a New Role for the Rural Woman: Home Demonstration Work in Augusta County, Virginia, 1917–1940" (PhD diss., Brown University, 1976), 137; Barbara R. Cotton, *The Lamplighters, Black Farm and Home*

Demonstration Agents in Florida, 1915–1965 (Tallahassee: US Dept. of Agriculture in cooperation with Florida Agricultural and Mechanical University, 1982), 49; *Oklahoma Annual Report Extension Division 1927*, Circular 251 (Stillwater: Oklahoma Agricultural and Mechanical College, 1927), 80–81.

13. Mary Jean Houde, *Reaching Out: A Story of the General Federation of Women's Clubs* (Chicago: Mobium Press, 1989), 232.

14. Stella Blum, ed., *Everyday Fashion of the Twenties as Pictured in Sears and Other Catalogs* (New York: Dover, 1981), 147; Edna Woolman Chase and Ilka Chase, *Always In Vogue* (New York: Doubleday, 1954), 219.

15. Mildred Graves Ryan, *Your Clothes and Personality*, rev. ed. (New York: D. Appleton-Century, 1942), 169.

16. Lucretia Hunter, *The Girl Today, the Woman Tomorrow* (Boston: Allyn and Bacon, 1932), 57.

17. Ryan, *Your Clothes and Personality*, 171; Mabel B. Trilling and Florence Williams, *Art in Home and Clothing* (Chicago: J. B. Lippincott, 1936), 426.

18. Lawrence A. Cremin, *American Education: The Metropolitan Experience, 1876–1980*, vol. 3 of *American Education* (New York: Harper and Row, 1988), 546–548.

19. Baxter and Laztke, *Modern Clothing*, 506–507.

20. Helen Goodrich Buttrick, *Principles of Clothing Selection* (New York: Macmillan, 1923), 107; Mildred Graves Ryan and Velma Phillips, *Clothes for You*, 2nd ed. (New York: Appleton-Century-Crofts, 1954), 210.

21. Trilling and Williams, *Art in Home and Clothing*, 426.

22. Buttrick, *Principles of Clothing Selection*, 107; Alpha Latzke and Beth Quinlan, *Clothing: An Introductory College Course* (Chicago: J. B. Lippincott, 1935), 258–259.

23. Ellen Beers McGowan and Charlotte A. Waite, *Textiles and Clothing* (New York: Macmillan, 1919), 229–230.

24. Jessie E. Gibson, *On Being a Girl* (New York: Macmillan, 1927), 307 (Appendix).

25. Mary A. Laselle, *The Young Woman Worker* (Boston: Pilgrim Press, 1914), 92.

26. Grace Margaret Morton, *The Arts of Costume and Personal Appearance* (New York: John Wiley and Sons, 1943), 198; Junior Vogue Patterns, *Vogue Pattern Book*, February–March 1946, 16–19, 18; *Vogue Pattern Book*, April–May 1946, 24–25.

27. Laurene Hempstead, *Color and Line in Dress* (New York: Prentice-Hall, 1936), 299.

28. Quoted in Deirdre Clemente, "'Prettier Than They Used to Be': Fashion, Femininity, and the Recasting of Radcliffe's Reputation, 1900–1950," *New England Quarterly* 82, no. 4 (2009): 637–666, esp. 646, 658.

29. Elizabeth Hawes, *Why Is a Dress: Who? What? When? Where?* (New York: Viking Press, 1942), 35.

30. Christine Stansell, *City of Women: Sex and Class in New York, 1789–1860* (Urbana: University of Illinois Press, 1987), 93; Julie Berebitsky, *Sex and the Office: A History of Gender, Power, and Desire* (New Haven, CT: Yale University Press, 2012), 21–59.

31. Baxter and Laztke, *Modern Clothing*, 26; quoted in JoAnne Olian, ed., *Everyday Fashions 1909–1920 as Pictured in Sears Catalogs* (New York: Dover, 1995), iii. On men's fashions as simple and dignified, see Sally Helveston, "Popular Advice for the Well-Dressed Woman in the 19th Century," *Dress* 6 (1980): 31–46, esp. 33.

32. S. J. Kleinberg, "Women's Employment in the Public and Private Spheres, 1880–1920," in Janet Floyd, R. J. Ellis, and Lindsey Traub, eds., *Becoming Visible: Women's Presence in Late Nineteenth-Century America* (Amsterdam: Rodopi, 2010), 96; William R. Leach, "Transformations in a Culture of Consumption: Women and Department Stores, 1890–1925," *Journal of American History* 71, no. 2 (1984): 319–342, esp. 332; Susan Porter Benson, *Counter Cultures: Saleswomen, Managers, and Customers in American Department Stores, 1890–1940* (Urbana: University of Illinois Press, 1986), 177–226.

33. Buttrick, *Principles of Clothing Selection*, 4.

34. Margaret Story, *Individuality and Clothes: The Blue Book of Personal Attire* (New York: Funk and Wagnalls, 1930), xxi.

35. Samuel Haber, *Efficiency and Uplift: Scientific Management in the Progressive Era, 1890–1920* (Chicago: University of Chicago Press, 1964).

36. US Department of Agriculture, *Domestic Needs of Farm Women*, Report 104 (Washington, DC: US Government Printing Office, 1915), 8.

37. Mary Brooks Picken, *The Secrets of Distinctive Dress* (Scranton, PA: International Textbook Company, 1918).

38. Laura I. Baldt, *Clothing for Women: Selection, Design, Construction* (Philadelphia: J. B. Lippincott, 1916), 83, 57; Helen Louise Johnson, "Should Women Wear Trousers?" *Atlanta Constitution*, February 25, 1923; Lucile Babcock, "What Should the Business Woman Wear?" *Delineator*, April 1930, 36, 48.

39. Quoted in Alpha Latzke and Helen P. Hostetter, *The Wide World of Clothing: Economics, Social Significance, Selection* (New York: Ronald Press, 1968), 4; Margaretta Byers and Consuelo Kamholz, *Designing Women: The Art, Technique, and Cost of Being Beautiful* (New York: Simon and Schuster, 1938), 152; Hazel Rawson Cades, *Any Girl Can Be Good Looking* (New York: D. Appleton, 1927), 73.

40. Wendy Gamber, *The Female Economy: The Millinery and Dressmaking Trades, 1860–1930* (Urbana: University of Illinois Press, 1997), 129, 216; Marie Downs and Florence O'Leary, *Elements of Costume Design for High School Students* (Milwaukee: Bruce, 1923), 41–42; Florence Hull Winterburn, with chapters by Jean Worth and Paul Poiret, *Principles of Correct Dress* (New York: Harper and Brothers, 1914), 111.

41. Paul H. Nystorm, *Economics of Fashion* (New York: Ronald Press, 1928), 375.

42. Latzke and Quinlan, *Clothing*, 232.

43. Francis Benton, *Complete Etiquette: The Complete Modern Guide for Day-to-Day Living the Correct Way* (New York: Random House, 1956), 45.

44. Morton, *Arts of Costume and Personal Appearance*, 199; Lucretia Hunter, *The Girl Today, the Woman Tomorrow* (Boston: Allyn and Bacon, 1932), 205.

45. Quoted in Benson, *Counter Cultures*, 236.

46. Laztke and Quinlan, *Clothing*, 236; Annette J. Warner, *Artistry in Dress*, Cornell Bulletin for Homemakers (New York: New York State College of Home Economics at Cornell University, 1926), 10.

47. Baldt, *Clothing for Women*, 4–5.

48. Warner, *Artistry in Dress*, 66; Milton Blum and Beatrice Candee, *Family Behavior, Attitudes, and Possessions* (New York: John B. Pierce Foundation, 1944), 59.

49. Christina Binkley, "Law Without Suits," *Wall Street Journal*, January 31, 2008.

50. Elizabeth Burris-Meyer, *Color and Design in the Decorative Arts* (New York: Prentice-Hall, 1935), 473.

51. Laselle, *Young Woman Worker*, 91.

52. Quoted in George Van Ness Dearborn, *Psychology of Clothing*, vol. 26 of *Psychological Monographs*, James Rowland Angell, Howard C. Warren, John B. Watson, Shepherd I. Franz, and Madison Bentley, eds. (Princeton, NJ: Psychological Review Company, 1918), 58; Laselle, *Young Woman Worker*, 93; Bernice G. Chambers, *Color and Design: Fashion in Men's and Women's Clothing and Home Furnishings* (New York: Prentice-Hall, 1951), 548.

53. Chambers, *Color and Design*, 238.

54. Mabel B. Trilling and Florence Williams, *Art in Home and Clothing* (Chicago: J. B. Lippincott, 1928), 455; Trilling and Williams *Art in Home and Clothing* (1936), 428.

55. Buttrick, *Principles of Clothing Selection*, 105.

56. Baxter and Laztke, *Modern Clothing*, 79; Story, *Individuality and Clothes*, 303; *Pictorial Printed Patterns*, August 1933, 3; Lucy Rathbone, Elizabeth Tarpley, Marjorie

Easts, and Nell Giles Ahern, *Fashions and Fabrics* (New York: Houghton Mifflin, 1962), 366–367.

57. Morton, *Arts of Costume and Personal Appearance*, 41; Buttrick, *Principles of Clothing Selection*, 105; Trilling and Williams, *Art in Home and Clothing* (1936), 427.

58. Ryan, *Your Clothes and Personality*, book jacket; "Flashes from Our Advertisers and Exhibitors," *Journal of Home Economics* 51, no. 6 (1959): 500.

59. Ryan, *Your Clothes and Personality*, 187, 188–189; F. Anthea Jarvis, "The Dress Must Be White, and Perfectly Plain and Simple: Confirmation and First Communion Dress, 1850–2000," *Costume* (2007): 83–98.

60. Ruth La Ferla, "The Bride Wore Very Little," *New York Times*, February 21, 2008; "Mildred Graves Is Wed in Albany," *New York Times*, April 28, 1935.

61. Helen Kinne and Anna M. Cooley, *Shelter and Clothing: A Textbook of the Household Arts* (New York: Macmillan, 1914), 1, 10; Dulcie G. Donovan, *The Mode in Dress and Home* (Boston: Allyn and Bacon, 1935), 397.

62. American School of Home Economics, *The Profession of Home Making: A Condensed Home-Study Course* (Chicago: American School of Home Economics, 1911), 3; Dulcie G. Donovan, *The Mode in Dress and Home* (Boston: Allyn and Bacon, 1935), 345.

63. Baxter and Laztke, *Modern Clothing*, 487.

64. "Daytime Frocks of New Prints Choose Modish Trims," *Fashion Service: Woman's Institute Magazine*, March 1928, 10.

65. Woman's Institute of Domestic Arts and Sciences, *Harmony in Dress* (Scranton, PA: International Educational Textbook, 1924), 2:8; Ella Mae Washington, *Color in Dress (For Dark-Skinned Peoples)* (Langston, OK: Ella Mae Washington, 1949), 80.

66. "The Morning Mode for Autumn," *Fashion Service: Woman's Institute Magazine*, October 1928, 7; Stella Blum, ed., *Everyday Fashion of the Thirties as Pictured in Sears and Other Catalogs* (New York: Dover, 1986), 61.

67. Eve Merriam, *Figleaf: The Business of Being in Fashion* (Philadelphia: J. B. Lippincott, 1960), 16; Story, *Individuality and Clothes*, 388.

68. Kinne and Cooley, *Shelter and Clothing*, 11.

69. Buttrick, *Principles of Clothing Selection*, 108.

70. Dorée Smedley, *You're Only Young Twice: The Art and Technique of Transforming Your Appearance* (New York: Simon and Schuster, 1941), 200.

71. Woman's Institute of Domestic Arts and Sciences, *Harmony in Dress* (Scranton, PA: International Educational Textbook, 1936), "Clothes Suitability," 4.

72. Helen Hall, *Correct Styles of the Individual: Pattern Making* (St. Louis: Sye Foundation, 1931), 11.

73. Patricia Campbell Warner, *When the Girls Came Out to Play: The Birth of American Sportswear* (Amherst: University of Massachusetts Press, 2006), 5. My chronology of women and sports relies upon Warner.

74. Warner, *When the Girls Came Out to Play*, 209; JoAnne Olian, ed., *Everyday Fashions 1909–1920 as Pictured in Sears Catalogs* (New York: Dover, 1995), 20.

75. Baxter and Laztke, *Modern Clothing*, 71.

76. Burris-Meyer, *Color and Design in the Decorative Arts*, 189.

77. Story, *Individuality and Clothes*, 357.

78. Buttrick, *Principles of Clothing Selection*, 107.

79. Mildred Graves Ryan, *Your Clothes and Personality*, rev. ed. (New York: D. Appleton-Century, 1942), 175.

80. Barbara Clark Smith and Kathy Peiss, *Men and Women: A History of Costume, Gender, and Power* (Washington, DC: National Museum of American History, 1989), 9.

81. See Patricia A. Cunningham, *Reforming Women's Fashion, 1850–1920* (Kent, OH: Kent State University Press, 2003), 44; Stella Mary Newton, *Health, Art and Reason: Dress Reformers of the 19th Century* (London: John Murray, 1974), 3.

82. Quoted in Emily Burbank, *Woman as Decoration* (New York: Dodd, Mead, 1925), 82, 87; Cheryl Buckley, "'De-Humanised Females and Amazonians': British Wartime Fashion and Its Representation in *Home Chat*, 1914–1918," *Gender & History* 14 (2002): 516–536.

83. "Standard Dresses Urged for Women," *New York Times*, January 21, 1920; Joanne Olian, ed., *Everyday Fashions 1909–1920 as Pictured in Sears Catalogs* (New York: Dover, 1995), 106; Johnson, "Should Women Wear Trousers?"

84. Harriet Pepin, *Modern Pattern Design* (New York: Funk and Wagnalls, 1942), 205; Lisa Ticknor, "Women and Trousers: Unisex Clothing and Sex Role Changes in the Twentieth Century," in *Leisure in the Twentieth Century: History of Design* (London: Design Council Publications, 1977), 56–67; "On the Trail," *Butterick Fashion Magazine*, Summer 1937, 6–7.

85. Emily C. Davis, "Defense Fashions," *Science News-Letter*, July 19, 1941, 45, 39.

86. Mimi Blaker, "Fashions in 1943," *Journal of Home Economics* 35, no. 2 (1943): 75.

87. *Vogue Pattern Book*, February-March 1934, 30–31, December-January 1954–1955, 19; "Dude Ranch," *Pictorial Fashion Book*, Summer 1938, 12–13.

88. Katina Bill, "Attitudes Towards Women's Trousers: Britain in the 1930s," *Journal of Design History* 6 (1993): 45–54, esp. 49.

89. Juliana Albrecht, Jane Farrell-Beck, and Geltel Winakor, "Function, Fashion, and Convention in American Women's Riding Costume, 1880–1930," *Dress* 14 (1988): 56–67, esp. 60; Byers and Kamholz, *Designing Women*, 66; Harriet Pepin, *Modern Pattern Design* (New York: Funk and Wagnalls, 1942), 213–214; Mildred Graves Ryan and Velma Phillips, *Clothes for You*, 2nd ed. (New York: Appleton-Century-Crofts, 1954), 225.

90. Blum and Candee, *Family Behavior*, 63 (Table 45), 59 (Table 42); Ryan and Phillips, *Clothes for You*, 295.

91. Burris-Meyer, *Color and Design in the Decorative Arts*, 189.

92. Baxter and Laztke, *Modern Clothing*, 80; Story, *Individuality and Clothes*, 325; Latzke and Quinlan, *Clothing*, 216.

93. Burris-Meyer, *Color and Design in the Decorative Arts*, 190; Baldt, *Clothing for Women*, 57; Harriet T. McJimsey, *Art in Clothing Selection* (New York: Harper and Row, 1963), 120.

94. Quoted in Tera W. Hunter, *To Joy My Freedom': Southern Black Women's Lives and Labors After the Civil War* (Cambridge, MA: Harvard University Press, 1997), 182.

95. *Vogue Pattern Book*, February-March 1934, 49.

96. Morton, *Arts of Costume and Personal Appearance*, 358; Burris-Meyer, *Color and Design in the Decorative Arts*, 187.

97. *Butterick Pattern Book*, Spring 1957, 63.

98. Burris-Meyer, *Color and Design in the Decorative Arts*, 190; Mary Lynch, *Sewing Made Easy* (Garden City, NY: Garden City Books, 1950), 183.

99. Latzke and Quinlan, *Clothing*, 220; Picken, *The Secrets of Distinctive Dress*, 82–86.

100. Morton, *Arts of Costume and Personal Appearance*, 373–375; Anne Hull Rittenhouse, *The Well-Dressed Woman* (New York: Harper and Brothers, 1924), 77.

101. "Mrs. C. K. Hermer Becomes a Bride," *New York Times*, May 7, 1949, 8.

102. Byers and Kamholz, *Designing Women*, 224–225, 226.

103. Latzke and Quinlan, *Clothing*, 216; Rittenhouse, *Well-Dressed Woman*, 198; Byers and Kamholz, *Designing Women*, 108.

104. *Singer Design Digest*, Fall-Winter 1940, 14.

105. Baxter and Laztke, *Modern Clothing*, 93.

106. Woman's Institute of Domestic Arts and Sciences, *Harmony in Dress* (1924), 2:8.

107. *Manhattan Trade School for Girls* (1911), in *Treasures III: Social Issues in American Film, 1900–1934* (San Francisco: National Film Preservation Foundation, 2007).

108. Rittenhouse, *Well-Dressed Woman*, 182–183.

109. Paul H. Nystrom, quoted in "Women's Hats Seen as Cure for Blues," *New York Times*, February 18, 1932; Story, *Individuality and Clothes*, 320.

110. Maureen E. Lynn Reilly and Mary Beth Detrich, "Seven Rules of Rationing," in *Women's Hats of the Twentieth Century* (Atglen, PA: Schiffer, 1997), 111; Elizabeth Penrose Howkins, "Hatlessness May Wane; New Fashions a Factor," *New York Times*, January 19, 1959; Pat Kirkham, "Keeping Up Home Front Morale: 'Beauty and Duty' in War Time Britain," in Jacqueline M. Atkins, ed., *Wearing Propaganda: Textiles on the Home Front in Japan, Britain, and the United States, 1931–1945* (New Haven, CT: Yale University Press, 2005), 218; "John Fredrics Gives Away a Secret," *Vogue Pattern Book*, August-September 1954, 40–41.

111. Winifred Rauschenbush, *How to Dress in Wartime* (New York: Coward-McCann, 1942), 110–111; Blum and Candee, *Family Behavior*, 59.

112. Chambers, *Color and Design*, 4.

113. Aage Thaarup and Dora Shackell, *How to Make a Hat* (London: Cassell and Company, 1957), 8.

114. Chambers, *Color and Design*, 316.

115. Smedley, *You're Only Young Twice*, 151.

116. Hempstead, *Color and Line in Dress*, 1.

117. Ibid., 265.

118. Story, *Individuality and Clothes*, 303.

Chapter 4: Thrift: Much for Little

1. Helen Goodrich Buttrick, *Principles of Clothing Selection* (New York: Macmillan, 1923), 119; Elizabeth Todd, *Clothes for Girls: Their Selection, Construction, and Care* (Boston: D. C. Heath, 1947), 120.

2. Grace Margaret Morton, *The Arts of Costume and Personal Appearance* (New York: John Wiley and Sons, 1943), 357.

3. Margaret Story, *Individuality and Clothes: The Blue Book of Personal Attire* (New York: Funk and Wagnalls, 1930), 302; Jon Mooallem, "The Self-Storage Self," *New York Times Magazine*, September 6, 2009; Theodore Caplow, Louis Hicks, and Ben J. Wattenberg, *The First Measured Century* (Washington, DC: AEI Press, 2001), 166–167.

4. Mary Schenck Woolman, *Clothing: Choice, Care, Cost* (Philadelphia: J. B. Lippincott, 1920), 1, 11, 12, 129, v.

5. Anna M. Cooley, "Mary Schenck Woolman, 1860–1940," *Journal of Home Economics* 32, no. 9 (1940): 585–588; "Notes," *Journal of Home Economics* 12, no. 4 (1920): 192.

6. Quoted in David M. Tucker, *The Decline of Thrift in America: Our Cultural Shift from Saving to Spending* (New York: Praeger, 1991), 35; "The Influence of Fashions," *Ladies' Magazine and Literary Gazette* 5, no. 1 (1832): 1.

7. Ellen H. Richards, *The Cost of Living as Modified by Sanitary Science*, 1st ed. (New York: Wiley and Sons, 1910), 12.

8. Meg Jacobs, "State of the Field: The Politics of Consumption," *Reviews in American History* 39, no. 3 (2011): 561–573; Stuart Ewen, *Captains of Consciousness: Advertising and the Social Roots of the Consumer Culture* (New York: McGraw-Hill, 1976), 159–184; Rayna Rapp and Ellen Ross, "The 1920s: Feminism, Consumerism, and Political Backlash in the United States," in Judith Friedlander, Blanche Wiesen Cook, Alice Kessler-Harris,

and Carroll Smith-Rosenberg, eds., *Women in Culture and Politics: A Century of Change* (Bloomington: Indiana University Press, 1986): 52–61.

9. Daniel Horowitz, *The Morality of Spending: Attitudes Toward the Consumer Society in America, 1875–1940* (1985; reprint, Chicago: Ivan R. Dee, 1992), 90–92.

10. Quoted in Tucker, *Decline of Thrift in America*, 69; "Pushcarts Burned in Riots over Food," *New York Times*, February 20, 1917.

11. G. Lynn Sumner, *How I Learned the Secrets of Success in Advertising* (New York: Prentice-Hall, 1952), 79.

12. Ibid.

13. *Woman's Institute of Domestic Arts and Sciences Catalogue* (Scranton, PA: Woman's Institute of Domestic Arts and Sciences, 1922), back cover; "The Woman's Institute of Domestic Arts and Sciences," *Manual Training Magazine*, 1921, 161–163.

14. Sumner, *How I Learned*, 81; *Woman's Institute Catalogue*, 81.

15. Olive Carter, "Eleanor Finds a Way," *Cosmopolitan*, October 1920, 133.

16. *Woman's Institute Catalogue*, 16, 15, 21.

17. "The Envelope," *The Silent Partner*, November 1915, 362.

18. *Woman's Institute Catalogue*, 19, 23; *What the Woman's Institute Means to Me* (Scranton, PA: Woman's Institute, 1921), 8–9.

19. Mary A. LaSelle and Katherine E Wiley, *Vocations for Girls* (Boston: Houghton Mifflin, 1913).

20. W. E. Burghardt Du Bois, ed., *The Negro Artisan* (Atlanta: Atlanta University Press, 1902), 28; Tera W. Hunter, *To 'Joy My Freedom': Southern Black Women's Lives and Labors After the Civil War* (Cambridge, MA: Harvard University Press, 1997), 111–112; quoted in Wendy Gamber, *The Female Economy: The Millinery and Dressmaking Trades, 1860–1930* (Urbana: University of Illinois Press, 1997), 1.

21. *Woman's Institute Catalogue*, 80.

22. Mary Brooks Picken, *Modern Dressmaking Made Easy* (New York: Funk and Wagnalls, 1940), section 5, 1.

23. US Department of Agriculture (USDA), *Report of Extension Work in Agriculture and Home Economics in the United States* (Washington, DC: USDA, 1933), 16.

24. US Department of Agriculture (USDA), *Report of Extension Work in Agriculture and Home Economics in the United States* (Washington, DC: USDA, 1931), 59; US Department of Agriculture (USDA), *Report of Extension Work in Agriculture and Home Economics in the United States* (Washington, DC: USDA, 1932), 17.

25. Quoted in Carmen Harris, "Grace Under Pressure: The Black Home Extension Service in South Carolina, 1919–1966," in Sarah Stage and Virginia B. Vincenti, eds., *Rethinking Home Economics: Women and the History of a Profession* (Ithaca, NY: Cornell University Press, 1997), 203–228, esp. 206; Debra A. Reid, *Reaping a Greater Harvest: African Americans, the Extension Service, and Rural Reform in Jim Crow Texas* (College Station: Texas A&M University Press, 2007), xxiv–xxv; Harris, "Grace Under Pressure," 217; Barbara R. Cotton, *The Lamplighters: Black Farm and Home Demonstration Agents in Florida, 1915–1965* (Tallahassee: US Department of Agriculture, in cooperation with Florida Agricultural and Mechanical University), 48.

26. USDA, *Report* (1933), 25; Ann Elizabeth McCleary, "Shaping a New Role for the Rural Woman: Home Demonstration Work in Augusta County, Virginia, 1917–1940" (PhD diss., Brown University, 1996), 148.

27. Quoted in LuAnn Jones, *Mama Learned Us to Work: Farm Women in the New South* (Chapel Hill: University of North Carolina Press), 177.

28. "News Notes: The University of Alabama," *Journal of Home Economics* 21, no. 1 (1929): 73–74; McCleary, "Shaping a New Role," 147; Henrietta Mary Thompson, "What

Belongs in High School Clothing Courses," *Journal of Home Economics* 25, no. 1 (1933): 19–23, esp. 19.

29. Henrietta May Thompson, "High Style on a Low Income," *Practical Home Economics*, May 1941, 167; Todd, *Clothes for Girls*, 131.

30. Dorothy S. Day, "$35 Does It," *Practical Home Economics*, June 1941, 211; US Department of Agriculture (USDA), Office of Extension Work, *Recommendations for Clothing Club Demonstration Work* (Washington, DC: USDA, 1918), 17; Laura I. Baldt, *Clothing for Women: Selection, Design, Construction* (Philadelphia: J. B. Lippincott, 1916), 7–8; Ellen Beers McGowan and Charlotte A. Waite, *Textiles and Clothing* (New York: Macmillan, 1919), 235; Alpha Laztke and Laura Baxter, *Modern Clothing: A Text for the High School Girl* (Philadelphia: J. B. Lippincott, 1938), 175.

31. Cited in Mildred Graves Ryan and Velma Phillips, *Clothes for You*, 2nd ed. (New York: Appleton-Century-Crofts, 1954), 310.

32. Susan K. Cahn, *Sexual Reckonings: Southern Girls in a Troubling Age* (Cambridge, MA: Harvard University Press, 2007), 135–136; USDA, *Report* (1933), 24.

33. The Shreveport story is told in Lynne Anderson Rieff, "'Rousing the People of the Land': Home Demonstration Work in the Deep South" (PhD diss., Auburn University, 1995), 133; quoted in McCleary, "Shaping a New Role," 410.

34. Sara B. Marcketti, "The Sewing-Room Projects of the Works Progress Administration," *Textile History* 41, no. 1 (2010): 28–49, esp. 30.

35. *Paris Frocks at Home* (New York: Butterick, 1930), 2.

36. Quoted in Mildred White Wells, *Unity in Diversity: The History of the General Federation of Women's Clubs* (Washington, DC: General Federation of Women's Clubs, 1953), 183; quoted in Mary Jean Houde, *Reaching Out: A Story of the General Federation of Women's Clubs* (Chicago: Mobium Press, 1989), 121.

37. Robin W. Doughty, *Feather Fashions and Bird Preservation: A Study in Nature Protection* (Berkeley: University of California Press, 1975).

38. Houde, *Reaching Out*, 7; quoted in Wells, *Unity in Diversity*, 32; "Short Skirts and Law Expense Bills for Politicians, Say Women," *New York Tribune*, October 21, 1922.

39. Helen Louise Johnson, "For the Homemaker: Women and Clothes. What the Clubs Are Doing in the Matter of Standardization," *Journal of Home Economics* 9, no. 3 (1917): 127, 129, 132, 129.

40. Woolman, *Clothing*, 124.

41. "Standard Dresses Urged for Women," *New York Times*, January 21, 1920.

42. Johnson, "For the Homemaker," 132.

43. "Women Advised to Run Their Housekeeping on a Budget Plan," *New York Times*, March 18, 1917; Johnson, "For the Homemaker," 133.

44. See Amy De La Haye and Shelley Tobin, *Chanel: The Couturiere at Work* (Woodstock, NY: Overlook Press, 1996), 18.

45. Ethel Ronzone, "Standardized Dress," *Journal of Home Economics* 10, no. 9 (1918): 426–428; Ethel Ronzone, "Standard Dress at Last," *Boston Daily Globe*, April 9, 1916; "Stanford Club Favors Missouri Dress Reform," *San Francisco Chronicle*, January 23, 1917; Lelia R. Gaddis, "Standardization of Dress," *Purdue Agriculturalist* (1919): 516–517; Hannah Mitchen, "How Shall the Businesswoman Dress for the Office," *New York Tribune*, May 9, 1920.

46. Sophonisba Preston Breckinridge, *New Homes for Old* (New York: Harper and Brothers, 1921), 140; James Mickel Williams, *Principles of Social Psychology* (New York: Alfred A. Knopf, 1922), 82–83; Anna L. Cobb, "Why We Should Conserve and Standardize Dress," *School Arts* 17, no. 8 (1918): 354.

47. Helen Louise Johnson, "Should Women Wear Trousers?" *Atlanta Constitution*, February 25, 1923.

48. Claire Giles, "Fewer Typewriters and More Sewing Machines the Salvation of the Modern Girl, Says French Modiste," *Atlanta Constitution*, June 25, 1922; Lily Dashé, *Talking Through My Hats*, ed. Dorothy Roe Lewis (New York: Coward-McCann, 1946), 46.

49. "Bibliography of the Economics of Textiles and Clothing," *Library Bulletin*, no. 6, August 1918, 5.

50. Dorothy Dix, "Feminine Frills Will Never Be Outlawed," *Boston Daily Globe*, September 9, 1925.

51. Ibid. On the survival of dress as a test of character, see Anne Summers, "On Begging to Be a Bridesmaid in a Ballerina Dress: Some Meanings of British Fashion in the 1950s," *History Workshop Journal* 44 (Autumn 1997): 226–232.

52. "'Standardized' Dress," *Detroit Free Press*, January 25, 1920; Leona Hope, *Fashion, Its Use and Abuse*, Extension Circular no. 33 (Urbana: University of Illinois, College of Agriculture, Extension Service in Agriculture and Home Economics, 1919), 6; "The Merchant's Point of View," *New York Times*, July 22, 1917; "Standardized Raiment," *New York Times*, January 25, 1920.

53. "Women in Wartime," *Chicago Daily Tribune*, April 3, 1918; "Clubs Discuss Dress," *New York Times*, May 5, 1918.

54. "Miss Helen Johnson Dies," *New York Times*, March 6, 1926, 15.

55. Mary Brooks Picken, *The Secrets of Distinctive Dress* (Scranton, PA: International Textbook Company, 1918), 212.

56. Mabel D. Erwin, *Practical Dress Design: Principles of Fitting and Pattern Making* (1933; reprint, New York: Macmillan, 1940), 97, 430; Harriet Pepin, *Modern Pattern Design* (New York: Funk and Wagnalls, 1942), 144.

57. "What Every Woman Needs: One Perfect Basic Dress," *McCall's Pattern Fashions*, Fall-Winter 1961, 76–77; Ryan and Phillips, *Clothes for You*, 255; Dulcie G. Donovan, *The Mode in Dress and Home* (Boston: Allyn and Bacon, 1935), 290; Hazel Rawson Cades, *Any Girl Can Be Good Looking* (New York: D. Appleton, 1927), 75.

58. Ryan and Phillips, *Clothes for You*, 253.

59. Stella Blum, ed., *Everyday Fashion of the Thirties as Pictured in Sears and Other Catalogs* (New York: Dover, 1986), 105 (for a similar model in 1938, see p. 113); Kay Hardy, *Costume Design* (New York: McGraw-Hill, 1948), 82; "Unmarked Clothes Make Their Mark with Accessories," *Vogue Pattern Book*, October-November 1952, 11.

60. Morton, *Arts of Costume and Personal Appearance*, 370; Avery Strakosch, "Not Another Stitch," *Colliers*, October 8, 1938, 18, 29.

61. Quoted in Virginia Smith, *Clean: A History of Personal Hygiene and Purity* (Oxford: Oxford University Press, 2007), 52. On the Greeks, see Constance Classen, David Howes, and Anthony Synnott, *Aroma: The Cultural History of Smell* (London: Routledge, 1994), 31.

62. Suellen Hoy, *Chasing Dirt: The American Pursuit of Cleanliness* (New York: Oxford University Press, 1996), 59; Nancy Tomes, *Gospel of Germs: Men, Women and the Microbe in American Life* (Cambridge, MA: Harvard University Press, 1998), 145; Hoy, *Chasing Dirt*, 153.

63. Picken, *Secrets of Distinctive Dress*, 15, 43.

64. Milton B. Jensen, Mildred R. Jensen, and Louisa Ziller, *Fundamentals of Home Economics* (New York: Macmillan, 1935), 44; Nora A. Talbot, Florence L. Lytle, Millie V. Pearson, and Anna May Johnson, *Practical Problems in Home Life for Boys and Girls* (New York: American Book Company, 1936), 176; "How to Worry All Day," *Pictorial Review*, September 1935, 31.

65. *Care of Clothing*, vol. 3 of *Woman's Institute Library of Dressmaking* (Scranton, PA: Woman's Institute of Domestic Arts and Sciences, 1926), 27; Jensen et al., *Fundamentals of Home Economics*, 46.

66. Claire B. Shaeffer, *Couture Sewing Techniques* (Newtown, CT: Taunton Press, 1993), 132–133; "Protect It Here and Double the Wear," Kleinert's ad, *Butterick Quarterly*, Winter 1929, 47; Baldt, *Clothing for Women*, 13.

67. Milton Blum and Beatrice Candee, *Family Behavior, Attitudes, and Possessions* (New York: John B. Pierce Foundation, 1944), 64.

68. "A Perfect Wardrobe," *McCall Fashion Book*, Winter 1936–1937, 8.

69. "84 Things You Need for the Perfect Wardrobe," *Glamour*, September 2005, 124; Nina Garcia, *The One Hundred: A Guide to the Pieces Every Stylish Woman Must Own* (New York: HarperCollins, 2008); "A Month of Outfits," *Lucky*, November 2007, 232–237.

70. *Vogue Pattern Book*, April-May 1938, 34–35.

71. Florence Hull Winterburn, Jean Worth, and Paul Poiret, *Principles of Correct Dress* (New York: Harper and Brothers, 1914), 111; Anne Rittenhouse, *The Well-Dressed Woman* (New York: Harper and Brothers, 1924), 4.

72. Lucile Babcock, "What Should the Business Woman Wear?" *Delineator*, April 1930, 36, 45; Ryan and Phillips, *Clothes for You*, 248.

73. "Has Daughter Jailed for Charging Goods," *New York Times*, January 19, 1933.

74. William R. Leach, "Transformations in a Culture of Consumption: Women and Department Stores, 1890–1925," *Journal of American History* 71 (1984): 319–342; Hazel Rawson Cades, *Any Girl Can Be Good Looking* (New York: D. Appleton, 1927), 90.

75. Louis Hyman, *Debtor Nation: The History of America in Red Ink* (Princeton, NJ: Princeton University Press, 2011), 13–14, 17–18, 19, 148–156.

76. Eric Hoover, "The Lure of Easy Credit Leaves More Students Struggling with Debt," *Chronicle of Higher Education*, June 15, 2001; Juliet B. Schor, *The Overspent American: Why We Want What We Don't Need* (New York: HarperCollins, 1998), 72–73.

77. Todd, *Clothes for Girls*, 154 (italics in original).

78. Baxter and Laztke, *Modern Clothing*, 512; Sidonie Matsner Gruenberg and Benjamin C. Gruenberg, *Parents, Children and Money: Learning to Spend, Save, and Earn* (New York: Viking Press, 1933), 69.

79. Baxter and Laztke, *Today's Clothing*, 168.

80. Lucy Rathbone and Elizabeth Tarpley, *Fabrics and Dress*, rev. ed. (Boston: Houghton Mifflin, 1948), 252; Baxter and Laztke, *Modern Clothing*, 93; Talbot et al., *Practical Problems in Home Life*, 179, 383.

81. Baxter and Laztke, *Modern Clothing*, 103.

82. Suzy Gershman, *Best Dressed: The Born to Shop Lady's Secrets for Building a Wardrobe* (New York: Clarkson Potter, 1999), cited in Nina Willdorf, *City Chic: An Urban Girl's Guide to Livin' Large on Less* (Naperville, IL: Sourcebooks, 2003), 199–200; Harris Interactive, Inc., Public Relations Research, *2012 Consumer Financial Literacy Survey* (Rochester, NY: Harris Interactive, Inc., 2012), 3; Council for Economic Education, *Survey of the States: Economic and Personal Finance Education in Our Nation's Schools 2011* (New York: Council for Economic Education, 2012), 1.

83. "My Classroom Economy," *Vanguard Volunteers*, last modified in 2012, www.my classroomeconomy.org/home.html.

84. Ethel Lee Parker, "How Effective Is the Teaching of Home Economics? A Summary of a Study of Changes in Home Living Attributable to High-School Home Economics," *Bulletin of School Service* (University of Kentucky, College of Education) 17 (June 1945): 49–51.

85. Alpha Latzke and Beth Quinlan, *Clothing: An Introductory College Course* (Chicago: J. B. Lippincott, 1935), 319; Beulah I. Coon, *Home Economics Instruction in the Secondary Schools* (Washington, DC: Center for Applied Research in Education, 1964), 74; Ryan and Phillips, *Clothes for You*, 355.

86. Todd, *Clothes for Girls*, xii; Gruenberg and Gruenberg, *Parents, Children and Money*, vii.

87. Grace Margaret Morton and Marjorie Ruth Clark, "Income and Expenditures of Women Faculty Members in the University of Nebraska," *Journal of Home Economics* (1930): 656; Morton, *Arts of Costume and Personal Appearance*, 365–367.

88. *Dying, Remodeling, Budgets* (Scranton, PA: Woman's Institute of Domestic Arts and Sciences, 1931), "The Budget," 2.

89. Quoted in Elisa Miller, "In the Name of the Home: Women, Domestic Science, and American Higher Education, 1865–1930" (PhD diss., University of Illinois at Urbana-Champaign, 2004), 103; quoted in Susan Porter Benson, *Counter Cultures: Saleswomen, Managers, and Customers in American Department Stores, 1890–1940* (Chicago: University of Illinois Press, 1986), 135.

90. Quoted in Joanne J. Meyerowitz, *Women Adrift: Independent Wage Earners in Chicago, 1880–1930* (Chicago: University of Chicago Press, 1988), 103; quoted in Morton, *Arts of Costume and Personal Appearance*, 6.

91. Picken, *Secrets of Distinctive Dress*, 50.

92. Nan Enstad, *Ladies of Labor, Girls of Adventure: Working Women, Popular Culture, and Labor Politics at the Turn of the Twentieth Century* (New York: Columbia University Press, 1999), 77–83; Mary A. Laselle, *Dress for the Young Woman* (Boston: Pilgrim Press, 1914), 90–91.

93. Dorée Smedley, *You're Only Young Twice: The Art and Technique of Transforming Your Appearance* (New York: Simon and Schuster, 1941), 38–40.

94. Ibid.; Morton, *Arts of Costume and Personal Appearance*, 362.

95. Smedley, *You're Only Young Twice*, 45.

96. Latzke and Quinlan, *Clothing*, 314.

97. Ibid, 235.

98. Morton, *Arts of Costume and Personal Appearance*, 361; "Mrs. Exeter Plans Her Autumn Clothes," *Vogue*, August 1, 1948, 120–121, 144.

99. Rittenhouse, *Well-Dressed Woman*, 34.

100. Edna Woolman Chase and Ilka Chase, *Always In Vogue* (New York: Doubleday, 1954), 217; "7 Key Colours for Fall and 7 Ways to Key Them to a Wardrobe," *Vogue Pattern Book*, August-September 1955, 44–57; "A Perfect Wardrobe," *McCall's Pattern Book*, Winter 1936–1937, 3.

101. Mildred Graves Ryan, *Your Clothes and Personality*, rev. ed. (New York: D. Appleton-Century, 1942), vii.

102. Chase and Chase, *Always In Vogue*, 217, 216; *Vogue*, November 15, 1936, cover.

103. Winifred Raushenbush, *How to Dress in Wartime* (New York: Coward-McCann, 1942), 1, 46.

104. *Make and Mend for Victory* (New York: The Spool Company, 1942); US Department of Agriculture (USDA), Bureau of Home Economics, *Bureau of Home Economics in Wartime* (Washington, DC: USDA, Bureau of Home Economics, 1942), 10; Morton, *Arts of Costume and Personal Appearance*, 359.

105. Margaret Brew, US Department of Agriculture, Agricultural Research Service, Household Economics Research Branch, *Exploratory Studies of Measuring Money Savings and Time Costs of Homemade Clothing*, ARS 62–8 (Washington, DC: USDA, 1958).

106. Edna Bryte Bishop and Majorie Stotier Arch, *The Bishop Method of Clothing Construction* (Philadelphia: J. B. Lippincott, 1959), 193.

107. Ryan and Phillips, *Clothes for You*, 239.

108. "Editor's Letter: The Big Deal," *Lucky*, July 2009, 26.

109. "Elle Editor's Letter: Style-O-Nomics," *Elle*, February 2009; "Editor's Letter: Recessionistas Rule," April 2009, 17.

110. "The Month in Outfits," *Glamour*, September 2012, 164–165.

111. Morton, *Arts of Costume and Personal Appearance*, 357.

Chapter 5: Revolt: The Fall of the Dress Doctors

1. Hazel Rawson Cades, *Any Girl Can Be Good Looking* (New York: D. Appleton, 1927), 111.

2. Alpha Latzke and Beth Quinlan, *Clothing: An Introductory College Course* (Chicago: J. B. Lippincott, 1935), 260; Adelaide Laura Van Duzer, Edna M. Andrix, Ethelwyn L. Bobenmyer, et al., *Everyday Living for Girls* (Chicago: J. B. Lippincott, 1936), 5.

3. Henry J. Taylor, "Youth Is a Condition, It's Not a Possession," *Los Angeles Times*, May 20, 1966, A5.

4. Garda W. Bowman, N. Beatrice Worthy, and Stephen A. Greyser, "Are Women Executives People?" *Harvard Business Review*, July-August 1965, 14–28, 164–178.

5. Betty Friedan, *The Feminine Mystique* (1963; New York: Dell, 1974), 7, front material.

6. Quoted in Elisa Miller, "In the Name of the Home: Women, Domestic Science, and American Higher Education, 1865–1930" (PhD diss., University of Illinois at Urbana-Champaign, 2003), 251; US Department of the Interior, Office of Education, *Survey of Land-Grant Colleges and Universities*, 2 vols. (Washington, DC: US Government Printing Office, 1930), 1:852, 863.

7. Beth Ann Krier, "Feminists Put Off by What They Put On," *Los Angeles Times*, August 6, 1972; Alan Cartnal, "Women Libers Refuse Chat with Nation's Fashion Media in Los Angeles," *Sunday Oregonian*, September 27, 1979.

8. Gregory Duhé, "The FBI and Students for a Democratic Society at the University of New Orleans, 1968–1971," *Louisiana History* 43, no. 1 (2002): 55.

9. Robert J. Rubel, *The Unruly School: Disorders, Disruptions, and Crimes* (Lexington, MA: D. C. Heath, 1977), 89.

10. "General Sessions Speakers for AHEAA 62nd Annual Meeting," *Journal of Home Economics* 63, no. 4 (1971): 237; "What Robin Morgan Said at Denver," *Journal Home Economics* 65, no. 1 (1973): 13; "Letters to the Editor," *Journal of Home Economics* 65, no. 2 (1973): 2.

11. Maresi Nerad, *The Academic Kitchen: A Social History of Gender Stratification at the University of California, Berkeley* (Albany: State University of New York Press, 1999), 101–103.

12. Margaret W. Rossiter, "The Men Move In: Home Economics, 1950–1970," in Sarah Stage and Virginia B. Vincenti, eds., *Rethinking Home Economics: Women and the History of a Profession* (Ithaca, NY: Cornell University Press, 1997), 96–117; Margaret Rossiter, *Women Scientists in America: Before Affirmative Action, 1940–1972* (Baltimore: Johns Hopkins University Press, 1995), 284, 175–185.

13. "The Women's Role Committee Speaks Out," *Journal of Home Economics* 65, no. 1 (1973): 10, 11. Nancy F. Cott sees the Bureau of Home Economics' staff in an "anomalous position" from the first as career women advocating the home as the greatest profession, in *The Grounding of Modern Feminism* (New Haven, CT: Yale University Press, 1987), 163.

14. Virginia Y. Trotter, "The Women's Role Committee Speaks Out," *Journal of Home Economics* 65, no. 1 (1973): 14.

15. Quoted in Letitia A. Combs, "Conflict and Resolution: 1976 Congressional Legislation for Consumer and Homemaking Education," *Journal of Vocational and Technical Education* 1 (1985): 17–24, esp. 18.

16. Friedan, *Feminine Mystique*, 369; Kathleen C. Berkeley, *The Women's Liberation Movement in America* (Westport, CT: Greenwood Press, 1999), 28–31.

17. US House of Representatives, *Sex Discrimination and Sex Stereotyping in Vocational Education: Hearings Before the Subcommittee on Elementary, Secondary, and Vocational Education of the Committee on Education and Labor*, 94th Cong., 1st sess. (Washington, DC: US Government Printing Office, 1975).

18. Ibid., 26, 54; Marcia Federbush, *Let Them Aspire! A Plea and Proposal for Equality of Opportunity for Males and Females in the Ann Arbor Public Schools* (Ann Arbor, MI: Committee to Eliminate Sex Discrimination in the Public Schools, 1973), 13, 7, 21 (Table 4); US House, *Sex Discrimination*, 65.

19. US House, *Sex Discrimination*, 125, 126, 42. Office training came in second for girls and the manual trades and industry third. The 1950s rate of 9 divorces per 1,000 married women climbed to 20.3 by 1975, hitting a high of 22.6 in 1981. National Center for Health Statistics, *Vital Statistics of the United States*, vol. 3, *Marriage and Divorce* (Hyattsville, MD: National Center for Health Statistics, 1988), sec. 2, 1.

20. See Elaine Tyler May, *Homeward Bound: American Families in the Cold War Era* (New York: Basic Books, 1988); Joanne Meyerowitz, "Beyond the *Feminine Mystique*: A Reassessment of Postwar Mass Culture, 1946–1958," in Joanne Meyerowitz, ed., *Not June Cleaver: Women and Gender in Postwar America, 1945–1960* (Philadelphia: Temple University Press, 1994), 235; "The Long, Smooth Look . . . Career-Bound," *Butterick Pattern Book*, Fall-Winter 1955, 18–19; "On the Job: A Wardrobe Plan for Young Career Women," *Vogue Pattern Book*, February-March 1959, 66; "Beauty Is My Business," *Vogue Pattern Book*, December-January 1960, 10–13. By the 1980s, women did not end wage work when they reached the age of motherhood. Drucilla K. Barker and Susan Feiner, *Liberating Economics: Feminist Perspectives on Families, Work, and Globalization* (Ann Arbor: University of Michigan Press, 2004), 60 (Figure 4.1).

21. Arlene C. Cooper, "Casual, But Not *That* Casual: Some Fashions of the 1950s," *Dress* (1985): 45–56; "Sportswear: For Campus, Country, Suburbia," *Simplicity Pattern Book*, Fall-Winter 1956, 50–55.

22. "From California: A Way to Wear the Big Splash," *Simplicity Pattern Book*, Spring 1952, 34–35; Hoffman advertisement, "Viva California," *Vogue Pattern Book*, April-May 1949, 13.

23. "Fashion: The American Look," *Time*, May 2, 1955.

24. See "Capsule Wardrobe for a Sun Spot," *Vogue Pattern Book*, June-July 1946, 23–27.

25. "For Suburban Living," *Vogue Pattern Book*, October-November 1959, 38–41; Harriet T. McJimsey, *Art in Clothing Selection* (New York: Harper and Row, 1963), 31; Flyer, *Vogue Patterns*, January 15, 1955, 4.

26. "Guidebook Tutors College Men on Behavior at Girl's Campuses," *New York Times*, April 19, 1951; Mary Shaw Ryan, *Clothing: A Study in Human Behavior* (New York: Holt, Rinehart and Winston, 1966), 273; "College Requirements," *Vogue Pattern Book*, August-September 1955, 19.

27. "Ban on Shorts Threatens Classic Barnard Couture," *New York Times*, April 28, 1960.

28. "Ban on Shorts Threatens Classic Barnard Couture," *New York Times*, April 28, 1960; "Barnard Students to Meet to Protest Shorts Ban Today," *New York Times*, April 29, 1960; "Barnard Students Ask Right to Rule on School Clothes," *New York Times*, April 30, 1960; "Barnard Students Win Right to Wear Shorts on Campus," *New York Times*, September 7, 1960.

29. "Only the Slim Dare to Wear Shop's Styles," *New York Times*, July 8, 1960; "Ban on Shorts Threatens Classic Barnard Couture," *New York Times*, April 28, 1960.

30. Alpha Latzke and Helen P. Hostetter, *The Wide World of Clothing: Economics, Social Significance, Selection* (New York: Ronald Press, 1968), 13; James P. Sterba, "Schools Clar-

ify Girl Slacks Rule," *New York Times*, December 31, 1968; "Stretching the Rules," *South Bend Tribune*, March 11, 2012.

31. Quoted in Latzke and Hostetter, *Wide World of Clothing*, 15; Enid Nemy, "Restaurateurs Cave In Before the Pants Suit Onslaught," *New York Times*, April 25, 1969.

32. Marci Greenwald, "About Those Trousers," *Chicago Tribune*, December 15, 1969; Marylin Bender, "Pants-Ban Tempest at C.B.S.," *New York Times*, January 21, 1970.

33. "Rights," *The New Yorker*, February 17, 1968, 24–25; Richard C. Shepard, "On a Cold Day, a Hot Debate," *New York Times*, January 13, 1968; James P. Sterba, "Schools Clarify Girl Slacks Rule," *New York Times*, December 31, 1968.

34. McJimsey, *Art in Clothing Selection*, 47.

35. Stephanie V. Siek, "Adele P. Margolis: A Legacy, Stitched Together," *Boston Globe*, December 28, 2006; Adele P. Margolis, *How to Make Clothes That Fit and Flatter* (Garden City, NY: Doubleday, 1969), 170; *Fashion Sewing for Everyone* (Garden City, NY: Doubleday, 1974), 184.

36. "Pants Suits Unlimited," *McCall's Patterns*, Fall-Winter 1967–1968, 44–49; "Problems in Pants," *Time*, April 18, 1969, 97.

37. Quoted in Elizabeth Ewing, *History of Twentieth Century Fashion*, revised and updated by Alice Masckrell (Lanham, MD: Barnes and Noble Books, 1992), 179; Maureen Cleave, "Mary Quant, Limited—Kinky Success Story," *New York Times*, March 19, 1967.

38. See Sonia Ashmore, "'I Think They're All Mad': Shopping in Swinging London," in Christopher Breward, David Gilbert, and Jenny Lister, eds., *Swinging Sixties: Fashion in London and Beyond, 1955–1970* (London: V&A Publications, 2006), 58–77; Ewing, *History of Twentieth Century Fashion*, 183–187.

39. See "Summer in the Sun," *Chicago Tribune*, May 24, 1955; "On the Sunnier Shores of Fashion—Black Silk Sweaters and Mini-Skirts," *Vogue*, January 15, 1965, 84; "The New York Collections American Fashion to Go Out and Buy Now," *Vogue*, September 1, 1966, 234; Marylin Bender, "The Fashion Decade: As Hems Rose, Barriers Fell," *New York Times*, December 9, 1969.

40. "Vatican Bars Miniskirts," *New York Times*, September 15, 1967; "Miniskirts Bar Journalists," *New York Times*, May 22, 1970; "Dr. Ernst Dichter Examines Motivations Behind Miniskirt and Erogenous Fashions," *American Fabrics* 76 (1967): 87; "Legislators Ban the Mini Skirt," *Washington Post*, January 12, 1969; "Miniskirt Arrests in Congo," *New York Times*, April 17, 1968; "Ban in Miniskirt Spread in World," *New York Times*, December 1, 1968; "Wears Mini-Skirt, Is Slain by Brother," *Chicago Tribune*, January 18, 1968.

41. "Miniskirts Have Been Slipping by British Sales Tax," *New York Times*, July 16, 1968; Valerie Steele, *Fifty Years of Fashion: New Look to Now* (New Haven, CT: Yale University Press, 1997), 87.

42. Quoted in Jonathan Aitken, *The Young Meteors* (New York: Atheneum, 1967), 35; quoted in Mary Quant, *Quant by Quant* (New York: G. P. Putnam's Sons, 1966), 74.

43. "Up, Up, & Away," *Time*, Dec. 1, 1967, 78; Robert Musel, "Bad News, Fellas, the Hem's Coming Down," *Chicago Tribune*, December 21, 1967; Lucille Enix, "Business Men Tell Low Opinion of High Minis," *Chicago Tribune*, June 12, 1967; Ray Walker, "A Pretty Leg Is What They're Out to See," *Chicago Tribune*, August 19, 1968; Ken Lubas, "Girl Watchers International: Furtive Leer Comes Out in Open," *Los Angeles Times*, August 7, 1969; Charitey Simmons, "Compliments: Life's Sweet Supplement," *Chicago Tribune*, June 18, 1978; "New Watchers Say Midi 'Un-American,'" *Dallas Morning News*, March 27, 1970.

44. Latzke and Hostetter, *The Wide World of Clothing*, 54.

45. Bernadine Morris, "After the Decision to Raise the Hem: How to Live With It," *New York Times*, April 6, 1966.

46. Ibid.; "Fashion Show in the Office," *Time*, August 2, 1968, 76; Morris, "After the Decision to Raise the Hem." See also "Up, Up, & Away," 78; "And Now Bloomers Become Haremized," *Los Angeles Times*, March 28, 1968.

47. Sara Evans, *Personal Politics: The Roots of Women's Liberation in the Civil Rights Movement and the New Left* (New York: Vintage Books, 1979), 189–192.

48. "The Mini Goes Max," *Forbes*, May 15, 1967, 66–67.

49. *McCall Pattern Book*, Winter 1936–1937, 58–59.

50. Marylin Bender, "7th Ave. Looks to Sandbox Set for Summer Fashions," *New York Times*, February 18, 1966; "Welfare Boss Declares Ban on Mini-skirts," *Chicago Tribune*, July 6, 1967; Marilyn J. Horn, *The Second Skin: An Interdisciplinary Study of Clothing* (Boston: Houghton Mifflin, 1968), 289.

51. "People: The Adventurous Ones," *Vogue*, August 1, 1963, 75.

52. Evelyn Livingstone, "'Queen Mother' of Mini-Skirts Pushes Brevity," *Chicago Tribune*, January 18, 1967; Quant, *Quant by Quant*, 157; quoted in Steele, *Fifty Years of Fashion*, 51.

53. "Up, Up, & Away"; "The Mini Goes Max," 66–67; Sara Jane Goodyear, "Hemlines Fall at Bogan H.S.: Parents Police the Mini Skirt," *Chicago Tribune*, January 27, 1968.

54. "Miniskirt Polls Highest in Under-30 Age Group," *New York Times*, September 6, 1970.

55. Marci Greenwald, "About Those Trousers," *Chicago Tribune*, December 15, 1969.

56. Sylvie Reice, "New York Ogles the London Look," *Los Angeles Times*, July 17, 1966.

57. Larch Cody, "What They Wear Under Mini-Skirts," *Chicago Tribune*, January 2, 1968.

58. "Nights of the Garter Are Over, 1959," *Wall Street Journal*, August 25, 1989; George Stein, "Textile Giants Slugging It Out in Pantyhose," *New York Times*, November 16, 1975.

59. Mildred Graves Ryan, *Junior Fashions* (New York: D. Appleton-Century, 1944), 120; Mildred Graves Ryan and Velma Phillips, *Clothes for You*, 2nd ed. (New York: Appleton-Century-Crofts, 1954), 256.

60. Jane Farrell-Beck, "Lifeblood of the Business: Fitters in American Foundations Departments, 1910s–1950s," *Textile History* 34, no. 1 (2003): 1–20; Joanne Olian, ed., *Everyday Fashions 1909–1920 as Pictured in Sears Catalogs* (New York: Dover, 1995), 69; "You're Only Young Twice," *Good Housekeeping*, February 1941, 46–55, esp. 55.

61. Dorée Smedley, *You're Only Young Twice: The Art and Technique of Transforming Your Appearance* (New York: Simon and Schuster, 1941), xx–xxi.

62. Margaret Story, *Individuality and Clothes: The Blue Book of Personal Attire* (New York: Funk and Wagnalls, 1930), 304; Helen Goodrich Buttrick, *Principles of Clothing Selection* (New York: Macmillan, 1923), 126.

63. Ellen B. McGowan and Charlotte A. Waite, *Textiles and Clothing* (New York: Macmillan, 1919), 250. See Stella Blum, ed., *Everyday Fashion of the Thirties as Pictured in Sears and Other Catalogs* (New York: Dover, 1986), 123.

64. "Test . . . the Perfolastic Girdle . . . at Our Expense!" *Pictorial Review*, September 1935, 65; Latzke and Quinlan, *Clothing*, 229; quoted in Joan Cook, "Figure Control Builds Billion-Dollar Industry," *New York Times*, February 8, 1960.

65. Lilian Rixeym, "Shape of Women," *Life*, March 9, 1942, 12, 14–15; Milton Blum and Beatrice Candee, *Family Behavior, Attitudes and Possessions* (New York: John B. Pierce Foundation, 1944), 63; Sylvia S. Silverman, *Clothing and Appearance: Their Psychological Implications for Teenage Girls* (New York: Teachers College, Columbia University, 1945), 38–39; Ryan and Phillips, *Clothes for You*, 301.

66. "Veruschka: Set to Music," *Vogue*, September 15, 1965, 154–163; "'Stars 'n' Stripes' Girdle Banned on D.A.R. Protest," *New York Times*, August 26, 1965; Leonard Sloane, "New Girdle Is Aimed at Teens," *New York Times*, December 29, 1968.

67. "Wyomissing Sees a Skid in Year's Operating Net, Cites Girdle Sales Slump," *Wall Street Journal*, December 22, 1969; "Hers: Sex Appeal in New Marketing Strategy," *New York Times*, September 12, 1976, 117; quoted in Kaori O'Connor, "The Body and the Brand: How Lycra Shaped America," in Regina Lee Blaszczyk, ed., *Producing Fashion: Commerce, Culture, and Consumers* (Philadelphia: University of Pennsylvania Press, 2008), 222.

68. Gloria Steinem, "Gernreich's Progress; or, Eve Unbound," *New York Times Sunday Magazine*, January 31, 1965, 18.

69. Judy Klemesrud, "Braless Look: 2 Years Ago a Daring Fad, But Now It's a Trend," August 5, 1970; quoted in Isadore Barmash, "Bra Industry Reacts to Women's Lib," *New York Times*, September 13, 1970.

70. Herbert Koshetz, "Brassieres: The Soft Look," *New York Times*, July 30, 1972.

71. Barbara Rose, *American Art Since 1900: A Critical History* (New York: F. A. Praeger, 1967), 177; "Chimp's Realistic Touch in Abstract Art Finds Market," *New York Times*, March 12, 1957, citing *Baltimore News Post*; "Topics: Monkeyshines in Art," *New York Times*, November 9, 1961; Angelina Hawley-Dolan and Ellen Winner, "Seeing the Mind Behind the Art: People Can Distinguish Abstract Expressionist Painting from Highly Similar Paintings by Children, Chimps, Monkeys, and Elephants," *Psychological Science* 22 (2011): 435–441.

72. Quoted in Bernice G. Chambers, *Color and Design: Fashion in Men's and Women's Clothing and Home Furnishings* (New York: Prentice-Hall, 1951), 34; "The New Law She Pictures Herself in Modern Master Prints," *Butterick Pattern Book*, Spring 1957, 20–21.

73. William O'Neill, *Coming Apart: An Informal History of America in the 1960s* (New York: Times Books, 1971), 202; Steven Henry Madoff, "*Wham! Blam!* How Pop Art Stormed the High-Art Citadel and What the Critics Said," in Steven Henry Madoff, ed., *Pop Art: A Critical History* (Berkeley: University of California Press, 1997), xv; Horn, *Second Skin*, 285.

74. Sarah Doris, *Pop Art and the Contest over American Culture* (Cambridge, UK: Cambridge University Press, 2007), 171; Joel Lobenthal, *Radical Rags: Fashions of the Sixties* (New York: Abbeville Press, 1990), 81.

75. Quoted in Rene Parola, *Optical Art: Theory and Practice* (New York: Reinhold, 1969), 9; Horn, *Second Skin*, 196, 286; John Borgzinner, "Op Art: Pictures That Attack the Eye," *Time*, October 23, 1964, 78; "Blast-Off into Print," *McCall's Patterns*, Fall-Winter 1967–1968, 39.

76. McJimsey, *Art in Clothing Selection*, 137; Latzke and Quinlan, *Clothing*, 207; "Fashion Op. from Toe to Top: The Newest Style in Clothes Takes After the Newest Style in Art," *Life*, April 16, 1965, 52–55.

77. Flyer, *Simplicity Fashion News*, November 1967, cover; Jessica Daves, *Ready-Made Miracle: The American Story of Fashion for the Millions* (New York: G. P. Putnam's Sons, 1967), 233; Florence Hull Winterburn, with chapters by Jean Worth and Paul Poiret, *Principles of Correct Dress* (New York: Harper and Brothers, 1914), 142.

78. Quoted in Martin Harrison, *Appearances: Fashion Photography Since 1945* (New York: Rizzoli, 1991), 16.

79. Agnes de Mille, "Whatever Has Become of Mommy?" *Horizon* 8, no. 3 (1966): 10.

80. "Dress for Non-Seamstresses: Glue-It-Yourself," *Life*, July 29, 1966, 68–70.

81. De Mille, "Whatever Has Become of Mommy?" 13. See *McCalls' Patterns*, Fall-Winter 1967–1968; quoted in Lobenthal, *Radical Rags*, 83.

82. Quant, *Quant by Quant*, 17–18, 151; Clara Pierre, *Looking Good: The Liberation of Fashion* (New York: Reader's Digest Press, 1976), 165.

83. Cades, *Any Girl Can Be Good Looking*, 13.

84. Charlotte Curtis, "Miss America Is Picketed by 100 Women," *New York Times*, September 8, 1968.

85. Maxine Leeds Craig, *Ain't I a Beauty Queen? Black Women, Beauty, and the Politics of Race* (New York: Oxford University Press, 2002); Kathy Peiss, *Hope in a Jar: The Making of America's Beauty Culture* (New York: Henry Holt, 1998), 42, 205; Laila Haidarali, "Polishing Black Diamonds: African American Women, Popular Magazines, and the Advent of Modeling in Early Postwar America," *Journal of Women's History* 17, no. 1 (2005): 10–37; Malia McAndrew, "A Twentieth-Century Triangle Trade: Selling Black Beauty at Home and Abroad, 1945–1965," *Enterprise & Society* 11 (2010): 784–810.

86. Phyl Garland, "The Natural Look: Many Negro Women Reject White Standards of Beauty," *Ebony*, June 1966, 142–144, 146, 148, 143; Cal Patterson, "Femingenuity: Black Women Go Natural Exposing True Beauty," *Milwaukee Star*, October 5, 1968.

87. "Miss Black America Beauty Pageant Becomes a Reality," *Milwaukee Star*, April 19, 1969; quoted in Judy Klenesrud, "There's Now Miss Black America," *New York Times*, September 9, 1968; "Black Look in Beauty," *Time*, April 11, 1969, 90; "Black Models Take Center Stage," *Life*, October 17, 1969; "Girl Discovers Pride; Wins Beauty Contest," *Milwaukee Star*, March 8, 1969; "Why Is Black Beautiful?" *Milwaukee Star*, November 7, 1970.

88. Mary Mark Sturm and Edwina H. Grieser, *Guide to Modern Clothing* (New York: McGraw-Hill, 1962).

89. Eventually the franchise published Doris Pooser, *Always in Style with Color Me Beautiful* (Washington, DC: Acropolis Books, 1985).

90. Gloria Emerson, "Paris Fashion Designers Said Losing Influence," *Oregonian*, January 30, 1968, 1.

91. Peggy J. Murrell, "Bonwit Teller Memo Urging Switch to Midi Puts Staff in a Tizzy," *Wall Street Journal*, July 31, 1970, 17; Ann Hencken, "Pants Great All-American Cop Out in Midi Battle," *Dallas Morning News*, October 15, 1970, 1

92. Marie-France Pochna, *Christian Dior: The Biography* (New York: Overlook Duckworth, 2008), 152.

93. Paul H. Nystrom, *Economics of Fashion* (New York: Ronald Press, 1928), 379–381.

94. Quoted in Aitken, *Young Meteors*, 10.

95. Daves, *Ready-Made Miracle*, 223.

96. Megan Elias, *Stir It Up: Home Economics in American Culture* (Philadelphia: University of Pennsylvania Press, 2008), 170; Linda Marie Fritschner, "The Rise and Fall of Home Economics: A Study with Implications for Women, Education, and Change" (PhD diss., University of California at Berkeley, 1973), 157; Ruth Anne Mears, "Home Economics Degrees Granted: Perspective from the Seventies," in Elizabeth M. Ray, ed., *Sixty Significant Years: Home Economics Teacher Education* (Washington, DC: American Home Economics Association, 1981), 129–151, esp. 135.

97. Horn, *The Second Skin: An Interdisciplinary Study of Clothing* (Boston: Houghton Mifflin, 1975), preface.

Chapter 6: Aftermath: Tyrannies of Age and Size

1. Quoted in Joel Lobenthal, *Radical Rags: Fashions of the Sixties* (New York: Abbeville Press, 1990), 23.

2. Agnes de Mille, "Whatever Has Become of Mommy?" *Horizon* 8, no. 3 (1966): 9; Zena Smith Blau, *Old Age in a Changing Society* (New York: New Viewpoints, 1973), 100.

3. David Hackett Fischer, *Growing Old in America* (Oxford: Oxford University Press, 1977), 3.

4. Mary Quant, quoted in Jonathan Aitken, *The Young Meteors* (New York: Atheneum, 1967), 13.

5. Mildred Graves Ryan and Velma Phillips, *Clothes for You,* 2nd ed. (New York: Appleton-Century-Crofts, 1954), 210; "How to Choose a Becoming Style," *Woman's Home Companion*, April 1937, 82–83; *Butterick Quarterly,* Winter 1929, 46.

6. Editors of Time-Life Books, *The Art of Sewing: Boutique Attire* (New York: Time-Life Books, 1975), 10; quoted in Sara Doris, *Pop Art and the Contest over American Culture* (Cambridge, UK: Cambridge University Press, 2007), 172; Vivienne Colle and Marjorie P. Katz, *Vivienne Colle's Make-It-Yourself Boutique* (New York: M. Evans,1967), book jacket.

7. Quoted in Lobenthal, *Radical Rags*, 96.

8. Mary Brooks Picken, *The One Hour Dress* (Scranton, PA: Woman's Institute of Domestic Arts, 1924); San Francisco Board of Supervisors, *Journal of Proceedings, Board of Supervisors, City and County of San Francisco,* vol. 19 (San Francisco: Recorder Printing and Publishing Company, 1924), 660.

9. "Patsy Planner," *Treasure Chest of Fun and Fact* 18, no. 12 (1963): 16–17.

10. Maureen Cleave, "Mary Quant, Limited—Kinky Success Story," *New York Times*, March 19, 1967.

11. Sharon Rosenberg and Joan Wiener, *The Illustrated Hassle-Free Make Your Own Clothes Book* (New York: Avenal Books, 1971), 44.

12. Laura Torbet, *Clothing Liberation: Out of the Closets and Into the Streets* (New York: Ballantine, 1973), v, 25.

13. Editors of *Mademoiselle* Magazine, *You Make It* (New York: Lancer Books, 1973), 128–147; Editors of Time-Life Books, *Boutique Attire*, 77.

14. Editors of Time-Life Books, *The Art of Sewing: Shortcuts to Elegance* (New York: Time-Life Books, 1973), 9–10; Colle and Katz, *Vivienne Colle's Make-It-Yourself Boutique*, 11.

15. Editors of Time-Life, *Shortcuts to Elegance*, 57, 59; Hazel Rawson Cades, *Any Girl Can Be Good Looking* (New York: D. Appleton, 1927), 65.

16. Jessica Daves, *Ready-Made Miracle: The American Story of Fashion for the Millions* (New York: G. P. Putnam's Sons, 1967), 161, 132.

17. Harriet Pepin, *Modern Pattern Design* (New York: Funk and Wagnalls, 1942), 165.

18. Mary Brooks Picken, *The Language of Fashion* (New York: Funk and Wagnalls, 1939), 102; *Vogue Patterns Counter Catalogue,* June 1969, #2151.

19. Patricia A. Cunningham, "Dressing for Success: The Re-Suiting of Corporate America in the 1970s," in Linda Welters and Patricia A. Cunningham, eds., *Twentieth-Century American Fashion* (Oxford, UK: Berg, 2005): 191–208; "The Year of the Dress?" *Forbes*, March 15, 1974, 28.

20. *Tinker v. Des Moines Independent Community School District*, 393 US 503 (1969); "Safe, Disciplined and Drug-Free Schools," in President Bill Clinton's "Call to Action for American Education in the 21st Century," 1997; David L. Brunsma, *The School Uniform Movement and What It Tells Us About American Education: A Symbolic Crusade* (Lanham, MD: Scarecrow Education, 2004), 12; *Canady v. Bossier*, 240 F. 3rd 437 (2001), US Court of Appeals for the Fifth Circuit; *Littlefield et al. v. Forney Independent School*, 108 F. Supp. 2d 681 (2000), USDC North District of Texas; *Littlefield et al. v. Forney Independent School District*, 268 F. 3d 275 (2001); National Center for Education Statistics, *Indicators of School Crime and Safety 2007* (Washington, DC: US Department of Education, 2008), Table 20.2.

21. Kim R. Kaye, ed., *National College Databank*, 4th ed. (Princeton, NJ: Peterson's Guide, 1987), 136–139; Thomas Bartlett, "Black Colleges React to Low Point in Fashion," *Chronicle of Higher Education*, November 8, 2009, A1, A20–21.

22. Bernadine Morris, "Plenty of Clothes to Please the Post-Puberty Set," *New York Times*, November 2, 1972, 53.

23. Bernadine Morris, "Diane Von Furstenberg: Making Some Changes," *New York Times*, June 17, 1978, 10.

24. John T. Molloy, *Dress for Success* (New York: Peter H. Wyden, 1975).

25. Lawrence Van Gelder, "What's in a Designer's Name? More Men Say It Spells Style," *New York Times*, December 16, 1975, 52.

26. "Year of the Dress," *Forbes*, 29; John T. Molloy, *The Woman's Dress for Success Book* (Chicago: Follett, 1977), 19.

27. Esther B. Fein, "Redefining Office Style," *New York Times*, March 3, 1985, SMA64.

28. Ibid.; Judith Keith, *"I Haven't a Thing to Wear"* (New York: Avon, 1980), 93–148.

29. Sara B. Marcketti and Jane Farrell-Beck, "'Look Like a Lady; Act Like a Man; Work Like a Dog': Dressing for Business Success," *Dress* 35 (2008/2009): 63.

30. Helen L. Brockman, *Theory of Fashion Design* (New York: Wiley, 1965), 26; Marcia Sullivan, "Former Instructor Recalls Past Careers in Language, Design," *Kansas State Collegian*, June 19, 1986, 3.

31. Harriet T. McJimsey, *Art in Clothing Selection* (New York: Harper and Row, 1963), 28; De Mille, "Whatever Has Become of Mommy?" 9.

32. Edward John Tilt, *The Change of Life in Health and Disease* (Philadelphia: Lindsay and Blakiston, 1871), 130, quoted in Lois W. Banner, *In Full Flower: Aging Women, Power, and Sexuality* (New York: Knopf, 1992), 281; Florence Hull Winterburn, with chapters by Jean Worth and Paul Poiret, *Principles of Correct Dress* (New York: Harper and Brothers, 1914), 161.

33. Helen Koves, "Mother, Why Can't You Look Smart?" *Good Housekeeping*, February 1939, 45–52; "You're Only Young Twice," *Good Housekeeping*, February 1941, 46–55, esp. 47.

34. Frieda Steinmann Curtis, *How to Give a Fashion Show* (New York: Fairchild Publications, 1950), 19; Dorée Smedley, *You're Only Young Twice: The Art and Technique of Transforming Your Appearance* (New York: Simon and Schuster, 1941), xiv.

35. Koves, "Mother, Why Can't You Look Smart?" 45–52; "Mother Answers Back," *Good Housekeeping*, October 1939, 58–61.

36. Alpha Latzke and Beth Quinlan, *Clothing: An Introductory College Course* (Chicago: J. B. Lippincott, 1935), 255; "Faculty Biography, Bernice Gertrude Chambers," Summer 1942 and October 23, 1951, New York University Archives, Esther Holmes Bobst Library.

37. Woman's Institute of Domestic Arts and Sciences, *Harmony in Dress* (Scranton, PA: International Educational Textbook, 1936), 7:3; Latzke and Quinlan, *Clothing*, 255.

38. Smedley, *You're Only Young Twice*, 339.

39. Anne Rittenhouse, *The Well-Dressed Woman* (New York: Harper and Brothers, 1924), 56.

40. Charla Krupp, *How Not to Look Old* (New York: Springboard Press, 2008), 26–27.

41. Margaret Story, *Individuality and Clothes: The Blue Book of Personal Attire* (New York: Funk and Wagnalls, 1930), 61.

42. Laurene Hempstead, *Color and Line in Dress* (New York: Prentice-Hall, 1936), 325.

43. Mildred Graves Ryan, *Junior Fashions* (New York: D. Appleton-Century, 1944), 62.

44. Woman's Institute of Domestic Arts and Sciences, *Harmony in Dress*, 9:5; Winterburn, *Principles of Correct Dress*, 151.

45. Ryan and Phillips, *Clothes for You*, 251; Story, *Individuality and Clothes*, 84; Hempstead, *Color and Line in Dress*, 290, 288, 285; Ryan and Phillips, *Clothes for You*, 210; Rittenhouse, *Well-Dressed Woman*, 185.

46. "I Want a Spring Suit," *Good Housekeeping*, February 1941, 56–58; "Patterns for Youth," *Vogue Pattern Book*, October-November 1955, 60–61.

47. Rittenhouse, *Well-Dressed Woman*, 158, 160.

48. Dulcie G. Donovan, *The Mode in Dress and Home* (Boston: Allyn and Bacon, 1935), 98; Leona Hope, *Fashion: Its Use and Abuse*, Extension Circular no. 33 (Urbana: University of Illinois, College of Agriculture, Extension Service in Agriculture and Home Economics, 1919), 7.

49. Jeannette Throckmorton, "Fashions as Affecting Public Health," *Public Health* (1918): 817–820.

50. Martha McPheeters and Cleora C. Helbing, "Suggestions for Conducting 4-H Club Girls Judging Contests," Circular 258 (Oklahoma City: State of Oklahoma Cooperative Extension Work in Agriculture and Home Economics, 1929), 3–4; "Score Cards for Food and Clothing," Extension Circular 257 (Oklahoma City: State of Oklahoma Cooperative Extension Work in Agriculture and Home Economics, 1929), 8.

51. Ethel Henley Caldwell [?] to President James Blaisdell, May 11, 1927, Gibson personnel file, Pomona College Archives; Jessie Gibson, *On Being a Girl* (Philadelphia: Macmillan, 1927), 28, 29.

52. Joan J. Brumburg, *The Body Project: An Intimate History of American Girls* (New York: Random House, 1997), 98; Beth L. Bailey, *From Front Porch to Back Seat: Courtship in Twentieth Century America* (Baltimore: Johns Hopkins University Press, 1988).

53. Elizabeth Hawes, *Why Is a Dress: Who? What? When? Where?* (New York: Viking Press, 1942), 41.

54. Story, *Individuality and Clothes*, 359; Hempstead, *Color and Line in Dress*, 305; Geneviève Antoine Dariaux, *Elegance: A Complete Guide for Every Woman Who Wants to Be Well and Properly Dressed on All Occasions* (New York: Doubleday, 1964), 6.

55. Hempstead, *Color and Line in Dress*, 305.

56. Ryan and Phillips, *Clothes for You*, 213.

57. Ibid., 213, 215; Latzke and Quinlan, *Clothing*, 256; Hempstead, *Color and Line in Dress*, 315.

58. Grace Margaret Morton, *The Arts of Costume and Personal Appearance* (New York: John Wiley and Sons, 1943), 163; "Grace Margaret Morton, Associate Professor of Home Economics, July 24, 1884–December 3, 1945," University Archives/Special Collections, University of Nebraska at Lincoln.

59. Hempstead, *Color and Line in Dress*, 313.

60. Elizabeth Penrose Howkins, "Hatlessness May Wane; New Fashions a Factor," *New York Times*, January 19, 1959; Jacqueline du Pasquier, *A Guide to Elegance* (London: Staples Press, 1956), 173.

61. Jody Shields, *Hats: A Stylish History and Collector's Guide* (New York: Clarkson Potter, 1991), 90; Dariaux, *Elegance*, 118; Mabel D. Erwin and Lila A. Kincher, *Clothing for Moderns*, 4th ed. (Toronto: Macmillan, 1969), 66–67; Francis Benton, *Complete Etiquette: The Complete Modern Guide for Day-to-Day Living the Correct Way* (New York: Random House, 1956), 44; Isadore Barmash, "Hats Are Coming Back Once Again," *New York Times*, May 7, 1967.

62. Jane Mulvagh, "Obituary: John P. John," *The Independent*, July 2, 1993.

63. Barmash, "Hats Are Coming Back Once Again."

64. Jane Loewen, *Millinery* (New York: Macmillan, 1926), 126.

65. Bernice G. Chambers, *Color and Design: Fashion in Men's and Women's Clothing and Home Furnishings* (New York: Prentice-Hall, 1951), 315.

66. Christina Binkley, "Fashion Nation: What Retailers Know About Us," *Wall Street Journal*, July 28, 2010.

67. Margaretta Byers and Consuelo Kamholz, *Designing Women: The Art, Technique, and Cost of Being Beautiful* (New York: Simon and Schuster, 1938), 172; Benton, *Complete Etiquette*, 45.

68. Smedley, *You're Only Young Twice*, 109–110; Elizabeth Burris-Meyer, *Color and Design in the Decorative Arts* (New York: Prentice-Hall, 1935), 151.

69. Hempstead, *Color and Line in Dress* (New York: Prentice-Hall, 1936), 59.

70. For the history of the color black in the European tradition, see Anne Hollander, *Seeing Through Clothes* (New York: Viking Press, 1978), 365–390.

71. Hempstead, *Color and Line in Dress*, 336–337; Mary Brooks Picken, *The Secrets of Line and Dress* (Scranton, PA: International Textbook Company, 1918), 141; Story, *Individuality and Clothes*, 168.

72. Chambers, *Color and Design*, 315.

73. Mary Mahon, "Hatting the Matron Becomingly," *Fashion Service*, April 1928, 4.

74. Ryan and Phillips, *Clothes for You*, 216; Latzke and Quinlan, *Clothing*, 205–206; Annette J. Warner, *Artistry in Dress*, Cornell Bulletin for Homemakers (New York: New York State College of Home Economics at Cornell University, 1926), 47.

75. Hempstead, *Color and Line in Dress*, 334.

76. Rittenhouse, *Well-Dressed Woman*, 90. But Hempstead disagreed in *Color and Line in Dress*, 336.

77. Edna Woolman Chase and Ilka Chase, *Always In Vogue* (New York: Doubleday, 1954), 217–218.

78. Elizabeth Penrose Howkins, "First Lady of Fashion, Still a Great Influence, Marks Eightieth Year," *New York Times*, March 13, 1957, 28.

79. "Fifty-Odd and Still in the Swim," *Vogue*, June 1, 1948, 140.

80. Zillah Halls on the British edition, "Mrs. Exeter—The Rise and Fall of the Older Woman," *Costume* 34 (2000): 105–112, esp. 109; "Introducing Mrs. Exeter," *Vogue Pattern Book*, October-November 1955, 33; "Mrs. Exeter Takes a Trip," *Vogue Pattern Book*, February-March 1959, 49.

81. "Style Counsel: The Return of Mrs. Exeter," *Vogue*, December 1, 2001, 180–182, 184.

82. Lance Schwuist, "Resident Recalls Design Career," *Kansas State Collegian*, April 20, 1989, 1, 8.

83. Smedley, *You're Only Young Twice*, 328.

84. Acme Dress Form Advertisement, *Butterick Pattern Book*, Spring 1957, 72.

85. Helen Goodrich Buttrick, *Principles of Clothing Selection* (New York: Macmillan, 1923), 58, 57, 55.

86. Rittenhouse, *Well-Dressed Woman*, 80, 83, 82.

87. "The Smart Woman Plans Her Winter Wardrobe," *Vogue Fashion Bi-Monthly*, October-November 1926, 1–9, 86.

88. Mary Louise Roberts, "Samson and Delilah Revisited: The Politics of Women's Fashion in 1920s France," *American Historical Review* 98, no. 3 (1993): 657–684; Margaret A. Lowe, *Looking Good: College Women and Body Image, 1875–1930* (2003; reprint, Baltimore: Johns Hopkins University Press, 2006), 144.

89. Stella Blum, ed., *Everyday Fashion of the Twenties as Pictured in Sears and Other Catalogs* (New York: Dover, 1981), 95.

90. Elizabeth Hawes, *Fashion Is Spinach* (New York: Random House, 1938), 139.

91. "Smart Styles Feature Long Lines," *Fashion Service*, January 1930, 8; Blum, *Everyday Fashion of the Twenties*, 143; Celia Caroline Cole, "Reach Up Your Hands," *Delineator*, February 1930, 25, 48; Paul H. Nystrom, *Fashion Merchandising* (New York: Ronald Press, 1932), 45.

92. Byers and Kamholz, *Designing Women*, 11; Story, *Individuality and Clothes*, 121. Five feet, four inches was the average height for a woman born in 1930. Richard Steckel, "A History of the Standard of Living in the United States," *EH.Net Encyclopedia*, ed. Robert Whaples, July 21, 2002, http://eh.net/encyclopedia/article/steckel.standard.living.us.

93. Ruth O'Brien and William C. Shelton, *Women's Measurements for Garment and Pattern Construction*, USDA Miscellaneous Publication no. 454 (Washington, DC: US Government Printing Office, 1941); Lilian Rixey, "Shape of Women," *Life*, March 9, 1942, 12; Mildred Graves Ryan and Velma Phillips, *Clothes for You* (New York: Appleton-Century-Crofts, 1947), 114.

94. Rixey, "Shape of Women," 14.

95. Singer Educational Department, *Singer Dressmaking Course in 8 Easy Steps* (New York: Singer Company, 1961), 131.

96. June Wood, "Twiggy Makes Me Look Like Betty Grable," *Chicago Tribune*, May 14, 1967; Lobenthal, *Radical Rags*, 23–24; quoted in Ina Zweiniger-Bargielowska, *Austerity in Britain: Rationing, Controls, and Consumption, 1939–1955* (Oxford, UK: Oxford University Press, 2000), 44.

97. Quoted in Aitken, *Young Meteors*, 51.

98. "Cellulite, the New Word for Fat You Couldn't Lose Before," *Vogue*, April 15, 1968, 110–111, 144.

99. Beth Ann Krier, "What's All the Flap About Cellulite," *Los Angeles Times*, January 24, 1975, H1.

100. Clara Pierre, *Looking Good: The Liberation of Fashion* (New York: Reader's Digest Press, 1976), 57–58; Megan Kathy, "Experts Clash over Cellulite," *New York Amsterdam News*, February 24, 1969.

101. David M. Garner, Paul E. Garfinkel, D. Schwartz, and M. Thompson, "Cultural Expectations of Thinness in Women," *Psychological Reports* 47 (1980): 483–491.

102. Brett Silverstein, Lauren Perdue, Barbara Peterson, and Eileen Kelly, "The Role of the Mass Media in Promoting a Thin Standard of Bodily Attractiveness for Women," *Sex Roles* 14, no. 9 (1986): 519–532, esp. 530.

103. Kaori O'Connor, "The Body and the Brand," in Regina Lee Blaszczyk, ed., *Producing Fashion: Commerce, Culture, and Consumers* (Philadelphia: University of Pennsylvania Press, 2008), 207–227, esp. 222–225.

104. Larch Cody, "What They Wear Under Mini-Skirts," *Chicago Tribune*, January 22, 1968.

105. Caterine Millinaire and Carol Troy, *Cheap Chic* (New York: Harmony Books, 1975), 9, 11; "Body Basics," *Simplicity*, Spring 1972, 96.

106. Pierre, *Looking Good*, 11, book jacket, 71.

107. Holly Brubrach, *A Dedicated Follower of Fashion* (London: Phaidon Press, 1999), 46.

108. Brumberg, *Body Project*, 119–120.

109. *Seventeen*, June/July 2010, August 2010.

110. Beverly Stephen, "Women Are Losing Their Shirts," *Los Angeles Times*, May 15, 1980.

111. Body Issue, *Elle*, June 2011, 178, 48.

112. Shaun Dreisbach, "5 Secrets of Rock Star Abs," *Glamour*, June 2011, 128; "Calories Burned Calculator," *Calorie Count*, accessed August 27, 2012, http://caloriecount.about .com/cc/calories-burned.

113. *Elle*, July 2010, 28; Emma Seifrit Weilgey, "Average? Ideal? Desirable? A Brief Overview of Height-Weight Tables in the United States," *Journal of the American Dietetic Association* 84 (1984): 417–423. Grace Margaret Morton cites John Powers, who ran the first important modeling agency, in *The Arts of Costume and Personal Appearance*, 3rd ed. (New York: John Wiley and Son, 1964), 38.

114. Buttrick, *Principles of Clothing Selection*, 61; Morton, *Arts of Costume and Personal Appearance* (1943), 250.

115. Hempstead, *Color and Line in Dress*, 224; Byers and Kamholz, *Designing Women*, 31; Mabel B. Trilling and Florence Williams, *Art in Home and Clothing* (Chicago: J. B. Lippincott, 1936), 415.

116. American Society of Plastic Surgeons, *Report of the 2010 Plastic Surgery Statistics*, 2011, 7.

117. Hempstead, *Color and Line in Dress*, 187; Latzke and Quinlan, *Clothing*, 130; Byers and Kamholz, *Designing Women*, 43; Chase and Chase, *Always In Vogue*, 215.

118. *Paris Frocks at Home* (New York: Butterick, 1930), 27; Barbara E. Scott Fisher, "Standard Sizing of Garments Predicted by Miss Chambers," *Christian Science Monitor*, January 13, 1943.

119. Charity M. Prelipp, "The Effects of Vanity Sizing on Consumer Satisfaction with Fit and Body-Cathexism" (master's thesis, University of North Carolina at Greensboro, 2000).

120. Jane Warren Wells, *Dress and Look Slender* (Scranton, PA: Personal Arts Company, 1924).

121. Hawes, *Why Is a Dress*, 118, 117.

122. Peter Stearns, "The Rise and Fall of American Posture," *American Historical Review* 103, no. 4 (1998): 1057–1095; Carmen Gorman, "Educating the Eye: Body Mechanics and Streamlining in the United States, 1925–1950," *American Quarterly* 58, no. 3 (2006): 839–868; White House Conference on Child Health and Protection, *Body Mechanics: Education and Practice* (New York: Century Company, 1932), 41.

123. Essie M. Heyle, *4-H Clothing Club III: Winter Clothes for Girls*, Circular 4-H 24 (Columbia: Cooperative Extension Work in Agriculture and Home Economics, University of Missouri College of Agriculture, 1929), 11; Latzke and Quinlan, *Clothing*, 60.

124. Li Huang, Adam D. Galinsky, Deborah H. Gruenfeld, and Lucia E. Guillory, "Powerful Postures Versus Powerful Roles: Which Is the Proximate Correlate of Thought and Behavior?" *Psychological Science* 22, no. 1 (2011): 95–102; Pablo Briñol, Richard E. Petty, and Benjamin Wagner, "Body Posture Effects on Self-Evaluation: A Self-Validation Approach," *European Journal of Social Psychology* 39, no. 6 (2009): 1053–1064; "The Power of Posture," *The Economist*, January 15, 2011, 90.

125. Helen Powell Smith, *The Woman and Her Posture*, Cornell Bulletin for Homemakers 535 (Ithaca, NY: Cornell University, 1942), 2.

126. Eve Merriam, *Figleaf: The Business of Being in Fashion* (New York: J. B. Lippincott, 1960), 203.

127. Quoted in Lobenthal, *Radical Rags*, 129; Eugenia Sheppard, "Something New Added: Shake-up of the Best Dressed List," *Los Angeles Times*, January 2, 1968.

128. Wina Sturgeon, "A Woman's Invisible Years Are Frightening to See," *Los Angeles Times*, January 7, 1980.

129. Ari Seth Cohen, *Advanced Style* (Brooklyn: Powerhouse Books, 2012), "Introduction."

130. Ryan and Phillips, *Clothes for You* (1947), 6.

131. Ryan and Phillips, *Clothes for You* (1954), 297.

Epilogue: Legacies

1. Megan Elias, *Stir It Up: Home Economics in American Culture* (Philadelphia: University of Pennsylvania Press, 2008), 173–174.

2. "Grace Margaret Morton, Associate Professor of Home Economics, July 24, 1884–December 3, 1945," University Archives/Special Collections, University of Nebraska at Lincoln.

3. Steven Rosen, "As Eric Lee Departs, Taft Museum Has a Hit," *City Beat*, March 11, 2009; "Alexander McQueen: Savage Beauty Exhibition Extended," May 31, 2011, press release, Metropolitan Museum of Art; Kate Murphy, "This Old Thing? Actually, It's New," *New York Times*, February 2, 2011; David Colman, "Dressing for Success, Again," *New York Times*, December 17, 2009; Claire Cain Miller, "Techies Break a Fashion Taboo," *New York Times*, August 3, 2012; Andy Jordon, "If You Really Want to Defy Conformity, Dress Up on Fridays," *Wall Street Journal*, January 3, 2013.

4. Author interview with Catherine Stephenson of the Association of Sewing and Design Professionals, October 2009.

5. Ruth O'Brien, *Present Trends in Home Sewing*, Miscellaneous Publication no. 4 (Washington, DC: US Department of Agriculture, 1927), 9; Laura MacFarlane, "Happy New Year," *Fashion Service*, January 1930, 1; quoted in Barbara Burman, "Made at Home by Clever Fingers: Home Dressmaking in Edwardian England," in Barbara Burman, ed., *The Culture of Sewing: Gender, Consumption and Home Dressmaking* (Oxford, UK: Berg, 1999), 33–53, esp. 37; Doris Johnson, "A New Direction in Clothing Construction," *Journal of Home Economics* 52, no. 9 (1960): 752–753.

6. Biographical information provided to author by Helen Long Devitt.

7. "Introduction: Home Economics: What's in a Name?" in Sarah Stage and Virginia B. Vincenti, eds., *Rethinking Home Economics: Women and the History of a Profession* (Ithaca, NY: Cornell University Press, 1997), 1–13, esp. 9; Jane Bernard Powers, *The "Girl Question" in Education: Vocational Education for Young Women in the Progressive Era* (London: Falmer Press, 1992), 3. Laura Shapiro calls the home economists "modern," but not "feminist," in *Perfection Salad: Women and Cooking at the Turn of the Century* (New York: Modern Library, 2001).

8. Quoted in Amy Sue Bix, "Equipped for Life: Gendered Technical Training and Consumerism in Home Economics, 1920–1980," *Technology and Culture* 43, no. 4 (2002): 728–754, esp. 741.

9. Catherine Hill and Andresse St. Rose, *Why So Few? Women in Science, Technology, Engineering, and Mathematics* (Washington, DC: American Association of University Women, 2010).

10. Constance Talbot, *The Complete Book of Sewing* (New York: Book Presentations, 1943), 190, 188; *Alumnus* (published by the Carnegie Institute of Technology, Alumni Federation), June 1944, 5, Carnegie Mellon University Archives.

11. *McCall's Fashion Book*, Winter 1936–1937, 68.

12. American Home Economics Association, *Lake Placid Conference Proceedings* 6 (1904), 31.

13. Annette J. Warner, "Art in the Home," *Journal of Home Economics* 7, no. 1 (1915): 8–16, esp. 16 (quoting Psalm 90:17), 8.

14. Mildred Graves Ryan and Velma Phillips, *Clothes for You*, 2nd ed. (New York: Appleton-Century-Crofts, 1954), 280.

15. Character did not apply to women: see Warren I. Susman, "'Personality and the Making of Twentieth Century Culture," in his *Culture as History: The Transformation of American Society in the Twentieth Century* (New York: Pantheon Books, 1984), 271–285, esp. 273–274, 277.

16. Adelaide Laura Van Duzer, Edna M. Andrix, Ethelwyn L. Bobenmyer, et al., *Everyday Living for Girls* (Chicago: J. B. Lippincott, 1936), 353 (emphasis added); Grace Margaret Morton, "Related Art in Clothing Selection," *Journal of Home Economics* 18, no. 1 (1926): 25–28. For an account of how menswear manufacturers bridged this divide as well, see Rob Schorman, "The Truth About Good Goods: Clothing, Advertising, and the Representation of Cultural Values at the End of the Nineteenth Century," *American*

Studies 37, no. 1 (1996): 23–49. Nan Enstad challenges Warren I. Susman's division in *Ladies of Labor, Girls of Adventure: Working Women, Popular Culture, and Labor Politics at the Turn of the Twentieth Century* (New York: Columbia University Press, 1999), 19–20, 203–204. The Picken quotation is from Mary Brooks Picken, *Modern Dressmaking Made Easy* (New York: Funk and Wagnalls, 1940), cover of Part 6; the "wrong impression" quotation is from Lillian C. W. Baker, *Clothing Selection and Purchase* (1931; reprint, New York: Macmillan, 1932), 46.

17. Jane Loewen, *Millinery* (New York: Macmillan, 1925), 180.

18. Van Duzer et al., *Everyday Living for Girls*, 2, v.

19. Mabel B. Trilling and Florence Williams Nicholas, *Clothing Study: A Workbook for High School Girls* (Chicago: J. B. Lippincott, 1935), 203–204.

20. Ryan and Phillips, *Clothes for You*, i.

INDEX

Morris, William, 8, 20
Morton, Grace Margaret
  on angular figure, 271–272
  on campus clothing, 86
  on character, 286
  as *éminence grise,* 244
  on emphasis, 70, 71
  on evening clothing, 121
  on harmony of color, 47, 49–50, 55
  life and career of, 10, 280
  on rhythm, 59
  Thrift Movement and, 162, 174, 183, 186
  on wardrobes, 132, 177–178
  on work clothing segue to afternoon clothing, 119
Movies, 90, 97–98, 107, 127, 160, 175–176, 199
Mrs. 'Arris Goes to Paris (Gallico), 179
My Classroom Economy program, 172

National Association for the Advancement of Colored People (NAACP), 188, 221
National Education Association, 136
National Organization of Women, 195
Nature
  color and, 46, 48–49
  proportion and, 65–66
Negra woman, 57–58
Neiman Marcus, 31
Neutral colors, 45–46
New Deal, 145, 149, 265
New Look, 31, 224–225, 260, 265, 273
New Woman, 241
New York Civil Liberties Union, 201
New York Times, 28, 158, 167, 212, 213
New York Tribune, 243
New York University, 11, 52, 53, 117, 129, 242, 256
Newton, Isaac, 43
9 Heads (illustration book), 69
Nineteenth Amendment, xii
Norell, Norman, 200
Novelty, 130, 160, 225
Nystrom, Paul H., 225

O magazine, 27
Obama, Michelle, 34–35

O'Brien, Ruth
  on children's clothing, 81
  life and career of, 5
  sewing machine survey by, 281
  standardized sizing and, 10, 265, 273, 274
Occasions. *See* Six Occasions for Dress
Occult, 62
Occupational shoes, 107
Oklahoma State University, 82, 247
Ombré fabrics, 61
One Hour Dress, 230
Op art, 216
Oregon Agricultural College (now Oregon State University), 11
Outfits
  assembling, xiii
  evaluation of, 23
  month of, 166, 186
  Story on, 132
Overalls, 19, 114
Owen, Ruth Bryan, 15

Pajamas, 123–124
  beach, 113–114
Pants, 111–116, 198–202, 231–232
  See also Trousers
Pantsuits, 200
Pantyhose, 208–209
Parents, Children and Money (Gruenberg and Gruenberg), 173
Paris Frocks at Home, 45
Parsons School of Design, 17, 33
Pastel colors, 45
Patou, Jean, 29–30, 150
Peel-Off pattern, 119
Pennsylvania State University, 11
Pepin, Harriet, 33, 115, 161, 234
Peplum, 272 (fig.)
Personal shoppers, 97, 239
Personality, 286
Petticoats, 79, 112
Phelps, Elizabeth Stuart, 24–25, 27
Phi (Φ), 66
Philadelphia Ledger, 74, 112
Phillips, Velma
  life and career of, 279
  philosophy of, 285, 287
  on wardrobes, 184

Index